HEALTHY HOME COOKING

*More than 200 easy, low-fat
recipes for you to enjoy*

MARGARET HOWARD B.Sc., R.P.Dt., P.H.Ec.
&
ELLIE TOPP B.A., M.Sc., P.H.Ec.

Macmillan Canada
Toronto

Canadian Cataloguing in Publication Data

Howard, Margaret, 1930–
  Healthy home cooking : more than 200 easy, low-fat recipes for you to enjoy

Includes bibliographical references and index.
ISBN 0-7715-9189-6

1. Low-fat diet – Recipes. I. Topp, Ellie, 1938–
II. Title.

RM237.7.H69 1993   641.5'638   C93-094088-1

Macmillan Canada wishes to thank the Canada Council for supporting its publishing program.

1 2 3 4 5 TG 97 96 95 94 93

COVER AND BOOK DESIGN: ArtPlus Limited/Brant Cowie
COVER AND INTERIOR PHOTOGRAPHS: Hal Roth
COVER PHOTO: Baked Lemon Garlic Chicken Breasts (page 96) and Bow-Tie Pasta with Zucchini and Peppers (page 78).

Macmillan Canada
A Division of Canada Publishing Corporation
Toronto, Ontario, Canada

Printed in Canada

Acknowledgements

The Canadian Home Economics Association.

Ellen Boynton, Executive Director, CHEA.

CHEA Liaison Committee members: Roxanne McQuilkin, Chairperson, Margaret Fraser and Barb Holland.

We are grateful to Claire Horsley, assisted by Carol Gulyas and Yvonne Tremblay, for their creative food styling expertise and also to Ontario Home Economists in Business (OHEIB) for their generous donation of food for the photographs.

Heather Nielsen, Chief, Nutrition Programs Unit, Health and Welfare Canada.

Pam Bouchard, R.P.Dt., for her nutrient analyses of the recipes.

Sheryl Conrad, R.P.Dt.,Communications Manager, National Institute of Nutrition, for her assistance with nutrition questions.

Clarke Topp for computer assistance, John Howard for editing assistance and, together, for their patience in tasting all the recipes during their development.

Bruce Topp for his assistance relaying E-mail faxes when his mother was in Australia during the final edit.

The critical and creative palates of our respective families, who joyfully sampled our recipes.

Food associates Shirley Ann Holmes, Cecile Moses and Rosalie Reese, who provided input during the book's development.

Fiona Lucas, Senior Domestic Interpreter, Historic Fort York, and Joyce Gillelan, formerly a historical interpreter at Colborne Lodge, Toronto Historical Board, for their guidance and advice on historical food references.

Ontario Ministry of Agriculture and Food.

Beef Information Centre.

Elizabeth Driver, author of A *Bibliography of Cookery Books from 1875-1914*, published in London, England, in 1989.

Everyone at Macmillan for their constant support and for being so pleasant to work with, and a special thanks to Denise Schon for her counsel and Jackie Rothstein for her dedication and editorial wisdom.

Canadian Home Economics Association Foods and Nutrition Committee

THE CANADIAN HOME ECONOMICS ASSOCIATION is pleased to recommend *Healthy Home Cooking*. This cookbook promotes the importance of food selection and preparation in achieving and maintaining good health.

Using the 1992 Canada's Food Guide to Healthy Eating (a copy of which appears inside), the authors have developed recipes that encourage enjoyment of a variety of foods, which ensures the intake of a balance of nutrients; choosing lower-fat foods and foods prepared with little or no fat; increased consumption of fruits, vegetables and grains; and limited use of salt.

Healthy Home Cooking contains more than 200 delicious recipes that are low in fat and high in fibre. The authors also make use of creative seasonings to promote the use of herbs and spices as substitutes for salt. A nutrient analysis accompanies each recipe, making this cookbook an even better tool in the effort to achieve and maintain a healthier diet. And as an added bonus, every section contains helpful tips and background information about food.

Healthy cooking was never so easy — healthy eating never tasted so good!

RUTH E. BERRY, P.H.Ec., Ph.D.
*President, Canadian Home
Economics Association*

Founded in 1939, the nearly 3,000-member strong Canadian Home Economics Association is the professional organization for graduates of university programs in home economics, human ecology, nutrition, and consumer and family studies. Its members work in diverse settings, primarily as educators, to actively promote improved quality of life for individuals and families in Canada and the developing world.

Contents

Preface

WE CONGRATULATE the Canadian Home Economics Association for providing a healthy eating cookbook based on Canada's Food Guide to Healthy Eating.

Canada's Food Guide has come a long way over the past 50 years. It was introduced in 1942 as Canada's Official Food Rules to respond to the needs of consumers during the Second World War. In 1944, it was renamed Canada's Food Rules and in 1961 became Canada's Food Guide.

From 1961 to 1982, revisions were made to the content and look of the guide. Content changes were made to keep pace with the latest scientific information about nutritional requirements and to allow for the many foods that became available to Canadians over that time period. As knowledge was gained about the ways Canadians learned about nutrition, adjustments were made to the design and presentation of the food guide. The 1982 version of Canada's Food Guide with four food groups around the sun found a place in many Canadian kitchens.

Today we have a new food guide — Canada's Food Guide to Healthy Eating. This food guide is based on updated information from nutrition and food science. To develop the food guide, research was conducted with consumers and consultations were held with more than 200 stakeholders from many disciplines and organizations. As a result, the food guide is designed to address those nutrition issues that affect today's consumers. The new rainbow design of graduated arcs corresponding to a food group's importance in our diet reflects current healthy eating messages.

We believe that Canada's Food Guide to Healthy Eating provides Canadians with a practical and realistic guide to selecting their foods.

Enjoy eating well. Put Canada's Food Guide to Healthy Eating in your kitchen next to *Healthy Home Cooking*.

HEATHER NIELSEN AND CARMEN CONNOLLY
Nutrition Programs Unit
Health Promotion Directorate
Health and Welfare Canada

Introduction

IMPORTANCE OF HEALTHY COOKING

HEALTHY COOKING IS the way we choose and prepare food to achieve an enjoyable, healthy eating style for ourselves, our families and our friends. It's what this book is all about.

Healthy eating starts with proper nutrition, long identified as a critical factor in growth and development. Research conducted throughout the 1970s and 1980s has established that healthy eating is a significant factor in reducing the risk of developing such nutrition-related problems as heart disease, cancer, obesity, hypertension (high blood pressure), osteoporosis, anaemia, dental decay and some bowel disorders. While reducing risk does not guarantee that a disease will be prevented, it does decrease the chance of developing a disease. Today we are becoming increasingly aware of the significant role nutrition plays in our overall sense of well-being and in our appearance, health and performance.

VARIETY, BALANCE, MODERATION

HEALTHY EATING EMBRACES the belief that all foods can be incorporated into a healthy diet. The intent of our book is to promote this belief by recommending the choice of a wide variety of foods, the achievement of a balance of energy (calories) and nutrients, and the exercise of moderation in choosing higher-fat, calorie-dense foods. Let's stop referring to foods as either good or bad. No one food can make or break an overall healthy diet. It's a person's total diet that is important to good health, not the content of one meal or even one day's meals. Healthy eating is the sum of all foods eaten over time. We achieve a healthy eating pattern by making better food choices *most* of the time.

The new Canada's Food Guide to Healthy Eating[1] expresses our personal philosophy. What better basis for a healthy eating recipe book?

WHAT IS CANADA'S FOOD GUIDE TO HEALTHY EATING?

CANADA'S NEW FOOD GUIDE comes complete with a new name, a new look, and a new approach to healthy eating! Health and Welfare Canada introduced the guide in the fall of 1992 to promote better health among Canadians through wise eating choices.

This new food guide is based on Health and Welfare's own Guidelines for Healthy Eating[2], published in 1989, which are:

- Enjoy a VARIETY of Foods.
- Emphasize cereals, breads, other grain products, vegetables and fruits.
- Choose lower-fat dairy products, leaner meats, and foods prepared with little or no fat.
- Achieve and maintain a healthy body weight by enjoying regular physical activity and healthy eating.
- Limit salt, alcohol and caffeine.

These guidelines evolved from a comprehensive scientific review of current nutritional knowledge.[3]

[1] Minister of Supply and Services Canada, 1992 Cat. No. H39—252/1992E.
[2] *Nutrition Recommendations... A Call for Action.* Summary Report of the Scientific Review Committee and the Communications/Implementation Committee. (Health and Welfare Canada, 1989).
[3] This review of the Scientific Review Committee resulted in the "Nutrition Recommendations for Canadians" which would serve as the foundation for all nutrition and healthy eating programs in Canada. Their report is found in *Nutrition Recommendations.* The Report of the Scientific Review Committee. (Health and Welfare Canada, 1990).

The Food Guide

For the first time in Canada we have a food guide designed specifically to help consumers select foods consistent with their varying needs for energy (calories) and essential nutrients. It is not designed, however, to meet the needs of people with special dietary requirements or for children under four years of age. The number of servings and serving sizes in the guide are too large for toddlers and preschoolers.

The overall pattern for healthy eating promoted by the new food guide is referred to as a *total diet approach*. You *don't* have to give up foods you love for the sake of your health. But you *do* need to aim for moderation and a variety of foods containing essential nutrients.

This total diet approach responds more effectively to today's nutritional concerns than did earlier guides.[4] Earlier guides met only minimum nutrition needs and so fell short of meeting the energy needs of most people. Furthermore, they did not offer guidance on all daily food choices.

The new food guide is just that, a guide. Throughout it uses the term "choose...more often" when discussing choices from the various food categories. This is in keeping with the philosophy of the total diet approach, making better choices most of the time.

Canada's Food Guide to Healthy Eating (pictured between pages 152 and 153) is a two-sided document featuring a rainbow side and a bar side:

The rainbow side features four arcs depicting the four food groups: Grain Products, Vegetables and Fruit, Milk Products, and Meat and Alternatives. All four food groups are important to healthy eating but the amounts needed from each group vary.

The bar side tells us the appropriate number of servings per person per day for each of the four major food groups. Foods chosen provide 1,800 to 3,200 calories (7,500–13,400 kj), depending on the number and types of servings selected from each food group. Although there is an increase in the number of servings for Grain Products and Vegetables and Fruit from past guides, this doesn't mean everyone is to aim for the upper range of servings. Remember, this guide is for a wide range of people and it is up to you to decide what level is appropriate.

And there is an additional food category, Other Foods. This category contains the wide range of dietary items and beverages that add to the enjoyment of eating but do not fit into any of the four food groups. There is no suggested number of servings or serving sizes except for recommendations of moderation in the use of some items.

The bar side also displays the Vitality message. This message encourages Canadians to enjoy total well-being through the integration of eating well, being active and feeling good about themselves.

USING CANADA'S FOOD GUIDE TO HEALTHY EATING

Enjoy a Variety of Foods

VARIETY IS THE SPICE of life! Choosing a variety from each of the four food groups every day in the proportions the guide suggests gives you an adequate intake of the essential nutrients you require. By choosing lower-fat foods from each group every day as well as smaller amounts of higher-fat foods, you'll enjoy the foods you love, yet eat well. Eat different kinds of foods, prepare them in different ways, and you will enjoy the pleasure of exploring a wide range of foods varying in colour, flavour and texture.

The following chart explains where macronutrients (proteins, fats and carbohy-

---

[4] *Canada's Food Guide* (Health and Welfare Canada, 1983). *Canada's Food Rules* (Canada's Department of Health and Welfare, 1942).

KEY NUTRIENTS IN CANADA'S FOOD GUIDE TO HEALTHY EATING

Grain Products	+	Vegetables & Fruit	+	Milk Products	+	Meat & Alternatives	=	The Food Guide
protein				protein		protein		protein
				fat		fat		fat
carbohydrate		carbohydrate						carbohydrate
fibre		fibre						fibre
thiamin		thiamin				thiamin		thiamin
riboflavin				riboflavin		riboflavin		riboflavin
niacin				niacin				niacin
folacin		folacin				folacin		folacin
				vitamin B12		vitamin B12		vitamin B12
		vitamin C						vitamin C
		vitamin A		vitamin A				vitamin A
				vitamin D				vitamin D
				calcium				calcium
iron		iron				iron		iron
zinc				zinc		zinc		zinc
magnesium		magnesium		magnesium		magnesium		magnesium

drates) and micronutrients (vitamins and minerals) are found in food. It illustrates how variety ensures the proper balance of nutrient intake. Each food group is essential because each provides its own set of key nutrients.

Ways to Enjoy a Variety of Foods

This is really easy to do! Here are some suggestions for introducing variety into your life:

- Choose different foods from each food group every day.
- Try new foods.
- Experiment with new recipes.
- Use foods and cuisines enjoyed by different ethnic and cultural groups.
- Vary the form of food (fresh, frozen, canned, dry).
- Vary the ways you prepare food (raw, baked, steamed, braised, broiled).
- Vary the way you serve food (with and without sauces, condiments and accompaniments).

Emphasize Cereals, Breads, Grains, Vegetables and Fruits

The food guide recommends we choose whole grain and enriched products, dark green and orange vegetables and orange fruit more often for the following reasons:

- They are all complex carbohydrates (starch) and contain fibre—but more about that later.
- Enriched foods have some vitamins and minerals added to them.
- Dark green and orange vegetables, and orange fruit are higher in certain key nutrients, such as vitamin A and folacin, than other vegetables and fruit. Dark green and orange vegetables include broccoli, spinach, carrots, squash and sweet potatoes. Orange fruits include peaches, cantaloupe and orange juice.

Grain Products and Vegetables and Fruit are so significant to proper nutrition that they occupy the two largest arcs of the rainbow. According to the Nutrition Recommendations for Canadians,

"The Canadian diet should provide 55% of energy as carbohydrate (138 g/1,000 kcal or 165 g/ 5,000 kcal) from a variety of sources. Sources should be selected that provide complex carbohydrates, a variety of dietary fibre and ß carotene."[5] This doesn't mean you should increase your overall caloric intake. Rather, you should shift the balance—obtain more calories from complex carbohydrates and fewer calories from fat and protein. The Report of the Scientific Review Committee[6] recommends a diet providing 13% to 15% of calories as protein. Most Canadians consume more than that amount of protein.

Assuming you don't need to reduce your energy intake, calories lost from reducing fat intake must come from some other macronutrient source. The best source is complex carbohydrates.

Four Cheers for Complex Carbohydrates!
- Eating patterns that are high in complex carbohydrates are associated with lower incidence of heart disease and certain types of cancers.
- ß carotene, found in certain vegetables and fruits, may help reduce the risks of some cancers.
- Foods containing complex carbohydrates also contain dietary fibre.
- Gram for gram, complex carbohydrates provide less than half the calories of fat.

Where You'll Find Complex Carbohydrates
- Grains: wheat, oats (oatmeal), rice, wild rice, barley, buckwheat (kasha)
- Grain-based foods: breads, rolls, muffins, cereals, pasta
- Vegetables: potatoes, sweet potatoes, peas, corn
- Legumes: dried peas, beans, lentils.

Starch Gets a Bad Rap
But aren't starchy foods fattening? you say. Not so. In fact, plain starchy foods, such as rice,

pasta, potatoes, bread and most legumes, are very low in fat. A meal based on starchy foods can be low in calories and still satisfy hunger. It is the combination of fats with starches found in such foods as croissants, cookies, pasta with rich sauces, french fries, and potatoes with butter and sour cream, that is fattening and gives starch its bad reputation.

The Fuss about Fibre
There is a lot of media attention given to fibre these days. But what exactly are they talking about? Fibre is a component of plants that is either partially or completely undigested, depending on the type. Soluble fibre is the partially digested, softer type that is thought to help control the levels of blood sugar and blood cholesterol. Insoluble fibre, sometimes called roughage, is generally undigested and helps to regulate bowel function and may have other health benefits.

Increases in fibre intake should be gradual and accompanied by larger intakes of fluid. This may help avoid the excessive intestinal gas and bloating that affects some people.

Where You'll Find Dietary Fibre
- Whole grains such as whole wheat, brown rice, whole rye, barley
- Bran of wheat and oats
- Vegetables
- Fruit
- Legumes such as dried peas, beans, lentils.

Choose Lower-Fat Foods More Often
The food guide recommends choosing lower-fat milk products, leaner meats, poultry, fish and meat alternatives more often. It does so to help you decrease your fat intake yet still obtain the nutrients essential to healthy eating.

Fat found in food is made up of fatty acids, which are either saturated, monounsaturated or polyunsaturated. The saturation of the fat relates to the number of hydrogen atoms added

[5]*Nutrition Recommendations*, 5.
[6]*Nutrition Recommendations*, 80.

to the fatty acids in the fat molecule. Let's take a closer look at these three kinds of fats:

Saturated fats are closely related to elevated blood cholesterol levels. The main sources of saturated fats are animal fats and palm and coconut oils.

Monounsaturated fats may actually lower blood cholesterol, especially the LDL cholesterol, according to recent research. Olive and canola oils are high in monounsaturated fat.

Polyunsaturated fats are also associated with lowered blood cholesterol levels. Sunflower, safflower, soybean and corn oils are high in polyunsaturated fats. Omega-3 fats, found in certain fish such as salmon, are made up of polyunsaturated fatty acids which have been associated with lowered blood triglyceride levels, another type of blood fat that is linked to the risk of heart disease.

The proportions of these fatty acids in food varies. Meat and milk products are higher in saturated fat, whereas most vegetable oils are higher in monounsaturated and polyunsaturated fats.

High-fat eating patterns are linked with increased incidence of heart disease and certain types of cancer. The amount of saturated fat in the diet is closely allied with the elevated blood cholesterol levels associated with risk of heart disease and stroke.

The chart below shows the proportion of the saturated, polyunsaturated and monounsaturated fatty acids in oils and fats.

What About Cholesterol?
Cholesterol is a substance that is made by all animals, including humans, and is an essential component of cell membranes and some hormones. It is not an essential nutrient because the body produces what it needs. It is very important, therefore, to distinguish between blood cholesterol made by the body and dietary cholesterol found in foods.

As we've already suggested, keeping blood cholesterol levels under control is a key factor in reducing the risk of heart disease and stroke. While dietary cholesterol can affect blood

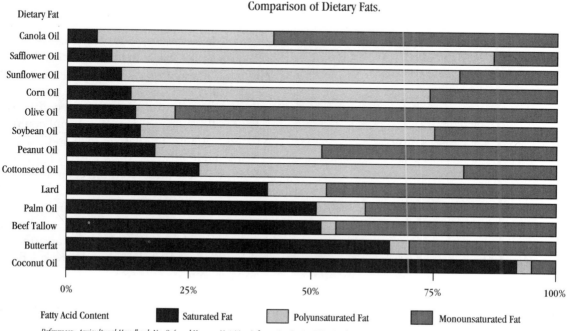

Comparison of Dietary Fats.

Dietary Fat
Canola Oil
Safflower Oil
Sunflower Oil
Corn Oil
Olive Oil
Soybean Oil
Peanut Oil
Cottonseed Oil
Lard
Palm Oil
Beef Tallow
Butterfat
Coconut Oil

0%   25%   50%   75%   100%

Fatty Acid Content   ■ Saturated Fat   ▨ Polyunsaturated Fat   ▨ Monounsaturated Fat

References: Agricultural Handbook No. 8-4 and Human Nutrition Information Service USDA, Washington, D.C., 1979.

cholesterol levels, it is not as significant a factor as the total amount of fat, especially saturated fat, in your diet. Most experts agree that the key dietary strategy for controlling blood cholesterol is to reduce the *total fat* and, specifically, saturated fat in the diet.

Cholesterol is a different substance from fat. It is not considered part of the nutrient analysis for total fat. Dietary cholesterol comes from animal fats which are also, with a few exceptions such as eggs, high in saturated fats. Remember, it's the total fat content that is important. The potato chips labelled "cholesterol-free" are still loaded with fat.

How Much Fat Per Day?
The Nutritional Recommendations for Canadians states that "The Canadian diet should include no more than 30% of energy as fat, and no more than 10% as saturated fat."[7] Data from 1986 shows that Canadians received 38% of their daily energy (calories) from fat, 13% of which was in the form of saturated fat.

The box below outlines two formulas for estimating the approximate amount of fat that represents 30% of calories consumed.

APPROXIMATE GRAMS OF FAT PER DAY FOR A HEALTHY DIET

- Divide healthy weight in pounds by 2 to give grams of fat per day
- Divide calories required per day to maintain healthy weight by 30 to give grams of fat per day

---

For example, if you weigh 140 pounds and require 2,100 calories per day, you probably should limit daily fat intake to 70 grams.

What About Margarine and Butter?
Margarines contain varying amounts of saturated fats, but no cholesterol. Some margarines are made by a process called hydrogenation. This process adds hydrogen to vegetable oils to make them solid. It also converts the monounsaturated and polyunsaturated fats in the oils to saturated fats. As a result, solid margarine is a significant dietary source of saturated fat. Margarine can also be made by adding a small amount of a naturally occurring saturated fat such as palm oil. This makes the margarine solid without the hydrogenation process which may mean that it contains less saturated fat than those made by hydrogenation.

The softer the margarine, the less saturated fat it contains. Look for a soft margarine with at least a two-to-one ratio of polyunsaturated fat to saturated fat. So, check the label.

You've probably guessed this, but butter is even higher in saturated fat than most margarines. And because it is an animal fat, it is also high in dietary cholesterol.

Trimming the Fat from Your Diet
- Choose lower-fat dairy products such as 1% and 2% yogurt and cottage cheese; lower-fat cheeses; frozen yogurt; skim, 1% or 2% milk.
- Spread less butter or margarine on bread, bagels or buns.
- Choose leaner meats, poultry or fish, such as lean beef, pork loin and skinless chicken breast.
- Remove and discard all visible fat from meat and poultry.
- Remove and discard all skin from poultry.
- Eat smaller portions of meat, fish and poultry.
- Choose protein alternatives such as dried beans and lentils.
- Enjoy eggs as a meat alternative, but not every day.
- Increase portions of vegetables, starches and fruits.
- Serve vegetables without butter, margarine or rich sauces; replace them with herbs, spices and lemon juice.
- Prepare food using low-fat cooking methods such as microwaving, baking or broiling.

---

[7]*Nutrition Recommendations*, 5.

- Prepare foods using less oil and fat.
- Balance your daily intake of higher-fat foods with lower-fat choices.
- Read labels for the content of total fat per serving.
- Choose lower-fat dressings for salads or use less of the higher-fat variety.
- Eat fried or deep-fried foods less often.
- Eat snacks such as chips or chocolate bars less often.

This may seem disconcerting — all this low-fat talk — but you'll find that today's supermarkets are carrying a wide (and it's getting wider) variety of good tasting, lower-fat foods.

The Other Foods

Although they do not belong in any of the four food groups, Other Foods play a role in everyday eating by providing taste, enjoyment and energy (calories). Some of these foods should be consumed in moderation because they are high in fat and calories. Others, such as caffeine, salt and alcohol, may have adverse health effects when consumed in excess. Other Foods include:

- Foods that are mostly fats and oils: butter, margarine, cooking oils, mayonnaise, oil-based salad dressings, shortening, lard.
- Foods that are mostly sugar: most jams, jelly, honey, candy, syrup.
- High-fat and/or high-salt snack foods: potato chips, pretzels, corn chips, cheese-flavoured puffs.
- Beverages: water, tea, coffee, soft drinks, fruit-flavoured drinks, alcohol.
- Herbs, spices and condiments: oregano, pepper, salt, mustard, relish, ketchup, steak sauces, horseradish, chili sauce, pickles, soy sauce.

Limit the Use of Salt, Alcohol and Caffeine

Many of us consume more salt than we need. Moderation is recommended because of salt's association with hypertension (high blood pressure). Our taste for salt has been acquired over many years of preparing and eating foods containing salt. By cutting back gradually, you'll realize one day you don't really miss salt. Substituting herbs and spices to enhance natural food flavours, choosing highly salted snack foods less often and checking food labels for lower-salt foods are other ways you can moderate salt intake.

The guide recommends a sensible approach to alcohol because of its undesirable effects on hypertension. This means using alcohol in moderation and choosing non-alcoholic beverages most often. Canada's Drug Strategy suggests moderate consumption is one drink a day and no more than 7 drinks a week. One drink is considered to be 1 bottle (12 oz/350 mL) of beer (5% alcohol); 5 oz/150 mL of wine(10%–14% alcohol); or 1 1/2 oz/50 mL of spirits containing 40% alcohol. Abstinence is recommended for pregnant women.

Coffee, tea, cola, cocoa products and a number of medications contain caffeine. Moderation in the consumption of caffeine is recommended. Intakes of up to 400 to 450 mg of caffeine per day does not increase the risk of heart disease or hypertension for most people or have adverse effects on pregnant women or their fetuses. Limiting your coffee to no more than four regular cups (6 oz/175 mL) a day meets this recommendation.[8]

Factors Influencing Energy and Nutrient Needs

The food guide recognizes that different people require different amounts of food and have differing nutritional needs. Differences depend on:

- Age — at certain stages of the life cycle energy and nutrient needs differ.
- Body size — energy and nutrient needs are greater for those with a larger body size.
- Gender — males, with their larger body size and greater muscle mass, generally have higher

[8]Caffeine. Issue paper available from Health Protection Branch, Health and Welfare Canada (1992).

nutrient and energy needs. Females have special nutrient needs too, particularly for calcium and iron.

• Pregnancy and breast-feeding — these stages in a woman's life increase nutrient and energy needs.
• Activity level — increased activity levels can increase energy and nutrient needs.
• Basal metabolic rate — this is our calorie transformer and will adapt fairly quickly to a reduction in calories.
• Individual variation — there is a natural variation in the need for energy and nutrients from person to person even when factors such as age, body size, gender, and activity levels are similar.

Foods chosen according to the food guide provide between 1,800 and 3,200 calories (7,500 and 13,400 kj) depending on:

• The number of servings selected from each food group.
• Choices made from the Other Foods category.
• The size of the portions chosen.

Most of us will meet our energy and nutrient needs by choosing a number of servings falling somewhere between the lower and upper end of the servings range.

Putting It All Together

Vitality
Many Canadians are preoccupied with their weight and body image. The food guide's Vitality principle is meant to shift that focus to a more positive approach to health. Its message is to *enjoy eating well, being active and feeling good about yourself.*

Enjoy eating well. After all, food is one of life's great pleasures! Make wise food choices from Canada's Food Guide to Healthy Eating. The message is healthy eating instead of dieting.

Enjoy being active. Make some form of physical activity a part of your everyday life.

Activities such as riding a bike, walking the dog, even washing the car, mowing the lawn, or shovelling snow help you manage your weight as well as strengthen your lungs, heart and body.

Feel good about yourself. Appreciate the importance of taking charge of your life and learn to like, accept and respect yourself. Having a healthy self and body image gives you more control over your life and makes you feel and look happier. A healthy body image is the realization that healthy bodies come in a variety of shapes and sizes. A good weight is a healthy weight, not just a lower weight. A healthy weight helps you stay active and lowers the risk of health problems.

The Balancing Act

Now that you are familiar with Canada's Food Guide to Healthy Eating and know that healthy eating is the average of what is eaten over time, you can start to put it all together. Begin by asking yourself these questions to see how you are getting along in your overall healthy eating pattern.

• Have I eaten foods from all four food groups today?
• Was there at least one Grain Product and one Vegetables and Fruit choice in each meal or snack?
• How many servings from each food group did I get?
• Is the meal or snack high in fat? Can I balance it in subsequent meals with lower-fat foods?
• Am I moderate in my use of salt, alcohol and caffeine?
• Have I been physically active today?
• *The last and most important question*—what should my next few meals or snacks include to balance out what I have already eaten? Tracking the foods you have eaten to influence your subsequent food selection is the secret to a healthy eating pattern.

Food Labels
Healthy eating begins at the grocery store. Food labels provide important information to help us make better choices. You should look for these four pieces of significant information on a food label:

List of Ingredients — Ingredients in a product are listed in order of descending proportion of the total weight. When salt is first, watch out!

Descriptive Nutrition Claims — All nutrition claims must be supported by detailed facts relating to the claim. Some claims require interpretation. A food claiming to have "50% less salt" must contain half the salt of the food with which it is compared. It doesn't necessarily mean the product is low in salt. Half the salt can still be a lot of salt. "Cholesterol-free" may be accurate but the product may never have contained cholesterol. "Light" or "Lite" can mean different things, such as taste, texture *or* reduced fat or calories.

Selective Nutrition Information — Information specific to a particular product can be very helpful. The percentage on dairy labels, for example, 2% M.F., tells us the fat content of the product.

The Nutrition Label — Canada's nutrition labelling is a standardized presentation of nutrient content. The program is voluntary but more is appearing on packaging. The label describes the contents as purchased, not as they might be prepared or used. The stated serving size may or may not be the size you eat or the food guide serving size.

The nutrition label is useful for such comparisons as the fibre and calorie content of different brands of cereal. It also helps us be aware of the grams of fat we have consumed so we can monitor daily fat consumption.

HEALTHY COOKING

Low-Fat Cooking Methods
Today's cooking methods greatly affect the amount of fat and nutrients we obtain from food. We recommend the following methods.

- *Microwave* — Cooking by microwave energy is not only a very fast method, but it also allows cooking with little or no fat, since the heat is produced in the food. Nutrients are retained because little or no water is required in the cooking process.
- *Steaming and poaching* — Using water to cook food is an excellent fat-free method. It is a gentle means of cooking that helps avoid toughening of foods, especially delicate proteins like fish.
- *Broiling, barbecuing and grilling* — Cooking food with a high heat source allows browning for good flavour development without adding fat. Broiling and barbecuing have the added advantage of allowing some of the fat present in meat, poultry and fish to drain off.
- *Frying* — Traditionally, frying uses large amounts of fat for cooking and browning. This method can be adapted for low-fat cooking by using a nonstick skillet with very little or no oil, a non-stick cooking spray or by adding a little water to keep food from sticking.
- *Slow Cookers* — A slow cooker allows the long cooking required for the generally less tender, lower-fat meat cuts.

We have shown what we believe are the most appropriate cooking methods for our recipes — sometimes microwave, sometimes one of the conventional methods, and sometimes both.

Low-Fat Cooking Techniques
- Choose one of the low-fat cooking methods mentioned above.
- Drain all fat from cooked ground meat.
- Reduce the fat by ⅓ to ½ in recipes calling for shortening, margarine, butter or oil.

- Substitute oil in recipes calling for melting of solid fats.
- Prepare broth, soup and stew ahead of time, then chill it to allow the fat to rise to the top and solidify for easy removal. (Also, see *Trimming the Fat from Your Diet*, page xii.)

Recipe Nutrient Analysis

Pam Bouchard, R.P. Dt., of NutriProfile, University of Manitoba Department of Foods and Nutrition, provided the nutrient analysis of our recipes using Demeter software. Her analysis is based on the latest food composition data and Recommended Nutrient Intakes issued by Health and Welfare Canada (1991).

Any comments rating the calcium, iron and fibre content of our recipes are in accordance with the "Nutrition Labelling Handbook" from Consumer and Corporate Affairs Canada (Revised Edition, November 1992). A serving of a recipe must contain at least 5% of the Recommended Daily Intake (RDI) of calcium and iron to be considered a "source." It must contain 15% of the RDI to be considered a "good source" and 25% to be considered an "excellent source." The RDI reference values are based on the highest recommended intake for calcium and iron, omitting supplemental needs for pregnancy and lactation. A serving of a recipe must contain at least 2 grams of dietary fibre to be described as a "source" of fibre. It must contain a minimum of 4 grams of dietary fibre to be described as containing "high" amounts of fibre and 6 grams to be described as containing "very high" amounts of fibre.

All analysis is based on imperial measure. The numbers in the analyses are rounded off according to the Nutrition Labelling Guidelines. All recipes were tested and analysed using: 1% plain yogurt, 2% milk, 1% cottage cheese and part-skim cheeses where available. Of course, you can use lower-fat dairy products, if desired. Meat, fish and poultry serving sizes are 2 to 3 oz (50 to 100 g). Where two ingredients are listed, the first ingredient is the one analysed.

Garnishes and optional ingredients were not analysed. The small amounts of salt used in recipes were analysed. Salt is omitted from recipes where sufficient flavours are obtained from other seasonings.

All recipes that call for chicken or beef stock have been analysed using store-bought, low-sodium powdered bouillon products. Those recipes that call for "Homemade" stock have been analysed using the recipes on pages 38 and 40. These homemade stocks are even lower in sodium than the commercial low-sodium products. The advantage of making your own stock is that it allows you to control the amount of sodium.

Microwave recipes were tested in 800-watt microwave ovens. Microwave cooking time is affected by wattage, oven capacity and type of cookware used, so you may have to adjust suggested cooking times slightly. Our recipes use the following standard terms for power levels established by the International Microwave Power Institute:

High	(100%)
Medium-High	(70%)
Medium	(50%)
Medium-Low	(30%)
Low	(10%)

OUR COOKING HERITAGE

A final note.

Throughout the book we have included historical anecdotes taken from old cookbooks, most of them Canadian. Some of the tips and methods are very much in keeping with those used today. Many others are vastly different. The latter illustrate the differences between good nutrition practices then and now.

Enough talk...on to the food!

1

Morning Starts

The Way to a Healthy Start!

Some people are morning people, others are not. If you find breakfast unappealing, do not despair. Our fast-starts may be just what you need. ◆ *As sure as the sun is going to shine, breakfast will remain an important meal of the day—and one that should be eaten by everyone. Nutritionists say that breakfast is the most important meal of the day. Studies show that breakfast is associated with improved strength and endurance in the late morning, and a better attitude toward work and school.* ◆ *You know the old saying: eat like a king at breakfast, like a prince at lunch and like a pauper at dinner.*

Quick Tips to Help Avoid Being a Breakfast Skipper

No time? Why not build a breakfast around foods that are ready to eat or take little preparation: fresh and canned fruit, a small tub of yogurt, cottage cheese, our Fast Morning Starts (pages 17 to 18) or our muffins (pages 10 to 12). ◆ *On the run? We have two great fibreful cookies that you can eat as you go (page 9).* ◆ *Cold cereals? Why not! Sometimes a little perking up is all they need. Stir in some chopped nuts or fresh cut-up fruit and plain yogurt to enjoy as a desktop breakfast.* ◆ *Not hungry yet? Drink some juice, take a banana, a piece of cheese and crackers or some dried fruit to enjoy when you are awake enough to realize what you have missed.* ◆ *Just bored with the same old thing each morning? For a change, look at some of our innovative ideas, such as Hot Bulgur and Fruit Cereal (page 6).*

Breakfast Fruit Plates

THE MORE IDEAS for breakfast we can give you, the more enjoyment you will have from this most important meal of the day. Having fresh fruit, rather than fruit juice, is a "leg-up" on getting sufficient fibre each day.

RAINBOW-COLOURED FRUIT PLATE

2 cups	strawberries, hulled OR raspberries	500 mL
2 tbsp	granulated sugar	25 mL
4	grapefruit, peeled and sectioned	4
4	oranges, peeled and sectioned	4
$\frac{1}{2}$ cup	blueberries	125 mL
	Mint leaves (optional)	

COOKING TIPS:

To add some zing to a mixture of tropical fruit add some lime or lemon juice and rind and finely chopped gingerroot.

In food processor or blender container, purée berries until smooth; strain, if desired. Stir in sugar; set aside.

Arrange grapefruit and orange sections on a platter. Drizzle with berry mixture. Top with blueberries and mint leaves, if using.

MAKES 8 SERVINGS.

WARM SPICED GRAPEFRUIT

2	grapefruit	2
2 tbsp	brown or maple sugar	25 mL
$\frac{1}{8}$ tsp	ground nutmeg OR ginger	0.5 mL
2 tbsp	toasted unsweetened coconut	25 mL

NUTRIENT ANALYSIS

Fruit Plate
Per Serving

Calories		*98*
g	Protein	1.7
g	Total Fat	0.4
g	Carbohydrate	24
g	Fibre	4.4
mg	Sodium	1
mg	Potassium	356
mg	Calcium	46
mg	Iron	0.3

Grapefruit
Per Serving

Calories		*74*
g	Protein	0.9
g	Total Fat	1.3
g	Carbohydrate	16
g	Fibre	2.2
mg	Sodium	3
mg	Potassium	200
mg	Calcium	20
mg	Iron	0.3

Cut grapefruit crosswise in half; loosen segments. Place in baking pan (or microwavable dish).

Combine sugar and nutmeg; sprinkle sugar mixture and coconut over each grapefruit half. Broil for 3 to 4 minutes or microwave at High (100%) for 2 minutes or until grapefruit are warm.

MAKES 4 SERVINGS.

FRUIT TOPPINGS

The following are excellent to serve over other fresh fruit or pancakes, waffles or French toast.

Pineapple: In small saucepan, combine 1 can (8 oz/227 mL) undrained crushed pineapple, 1 tbsp (15 mL) cornstarch and 1 tsp (5 mL) grated orange rind. Cook over medium-low heat for about 5 minutes or until thickened. Cover and refrigerate until cool. Before serving, stir in ½ cup (125 mL) low-fat plain yogurt.

MAKES 1 ½ CUPS (375 ML).

Strawberry, Peach or Raspberry: In food processor or blender container, purée 1 cup (250 mL) sliced strawberries, peaches or raspberries, 1 tbsp (15 mL) granulated sugar, 1 tbsp (15 mL) frozen orange juice concentrate and 1 tsp (5 mL) lemon juice. Transfer to small microwavable container; microwave, covered, at High (100%) for 2 to 3 minutes. Serve warm or refrigerate and serve cold. If desired, add low-fat plain yogurt to make your own fresh strawberry yogurt.

MAKES ¾ CUP (175 ML).

WARM SPICED BANANAS

¼ cup	orange juice	50 mL
2 tbsp	lime juice	25 mL
2 tbsp	light cream cheese	25 mL
¼ tsp	curry powder	1 mL
Pinch	Each: ground cloves and ground ginger	Pinch
¼ cup	granulated sugar	50 mL
2 tbsp	chopped raisins	25 mL
4	medium bananas, sliced	4

In food processor or blender container, process orange and lime juice, cream cheese and seasonings until smooth. Pour into large skillet; add sugar and raisins and cook over medium heat until sugar melts.

Add bananas to skillet; cook for 30 seconds on each side. Serve with sauce.

MAKES 4 SERVINGS.

Hot Breakfast Cereals with a Difference

START YOUR DAY the healthy, delicious way with these easy-to-prepare whole grain cereals. They all cook in a bowl for fast individual servings. Enjoy with milk and fresh fruit or a little brown sugar.

ROLLED OATS

Prepare these oatmeal mixtures ahead of time and store as dry mixes to be quickly cooked at breakfast time. To 1 cup (250 mL) uncooked quick-cooking rolled oats add 1 of the following:

Oatmeal with Raisins: $\frac{1}{4}$ cup (50 mL) raisins, 2 tbsp (25 mL) maple or brown sugar and $\frac{1}{4}$ tsp (1 mL) ground cinnamon or nutmeg.

Coconut Citrus Oatmeal: 2 tbsp (25 mL) unsweetened coconut, 1 tsp (5 mL) grated lemon or orange rind and $\frac{1}{8}$ tsp (0.5 mL) ground ginger.

Seeds 'n' Oats: 2 tbsp (25 mL) pumpkin, squash, sesame or sunflower seeds.

Dried Fruit 'n' Nut Oatmeal: 2 tbsp (25 mL) chopped dried apricots, apples, prunes or raisins, 1 tbsp (15 mL) chopped peanuts, almonds, pecans or walnuts and pinch ground cardamon, allspice, nutmeg or ginger.

For Single Serving:

Microwave: In deep microwavable bowl, combine $\frac{1}{3}$ cup (75 mL) Oatmeal Mix and $\frac{2}{3}$ cup (150 mL) water or low-fat milk. Microwave, uncovered, at High (100%) for 1 $\frac{1}{2}$ to 2 minutes; stir once. Cereal thickens during standing.

Stovetop: In small saucepan, combine $\frac{1}{3}$ cup (75 mL) Oatmeal Mix and $\frac{2}{3}$ cup (150 mL) water or milk. Cook over medium-low heat for 3 to 5 minutes; stir frequently.

NUTRIENT ANALYSIS

Oatmeal with Raisins
Per Serving

Calories		*114*
g	Protein	3.4
g	Total Fat	1.3
g	Carbohydrate	23
g	Fibre	2.1
mg	Sodium	3
mg	Potassium	137
mg	Calcium	19
mg	Iron	1.1

Coconut Citrus Oatmeal
Per Serving

Calories		*105*
g	Protein	3.8
g	Total Fat	3.1
g	Carbohydrate	16
g	Fibre	2.3
mg	Sodium	2
mg	Potassium	95
mg	Calcium	13
mg	Iron	1.1

Seeds 'n' Oats
Per Serving

Calories		*98*
g	Protein	4.1
g	Total Fat	1.8
g	Carbohydrate	17
g	Fibre	2.2
mg	Sodium	1
mg	Potassium	99
mg	Calcium	13
mg	Iron	1.0

Dried Fruit 'n' Oatmeal
Per Serving

Calories		*107*
g	Protein	4.3
g	Total Fat	2.6
g	Carbohydrate	18
g	Fibre	2.5
mg	Sodium	12
mg	Potassium	143
mg	Calcium	15
mg	Iron	1.1

OAT BRAN

For Single Serving:

Microwave: In deep microwavable bowl, combine 3 tbsp (45 mL) oat bran and ½ cup (125 mL) water. Microwave, uncovered, at High (100%) for 2 ½ minutes; stir once.

Stovetop: In small saucepan, combine 3 tbsp (45 mL) oat bran and ½ cup (125 mL) water. Cook over medium-low heat for 3 to 5 minutes; stir frequently.

Optional Additions:
- 2 tbsp (25 mL) raisins, chopped dates or apricots
- 1 tbsp (15 mL) maple syrup
- 1 tbsp (15 mL) orange marmalade

COOKING TIPS:

When preparing plain rolled oats or oat bran, consider adding chopped raw apple, strawberries, blueberries, raspberries or peaches and a dash of vanilla, almond or coconut extract just before serving. Top with low-fat plain yogurt and a sprinkle of maple sugar for a pleasant change.

QUICK STARTS

English Muffin: Split muffin and toast; spread each half with 1 tbsp (15 mL) apple butter, top with 1 tbsp (15 mL) shredded Cheddar cheese. Microwave at High (100%) for 10 seconds or until cheese is melted.

Raisin Toast: Toast raisin bread and spread with 1 tsp (5 mL) peanut butter; top with diced apple and sprinkle lightly with cinnamon and brown sugar.

NUTRIENT ANALYSIS
Per Serving

Calories		85
g	Protein	4.6
g	Total Fat	1.9
g	Carbohydrate	12
g	Fibre	3.1
mg	Sodium	1
mg	Potassium	131
mg	Calcium	19
mg	Iron	1.7

 No instant breakfast in our pioneer ancestors' day! While they had several methods for cooking porridge, the preferred method was to make it in a covered double boiler, which was placed on the back of the kitchen range. It cooked all night and was ready for breakfast first thing in the morning. *(Canadian Prairie Homesteaders)* They knew that grains (complex carbohydrates) are energy boosters and therefore a good way to start the day.

Hot Bulgur and Fruit Cereal

BULGUR, a high source of fibre, is easily found in health food stores. Make this the evening before and cook quickly in the morning for an enjoyable change from more traditional hot cereals.

¹/₂ cup	bulgur	125 mL
¹/₄ cup	quick-cooking rolled oats	50 mL
2 tbsp	wheat germ	25 mL
2 tbsp	chopped dried apricots	25 mL
1 tbsp	brown sugar	15 mL
1 ¹/₂ cups	water	375 mL

In bowl, combine bulgur, oats, wheat germ, apricots and sugar; stir in water. Cover and refrigerate overnight or up to 3 days.

MAKES 4 SERVINGS.

For Single Serving:

Microwave: In deep microwavable bowl, microwave ¹/₂ cup (125 mL) bulgur mixture at High (100%) for 1 ¹/₂ to 2 minutes or until thickened and liquid is absorbed; stir once.

For 4 Servings:

Stovetop: In medium saucepan, cook bulgur mixture over medium heat for about 8 minutes or until mixture thickens; stir frequently.

COOKING TIPS:
Make extra servings of cereal and store in refrigerator for up to three days, cooking as needed.

VARIATIONS:
Replace brown sugar with 1 tbsp (15 mL) molasses; replace apricots with raisins, dates or dried apple.

NUTRIENT ANALYSIS		
Per Serving		
Calories		*114*
g	Protein	4.0
g	Total Fat	0.9
g	Carbohydrate	24
g	Fibre	4.6
mg	Sodium	5
mg	Potassium	190
mg	Calcium	15
mg	Iron	1.1

Fruit Muesli with Rolled Oats

QUICK STARTS

Bran Muffin: Split muffin in half; spread one half with 1 tsp (5 mL) light cream cheese and orange marmalade; top with several banana slices. Place other muffin half on top and microwave at High (100%) for 45 seconds.

Pineapple Bagel: Split bagel in half; spread each half with 1 tbsp (15 mL) light cream cheese and top with 1 pineapple slice. Sprinkle lightly with sugar and cinnamon; broil for about 1 minute.

Flour Tortilla: Toast tortilla until crisp; spread crisp tortilla with 1 tbsp (15 mL) light cream cheese; top with smoked salmon and sprinkle with chopped chives or green onion.

MUESLI, the national breakfast dish of Switzerland, is prepared by soaking raw rolled oats in water overnight. In the morning, fruit, cream and lemon juice are added, with sometimes a sprinkling of chopped nuts. Our version made with plain yogurt is a good source of calcium and has the same rich flavour and texture without the high fat.

1 cup	quick-cooking rolled oats	250 mL
1 cup	low-fat milk	250 mL
2 tbsp	liquid honey	25 mL
$\frac{1}{2}$ tsp	vanilla extract	2 mL
$\frac{1}{2}$ cup	low-fat plain yogurt	125 mL
$\frac{1}{4}$ cup	blueberries, raspberries OR sliced strawberries	50 mL
$\frac{1}{2}$	medium banana, chopped	$\frac{1}{2}$
2 tbsp	slivered almonds (optional)	25 mL
1 tsp	lemon juice	5 mL
	Ground cinnamon (optional)	

In bowl, combine oats, milk, honey and vanilla; stir well. Cover and refrigerate overnight.

In the morning, stir in yogurt, 1 of the berry choices, banana, nuts if using, and lemon juice. Sprinkle with cinnamon, if desired.

MAKES 3 SERVINGS, $\frac{3}{4}$ CUP (175 mL) EACH.

NUTRIENT ANALYSIS		
Per Serving		
Calories		*242*
g	Protein	9.6
g	Total Fat	4.1
g	Carbohydrate	43
g	Fibre	3.2
mg	Sodium	73
mg	Potassium	417
mg	Calcium	193
mg	Iron	1.4

Mixed Grain Granola

HOMEMADE GRANOLA frequently has less fat and sugar than commercial varieties. It is especially quick to make in a microwave oven. The secret for even browning is frequent stirring.

2 cups	large-flake oatmeal	500 mL
1 cup	wheat flakes	250 mL
1 cup	rye flakes	250 mL
½ cup	flaked unsweetened coconut	125 mL
½ cup	natural wheat bran	125 mL
¼ cup	shelled unsalted sunflower seeds	50 mL
¼ tsp	salt	1 mL
½ cup	liquid honey	125 mL
3 tbsp	vegetable oil	45 mL
½ cup	chopped dried apricots OR dates	125 mL

In 8-cup (2 L) microwavable container, combine oatmeal, wheat flakes, rye flakes, coconut, bran, seeds and salt.

In 1 cup (250 mL) measure, whisk together honey and oil. Pour over oatmeal mixture; mix well. Microwave at High (100%) for about 6 minutes; stir thoroughly every 2 minutes or until mixture is slightly brown.

Mix in fruit and cool; stir several times. Store in tightly covered container.

MAKES 18 SERVINGS, ⅓ CUP (75 mL) EACH.

NUTRIENT ANALYSIS

Per Serving

Calories		*157*
g	Protein	3.7
g	Total Fat	5.9
g	Carbohydrate	25
g	Fibre	3.3
mg	Sodium	40
mg	Potassium	131
mg	Calcium	10
mg	Iron	1.0

Eat-on-the-Run Cookies

BETTER TO EAT on the run on a busy morning than not to eat at all. We suggest keeping these cookies tucked away in the refrigerator or freezer for those very days.

FIBRE 'N' FRUIT COOKIES

4	medium bananas, mashed	4
1/3 cup	vegetable oil	75 mL
1/2 tsp	almond extract	2 mL
	Grated rind of 1 lemon	
1 1/2 cups	quick-cooking rolled oats	375 mL
3/4 cup	whole wheat flour	175 mL
1/2 cup	raisins	125 mL
1/2 cup	chopped apricots	125 mL
1/2 cup	chopped dates OR prunes	125 mL
1/2 cup	chopped pecans, walnuts OR almonds	125 mL

In large bowl, combine bananas, oil, extract and rind. Stir in oats, flour, raisins, apricots, dates and pecans; mix well.

Drop small spoonfuls onto lightly greased baking sheets; flatten with a fork.

Bake in 350°F (180°C) oven for about 20 minutes or until lightly browned. Remove cookies from sheets immediately. Cool completely and store in freezer or refrigerator.

MAKES 48 COOKIES.

GRANOLA BREAKFAST SQUARES

THESE EASY-TO-MAKE granola bars are lower in fat and sugar and less expensive than those you buy.

1/2 cup	corn syrup	125 mL
2 tbsp	granulated sugar	25 mL
1/4 cup	peanut butter	50 mL
3 1/2 cups	Mixed Grain Granola (page 8)	875 mL
1/4 cup	sunflower seeds	50 mL
1 tsp	ground cinnamon	5 mL

In large microwavable container, combine syrup and sugar. Microwave at High (100%) for 2 to 2 1/2 minutes or just until mixture is boiling; stir in peanut butter until smooth.

Quickly stir in granola, seeds and cinnamon, stirring just until mixture is combined. Spoon into greased 8-inch (2 L) square pan. Press mixture down firmly. Cut into squares when cool.

MAKES 16 SQUARES.

NUTRIENT ANALYSIS

Per Cookie

Calories		60
g	Protein	1.0
g	Total Fat	2.6
g	Carbohydrate	8.9
g	Fibre	1.0
mg	Sodium	1
mg	Potassium	101
mg	Calcium	5
mg	Iron	0.4

Per Square

Calories		177
g	Protein	3.9
g	Total Fat	7.1
g	Carbohydrate	27
g	Fibre	2.6
mg	Sodium	53
mg	Potassium	127
mg	Calcium	16
mg	Iron	1.4

Banana Date Bran Muffins

MOST PEOPLE consider muffins to be a healthy food, but store-bought muffins are often very high in fat. These great-tasting muffins can easily be made at home. They are low in fat and have lots of fibre — a great way to start the day.

1 1/4 cups	all-purpose flour	300 mL
1/2 cup	high-fibre bran cereal	125 mL
1 tsp	ground cinnamon	5 mL
1 tsp	baking powder	5 mL
1/2 tsp	baking soda	2 mL
1/4 tsp	salt	1 mL
1/2 cup	chopped dates	125 mL
3/4 cup	buttermilk OR sour milk	175 mL
1/4 cup	vegetable oil	50 mL
1	egg	1
1/3 cup	liquid honey	75 mL
1	medium banana, mashed	1

In large bowl, stir together flour, cereal, cinnamon, baking powder, baking soda, salt and dates.

In second bowl, combine buttermilk, oil, egg, honey and banana. Add to dry ingredients, stirring just until moistened; do not overmix.

Spoon into 12 medium paper-lined or nonstick muffin cups, filling 3/4 full. Bake in 400°F (200°C) oven for about 16 minutes or until muffins are lightly browned and firm to the touch.

MAKES 12 MUFFINS.

NUTRIENT ANALYSIS		
Per Muffin		
Calories		163
g	Protein	3.0
g	Total Fat	5.4
g	Carbohydrate	28
g	Fibre	2.1
mg	Sodium	184
mg	Potassium	158
mg	Calcium	40
mg	Iron	1.2

Blueberry Cornmeal Muffins

BLUEBERRY JAM WITH HONEY AND COINTREAU

Jam is easy to make in your microwave oven. This small batch can be kept covered in the refrigerator for several weeks.

1 ½ cups	fresh or frozen blueberries	375 mL
2 tbsp	fruit pectin crystals	25 mL
1 ½ cups	granulated sugar	375 mL
⅓ cup	liquid honey	75 mL
2 tsp	Cointreau OR	10 mL
	Grand Marnier OR	
	1 tsp (5 mL) orange extract	

In 8-cup (2 L) microwavable container, crush berries and combine with pectin crystals. Microwave at High (100%) for 3 minutes or until mixture reaches a full boil.

Stir in sugar and honey; microwave at High for 3 minutes or until boiling; stir. Microwave at High for 3 to 5 minutes longer or until jam is slightly thickened and syrupy. Stir in liqueur.

Pour into hot sterilized jars and seal. Process in boiling water canner for 5 minutes or refrigerate and use within several weeks.

MAKES 2 CUPS (500 ML).

CORNMEAL ADDS a wonderful crunch to these lemon-flavoured blueberry muffins.

1 cup	fresh OR frozen blueberries	250 mL
1 tsp	all-purpose flour	5 mL
1 ½ cups	whole wheat flour	375 mL
⅔ cup	granulated sugar	150 mL
⅓ cup	yellow cornmeal	75 mL
1 tsp	baking soda	5 mL
1 tsp	baking powder	5 mL
¼ tsp	salt	1 mL
¾ cup	low-fat plain yogurt	175 mL
¼ cup	vegetable oil	50 mL
1	egg	1
	Grated zest of 1 lemon	

In small bowl, toss blueberries with all-purpose flour; set aside.

In second bowl, stir together whole wheat flour, sugar, cornmeal, baking soda, baking powder and salt.

Combine yogurt, oil, egg and zest. Add to dry ingredients, stirring just until moistened; do not overmix. Stir in reserved blueberries.

Spoon into 12 medium paper-lined or nonstick muffin cups, filling ¾ full. Bake in 375°F (190°C) oven for 18 to 20 minutes or until muffins are lightly browned and firm to the touch.

MAKES 12 MUFFINS.

NUTRIENT ANALYSIS
Per Muffin

Calories		174
g	Protein	3.8
g	Total Fat	5.7
g	Carbohydrate	28
g	Fibre	2.6
mg	Sodium	210
mg	Potassium	118
mg	Calcium	47
mg	Iron	0.8

 Beet jam was a favourite breakfast spread of the early pioneers. It was prepared with raw grated beets, sugar, water, lemons, walnuts and candied ginger. (Pioneer Potpourri)

Double Bran Muffins

BOTH WHEAT BRAN and oat bran are combined in these tasty high-fibre raisin muffins. One Double Bran muffin for breakfast is a great way to increase your intake of complex carbohydrates, a recommendation of the new Canada's Food Guide to Healthy Eating.

1 cup	all-purpose flour	250 mL
1 cup	natural wheat bran	250 mL
1/2 cup	oat bran	125 mL
1/2 cup	granulated sugar	125 mL
1 tsp	baking soda	5 mL
1 tsp	baking powder	5 mL
1 cup	low-fat plain yogurt	250 mL
1/4 cup	molasses	50 mL
3 tbsp	vegetable oil	45 mL
1	egg	1
1/2 cup	raisins	125 mL

VARIATIONS:
Instead of raisins, add finely chopped apple, kiwifruit, dried dates, dried apricots or dried figs.

In large bowl, stir together flour, brans, sugar, baking soda and baking powder.

In second bowl, combine yogurt, molasses, oil and egg. Add to dry ingredients, stirring just until moistened; stir in raisins. Spoon into 12 large paper-lined or nonstick muffin cups, filling 3/4 full. Bake in 375°F (190°C) oven for 18 to 20 minutes or until muffins are lightly browned and firm to the touch.

MAKES 12 MUFFINS.

NUTRIENT ANALYSIS		
Per Muffin		
Calories		178
g	Protein	4.4
g	Total Fat	4.8
g	Carbohydrate	33
g	Fibre	3.4
mg	Sodium	164
mg	Potassium	405
mg	Calcium	108
mg	Iron	2.5

Cranberry Oat Bran Pancakes

CRANBERRIES AND BLUEBERRIES add a delightful tartness as well as colour to these breakfast pancakes. They are a wonderful high-fibre way to start your day.

Syrup:

2 tbsp	granulated sugar	25 mL
1 tbsp	cornstarch	15 mL
Pinch	ground ginger	Pinch
1 cup	cranberry juice	250 mL

Pancakes:

3/4 cup	oat bran	175 mL
1/2 cup	whole wheat flour	125 mL
1 tbsp	baking powder	15 mL
1 tbsp	granulated sugar	15 mL
1/4 tsp	salt	1 mL
1 cup	low-fat milk	250 mL
1 tbsp	vegetable oil	15 mL
1	egg	1
1/2 cup	chopped cranberries	125 mL
1/2 cup	fresh OR frozen blueberries	125 mL

Syrup: In small microwavable container, combine sugar, cornstarch and ginger; stir in juice. Microwave at High (100%) for 2 to 2 $\frac{1}{2}$ minutes or until mixture comes to a boil; stir several times. Keep warm while cooking pancakes.

Pancakes: In large bowl, stir together bran, flour, baking powder, sugar and salt.

In second bowl, combine milk, oil and egg. Add to dry ingredients; fold in berries.

Heat large nonstick skillet over medium heat until hot. Drop batter by spoonfuls into skillet to form rounds. Cook over medium-high heat until bubbles form on surface and underside is golden brown. Turn pancakes and cook just until second side is lightly browned.

MAKES 4 SERVINGS, THREE 3 $\frac{1}{2}$-INCH (9 CM) PANCAKES WITH $\frac{1}{4}$ CUP (50 ML) SYRUP EACH.

NUTRIENT ANALYSIS
Per Serving

Calories		278
g	Protein	9.0
g	Total Fat	7.6
g	Carbohydrate	52
g	Fibre	5.6
mg	Sodium	419
mg	Potassium	323
mg	Calcium	190
mg	Iron	2.1

Granola-Topped Brunch Cake

MARMALADE

Marmalade comes from the Portuguese word *marmelada*, which means quince jam. The original marmalades were made in Portugal from fresh quinces. Today, the most popular fruit for making marmalades is the Seville orange.

VARIATIONS:

Blueberry Brunch Cake: Add ½ cup (125 mL) blueberries to batter before pouring into baking pan.

Marmalade or Jam Brunch Cake: Before baking, spread ½ cup (125 mL) orange marmalade or raspberry or strawberry jam over batter; sprinkle with Mixed Grain Granola.

Candied Fruit Brunch Cake: Add ½ cup (125 mL) chopped candied fruit (cherries, pineapple or mixed fruit) to batter before pouring into baking pan.

THIS IS A HOLIDAY morning favourite. Granola adds great texture and flavour to this lower-fat coffee cake.

2 cups	cake and pastry flour	500 mL
1 tsp	baking powder	5 mL
1 tsp	baking soda	5 mL
1 tsp	ground cinnamon	5 mL
⅛ tsp	salt	0.5 mL
¼ cup	margarine OR butter	50 mL
1 cup	granulated sugar	250 mL
1	egg	1
2 tsp	vanilla extract	10 mL
1 cup	low-fat plain yogurt	250 mL
½ cup	Mixed Grain Granola (page 8)	125 mL

In large bowl, stir together flour, baking powder, baking soda, cinnamon and salt.

In second bowl, cream margarine and sugar. Add egg and vanilla; beat until light and fluffy. Stir dry ingredients into egg mixture alternately with yogurt.

Pour into lightly greased 8-inch (2 L) square baking pan. Sprinkle with granola.

Bake in 350°F (180°C) oven for 40 minutes or until cake springs back when lightly touched and tester inserted in centre comes out clean.

MAKES 12 SERVINGS.

NUTRIENT ANALYSIS

Per Serving

Calories		*207*
g	Protein	3.6
g	Total Fat	5.4
g	Carbohydrate	36
g	Fibre	0.5
mg	Sodium	234
mg	Potassium	93
mg	Calcium	57
mg	Iron	1.5

 Many kinds of wild berries were known by native peoples in the Maritime provinces. Blueberries, huckleberries and cranberries were eaten fresh and also were boiled and shaped into little cakes that were dried in the sun. *(Out of Old Nova Scotia Kitchens)* Funny how everything old is new again—dried cranberries are showing up in stores today.

Mushroom Broccoli Frittata

THE FLAVOURFUL vegetable filling of this frittata, or Italian omelette, is mixed into the eggs before they are cooked. The cheeses combine with the eggs to provide protein as well as extra calcium.

4	eggs, beaten	4
3 tbsp	low-fat milk	45 mL
1/4 tsp	salt	1 mL
	Freshly ground black pepper to taste	
2 tsp	vegetable oil	10 mL
3	green onions, thinly sliced	3
1 cup	sliced mushrooms	250 mL
1/2 cup	chopped broccoli	125 mL
1/3 cup	shredded Swiss cheese	75 mL
1/4 cup	freshly grated Parmesan cheese	50 mL

BROCCOLI

Broccoli is truly a wonder food, providing an excellent source of vitamin C, a good source of vitamin A and soluble fibre. The other good news is that 1 cup (250 mL) of cooked broccoli has only 48 calories. Isn't it great that a vegetable that tastes so good is so good for you?

In small bowl, combine eggs, milk, salt and pepper; set aside.

In large nonstick skillet, heat oil over medium-high heat; cook onions, mushrooms and broccoli for about 2 minutes or until vegetables are just tender, stirring frequently.

Reduce heat to medium-low. Pour egg mixture into skillet. As bottom begins to set, carefully lift with a spatula, letting uncooked egg flow underneath. Cook for about 2 minutes or until mixture begins to set but is still very moist.

Sprinkle cheeses over egg. Cover skillet handle with aluminum foil and place skillet under preheated broiler. Broil for about 2 minutes or until cheese is bubbly. To serve, cut into 6 wedges.

MAKES 6 SERVINGS.

NUTRIENT ANALYSIS

Per Serving

Calories		111
g	Protein	8.1
g	Total Fat	7.8
g	Carbohydrate	2.2
g	Fibre	0.4
mg	Sodium	240
mg	Potassium	138
mg	Calcium	137
mg	Iron	0.8

Sunday Brunch Vegetable Cheese Pie

SIMILAR TO QUICHE, this cheese pie uses cottage cheese to provide extra protein and calcium. The vegetables add colour and extra fibre.

3	eggs, lightly beaten	3
1	container (500 g) low-fat cottage cheese	1
1/2 cup	low-fat plain yogurt	125 mL
1/4 cup	whole wheat flour	50 mL
1/4 tsp	salt	1 mL
1/8 tsp	freshly ground black pepper	0.5 mL
1 cup	fresh whole wheat breadcrumbs	250 mL
1 cup	finely chopped mixed vegetables (carrot, zucchini, onion and mushroom)	250 mL
2	medium tomatoes, cut into thin wedges	2
Pinch	dried oregano	Pinch
Pinch	dried basil	Pinch

In bowl, mix together eggs, cheese, yogurt, flour, salt and pepper.

Stir 1/4 cup (50 mL) egg mixture into breadcrumbs; place in lightly greased 9-inch (23 cm) deep dish pie plate.

Add mixed vegetables to remaining egg mixture; pour over crumbs. Bake in 350°F (180°C) oven for about 35 minutes or until set in centre. Place tomatoes around outer edge, sprinkle with seasonings; bake for about 5 minutes longer to warm tomatoes. To serve, cut into 6 wedges.

MAKES 6 SERVINGS.

NUTRIENT ANALYSIS		
Per Serving		
Calories		162
g	Protein	17
g	Total Fat	4.2
g	Carbohydrate	15
g	Fibre	1.9
mg	Sodium	552
mg	Potassium	332
mg	Calcium	118
mg	Iron	1.2

 Early homesteaders would pack away any extra summer eggs, hoping to have enough to last through the winter. They might be packed in bran or salt, wrapped in brown paper or stored in a water glass solution and put down in the cellar. *(Canadian Prairie Homesteaders)*

It's a wonder anyone lived to tell about it after eating one of these old eggs!

NEXT PAGE: *Cranberry Oat Bran Pancakes (page 13)*.

Fast Morning Starts: Fruit Shakes

WE OFTEN PROMISE ourselves to get up just a little bit earlier so we'll have time for breakfast. After all, we know every day should start with a "break the fast" meal. But...another rushed morning. At least, try one of these fast beverage breakfasts. Prepare as much as possible the night before, then store in a blender container in the refrigerator for quick blending in the morning. Frozen peaches or berries may replace fresh for year-round use.

YOGURT WHIZ

1 cup	low-fat plain yogurt	250 mL
½ cup	low-fat milk	125 mL
1	medium banana, chopped	1
¾ cup	chopped peaches OR raspberries OR blueberries	175 mL
2 tsp	liquid honey	10 mL

In food processor or blender container, process all ingredients until smooth.

MAKES 3 SERVINGS, ⅔ CUP (150 mL) EACH.

ORANGE STRAWBERRY SMOOTHIE

¾ cup	sliced strawberries	175 mL
¼ cup	low-fat plain yogurt	50 mL
¼ cup	orange juice	50 mL
¼ cup	low-fat milk	50 mL
1 tbsp	strawberry jam	15 mL
½ tsp	vanilla extract	2 mL
Dash	almond extract	Dash

In food processor or blender container, process all ingredients until smooth.

MAKES 2 SERVINGS, ¾ CUP (175 mL) EACH.

NUTRIENT ANALYSIS

Yogurt Whiz
Per Serving

Calories		141
g	Protein	6.4
g	Total Fat	2.3
g	Carbohydrate	25
g	Fibre	1.5
mg	Sodium	79
mg	Potassium	497
mg	Calcium	206
mg	Iron	0.3

Orange Strawberry Smoothie
Per Serving

Calories		97
g	Protein	3.3
g	Total Fat	1.3
g	Carbohydrate	18
g	Fibre	1.5
mg	Sodium	39
mg	Potassium	282
mg	Calcium	107
mg	Iron	0.4

PREVIOUS PAGE: *Focaccia Bread Pizza Squares (page 29)*.

APRICOT PINEAPPLE SIPPER

½ cup	chilled apricot nectar	125 mL
½ cup	low-fat plain yogurt	125 mL
½ cup	unsweetened crushed pineapple, with juice	125 mL
1 tsp	liquid honey	5 mL
⅛ tsp	almond extract	0.5 mL

In food processor or blender container, process all ingredients until smooth.

MAKES 2 SERVINGS, ¾ CUP (175 mL) EACH.

APPLE-BERRY FIZZ

1 cup	apple juice	250 mL
½ cup	sliced strawberries OR raspberries	125 mL
½ cup	low-fat plain yogurt	125 mL
½ cup	low-fat milk	125 mL
½ cup	ice cubes	125 mL
⅓ cup	oat bran	75 mL
1 tbsp	liquid honey	15 mL
Pinch	ground cinnamon	Pinch

In food processor or blender container, process all ingredients until smooth. Sprinkle each serving with cinnamon.

MAKES 3 SERVINGS, 1 CUP (250 mL) EACH.

MELON MILK SHAKE

2 cups	melon pieces	500 mL
1 cup	low-fat milk	250 mL
½ cup	high-fibre bran cereal	125 mL
½ cup	unsweetened crushed pineapple, with juice	125 mL
2 tbsp	liquid honey	25 mL
1 tsp	vanilla extract	5 mL

In food processor or blender container, process all ingredients until smooth. Serve at once as beverage continues to thicken.

MAKES 3 SERVINGS, 1 CUP (250 mL) EACH.

NUTRIENT ANALYSIS

Apricot Pineapple Sipper
Per Serving

Calories		124
g	Protein	3.8
g	Total Fat	1.1
g	Carbohydrate	26
g	Fibre	1.0
mg	Sodium	46
mg	Potassium	297
mg	Calcium	127
mg	Iron	0.5

Apple-Berry Fizz
Per Serving

Calories		142
g	Protein	5.6
g	Total Fat	2.4
g	Carbohydrate	29
g	Fibre	2.3
mg	Sodium	53
mg	Potassium	368
mg	Calcium	142
mg	Iron	1.1

Melon Milk Shake
Per Serving

Calories		180
g	Protein	5.3
g	Total Fat	2.1
g	Carbohydrate	40
g	Fibre	4.9
mg	Sodium	154
mg	Potassium	640
mg	Calcium	128
mg	Iron	2.0

2 Appetizers

Appetizers are foods served before a meal to excite the palate for what is to follow. They are like the prologue to a play, preparing us for further and even greater joys to come. ◆ *We believe we have come up with a few meal starters to stimulate your palate. In keeping with the new Canada's Food Guide to Healthy Eating, we have developed recipes that include all the food groups. From yogurt Skinny Dips (page 22), to Bean and Lentil Pâté (page 26), to Marinated Vegetables (page 24), we're sure you will find one to suit the occasion.* ◆ *Some of our appetizers can be prepared ahead and stored frozen or refrigerated for busy days. Others require more last-minute preparation. Some will also be useful for lunches or late-evening snacks. All are low-fat, delicious and are offered in small amounts to save the appetite for the meal to come. Well, the serving sizes are small — how many you eat is up to you.*

Boursin-Style Cheese Spreads

BOURSIN CHEESE is a soft, expensive French triple-cream cheese with a buttery texture. Yogurt Cheese provides a wonderful creamy base for lower-fat Boursin-style spreads. Serve these spreads on an assortment of crackers. They make welcome hostess and holiday gifts.

Yogurt Cheese:

| 4 cups | low-fat plain yogurt | 1 L |

Pour yogurt into a sieve lined with cheesecloth or a coffee filter paper set over a medium bowl. Cover and refrigerate overnight or up to 24 hours. Gather edges of cheesecloth together and gently squeeze out any remaining liquid. Transfer cheese to a bowl; cover and refrigerate until ready to use (up to 1 week). Discard remaining whey liquid.

MAKES ABOUT 1 $\frac{1}{2}$ CUPS (375 mL).

Variations:

To $\frac{3}{4}$ cup (175 mL) Yogurt Cheese add:

Garlic Cheese: 1 tsp (5 mL) garlic powder, and pinch each of freshly ground pepper, granulated sugar and paprika.

Peppery Cheese: $\frac{1}{2}$ tsp (2 mL) pepper, $\frac{1}{4}$ tsp (1 mL) hot pepper sauce and $\frac{1}{4}$ tsp (1 mL) Worcestershire sauce.

Herbed Cheese: 1 tsp (5 mL) dried basil, $\frac{1}{2}$ tsp (2 mL) dried oregano, $\frac{1}{4}$ tsp (1 mL) Worcestershire sauce, pinch dry mustard and paprika.

MAKES $\frac{3}{4}$ CUP (175 mL) PER VARIATION.

SHERRY CHEDDAR CHEESE

Combine $\frac{1}{2}$ cup (125 mL) finely shredded light old Cheddar cheese, 2 tbsp (25 mL) dry sherry, 1 tsp (5 mL) light soy sauce, pinch dry mustard and dash hot pepper sauce.

MAKES 1 $\frac{1}{4}$ CUPS (300 mL).

NUTRIENT ANALYSIS		
Garlic, Peppery, Herbed		
Per 2 Tbsp (25 mL)		
Calories		48
g	Protein	4.0
g	Total Fat	1.2
g	Carbohydrate	5.4
g	Fibre	0
mg	Sodium	54
mg	Potassium	181
mg	Calcium	137
mg	Iron	0.1

Light Cheddar Cheese Spread

QUICK TO PREPARE, this lighter spread has all the great flavour of higher-fat spreads. Serve on whole wheat crackers for added fibre.

1 cup	shredded light old Cheddar cheese	250 mL
$\frac{1}{3}$ cup	light cream cheese	75 mL
$\frac{1}{4}$ tsp	dry mustard	1 mL
$\frac{1}{4}$ tsp	Worcestershire sauce	1 mL

In food processor container or with an electric beater, process Cheddar cheese, cream cheese and seasonings until smooth. Cover and refrigerate for up to 2 weeks or freeze for longer storage.

MAKES ABOUT 1 $\frac{1}{4}$ CUPS (300 mL).

CHEDDAR

Light Cheddar cheese provides less fat than regular Cheddar. Today you can find a variety of good lighter cheeses. Be sure to check the label for actual percentage of fat.

VARIATIONS:

Cheddar Cheese Ball: Form mixture into a ball. Roll in chopped fresh cilantro, parsley or dill.

Vegetable Cheese Spread: Add 1 cup (250 mL) finely chopped cooked broccoli, $\frac{1}{2}$ cup (125 mL) finely chopped celery, $\frac{1}{2}$ cup (125 mL) finely chopped red pepper and 1 finely chopped green onion. Spread on slices of rye bread and bake in 350°F (180°C) oven until hot.

Cheese-Stuffed Dates: For a fibre-rich appetizer, use Light Cheddar Cheese Spread to fill pitted dates.

NUTRIENT ANALYSIS

Per 2 Tbsp (25 mL)

Calories		51
g	Protein	4.1
g	Total Fat	3.8
g	Carbohydrate	0.5
g	Fibre	0
mg	Sodium	127
mg	Potassium	23
mg	Calcium	90
mg	Iron	0.1

Skinny Dips

DIPS TO ENHANCE raw vegetables or crackers don't have to be high in fat. Try these skinny dips the next time you are preparing a vegetable platter. They are also nice with pita bread, cut into triangles to make dippers.

CREAMY DIP

1 cup	low-fat cottage cheese	250 mL
1/2 cup	low-fat plain yogurt	125 mL
1 tbsp	finely chopped sweet red pepper	15 mL
1 tbsp	finely chopped fresh parsley	15 mL
2	green onions, finely chopped	2
2	drops hot pepper sauce	2

In food processor or blender container, process cheese and yogurt until very smooth. Remove and stir in remaining ingredients. Cover and refrigerate for up to 4 days.

MAKES 1 1/2 CUPS (375 mL).

CURRIED LENTIL JALAPEÑO DIP

1 tsp	olive oil	5 mL
1	large onion, chopped	1
1	clove garlic, minced	1
2 cups	chicken stock	500 mL
1 cup	dried green lentils, washed	250 mL
1	jalapeño pepper, chopped	1
2 tbsp	chopped fresh parsley	25 mL
1 tsp	ground cumin	5 mL
1 tsp	curry powder	5 mL
1/4 cup	low-fat plain yogurt	50 mL

In large nonstick skillet, heat oil over medium heat; cook onion and garlic for 5 minutes or until soft, stirring frequently.

Add stock, lentils, pepper, parsley, cumin and curry powder. Cover and bring to a boil; reduce heat and simmer for 30 to 40 minutes or until lentils are soft. Cool slightly.

In food processor or blender container, process lentil mixture until smooth. Remove and stir in yogurt. Dip may be served warm or cold.

MAKES 3 CUPS (750 mL).

VARIATIONS:

Add any one of the following to Creamy Dip: 1/2 cup (125 mL) chopped crabmeat or small shrimp; 1/4 cup (50 mL) shredded light old Cheddar cheese; freshly grated Parmesan cheese; or hot bottled salsa.

Use red lentils in place of green lentils; they require only a 10-minute cooking time.

NUTRIENT ANALYSIS

Creamy Dip
Per 2 Tbsp (25 mL)

Calories		23
g	Protein	3.2
g	Total Fat	0.4
g	Carbohydrate	1.4
g	Fibre	0
mg	Sodium	94
mg	Potassium	48
mg	Calcium	33
mg	Iron	0.1

Curried Lentil Jalapeño
Per 2 Tbsp (25 mL)

Calories		37
g	Protein	2.7
g	Total Fat	0.4
g	Carbohydrate	5.8
g	Fibre	1.0
mg	Sodium	87
mg	Potassium	101
mg	Calcium	14
mg	Iron	0.9

Black Bean Dip with Tortilla Snacks

BLACK BEANS replace chick-peas in this version of the popular dip, hummus. Now that dried black turtle beans are becoming more readily available, they are a wonderful change from chick-peas. A bonus—the recipe makes a large quantity and it freezes well. The low-fat Flour Tortilla Snacks are wonderful accompaniments.

½ lb	dried black beans, washed	250 g
¼ cup	lime juice	50 mL
¼ cup	peanut butter	50 mL
2	large cloves garlic	2
½ cup	minced fresh cilantro	125 mL
1 tsp	hot pepper sauce	5 mL
¼ tsp	salt	1 mL
	Flour Tortilla Snacks (recipe below)	

COOKING TIPS:

To save time, prepare as much as you can in advance. Cook black beans ahead and freeze for later use. Make extra for the Warm Spinach Salad with Black Beans (page 57). Planning ahead means you are less likely to let slip your intentions for well-balanced nutritious meals.

In large saucepan, combine beans with 3 cups (750 mL) cold water. Cover and bring to a boil; boil for 2 minutes. Remove from heat and let stand for 1 hour; drain. Cover with cold water and bring to a boil; reduce heat and simmer for 40 minutes or until beans are tender; drain and reserve ½ cup (125 mL) liquid.

In food processor container, process lime juice, peanut butter and garlic until smooth. Add beans and enough reserved liquid to blend to a smooth consistency. Remove and stir in cilantro and seasonings. Cover and refrigerate. Serve with Flour Tortilla Snacks.

MAKES 14 SERVINGS, ¼ CUP (50 mL) DIP WITH 6 FLOUR TORTILLA SNACKS EACH.

Flour Tortilla Snacks: Using scissors, cut 1 pkg 8-inch (20 cm) flour tortillas into 10 wedges. Bake in 350°F (180°C) oven for about 20 minutes, or until golden and crisp. Cool and store in closed container.

NUTRIENT ANALYSIS		
Per Serving		
Calories		*155*
g	Protein	6.8
g	Total Fat	4.2
g	Carbohydrate	24
g	Fibre	1.8
mg	Sodium	203
mg	Potassium	308
mg	Calcium	62
mg	Iron	1.8

Marinated Italian-Style Vegetables

CHUNKS of colourful vegetables stimulate the appetite. Change the vegetables according to seasonal availability. This version may be used as a starter for a meal or as a salad accompaniment.

Vegetables:

2	large carrots, cut into 1-inch (2.5 cm) chunks	2
2 cups	broccoli OR broccoflower florets	500 mL
10	spears asparagus, cut into 2-inch (5 cm) lengths	10
1/2	sweet red pepper, cubed	1/2
1/2	sweet green pepper, cubed	1/2
1/2	sweet yellow pepper, cubed	1/2
10	medium mushrooms, halved	10
1	medium zucchini, cubed	1
2 cups	cubed eggplant	500 mL

Marinade:

1/4 cup	chopped fresh parsley	50 mL
1 tbsp	dried basil	15 mL
1/2 tsp	dried oregano	2 mL
1	clove garlic, minced	1
1/4 tsp	salt	1 mL
1/4 tsp	hot pepper sauce	1 mL
1/8 tsp	freshly ground black pepper	0.5 mL
2 tbsp	olive oil	25 mL
2 tbsp	water	25 mL
1 tbsp	balsamic vinegar	15 mL
1 tbsp	white wine vinegar	15 mL

Vegetables: In large shallow microwavable dish, arrange vegetables in a circular pattern with carrots on outside, then broccoli, asparagus, peppers, mushrooms, zucchini, ending in centre with eggplant. Sprinkle with 1 tbsp (15 mL) water. Cover and microwave at High (100%) for 8 minutes or until vegetables are tender-crisp; cool. Place vegetables in plastic bag.

Marinade: In bowl, stir together parsley, seasonings, oil, water and vinegars. Pour over vegetables, close bag and refrigerate for several hours for flavour to develop.

MAKES 10 SERVINGS, ABOUT 1/2 CUP (125 mL) EACH.

NUTRIENT ANALYSIS		
Per Serving		
Calories		*55*
g	Protein	2.1
g	Total Fat	3.0
g	Carbohydrate	6.7
g	Fibre	2.1
mg	Sodium	81
mg	Potassium	333
mg	Calcium	35
mg	Iron	1.0

Classic Antipasto

THIS IS A GREAT APPETIZER to have on hand. It is best made in the fall, when all the vegetables are inexpensive, and then stored in the freezer. The recipe multiplies easily — just be sure to increase the cooking time.

½ cup	tiny broccoli florets	125 mL
½ cup	cauliflower florets	125 mL
½ cup	chopped sweet red pepper	125 mL
½ cup	chopped sweet green pepper	125 mL
½ cup	thinly sliced mushrooms	125 mL
1	clove garlic, minced	1
1	small carrot, thinly sliced	1
1	can (198 g) tuna (packed in water), drained and flaked	1
¼ cup	chopped sweet pickled onions	50 mL
¼ cup	chopped black olives	50 mL
¼ cup	chopped stuffed green olives	50 mL
½ cup	tomato sauce	125 mL
¼ cup	chili sauce	50 mL
¼ tsp	hot pepper sauce	1 mL
¼ tsp	salt	1 mL
⅛ tsp	freshly ground black pepper	0.5 mL

Microwave: In 6-cup (1.5 L) microwavable dish, combine broccoli, cauliflower, peppers, mushrooms, garlic and carrot; sprinkle with 1 tsp (5 mL) water. Cover and microwave at High (100%) for 4 to 5 minutes or until vegetables are tender-crisp; stir several times.

Stir in tuna, onions, olives, tomato sauce, chili sauce, hot pepper sauce, salt and pepper. Cover and microwave at High for about 3 minutes or until mixture thickens; stir once and cool.

Spoon into glass jars and store in refrigerator for 1 week. Freeze for longer storage.

Stovetop: In large saucepan, combine all ingredients except tuna. Bring to a boil over medium heat, reduce heat and simmer for about 15 minutes or just until vegetables are tender-crisp; stir frequently. Remove from heat, stir in tuna and cool.

Spoon into glass jars and store in refrigerator for 1 week. Freeze for longer storage.

MAKES ABOUT 2 ½ CUPS (625 mL).

NUTRIENT ANALYSIS		
Per 2 Tbsp (25 mL)		
Calories		27
g	Protein	2.8
g	Total Fat	1.0
g	Carbohydrate	2.2
g	Fibre	0.6
mg	Sodium	214
mg	Potassium	121
mg	Calcium	11
mg	Iron	0.5

Bean and Lentil Pâté

COOKED OR CANNED lentils can be turned into an easy, time-saving vegetable pâté. Fibre-full and satisfying, this spread is excellent served warm or cold with a variety of crackers or whole wheat bread toasted and cut into squares.

$\frac{1}{2}$ cup	dried red lentils, washed	125 mL
1 cup	water	250 mL
1 tbsp	vegetable oil	15 mL
1 tbsp	chopped fresh parsley	15 mL
2	cloves garlic, minced	2
2 tsp	low-sodium chicken bouillon powder	10 mL
1	can (19 oz/540 mL) Roman OR pinto beans, drained and rinsed	1
2 tbsp	dry sherry	25 mL
1 tsp	Worcestershire sauce	5 mL
$\frac{1}{4}$ tsp	hot pepper sauce	1 mL
$\frac{1}{8}$ tsp	freshly ground black pepper	0.5 mL

In small saucepan, bring lentils and water to a boil; reduce heat, cover and simmer for 8 minutes or until lentils are just tender and water is absorbed.

In small nonstick skillet, heat oil over medium-high heat; cook parsley, garlic and bouillon for 2 to 3 minutes or until garlic is soft. In food processor or blender container, process parsley mixture, beans, lentils, sherry and seasonings until mixture is smooth.

Spoon into small containers; cover and chill until mixture is firm.

MAKES ABOUT 2 $\frac{1}{2}$ CUPS (625 mL).

NUTRIENT ANALYSIS
Per 2 Tbsp (25 mL)

Calories		42
g	Protein	2.2
g	Total Fat	0.8
g	Carbohydrate	6.2
g	Fibre	1.4
mg	Sodium	141
mg	Potassium	125
mg	Calcium	13
mg	Iron	0.8

Crostini with Summer Vegetables

CROSTINI generally refers to Italian croutons made from slices of bread covered with various kinds of cheese and baked. They are usually served as an hors d'oeuvre. We've added several vegetables to our crostini for their colour and nutrients.

1 tbsp	olive oil	15 mL
1	small onion, chopped	1
2	medium carrots, cut into 1-inch (2.5 cm) strips	2
1	medium sweet green pepper, chopped	1
1	clove garlic, minced	1
2	firm medium tomatoes, chopped	2
1	medium zucchini, cut into 1-inch (2.5 cm) strips	1
$\frac{1}{2}$ cup	chopped fresh basil leaves OR 2 tbsp (25 mL) dried	125 mL
$\frac{1}{8}$ tsp	freshly ground black pepper	0.5 mL
1 cup	shredded part-skim mozzarella cheese	250 mL
1	French baguette, cut into 24 thin slices	1

In large nonstick skillet, heat oil over medium heat; cook onion and carrots, covered, for 5 minutes or until softened. Add green pepper and garlic; cover and cook for 3 minutes or until pepper is softened. Add tomatoes and zucchini; cover and cook for about 5 minutes or until all vegetables are softened. Stir in basil and pepper.

Sprinkle cheese over vegetables; reduce heat. Cover for 3 minutes for cheese to melt; keep warm.

Toast or broil bread slices on each side until golden. Top each toasted slice with a portion of cooked vegetables and cheese. Serve at once on a small plate.

MAKES 12 SERVINGS, 2 SLICES EACH.

NUTRIENT ANALYSIS		
Per Serving		
Calories		141
g	Protein	6.0
g	Total Fat	3.8
g	Carbohydrate	21
g	Fibre	1.6
mg	Sodium	231
mg	Potassium	193
mg	Calcium	99
mg	Iron	1.2

Smoked Salmon Bites

QUICK SALMON SPREAD

Blend 1 can (7.5 oz/213 g), drained salmon with ½ cup (125 mL) low-fat cottage cheese, 1 chopped green onion, 1 chopped dill pickle, 1 tbsp (15 mL) lemon juice, dash hot pepper sauce and some chopped fresh parsley. Use as a spread for whole wheat toast squares or crackers.

MAKES ABOUT 1 ½ CUPS (375 mL).

SERVE THESE CRUSTLESS quiche-like squares, warm or cold, as finger food at a festive party. If smoked salmon is not in the budget, a small can of salmon may be used; choose sockeye for the best colour.

1 ½ cups	low-fat cottage cheese	375 mL
½	pkg (250 g) light cream cheese	½
3	eggs	3
1 tbsp	lemon juice	15 mL
1 tbsp	chopped fresh parsley	15 mL
½ tsp	dried thyme	2 mL
¼ tsp	hot pepper sauce	1 mL
1 cup	diced smoked salmon (about 5 oz/150 g)	250 mL
1 cup	shredded part-skim mozzarella cheese	250 mL
3	green onions, sliced	3

In food processor or blender container, process cottage cheese, cream cheese and eggs until smooth. Remove from container to bowl. Stir in juice, parsley, seasonings, salmon, mozzarella cheese and onions.

Microwave: Microwave egg mixture and vegetables in 8-inch (20 cm) microwavable dish, covered, at Medium-High (70%) for 11 to 14 minutes or until knife inserted in centre comes out clean; rotate every 3 minutes. Allow to stand for 5 minutes before cutting into bite-sized pieces.

Oven: Spray nonstick 8-inch (20 cm) square baking pan with cooking spray.

Bake egg mixture in pan in 350°F (180°C) oven for 45 to 50 minutes or until knife inserted in centre comes out clean. Allow to stand for 5 minutes before cutting.

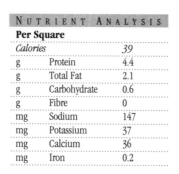

MAKES 36 APPETIZERS.

NUTRIENT ANALYSIS		
Per Square		
Calories		*39*
g	Protein	4.4
g	Total Fat	2.1
g	Carbohydrate	0.6
g	Fibre	0
mg	Sodium	147
mg	Potassium	37
mg	Calcium	36
mg	Iron	0.2

Focaccia Bread Pizza Squares

FOCACCIA is an Italian flatbread made with flour, salt and olive oil. Today in most grocery stores, you can find Italian-style flatbread that is very similar to the original focaccia. This bread comes in different herb flavours, but for this recipe it is preferable to use the plain one.

1	Italian-style gourmet flatbread (about 400 g)	1
1	can (7.5 oz/213 mL) tomato sauce	1
$\frac{1}{2}$ tsp	garlic powder	2 mL
$\frac{1}{2}$ tsp	dried oregano	2 mL
1	bottle (6 oz/170 mL) marinated artichoke hearts, drained and chopped	1
$\frac{1}{2}$	large sweet orange, yellow OR green pepper, cubed	$\frac{1}{2}$
1 cup	crumbled feta cheese	250 mL

Place flatbread on large baking sheet. Combine tomato sauce and seasonings; spread over bread. Top with artichokes, pepper and cheese.

Bake in 425°F (220°C) oven for 15 minutes or until crust is golden and cheese has softened. Cut into 36 bite-sized pieces.

MAKES 36 APPETIZERS.

PESTO APPETIZERS

Make lots of Light Pesto Sauce (page 80) and keep a supply in the freezer. Freeze in small amounts and use to make these fast and easy appetizers.

Pesto Toasts: Spread Light Pesto Sauce over slices of toasted French bread. Place on baking sheet and broil until spread starts to bubble.

Pesto Dip: Combine $\frac{1}{2}$ cup (125 mL) Light Pesto Sauce with 1/4 cup (50 mL) low-fat plain yogurt or light mayonnaise. Serve with fresh vegetables or pita triangles.

MAKES ¾ CUP (175 mL).

NUTRIENT ANALYSIS
Per Piece

Calories		41
g	Protein	2.0
g	Total Fat	1.1
g	Carbohydrate	6.0
g	Fibre	0.2
mg	Sodium	141
mg	Potassium	51
mg	Calcium	23
mg	Iron	0.4

Sweet Hot Mustard Appetizers

KEEP SWEET HOT MUSTARD on hand for an easy appetizer. It is also delicious served with cold meat and spread on ham during baking. We like to add extra crushed mustard seeds for a more grainy style of mustard. Small jars of this fancy mustard make a much appreciated hostess gift.

⅓ cup	Sweet Hot Mustard (recipe below)	75 mL
8	slices French bread	8
2 tbsp	freshly grated Parmesan cheese	25 mL

Spread mustard on bread slices, dividing evenly; place on baking sheet. Sprinkle with cheese and broil until bubbly. Serve at once.

MAKES 8 APPETIZERS.

SWEET HOT MUSTARD

¼ cup	dry mustard	50 mL
½ cup	loosely packed brown sugar	125 mL
⅓ cup	cider vinegar	75 mL
1 tbsp	vegetable oil	15 mL
1 tbsp	molasses	15 mL
¼ tsp	ground allspice	1 mL
¼ tsp	ground cloves	1 mL
¼ tsp	salt	1 mL
⅛ tsp	freshly ground black pepper	0.5 mL
1 tbsp	cornstarch	15 mL
2 tbsp	water	25 mL

In small saucepan, combine mustard, sugar, vinegar, oil, molasses and seasonings. Cook and stir over medium heat for 5 minutes or until hot.

Stir together cornstarch and water; stir into mustard mixture. Cook over low heat until smooth and thickened; stir frequently. Cool before storing in glass bottles. Refrigerate for up to 1 month.

MAKES ABOUT 2/3 CUP (150 mL).

NUTRIENT ANALYSIS
Per Appetizer

Calories		97
g	Protein	2.6
g	Total Fat	2.5
g	Carbohydrate	16
g	Fibre	0.5
mg	Sodium	156
mg	Potassium	98
mg	Calcium	53
mg	Iron	1.0

 For those who could afford them, a wide variety of spices was available by the start of the 19th century. Mustard was common, and fancy mustards were made at home. Pepper, cayenne and curry powders were also popular. Of course, today, the range of spices and herbs we enjoy is extensive, giving a boost to lower-fat cooking.

Red Pepper in Mushroom Caps

MICROWAVE NIBBLES

Toasting nuts and seeds to make delicious snacks is quick and easy in the microwave oven.

Pumpkin Seeds:

In a shallow microwavable dish, spread 1 cup (250 mL) washed and dried pumpkin seeds on a double thickness of dry paper towelling. Microwave at High (100%) for 10 to 12 minutes or until nicely toasted; stir several times. Add salt and butter, if desired.

MAKES 1 CUP (250 mL).

Chili Nuts:

In a microwavable container, combine 1 cup (250 mL) roasted peanuts, ¼ tsp (1 mL) chili powder, ¼ tsp (1 mL) garlic salt and a pinch of cayenne. Microwave at High (100%) for 3 to 4 minutes or until nuts just begin to turn brown.

MAKES 1 CUP (250 mL).

THESE MUSHROOMS are usually a favourite and disappear fast. So, make extra—they're quick and easy in the microwave oven.

18	large mushrooms	18
3	green onions, finely chopped	3
½ cup	finely chopped sweet red pepper	125 mL
1 tsp	olive oil	5 mL
2 tbsp	dried breadcrumbs	25 mL
⅓ cup	freshly grated Parmesan cheese	75 mL

Remove stems from mushrooms; set caps aside and chop stems.

In small microwavable container, microwave stems, onions, pepper and oil at High (100%) for 2 ½ to 3 minutes or until vegetables are just tender; stir once. Stir in breadcrumbs and cheese.

Spoon filling into caps. Arrange ½ of mushrooms in a circle on a microwavable plate. Microwave at High for 2 to 3 minutes or until mushrooms are hot, but not soft. Repeat with remaining mushrooms.

MAKES 18 APPETIZERS.

NUTRIENT ANALYSIS		
Per Serving		
Calories		*19*
g	Protein	1.3
g	Total Fat	0.9
g	Carbohydrate	1.7
g	Fibre	0.3
mg	Sodium	42
mg	Potassium	77
mg	Calcium	29
mg	Iron	0.3

Stacked Tortilla Wedges

PUT A STAR beside this recipe—it is probably the easiest you'll ever prepare.

6	8-inch (20 cm) flour tortillas	6
1 cup	shredded light Cheddar cheese	250 mL
2 tsp	chopped canned jalapeño peppers	10 mL
1	finely chopped green onion	1
1 tbsp	minced fresh marjoram OR 1 tsp (15 mL) dried	15 mL
½ tsp	olive oil	2 mL

Place 3 tortillas on baking sheet. Distribute cheese over tortillas. Sprinkle peppers, onion and marjoram evenly over cheese. Press remaining tortillas gently on top. Brush tops sparingly with oil.

Bake in 400°F (200°C) oven for about 6 minutes or until lightly browned and cheese is melted. To serve, cut each stack into 8 wedges.

MAKES 12 SERVINGS, 2 WEDGES EACH.

NUTRIENT ANALYSIS		
Per Serving		
Calories		89
g	Protein	4.6
g	Total Fat	3.5
g	Carbohydrate	11
g	Fibre	0
mg	Sodium	175
mg	Potassium	33
mg	Calcium	103
mg	Iron	0.9

Tostadas with Frijoles and Salsa

TOSTADAS are flat crisp-fried corn tortillas frequently served with refried beans, shredded lettuce, diced tomatoes and peppers, and grated cheese. Our version uses baked rather than deep-fried tostadas, an easy low-fat frijole, or bean, layer and a made-ahead salsa for a hearty Mexican-style appetizer that is high in fibre.

8	corn tortillas	8
1	recipe Frijoles (recipe below)	1
1 cup	Chunky Salsa (recipe below)	250 mL

Using scissors, cut each corn tortilla into 6 wedges. Bake in 350°F (180°C) oven for about 20 minutes or until crisp and lightly browned. Cool tostadas.

Spread frijoles in shallow serving dish. Spread with salsa, leaving a border of beans visible. Serve with tostadas.

MAKES 8 SERVINGS, ABOUT $\frac{1}{4}$ CUP (50 ML) BEANS AND 2 TBSP (25 ML) SALSA WITH 6 MINI TOSTADAS EACH.

FRIJOLES (BEANS)

FRIJOLES are an integral part of Mexican cuisine. When combined with cheese, they provide a complete protein and can make a valuable addition to your diet. You can also use this version as a filling for tacos, tortillas and enchiladas in place of higher-fat refried beans, or as a dip.

1	can (14 oz/398 mL) beans in tomato sauce	1
1 cup	shredded light Cheddar cheese	250 mL
2 tbsp	chopped onion	25 mL
1 tbsp	chili powder	15 mL
1	canned jalapeño pepper, seeded and diced	1

In food processor container, process beans, cheese, onion, chili powder and diced jalapeño until smooth. Serve warm or cold.

MAKES 2 $\frac{1}{4}$ CUPS (550 ML).

NUTRIENT ANALYSIS
Tostados with Frijoles and Salsa
Per Serving

Calories		175
g	Protein	9.4
g	Total Fat	4.5
g	Carbohydrate	27
g	Fibre	5.9
mg	Sodium	401
mg	Potassium	340
mg	Calcium	180
mg	Iron	2.1

CHUNKY SALSA

QUICK TEX-MEX
APPETIZERS

Salsa Dip: Mix 1 part Chunky Salsa with a bit of low-fat plain yogurt. Serve with vegetable dippers or mini tostadas.

Nachos: Sprinkle mini tostadas with grated cheese and chopped jalapeño peppers and bake just until cheese is melted.

WHEN TOMATOES are plentiful, make this wonderful salsa. For a fierier version, add more hot pepper.

8 cups	peeled chopped tomatoes	2 L
2 cups	chopped onions	500 mL
2	sweet green peppers, chopped	2
1	hot red or green pepper, minced	1
2	cloves garlic, minced	2
1/2 cup	chopped fresh parsley OR cilantro	125 mL
1	can (5.5 oz/156 mL) tomato paste	1
3/4 cup	white vinegar	175 mL
1 tbsp	granulated sugar	15 mL
1 tsp	salt	5 mL
1/2 tsp	ground cumin	2 mL

In large saucepan, combine tomatoes, onions, green and hot peppers, garlic, parsley, tomato paste, vinegar, sugar, salt and cumin. Bring to a boil, reduce heat and simmer, uncovered, for 2 hours or until salsa reaches desired consistency.

Store in refrigerator for up to 2 weeks or freeze for longer storage.

MAKES 10 CUPS (2.5 L).

3

Soups

Soups have that special "welcome home" quality, whether they are light, as a prelude to dinner, or heartier, to be served as a main course. A cold soup can be a refreshing entrée on a hot summer day. Hearty main course soups give us time-saving and budget-stretching meals. ◆ *Main course soups meet most of the dietary guidelines in the new Canada's Food Guide because they are usually made with vegetables, barley, rice, legumes or meat. Make these soups in larger quantities and freeze them for busier days. All you need to add to make a meal from one of these soups are a whole wheat roll or crusty Italian or French bread, a green salad and fresh fruit.* ◆ *Our recipes calling for stocks have been analysed using low-sodium powdered chicken or beef bouillon products. These stock concentrates are reduced in sodium by 30% from the regular concentrates but are still very high in sodium. You can add more water to them to reduce the sodium content even further. A few of the recipes call for Homemade stock, which has less sodium than the low-sodium commercial variety. Store these stocks in the refrigerator until chilled, then skim off all fat and refrigerate or freeze for longer storage.* ◆ *We have omitted salt in many recipes and used herbs, spices and vegetables for added flavour.*

Chilled Soups

FRESH TOMATO AND DILL SOUP

THIS UNCOOKED SOUP is easily prepared and has a vine-ripened tomato flavour. A swirl of extra yogurt in each bowl adds a nice touch.

3	large tomatoes, peeled and chopped	3
½ cup	low-fat plain yogurt	125 mL
1 tsp	dried dill weed OR	5 mL
	1 tbsp (15 mL) chopped fresh dill	
¼ tsp	salt	1 mL
Pinch	freshly ground pepper	Pinch
2 tbsp	chopped chives OR green onions	25 mL
	Garnish: Chopped tomatoes and dill sprigs, low-fat plain yogurt	

In food processor or blender container, process tomatoes, yogurt, dill weed and seasonings until smooth; stir in chives. Cover and refrigerate for 1 to 2 hours for flavour to develop. Serve with a choice of garnishes as desired.

MAKES 4 SERVINGS, 1 CUP (250 ML) EACH.

VARIATION:
Replace dill with ½ tsp (2 mL) curry powder and 1 tsp (5 mL) granulated sugar.

CHILLED HONEYDEW GAZPACHO

RIPE HONEYDEW MELON, cucumber and mint are blended for a refreshing and flavourful chilled soup. The tangy tartness of yogurt contrasts well with the sweetness of the fruit.

4 cups	chopped honeydew melon	1 L
1	medium seedless cucumber, peeled and cubed	1
1 cup	chopped celery	250 mL
¼ cup	chopped fresh mint	50 mL
1 cup	apple juice	250 mL
1 cup	low-fat plain yogurt	250 mL
⅓ cup	white wine vinegar	75 mL
1 tbsp	lemon juice	15 mL
½ tsp	salt	2 mL
¼ tsp	white pepper	1 mL
	Garnish: Mint sprigs, diced cucumber	

In food processor or blender container, coarsely chop melon, cucumber, celery and mint. Add apple juice, yogurt, vinegar, lemon juice and seasonings; purée until smooth.

NUTRIENT ANALYSIS

Tomato and Dill
Per Serving

Calories		50
g	Protein	2.9
g	Total Fat	1.0
g	Carbohydrate	8.8
g	Fibre	1.7
mg	Sodium	204
mg	Potassium	393
mg	Calcium	71
mg	Iron	0.8

Honeydew Gazpacho
Per Serving

Calories		100
g	Protein	3.2
g	Total Fat	0.9
g	Carbohydrate	22
g	Fibre	1.7
mg	Sodium	287
mg	Potassium	619
mg	Calcium	105
mg	Iron	0.6

Cover and refrigerate for 30 minutes or longer for flavour to develop. Serve with mint and cucumber garnish.

MAKES 6 SERVINGS, 1 CUP (250 mL) EACH.

MELON BERRY SWIRL SOUP

CHILLED SOUPS, especially fruit ones, are another way to add extra fruit and fibre to your daily meals.

8 cups	diced honeydew melon	2 L
$1/4$ cup	apple juice	50 mL
$1/4$ tsp	ground cinnamon	1 mL
$1/8$ tsp	ground cloves	0.5 mL
4 tsp	lemon juice, divided	20 mL
3 tbsp	chopped fresh mint	45 mL
1 cup	sliced strawberries	250 mL
$1/3$ cup	low-fat plain yogurt	75 mL
	Garnish: Mint leaves	

In food processor or blender container, process melon, apple juice, cinnamon, cloves, 2 tsp (10 mL) lemon juice and mint until smooth; cover and chill for 1 to 2 hours for flavour to develop.

In food processor or blender container, purée strawberries, remaining 2 tsp (10 mL) lemon juice and yogurt; cover and refrigerate for 1 to 2 hours.

Just before serving, pour melon mixture into 6 soup bowls, filling them $2/3$ full. Divide berry mixture and pour into centre of each bowl. Create a pattern, mixing the 2 soup purées, by using one circular motion with a spoon. Serve with mint as garnish.

MAKES 8 SERVINGS, ABOUT $3/4$ CUP (175 mL) EACH.

NUTRIENT ANALYSIS

Per Serving

Calories		77
g	Protein	1.5
g	Total Fat	0.4
g	Carbohydrate	19
g	Fibre	1.8
mg	Sodium	26
mg	Potassium	536
mg	Calcium	34
mg	Iron	0.3

 Advice from 1833 is still just as appropriate today when making soups: "Be careful and not throw in salt and pepper too plentifully; it is easy to add to it, and not easy to diminish." (The American Frugal Housewife)

Borscht in Minutes

THIS FAST VERSION of traditional borscht adds horseradish to canned beets for a bit of tang.

1 tsp	margarine	5 mL
1	small onion, chopped	1
1 cup	Homemade chicken stock (recipe at left)	250 mL
1	can (19 oz/540 mL) beets with juice	1
1 tbsp	horseradish	15 mL
$1/4$ cup	low-fat plain yogurt	50 mL

In 4-cup (1 L) microwavable bowl, combine margarine and onion. Microwave at High (100%) for 3 minutes or until onion is soft; stir once.

In food processor or blender container, process onion, stock, beets and horseradish until smooth. Return soup to bowl and heat to serving temperature. Garnish each serving with yogurt.

MAKES 4 SERVINGS, $3/4$ CUP (175 ML) EACH.

Harvest Pumpkin Soup

Use the hollowed-out pumpkin as a tureen for a dinner table conversation piece.

1 tsp	vegetable oil	5 mL
1	medium onion, chopped	1
1	large potato, diced	1
1 cup	sliced carrots	250 mL
2 cups	canned OR mashed cooked pumpkin	500 mL
3 cups	chicken stock	750 mL
$1/4$ tsp	ground cinnamon	1 mL
$1/4$ tsp	ground ginger	1 mL
	Freshly ground black pepper	
1 cup	low-fat milk	250 mL
	Garnish: Low-fat plain yogurt, chopped chives	

In large saucepan, heat oil over medium heat; sauté onion for 5 minutes or until soft. Add potato, carrots, pumpkin, stock and seasonings. Cover and bring to a boil; reduce heat and simmer for 20 minutes or until vegetables are tender.

In food processor or blender container, purée soup until smooth. Return soup to pan and add milk. Reheat to serving temperature. Serve with yogurt and chive garnish.

MAKES 6 SERVINGS, 1 CUP (250 ML) EACH.

HOMEMADE CHICKEN STOCK

This chicken stock has less sodium than commercial varieties. Store poultry bones in the freezer until you have accumulated enough to make a batch of stock for wonderful homemade soups. The stock can also be stored in the freezer until needed.

In large saucepan, place bones from 3 to 4 whole chicken breasts or the backs and wings from 2 or 3 chickens. Add enough cold water to cover bones by 1 inch (2.5 cm). Add 1 chopped onion, 2 stalks chopped celery and 2 sprigs parsley. Cover and bring to a boil; reduce heat and simmer for 2 hours or longer. Strain, discard bones and chill. When stock is cold, remove congealed fat on surface.

NUTRIENT ANALYSIS

Borscht
Per Serving

Calories		75
g	Protein	2.5
g	Total Fat	1.3
g	Carbohydrate	14
g	Fibre	2.2
mg	Sodium	396
mg	Potassium	306
mg	Calcium	58
mg	Iron	1.1

Harvest Pumpkin
Per Serving

Calories		107
g	Protein	4.0
g	Total Fat	2.5
g	Carbohydrate	19
g	Fibre	2.8
mg	Sodium	466
mg	Potassium	501
mg	Calcium	94
mg	Iron	1.6

Potato Leek Soup with Curry

THERE ARE SIMILARITIES between this soup and vichyssoise, except this delicious smooth soup is served hot accompanied by an apple garnish. The touch of curry is a pleasant variation.

1 tsp	vegetable oil	5 mL
1	leek, washed, trimmed and sliced	1
1 cup	diced raw potato	250 mL
2 cups	chicken stock	500 mL
$\frac{1}{4}$ tsp	curry powder	1 mL
1	apple, chopped	1
2	sprigs parsley, minced	2

In small nonstick skillet, heat oil over medium heat; sauté leek until soft. Transfer leek to medium saucepan, add potato, stock and curry powder. Cover and bring to a boil; reduce heat and simmer for 15 minutes or until potato is tender; cool slightly.

In food processor or blender container, purée soup until smooth. Return soup to saucepan and reheat to serving temperature. Sprinkle each serving with chopped apple and parsley.

MAKES 4 SERVINGS, $\frac{3}{4}$ CUP (175 mL) EACH.

NUTRIENT ANALYSIS		
Per Serving		
Calories		*89*
g	Protein	2.0
g	Total Fat	2.0
g	Carbohydrate	17
g	Fibre	1.8
mg	Sodium	441
mg	Potassium	316
mg	Calcium	31
mg	Iron	1.1

Tomato Bean Minestrone

HOMEMADE BEEF STOCK

Beef stock requires a bit more effort than does chicken stock. The bones need to be browned and longer cooking is required to develop the flavour and reduce the liquid. The flavour home-made beef stock adds to soups is well worth the effort. Make a large batch and freeze for future use.

Place about 4 lb (2 kg) beef bones, 2 onions, 3 carrots and 3 celery stalks in roasting pan; bake in 450°F (230°C) oven for 1 hour or until well browned. With a slotted spoon, transfer bones and vegetables to a large pot. Drain off fat; add 2 cups (500 mL) water to roasting pan and scrape loose the browned bits. Add liquid to pot, plus several sprigs parsley, 1 bay leaf, $\frac{1}{2}$ tsp (2 mL) dried thyme, 10 whole peppercorns, 2 unpeeled cloves garlic and 1 tomato (or $\frac{1}{2}$ cup/125 mL tomato juice). Add enough cold water to cover bones by 1 inch (2.5 cm). Bring to a boil; reduce heat and simmer, uncovered, for 3 hours or longer. Strain, discard bones and chill. When broth is cold, remove congealed fat on surface.

MINESTRONE, the national soup of Italy, is a thick vegetable soup that usually contains beans and pasta. This delicious version provides a very high source of fibre from both the beans and the variety of vegetables.

1 tbsp	olive oil	15 mL
1	large onion, chopped	1
2	cloves garlic, minced	2
1	large carrot, chopped	1
2	medium zucchini, chopped	2
1	stalk celery, sliced	1
1	can (19 oz/540 mL) kidney beans	1
1	can (19 oz/540 mL) tomatoes	1
4 cups	Homemade beef stock (recipe at left)	1 L
$\frac{1}{4}$ cup	tomato paste	50 mL
1 tsp	dried oregano	5 mL
1 tsp	dried basil	5 mL
2 cups	shredded cabbage	500 mL
1 cup	macaroni	250 mL
	Garnish: Chopped fresh parsley	

In large saucepan, heat oil over medium heat; cook onion and garlic for 5 minutes or until tender. Add carrot, zucchini and celery; cook for 5 minutes. Add beans, tomatoes, stock, tomato paste and seasonings. Cover and bring to a boil; reduce heat and simmer for about 30 minutes.

Add cabbage and macaroni; cook for 10 minutes or until macaroni is tender. Serve with parsley garnish.

MAKES 9 MAIN DISH SERVINGS, 1 $\frac{1}{2}$ CUPS (375 ML) EACH.

NUTRIENT ANALYSIS

Per Serving

Calories		*154*
g	Protein	7.0
g	Total Fat	2.4
g	Carbohydrate	28
g	Fibre	6.4
mg	Sodium	341
mg	Potassium	557
mg	Calcium	67
mg	Iron	2.0

Vegetable and Lentil Soup

THE MORE OFTEN YOU COOK with lentils, the more interesting ways you will find to use them. Red lentils are a product from our western provinces. They cook very quickly and are an excellent source of both iron and fibre.

1 $\frac{1}{4}$ cups	dried red lentils, washed	300 mL
8 cups	Homemade chicken stock (page 38)	2 L
1	bay leaf	1
2 cups	shredded cabbage	500 mL
1	medium onion, chopped	1
1 $\frac{1}{2}$ cups	chopped carrots (2 medium)	375 mL
1 cup	chopped celery	250 mL
$\frac{1}{4}$ lb	cubed ham or peameal bacon	125 g
1	can (28 oz/796 mL) diced tomatoes	1
1 tbsp	red wine vinegar	15 mL
1 tsp	Worcestershire sauce	5 mL
$\frac{1}{4}$ tsp	freshly ground black pepper	1 mL
Pinch	hot pepper sauce	Pinch

In large saucepan, combine lentils, stock, bay leaf, cabbage, onion, carrots, celery, ham, tomatoes, vinegar and seasonings. Cover and bring to a boil; reduce heat and simmer for 20 minutes or until vegetables are tender. Remove bay leaf.

MAKES 9 MAIN DISH SERVINGS, 1 $\frac{2}{3}$ CUPS (400 mL) EACH.

 The 19th century had its own convenience foods. "Portable Soup" must have been the first instant soup: stewing meats were simmered overnight, strained and boiled to a "gluey consistence." Shallow pots were then filled to the brim with this mixture and cooled. When cooled and set, they were turned out onto paper, allowed to dry and stored hanging in paper bags. To use, the cakes were dissolved in water. *(Out of Old Ontario Kitchens)*

No preservatives in this lot!

Black Bean and Sausage Soup

A HEARTY LUNCH includes a big bowl of this spicy black bean soup accompanied by crusty bread or cornmeal muffins. Each serving provides a very high source of fibre and an excellent source of iron. Great for après-ski.

1 lb	dried black turtle beans, washed	500 g
1 tsp	vegetable oil	5 mL
$\frac{3}{4}$ lb	hot sausage, cut into 1-inch (5 cm) slices	375 g
1	large onion, chopped	1
4	cloves garlic, minced	4
4	stalks celery, chopped	4
5	carrots, chopped	5
2 cups	sliced mushrooms	500 mL
1 to 2	jalapeño peppers, seeded and chopped	1 to 2
7 cups	Homemade chicken stock (page 38)	1.75 L
7 cups	water	1.75 L
1	can (5.5 oz/156 mL) tomato paste	1
1 tsp	dried oregano leaves	5 mL
$\frac{1}{2}$ tsp	ground cumin	2 mL
$\frac{1}{4}$ tsp	freshly ground black pepper	1 mL
$\frac{1}{2}$ cup	lime juice	125 mL
	Garnish: Chopped fresh cilantro, light sour cream or low-fat plain yogurt	

In large saucepan, cover beans with 6 cups (1.5 L) cold water. Cover and bring to a boil; boil for 2 minutes. Remove from heat and let stand for 1 hour; drain and reserve.

In large saucepan, heat oil over medium heat; cook sausage until browned. Drain fat, remove sausage and reserve. Add onion, garlic, celery, carrots and mushrooms; cook for about 10 minutes. Return sausage to pan.

Stir in peppers, stock, water, tomato paste, seasonings and reserved beans. Cover and bring to a boil; reduce heat and simmer for 2 hours or until beans are tender. Stir in lime juice.

Serve with cilantro, sour cream or yogurt.

MAKES 10 MAIN DISH SERVINGS, ABOUT 1 $\frac{1}{2}$ CUPS (375 ML) EACH.

NUTRIENT ANALYSIS

Per Serving

Calories		279
g	Protein	16
g	Total Fat	6.5
g	Carbohydrate	41
g	Fibre	11.5
mg	Sodium	250
mg	Potassium	1177
mg	Calcium	121
mg	Iron	5.5

Sopa de Mexico

CORN, PINTO BEANS, CHILI and oregano give this soup its distinctive flavour. All are ingredients commonly used in Mexican cooking.

1 cup	dried pinto beans, washed	250 mL
2 lb	boneless pork shoulder	1 kg
2 tsp	vegetable oil	10 mL
1 cup	chopped onion	250 mL
3	cloves garlic, minced	3
1 tbsp	chili powder	15 mL
1 tsp	dried oregano	5 mL
1 tsp	ground cumin	5 mL
$\frac{1}{4}$ tsp	freshly ground black pepper	1 mL
6 cups	beef stock	1.5 L
2 cups	sliced carrots	500 mL
2 cups	frozen corn kernels	500 mL
	Garnish: Light sour cream, corn tortilla chips, chopped avocado, tomato, green onion and cilantro	

In large saucepan, combine beans with 3 cups (750 mL) cold water. Cover and bring to a boil; boil for 2 minutes. Remove from heat and let stand for 1 hour; drain and reserve.

Cube pork, trim fat and discard. In large nonstick skillet, heat oil over medium-high heat; cook meat, onion and garlic for 10 minutes or until meat is browned. Add seasonings and cook for 2 minutes. Transfer meat mixture to large saucepan; add beans and stock. Cover and bring to a boil; reduce heat and simmer for about 1 $\frac{1}{2}$ hours or until beans are tender; stir occasionally.

Add carrots and corn; cook for about 10 minutes or until vegetables are tender. Serve each bowl with assorted garnishes.

MAKES 12 MAIN DISH SERVINGS, 1 CUP (250 mL) EACH.

NUTRIENT ANALYSIS
Per Serving

Calories		192
g	Protein	17
g	Total Fat	4.8
g	Carbohydrate	21
g	Fibre	3.6
mg	Sodium	476
mg	Potassium	639
mg	Calcium	49
mg	Iron	2.3

Cold Weather Fish Chowder

FISH CHOWDERS COOK QUICKLY compared with meat-based soups. This tasty version provides an excellent source of iron and makes a delicious meal following a day outdoors.

1 tbsp	vegetable oil	15 mL
1	medium onion, finely chopped	1
1	clove garlic, minced	1
3 cups	sliced carrots	750 mL
3 cups	sliced celery	750 mL
3	potatoes, diced	3
3 cups	Homemade chicken stock (page 38)	750 mL
$\frac{1}{2}$ tsp	dried rosemary	2 mL
$\frac{1}{4}$ tsp	freshly ground black pepper	1 mL
1	pkg (400g) frozen fish fillets (turbot, haddock, halibut), thawed and cubed	1
3 cups	low-fat milk	750 mL
3 tbsp	all-purpose flour	45 mL
1	can (5 oz/142 g) clams	1
	Garnish: Chopped fresh parsley	

In large saucepan, heat oil over medium-high heat; cook onion and garlic for about 4 minutes or until tender. Add carrots, celery, potatoes, stock and seasonings. Cover and bring to a boil; reduce heat and simmer for about 20 minutes or until vegetables are tender. Add fish and simmer for 5 to 7 minutes longer or until fish can be easily flaked with a fork. Blend together milk and flour; stir into soup. Add undrained clams. Bring to a boil over medium-high heat, stirring constantly; reduce heat and simmer for about 2 minutes. Serve with parsley garnish.

MAKES 6 MAIN DISH SERVINGS, 1 $\frac{1}{2}$ CUPS (375 mL) EACH.

NUTRIENT ANALYSIS
Per Serving

Calories		*271*
g	Protein	21
g	Total Fat	7.6
g	Carbohydrate	31
g	Fibre	3.6
mg	Sodium	272
mg	Potassium	1144
mg	Calcium	233
mg	Iron	4.6

 Our ancestors showed their thriftiness when making soups and chowders. The soup kettle was always on the back of the stove where any leftovers could be tossed in. Every part of the animal was used and they knew that in every pound of bones, there were 5 ounces of good gelatin to provide the soup with additional protein.

4

Salads

Go with the Greens   *It's only recently that salads have been widely eaten, even though they've been around for a long time. According to Homer, salads were a favoured food of the gods. A typical ancient Greek meal was meat, bread, cheese and dessert, followed by a crisp vegetable salad. Salads provide a light, lower-fat addition to a multi-course meal and give us a wider range of vitamins and minerals, plus lots of extra fibre.*

To Dress or Not to Dress?   *Many times those low-fat salads become laden with fat and extra calories from the dressings that are added. Instead, make our new and easy salad dressings the low-fat way. Keep them refrigerated and enjoy a salad with a different dressing each day of the week. Make your own fancy vinegars and try a drop or two of some of the newer exotic oils such as sesame, hazelnut or walnut. A very small amount of these oils will make a very large difference to a salad.*

Life after Iceberg   *Yes, there is life after iceberg lettuce! Today, the vast variety of colourful and nutritious salad greens available to us offer exciting flavours. From sharp endive to curly cabbage, pungent arugula to attractive red leaf lettuce, soft Bibb or Boston lettuce to peppery watercress, the choice is almost limitless. The darker green leaves are more nutritious. For example, romaine lettuce has eight times the ß carotene and five times the vitamin C of iceberg lettuce.   ◆   In wintertime, there is a reduced variety of inexpensive greens available. Consider substituting spinach and cabbage for some of the more expensive lettuces. Shredded red cabbage or beets can add colour when radicchio or red pepper is simply too expensive. Other additions add colour or texture: grated carrot, tiny broccoli florets, sliced raw fennel, kohlrabi, sprouts of all kinds.*

Do We Need an Oil Change?   *As we learned from the chart in the introduction, there are differences in proportion of saturated fatty acid levels in vegetable oils. Choose different oils for variety of flavour, but choose those low in saturated fat.*

Fancy Vinegars

COOKING TIPS:
Use fancy vinegars when preparing oil and vinegar dressings. For a traditional vinaigrette use 1 part vinegar to 3 parts oil. For a lower-fat version, use 1 part vinegar and 1 part water to 2 parts oil, or use extra vinegar for a stronger flavour. Add fresh or dried herbs, salt or a bit of Dijon mustard if desired.

The fruit vinegars are excellent served over fruit salads, tossed greens, spinach or watercress.

FANCY VINEGARS ARE EXPENSIVE. What fun to know that you can create these in your own kitchen with little effort and expense. They are wonderful for enhancing the taste of salads and as a replacement for salt and butter on cooked vegetables. Store all vinegars in a cool place (not in the refrigerator).

Garlic Vinegar: Separate 1 large head of garlic into cloves; cut into quarters and place several garlic quarters in each glass jar. Cover with red or white wine vinegar; seal and let stand for several days. Strain and bottle. Do not discard garlic, but add more vinegar and repeat. Use in salad dressings, for cooked beets, corn salad, or lentil or bean salad.

Tomato Vinegar: Chop 3 large tomatoes; place in glass container. Microwave 2 cups (500 mL) red wine vinegar at High (100%) until boiling; pour over tomatoes. Cover and set aside at room temperature for 4 to 5 days. Strain and bottle. Makes about 4 cups (1 L).

Herb Vinegar: Wash and dry whichever fresh herb you wish to use. Tuck these herbs into a bottle. Heat vinegar to boiling, pour into bottle. Allow vinegar to cool before sealing the bottle. Let stand in a sunny location. Taste after 2 weeks. When the taste is satisfactory, strain or leave herbs in the bottle, as preferred.

Raspberry Vinegar: Heat 1 cup (250 mL) white vinegar; pour over 1 cup (250 mL) fresh or frozen and thawed raspberries. Store at room temperature in covered glass container for 4 to 5 days. Microwave at High (100%) until boiling; strain and pour into clean container. Makes 1 cup (250 mL).

Strawberry Vinegar: Combine 4 cups (1 L) whole strawberries with 1 cup (250 mL) white vinegar. Allow to stand, covered, for 2 to 3 days. Strain; add 2 tsp (10 mL) granulated sugar. Microwave at High (100%) until boiling; pour into clean containers. Makes about 2 cups (500 mL).

Blueberry Vinegar: Microwave 2 cups (500 mL) white vinegar and 2 tbsp (25 mL) granulated sugar at High (100%) until boiling. Pour over 1 cup (250 mL) fresh or frozen and thawed blueberries. Cover and let stand at room temperature for 3 to 4 days. Strain and pour into clean container. Makes 2 cups (500 mL).

Zesty Low-Fat Salad Dressings

IT'S WORTHWHILE INVESTING some time to prepare several home-made dressings to keep in the refrigerator. This way you can have a different salad each day of the week. These dressings use chicken stock, fruit juice or water to replace a portion of the oil, thus lowering the fat content. Serve with an assortment of greens and other vegetables — strips of raw kohlrabi or fennel, tiny broccoli and cauliflower florets and a variety of sprouts.

ORIENTAL SALAD DRESSING

USE WITH COOKED CHICKEN, beef, pork or shredded cabbage.

⅓ cup	pineapple juice	75 mL
¼ cup	rice wine vinegar	50 mL
1 tbsp	light soy sauce	15 mL
2 tsp	granulated sugar	10 mL
1 ½ tsp	sesame oil	7 mL
¼ tsp	freshly ground black pepper	1 mL

In small jar, combine juice, vinegar, soy sauce, sugar, oil and pepper. Cover and shake well. Refrigerate for at least 15 minutes to allow flavour to develop.

MAKES ABOUT ½ CUP (125 mL).

GARLIC DRESSING

USE WITH ROMAINE lettuce or in a cold or hot potato salad.

2	cloves garlic	2
½	small onion	½
1	stalk celery	1
¼ cup	white vinegar	50 mL
¼ cup	safflower oil	50 mL
¼ cup	water	50 mL
2 tbsp	Dijon mustard	25 mL
½ tsp	salt	2 mL
¼ tsp	freshly ground black pepper	1 mL
¼ tsp	Worcestershire sauce	1 mL

In food processor or blender container, process garlic, onion, celery and vinegar until smooth. Add oil, water, mustard and seasonings; blend briefly. Pour into covered container and refrigerate until ready to use.

MAKES ABOUT 1 CUP (250 mL).

NUTRIENT ANALYSIS
Oriental
Per Tbsp (15 mL)

Calories		20
g	Protein	0.1
g	Total Fat	0.9
g	Carbohydrate	3.2
g	Fibre	0
mg	Sodium	62
mg	Potassium	26
mg	Calcium	3
mg	Iron	0.1

Garlic
Per Tbsp (15 mL)

Calories		35
g	Protein	0.2
g	Total Fat	3.6
g	Carbohydrate	0.8
g	Fibre	0.1
mg	Sodium	118
mg	Potassium	18
mg	Calcium	6
mg	Iron	0.1

RASPBERRY ORANGE VINAIGRETTE

USE WITH FRUIT and cottage cheese salads.

1/3 cup	orange juice	75 mL
2 tbsp	Raspberry Vinegar (page 46)	25 mL
1/4 cup	olive oil	50 mL
1/4 cup	water	50 mL
2 tsp	chopped fresh parsley	10 mL

In small jar, combine juice, vinegar, oil, water and parsley. Cover and shake well. Refrigerate until ready to use.

MAKES ABOUT 3/4 CUP (175 mL).

GINGER HONEY DRESSING

USE WITH LEAFY GREENS such as watercress, red leaf lettuce, radicchio.

1/4 cup	packed parsley leaves	50 mL
2	slices gingerroot	2
1	clove garlic	1
3 tbsp	white vinegar	45 mL
2 tbsp	liquid honey	25 mL
1 tbsp	lemon juice	15 mL
1 tsp	dry mustard	5 mL
1/4 tsp	salt	1 mL
1/4 tsp	freshly ground black pepper	1 mL
1/2 cup	chicken stock	125 mL
1/3 cup	olive oil	75 mL

In food processor or blender container, chop parsley, gingerroot and garlic. Add vinegar, honey, juice and seasonings; process briefly. Continue processing while gradually adding stock and oil. Pour into covered container and refrigerate until ready to use.

MAKES ABOUT 1 2/3 CUPS (400 mL).

NUTRIENT ANALYSIS
Raspberry Orange
Per Tbsp (15 mL)

Calories		53
g	Protein	0.1
g	Total Fat	5.5
g	Carbohydrate	1.1
g	Fibre	0
mg	Sodium	0
mg	Potassium	20
mg	Calcium	1
mg	Iron	0.1

Ginger Honey
Per Tbsp (15 mL)

Calories		32
g	Protein	0.1
g	Total Fat	2.9
g	Carbohydrate	1.6
g	Fibre	0
mg	Sodium	43
mg	Potassium	8
mg	Calcium	2
mg	Iron	0.1

NEXT PAGE: *Warm Steak Salad with Mandarin Oranges* (page 58), *Raspberry and Herb Vinegars (page 46).*

CREAMY LOW-CALORIE HERB DRESSING

AN EXCELLENT, fresh-tasting dressing for green salads or coleslaw, or to use as a dip.

2	green onions	2
1/2 cup	parsley leaves	125 mL
2 tbsp	fresh dill OR	25 mL
	1 tsp (5 mL) dried	
1 cup	buttermilk	250 mL
1/2 cup	low-fat cottage cheese	125 mL
1/2 cup	low-fat plain yogurt	125 mL
1 tsp	dried oregano	5 mL
1/4 tsp	salt	1 mL
1/4 tsp	freshly ground black pepper	1 mL

Finely chop onions, parsley and fresh dill; set aside. In food processor or blender container, process buttermilk, cheese, yogurt and seasonings until smooth. Remove and stir in onion and herb mixture. Pour into covered container and keep refrigerated for up to 1 week.

MAKES ABOUT 2 CUPS (500 mL).

VARIATION:

For a high-protein dressing, replace cottage cheese and yogurt with 1/4 lb (125 g) tofu. Prepare dressing as above. This will result in a thicker, but equally delicious, dressing.

PESTO RANCH SALAD DRESSING

Combine 1/4 cup (50 mL) Light Pesto Sauce (page 80) with 1/2 cup (125 mL) buttermilk.

NUTRIENT ANALYSIS
Per Tbsp (15 mL)

Calories		9
g	Protein	1.0
g	Total Fat	0.2
g	Carbohydrate	0.9
g	Fibre	0.1
mg	Sodium	49
mg	Potassium	32
mg	Calcium	21
mg	Iron	0.1

PREVIOUS PAGE: *Grilled Salmon with Fresh Tomato Salsa (page 114), Rice and Lentil Pilaf Mix (page 76).*

Watercress Salad

THIS FREQUENTLY OVERLOOKED spicy green is superb combined with tomatoes, chives or minced green onions and served with an interesting low-fat dressing. Another time, combine the watercress with diced oranges, pineapple tidbits and/or sliced strawberries.

2	bunches watercress, washed and trimmed	2
1	large firm tomato, cubed	1
3	green onions, sliced OR	3
	$^1/_4$ cup (50 mL) chopped chives	
1 cup	diced cucumber	250 mL

Dressing:

2 tbsp	olive oil	25 mL
1 tbsp	lime juice	15 mL
1 tbsp	red wine vinegar	15 mL
1 tbsp	chicken stock	15 mL
1	small clove garlic, minced	1
$^1/_2$ tsp	Dijon mustard	2 mL
Dash	hot pepper sauce	Dash

In large bowl, combine watercress, tomato, onions and cucumber.

Dressing: In small jar, shake together oil, juice, vinegar, stock and seasonings.

Drizzle dressing over salad and toss to coat.

MAKES 6 SERVINGS.

NUTRIENT ANALYSIS		
Per Serving		
Calories		59
g	Protein	0.9
g	Total Fat	4.8
g	Carbohydrate	4.1
g	Fibre	1.1
mg	Sodium	25
mg	Potassium	170
mg	Calcium	24
mg	Iron	0.3

Tomatoes and Cucumbers in Yogurt Vinaigrette

THIS IS A SIMPLE make-ahead salad to serve when fresh tomatoes and cucumbers are plentiful.

1	large tomato, sliced	1
1/2	English cucumber, thinly sliced	1/2
1/2	medium sweet onion, thinly sliced	1/2

Yogurt Vinaigrette:

1/3 cup	low-fat plain yogurt	75 mL
2 tbsp	lemon juice	25 mL
1 tbsp	balsamic vinegar	15 mL
1/2	clove garlic, minced	1/2
1 tsp	Dijon mustard	5 mL
1/8 tsp	freshly ground black pepper	0.5 mL

Arrange tomatoes, cucumber and onion in a flat serving dish.

Yogurt Vinaigrette: In small bowl, whisk together yogurt, juice, vinegar, garlic, mustard and pepper.

Pour dressing over salad. Cover and let stand in refrigerator for 20 minutes to several hours, if desired.

MAKES 4 SERVINGS.

VARIATIONS:

- For a creamier dressing, add a small amount of light mayonnaise.
- Replace mustard with dill and use to marinate thinly sliced cucumbers.
- Hollow out fresh whole tomatoes, dice pulp and mix with Yogurt Vinaigrette. Refill tomato shells.

NUTRIENT ANALYSIS		
Per Serving		
Calories		*40*
g	Protein	2.1
g	Total Fat	0.7
g	Carbohydrate	7.5
g	Fibre	1.2
mg	Sodium	41
mg	Potassium	261
mg	Calcium	54
mg	Iron	0.5

Panzanella Salad

THIS ITALIAN SALAD is similar in flavour to a Caesar salad; it has some of the same ingredients, but has much less fat. Most important, serve the salad at room temperature.

3	large firm tomatoes, cubed	3
³⁄₄ cup	diced cucumber	175 mL
1	clove garlic, minced	1
¹⁄₂ cup	chopped red onion	125 mL
¹⁄₄ cup	chopped fresh basil OR	50 mL
	1 tbsp (15 mL) dried	
2 tbsp	olive oil	25 mL
2 tbsp	red wine vinegar	25 mL
¹⁄₃ cup	freshly grated Parmesan cheese, divided	75 mL
¹⁄₄ tsp	salt	1 mL
Pinch	freshly ground black pepper	Pinch
1 cup	croutons	250 mL
3 cups	torn Romaine lettuce	750 mL

In large bowl, stir together tomatoes, cucumber, garlic, onion, basil, oil, vinegar and 2 tbsp (25 mL) cheese. Sprinkle with salt and pepper. Cover, let stand at room temperature for 2 hours.

Toss with remaining cheese, croutons and lettuce.

MAKES 6 SERVINGS.

COOKING TIPS:

Make your own low-fat croutons. Cut sliced bread into small cubes. Shake with a mixture of seasoned salt and assorted herbs. Spread on baking sheet and bake in 350°F (180°C) oven for 20 to 30 minutes or until lightly toasted; stir frequently.

NUTRIENT ANALYSIS		
Per Serving		
Calories		*125*
g	Protein	4.7
g	Total Fat	7.0
g	Carbohydrate	12
g	Fibre	2.1
mg	Sodium	277
mg	Potassium	364
mg	Calcium	118
mg	Iron	1.3

Mixed Marinated Vegetables

MARINATING IS A GREAT way to add flavour to crisp raw vegetables. If you keep the amount of oil low, you won't add too many calories. A neat tip to remember when marinating is to place all ingredients in a sealed plastic bag. This way you can turn bag occasionally to ensure all vegetables come in contact with marinade.

2	medium carrots, shredded	2
1 cup	frozen peas, thawed	250 mL
1 cup	cut-up green beans	250 mL
1 cup	cauliflower florets	250 mL
$\frac{1}{2}$	large sweet yellow or green pepper, cut into strips	$\frac{1}{2}$
$\frac{1}{4}$ cup	chopped red onion	50 mL
2 tbsp	chopped fresh parsley	25 mL

Dressing:

1 cup	tomato juice	250 mL
2 tbsp	red wine vinegar	25 mL
1 tbsp	olive oil	15 mL
1 tsp	dried oregano	5 mL
$\frac{1}{4}$ tsp	salt	1 mL
Pinch	freshly ground black pepper	Pinch

Place carrots, peas, beans, cauliflower, yellow pepper, onion and parsley in plastic bag.

Dressing: In jar, shake together juice, vinegar, oil and seasonings.

Pour dressing over vegetables. Marinate in refrigerator for several hours; turn bag occasionally.

MAKES 6 SERVINGS.

NUTRIENT ANALYSIS		
Per Serving		
Calories		73
g	Protein	2.7
g	Total Fat	2.5
g	Carbohydrate	11
g	Fibre	3.0
mg	Sodium	299
mg	Potassium	346
mg	Calcium	35
mg	Iron	1.3

Southern California Salad Layers

AVOCADO AND BLACK OLIVES are layered on mixed greens, shredded red cabbage and yellow pepper for a colourful, tasty salad. Since avocados are quite high in fat, each serving has just enough to add wonderful flavour.

4 cups	torn assorted lettuces	1 L
1 $\frac{1}{2}$ cups	shredded red cabbage	375 mL
1	small avocado, peeled and diced	1
1	sweet yellow pepper, cut into thin strips	1
1	firm large tomato, diced	1
$\frac{1}{2}$ cup	ripe olives, quartered	125 mL

Dressing:

$\frac{1}{4}$ cup	white wine vinegar	50 mL
$\frac{1}{4}$ cup	cold tea	50 mL
2 tbsp	olive oil	25 mL
2 tsp	granulated sugar	10 mL
$\frac{1}{4}$ tsp	dried rosemary	1 mL
$\frac{1}{4}$ tsp	dried marjoram	1 mL
$\frac{1}{4}$ tsp	freshly ground black pepper	1 mL
$\frac{1}{8}$ tsp	salt	0.5 mL

COOKING TIPS:

Consider growing some edible flowers to garnish a green or fruit salad. Nasturtiums, borage, sweet woodruff, pansies, violets and primroses are all edible and will grow in a window box, if you don't have a garden.

In large shallow salad bowl, arrange lettuces. Top with layers of cabbage, avocado, yellow pepper, tomato and olives. Cover and refrigerate for about 30 minutes.

Dressing: In jar, shake together vinegar, tea, oil, sugar and seasonings.

At serving time, pour dressing over layers; mix lightly.

MAKES 6 SERVINGS.

NUTRIENT ANALYSIS		
Per Serving		
Calories		135
g	Protein	1.9
g	Total Fat	11
g	Carbohydrate	9.5
g	Fibre	2.5
mg	Sodium	168
mg	Potassium	429
mg	Calcium	39
mg	Iron	1.5

Lentil and Brown Rice Salad with Mustard Dressing

WHEN USING RED LENTILS for a salad, cook them only briefly because they very quickly become mushy. This combination of brown rice and lentils is suitable for a main course salad meal that is high in fibre and a good source of iron. It also offers you the convenience of preparing it ahead of time.

$^1/_2$ cup	dried red lentils, washed	125 mL
1 $^1/_2$ cups	water	375 mL
1 $^1/_2$ cups	cooked brown rice ($^1/_2$ cup/125 mL uncooked)	375 mL
1 $^1/_2$ cups	broccoli florets, blanched	375 mL
$^1/_2$ cup	chopped celery	125 mL
$^1/_2$ cup	chopped sweet green pepper	125 mL
2	chopped green onions	2
1	medium carrot, thinly sliced	1
2 tbsp	chopped fresh parsley	25 mL

Dressing:

$^1/_4$ cup	rice vinegar	50 mL
2 tbsp	olive oil	25 mL
1 tbsp	lemon juice	15 mL
2 tsp	Dijon mustard	10 mL

In medium saucepan, bring lentils and water to a boil; reduce heat and simmer for 8 minutes or until lentils are soft. Drain and cool.

In large bowl, combine lentils, rice, broccoli, celery, green pepper, onions, carrot and parsley.

Dressing: Whisk together vinegar, oil, juice and mustard.

Pour dressing over salad and toss. Cover and refrigerate for several hours or overnight.

MAKES 6 SERVINGS, 1 CUP (250 mL) EACH.

PESTO PASTA SALAD

Stir $^1/_2$ cup (125 mL) Light Pesto Sauce (page 80) into 3 cups (750 mL) cooked rotini. Add chopped raw vegetables, as desired. Chill before serving. Makes 3 cups (750 mL).

NUTRIENT ANALYSIS
Per Serving

Calories		*174*
g	Protein	7.1
g	Total Fat	5.5
g	Carbohydrate	26
g	Fibre	4.0
mg	Sodium	52
mg	Potassium	374
mg	Calcium	40
mg	Iron	2.3

Peach, Basil and Chicken Salad

SUMMERTIME IN CANADA, when peaches are ripe and fresh basil plentiful, is the perfect time to make this wonderful main-course salad. Serve it with tossed greens and whole wheat rolls for a relaxed summer meal.

2 cups	slivered cooked chicken	500 mL
4	fresh peaches, peeled and sliced	4
1	orange, peeled and thinly sliced	1
½	medium red onion, thinly sliced	½
½ cup	coarsely chopped basil leaves	125 mL

Dressing:

2 tbsp	red wine vinegar	25 mL
2 tbsp	orange juice	25 mL
2 tbsp	olive oil	25 mL
1 tsp	Dijon mustard	5 mL
1	clove garlic, crushed	1
	Romaine lettuce leaves	

In medium bowl, combine chicken, peaches, orange, onion and basil.

Dressing: In jar, shake together vinegar, juice, oil, mustard and garlic.

Pour dressing over chicken mixture and stir lightly; chill for about 15 minutes.

Arrange lettuce on individual plates and spoon salad over.

MAKES 4 SERVINGS.

 Today, we use raspberry vinegar primarily for salad dressings and think we have found something new, but it was a favourite beverage of the early pioneers, though much sweeter than today's vinegar. Fresh raspberries were covered with vinegar and allowed to stand for 24 hours. Then they were strained and 1 cup of sugar was added for each cup of juice. The mixture was boiled for 20 minutes and then bottled. It would last for years. To make a drink, fresh water was added. *(Pioneer Potpourri)*

Warm Spinach Salad with Black Beans and Balsamic Vinegar

THIS COLOURFUL SALAD makes a superb lunch that is a pleasant change from a cold salad. It is also a good source of iron and high in fibre. Add a whole wheat roll to round out the meal.

1	pkg (10 oz/284 g) fresh spinach	1
2 tsp	vegetable oil	10 mL
1	large onion, chopped	1
1	clove garlic, minced	1
2	green onions, sliced	2
1/2	medium sweet red pepper, diced	1/2
1	can (15 oz/426 mL) black beans, drained	1
3 tbsp	balsamic vinegar	45 mL
2 tbsp	water	25 mL
1/8 tsp	salt	0.5 mL
1/8 tsp	freshly ground black pepper	0.5 mL

COOKING TIPS:

If you prefer to cook dried black beans, see recipe for Black Beans with Squash (page 132) for cooking directions. You will require about 3/4 cup (175 mL) dried beans to give the necessary amount of cooked beans for this recipe.

Wash and dry spinach, tear into bite-sized pieces and place in a salad bowl; set aside.

In small nonstick skillet, heat oil over medium heat; cook onion and garlic for 2 minutes or until soft. Add green onions and red pepper; cook for 1 minute. Add beans, vinegar, water, salt and pepper; bring to a boil, reduce heat and simmer for 2 minutes. Top spinach with beans and serve immediately.

MAKES 6 SERVINGS.

NUTRIENT ANALYSIS
Per Serving

Calories		106
g	Protein	6.2
g	Total Fat	2.0
g	Carbohydrate	18
g	Fibre	4.6
mg	Sodium	372
mg	Potassium	564
mg	Calcium	82
mg	Iron	2.8

Warm Steak Salad with Mandarin Oranges

MOST STEAKS provide more than enough protein for one serving. The next time you barbecue steak, cook a little extra to use in this warm salad. An excellent source of iron, this main-course salad is a wonderful way to make use of leftover meat.

½ lb	cooked steak or roast OR sliced deli meat	250 g
6 cups	mixed greens (spinach, lettuce, radicchio)	1.5 L
1	can (10 oz/284 mL) mandarin oranges, drained	1
¼	large red sweet onion, cut into thinly sliced rings	¼
2 tbsp	red wine vinegar	25 mL
1 tbsp	vegetable oil	15 mL
2 tsp	Worcestershire sauce	10 mL
1 tsp	granulated sugar	5 mL
1	clove garlic, minced	1
¼ tsp	chili powder	1 mL
¼ tsp	salt	1 mL
⅛ tsp	freshly ground black pepper	0.5 mL

COOKING TIPS:

For an easy side salad, combine several fruits and top with chopped dates, prunes or figs. Drizzle with one of the low-fat dressings at the beginning of this section.

Cut meat into thin slivers. Place greens in large salad bowl. Top with mandarin oranges, onion rings and beef.

In small microwavable container, whisk together vinegar, oil, Worcestershire, sugar, garlic and seasonings. Microwave at High (100%) for 30 seconds or until dressing comes to a boil. Pour over salad; toss lightly and serve.

MAKES 4 SERVINGS.

NUTRIENT ANALYSIS		
Per Serving		
Calories		187
g	Protein	20
g	Total Fat	6.8
g	Carbohydrate	13
g	Fibre	2.1
mg	Sodium	271
mg	Potassium	704
mg	Calcium	73
mg	Iron	3.5

5

Vegetables

Summer in Canada affords us a bountiful choice of home-grown produce. From May to the end of October, we can satisfy our inner need for fresh homegrown goodness. Fortunately, many of our favourite Canadian vegetables are kept in storage facilities so we can continue to enjoy them through the winter. Greenhouses also supply us with excellent winter crops of vegetables such as tomatoes, mushrooms and cucumbers.

Vegetable Cooking Methods *To ensure optimum keeping quality, wash all vegetables thoroughly just before cooking. For best flavour and retention of valuable nutrients, either steam or microwave vegetables. Cook just until they are tender yet still crisp.*

Substitutes for Fats and Salt *Margarine, butter, oils, mayonnaise, cream and salt are frequently used too liberally in preparing vegetables. Adopting the following substitutes to enhance the taste of vegetables cuts back on the use of fats and salt:*

Low-fat dairy products such as plain yogurt, light sour cream, light cream cheese and light or part-skim cheeses.

The many fresh herbs that are available today in both supermarkets and home gardens.

Dried herbs and blends.

Spices such as ginger, nutmeg, cinnamon.

Citrus juices and rinds, and other juices such as pineapple and apple.

Vinegars and wines.

Other fresh high-moisture vegetables such as mushrooms, onions, garlic, celery, green pepper, tomatoes.

Fresh fruits such as apples, apricots, pineapple.

Summer Vegetable Casserole

IF YOU ARE LOOKING for a very high fibre vegetable source, you need look no further. This recipe doubles easily, so you can make two and freeze one for another occasion. The wonderful selection of vegetables available today encourages us to find new and different ways to prepare them.

COOKING TIPS:
For those who miss salt on vegetables, try a few drops of lemon juice. It is especially effective in perking up vegetable flavours. The slightly sour taste works to enhance just a small shake of salt, making foods taste saltier.

1 tbsp	olive oil	15 mL
2	large onions, sliced	2
1	large sweet green pepper, sliced	1
2	cloves garlic, minced	2
1/2 cup	barley	125 mL
1 cup	beef stock	250 mL
4	small carrots, cut into chunks	4
2	large firm tomatoes, cut into wedges	2
2	medium zucchini, cut into chunks	2
1 1/2 cups	green beans, trimmed and cut in half	375 mL
1	pkg (300 g) frozen green peas OR 2 cups (500 mL) fresh green peas	1
2 tbsp	lemon juice	25 mL
1 tsp	paprika	5 mL
1/2 tsp	salt	2 mL

In large nonstick skillet, heat oil over medium-high heat; cook onions, green pepper and garlic for 5 minutes or until slightly brown. Set aside.

In 8-cup (2 L) casserole, combine barley and stock. Layer carrots, tomatoes, zucchini, beans and peas over barley. Spoon onion mixture over top.

Combine lemon juice and seasonings; pour over vegetables. Cover and bake in 400°F (200°C) oven for 1 hour or until barley and vegetables are tender.

MAKES 8 SERVINGS.

NUTRIENT ANALYSIS		
Per Serving		
Calories		151
g	Protein	5.6
g	Total Fat	2.5
g	Carbohydrate	29
g	Fibre	7.0
mg	Sodium	338
mg	Potassium	535
mg	Calcium	53
mg	Iron	1.8

 Lemon was a popular flavour in early kitchens. An early cookbook advised, "Never throw away the rind of a lemon. Keep a wide-mouthed bottle half full of brandy, and put into it all the lemon-rind that you do not immediately want. As the white part of the rind is of no use, it will be best to pare off the yellow very thin, and put that alone into the brandy, which will thus imbibe a very fine lemon flavour, and may be used for many nice purposes." *(Out of Old Ontario Kitchens)*

Zucchini Stuffed with Herbed Quinoa

QUINOA GIVES AN INTERESTING TEXTURE to this savory side dish. It can be prepared in advance and reheated in the microwave oven when the rest of the dinner is ready to be served.

2	medium zucchini	2
1 tbsp	olive oil	15 mL
2	green onions, minced	2
⅔ cup	chicken stock	150 mL
⅓ cup	quinoa, washed and drained	75 mL
2 tbsp	minced fresh parsley	25 mL
⅛ tsp	crushed saffron threads	0.5 mL
¼ tsp	salt	1 mL
⅛ tsp	freshly ground black pepper	0.5 mL

Cut zucchini in half lengthwise; with a spoon, remove centre, leaving ¼-inch (6 mm) shell. Chop pulp finely.

In large nonstick skillet, heat oil over medium heat; cook onions and zucchini pulp for 5 minutes or until soft and dry. Add stock, quinoa and seasonings. Cover and bring to a boil; reduce heat and simmer for 12 to 15 minutes or until liquid has been absorbed. Divide mixture between the 4 zucchini shells.

Microwave: Microwave zucchini shells on microwavable platter, covered, at High (100%) for 5 to 8 minutes (depending on size of zucchini) or until they are just soft.

Oven: Bake in 350°F (180°C) oven for about 30 minutes or until shells are tender.

MAKES 4 SERVINGS.

NUTRIENT ANALYSIS
Per Serving

Calories		*102*
g	Protein	3.3
g	Total Fat	4.6
g	Carbohydrate	13
g	Fibre	2.4
mg	Sodium	321
mg	Potassium	356
mg	Calcium	31
mg	Iron	1.9

 Squash is native to the New World and may have been domesticated as early as 7000 to 5000 B.C. There are two classes of squash: summer squash, such as zucchini, which is harvested before it is fully ripe and the skin is still tender, and winter squash such as acorn and butternut, which is harvested at full maturity, when the skin is hard. Winter squash was a staple for the early settlers since it could be kept over the winter months.

Tomatoes Stuffed with Bulgur and Fresh Herbs

BULGUR

A popular staple of Middle Eastern diets, bulgur is made by steaming wheat kernels, which are then dried and crushed. Bulgur has a wonderful tender, chewy texture.

TABBOULEH

Combine 1 cup (250 mL) washed bulgur with 1 1/4 cups (300 mL) boiling water and a pinch of salt. Let stand for 20 minutes or until water has been absorbed. Stir a dressing of 1 large clove garlic, crushed, 2 tbsp (25 mL) each of olive oil, lemon juice and water into bulgur and chill. Just before serving, add chopped tomatoes, green onions and parsley. Chopped mint is also a nice addition.

STUFFED TOMATOES makes a superb side dish. This one with bulgur and fresh herbs is a nourishing high-fibre interpretation of an old favourite.

4	large firm tomatoes	4
4	fresh basil leaves OR	4
	1 tsp (5 mL) dried	
1	fresh rosemary sprig OR	1
	$\frac{1}{4}$ tsp (1 mL) dried	
$\frac{1}{4}$ tsp	salt	1 mL
$\frac{1}{8}$ tsp	freshly ground black pepper	0.5 mL
1 tsp	olive oil	5 mL
1	medium onion, minced	1
1	clove garlic, minced	1
$\frac{1}{2}$ cup	bulgur, washed	125 mL
2 tbsp	freshly grated Parmesan cheese	25 mL

Core tomatoes; remove tops and reserve. Scoop out pulp, leaving $\frac{1}{2}$-inch (1 cm) wall. In food processor or blender container, purée pulp with seasonings until smooth. Add water to measure $1\frac{1}{2}$ cups (375 mL).

In large nonstick skillet, heat oil over medium heat; cook onion and garlic until soft. Add tomato purée and bulgur. Cover and bring to a boil; reduce heat and simmer for 10 minutes or until all liquid has been absorbed. Remove from heat; cover and let stand for 10 minutes.

Divide bulgur mixture among 4 tomato shells; sprinkle with cheese.

Bake in 375°F (190°C) oven for 30 minutes or until tops are browned and tomatoes are slightly soft.

MAKES 4 SERVINGS.

NUTRIENT ANALYSIS		
Per Serving		
Calories		124
g	Protein	4.8
g	Total Fat	2.6
g	Carbohydrate	23
g	Fibre	5.4
mg	Sodium	232
mg	Potassium	418
mg	Calcium	62
mg	Iron	1.2

Spaghetti Squash with Broccoli and Peppers

SPAGHETTI SQUASH IS ONE of the many varieties of squash available in supermarkets. It is a sweet, mild variety that can be used just like pasta. Season it with red or white sauce, or try a little garlic and olive oil. You can also combine it with other vegetables for a colourful side dish.

1	small spaghetti squash, about 2 lb(1 kg)	1
1	stalk broccoli, trimmed and cut into small pieces	1
1	medium sweet red pepper, cut into thin strips	1
1 tbsp	olive oil	15 mL
2	cloves garlic, minced	2
¼ cup	chopped black olives	50 mL
¼ cup	freshly grated Parmesan cheese	50 mL
Pinch	freshly ground black pepper	Pinch

Cut squash in half lengthwise and remove seeds. Place cut-side down on flat microwavable plate. Microwave at High (100%) for 10 minutes or until shells feel soft; let stand for 5 minutes.

Rinse broccoli and red pepper with water and place in small microwavable container. Cover and microwave at High for 2 to 3 minutes or until broccoli is tender-crisp.

With a fork, scrape squash from shell into serving bowl. Drain off any excess liquid.

Meanwhile, in small nonstick skillet, heat oil; cook garlic for 2 minutes. Add olives and cook for 1 minute. Gently stir in broccoli mixture; spoon over cooked squash. Sprinkle with cheese and pepper.

MAKES 6 SERVINGS.

NUTRIENT ANALYSIS
Per Serving

	Calories	95
g	Protein	3.1
g	Total Fat	5.7
g	Carbohydrate	9.4
g	Fibre	0.6
mg	Sodium	275
mg	Potassium	227
mg	Calcium	87
mg	Iron	0.8

Red and Yellow Stir-Fry

THIS SWEET AND SOUR combination is especially appropriate for sweet peppers. Serve them with grilled or barbecued chicken, pork or ham steaks. The zesty sauce from the vegetables is marvellous over cooked rice.

½ cup	unsweetened pineapple juice	125 mL
2 tbsp	white vinegar	25 mL
2 tbsp	tomato sauce	25 mL
1 tbsp	brown sugar	15 mL
1 tbsp	light soy sauce	15 mL
1 tbsp	cornstarch	15 mL
2 tsp	vegetable oil	10 mL
6	green onions, cut on diagonal	6
1	large sweet red pepper, cut into chunks	1
1	large sweet yellow pepper, cut into chunks	1
2	cloves garlic, crushed	2

In bowl, combine juice, vinegar, tomato sauce, sugar, soy sauce and cornstarch; set aside.

In large nonstick skillet, heat oil over medium-high heat; cook onions, peppers and garlic for 5 minutes or until slightly softened.

Stir pineapple mixture into skillet; cook, stirring constantly, for 5 minutes or until thickened.

MAKES 4 SERVINGS.

NUTRIENT ANALYSIS
Per Serving

Calories		76
g	Protein	1.0
g	Total Fat	2.4
g	Carbohydrate	14
g	Fibre	0.7
mg	Sodium	173
mg	Potassium	182
mg	Calcium	21
mg	Iron	0.6

 Progress in nutritional knowledge is nowhere more apparent than in the cooking of vegetables. In *Mrs. Beeton's Cookery and Household Management,* written in the 19th century, Mrs. Beeton specified that when vegetables sink to the bottom of the pot, they are "done enough." Her cooking times seem excessive — 20 to 40 minutes for peas, 1 to 2 hours for cauliflower — when compared with today's practice of cooking vegetables "tender-crisp." Frequently soda and a generous amount of salt were added to the cooking water. Soda helped to keep the green colour of vegetables but hastened the heat destruction of the vitamins. And today we suggest a host of other ways to season to avoid the overuse of salt (see page 72).

Harvest Succotash

SUCCOTASH is a favourite in the southern United States. The name comes from a Naragansett Indian word meaning "boiled whole kernels of corn" and usually includes lima beans, corn kernels and often chopped red or green sweet peppers. Either fresh or frozen vegetables can be used to make this high-fibre dish. In winter, when tomatoes are more expensive, use a little tomato juice instead.

1 tsp	vegetable oil	5 mL
1	small onion, chopped	1
1	clove garlic, minced	1
$\frac{1}{2}$	sweet red or green pepper, diced	$\frac{1}{2}$
1 cup	fresh lima beans OR	250 mL
	$\frac{1}{2}$ pkg (350 g) frozen lima beans	
1 cup	fresh or frozen corn	250 mL
1	small tomato, diced	1
1 $\frac{1}{2}$ tsp	fresh oregano, minced OR	7 mL
	$\frac{1}{2}$ tsp (2 mL) dried	
$\frac{1}{8}$ tsp	salt	0.5 mL
Pinch	freshly ground black pepper	Pinch

In large nonstick skillet, heat oil over medium heat; cook onion, garlic and peppers for 2 minutes or until soft.

Add beans, corn, tomato and seasonings. Cover and cook for about 5 minutes or until beans are tender.

MAKES 4 SERVINGS.

NUTRIENT ANALYSIS

Per Serving

Calories		109
g	Protein	4.7
g	Total Fat	2.1
g	Carbohydrate	20
g	Fibre	4.0
mg	Sodium	98
mg	Potassium	420
mg	Calcium	25
mg	Iron	1.8

 In Canada, over 21 varieties of corn were once cultivated. Interestingly, corn was rarely served as a plain vegetable. It was made into cornmeal and then turned into porridge, hominy, succotash, mush, Indian pudding, breads and even something resembling cheese. (A Cooking Legacy) They certainly put their harvest to good use.

Mixed Winter Squash Bake

WE COMBINED several squash from the fall harvest in this slowly baked casserole, which was inspired by flavours characteristic of southern France. It doubles perfectly to serve larger groups.

8 cups	peeled and cubed winter squash (acorn, buttercup, butternut OR turban)	2 L
3 tbsp	all-purpose flour	45 mL
1 tbsp	minced fresh parsley	15 mL
1 tsp	dried rosemary	5 mL
1 tsp	ground ginger	5 mL
$1/2$ tsp	dried thyme	2 mL
$1/4$ tsp	salt	1 mL
$1/8$ tsp	freshly ground black pepper	0.5 mL
$1/3$ cup	chicken stock	75 mL
2 tbsp	olive oil	25 mL
3	cloves garlic, minced	3

In large bowl, combine all squash. Toss squash with a mixture of flour and seasonings; place in 8-cup (2 L) casserole.

Combine stock, oil and garlic; pour over squash. Cover and bake in 350°F (180°C) oven for 1 hour or until squash is tender.

MAKES 6 SERVINGS.

SQUASH

Experiment with the many varieties of squash now available. Butternut squash has a buttery, sweet taste. It can be stuffed, glazed or used in stews. Acorn squash is sweet, dry and firm. It's great with sweet, nutty or spicy fillings. Buttercup, one of the varieties of turban squashes, so called because of the turban-like formation at the blossom end, has an interesting flavour and can be baked or steamed.

COOKING TIPS:

Squash is easy to cut and peel if you pre-cook it in the microwave oven. Microwave the whole squash at High (100%) for 2 to 5 minutes, depending on the size of the squash. Frozen cubed squash may also be used when time is short.

NUTRIENT ANALYSIS
Per Serving

Calories		*137*
g	Protein	2.7
g	Total Fat	5.1
g	Carbohydrate	23
g	Fibre	0.2
mg	Sodium	170
mg	Potassium	648
mg	Calcium	73
mg	Iron	1.6

 Sauces were a popular feayure in 19th-century cuisine. Usually high in fat, they no longer regularly fit into our lower-fat lifestyles. A favourite was "Melted Butter," a cream sauce made with milk, cream or water that often had the essence of anchovies, eggs, fennel, parsley, onion, celery, cucumber or mushrooms added. *(Out of Old Ontario Kitchens)*

Mediterranean Eggplant Casserole

PARMIGIANA DI MELANZANE, eggplant baked with tomatoes and cheese, is one of the most famous dishes of southern Italy. Variations are found throughout the Mediterranean. This casserole, similar to a quiche but crustless, can be made with zucchini, or even potatoes, as a replacement for the eggplant.

1	medium eggplant, peeled and sliced $1/2$-inch (1 cm) thick	1
	Salt	
1 tbsp	olive oil, divided	15 mL
2 cups	sliced mushrooms	500 mL
$1/4$ cup	chopped fresh parsley	50 mL
1 tsp	dried oregano	5 mL
$1/2$ tsp	dried thyme	2 mL
$1/4$ tsp	salt	1 mL
$1/4$ tsp	freshly ground black pepper	1 mL
3	large tomatoes, thinly sliced	3
1	small onion, chopped	1
$1/2$	medium sweet green pepper, chopped	$1/2$
$1/4$ lb	part-skim mozzarella cheese, thinly sliced	125 g
3	eggs, beaten	3
$1 1/2$ cups	low-fat milk	375 mL
$1/3$ cup	freshly grated Parmesan cheese	75 mL

Sprinkle eggplant slices with salt; let stand for 30 minutes on paper towels. Rinse thoroughly under running water and pat dry.

In large nonstick skillet, heat 2 tsp (10 mL) oil over medium-high heat; cook eggplant slices on each side until soft and golden-brown. Place slices in 13 x 9-inch (3.5 L) baking pan. (Overlap slices, if necessary.)

In 1 tsp (5 mL) oil, sauté mushrooms over medium-high heat for 5 minutes or until golden-brown. Place over eggplant. Sprinkle with parsley and seasonings. Top with tomato slices, onion and green pepper. Cover with cheese slices.

Combine eggs and milk; pour over vegetables. Sprinkle with Parmesan cheese and bake in 350°F (180°C) oven for 40 minutes or until firm and puffy. Allow to stand for a few minutes before cutting into squares.

MAKES 8 SERVINGS.

NUTRIENT ANALYSIS		
Per Serving		
Calories		153
g	Protein	11
g	Total Fat	8.5
g	Carbohydrate	9.3
g	Fibre	1.8
mg	Sodium	293
mg	Potassium	378
mg	Calcium	249
mg	Iron	1.2

Polish Beets

MUSTARD YOGURT
SAUCE

Try this quick and easy sauce over steamed vegetables.

1 cup	low-fat plain yogurt	250 mL
2 tbsp	all-purpose flour	25 mL
2 tsp	Dijon mustard	10 mL
2 tbsp	freshly grated	25 mL
	Parmesan cheese	
	Paprika	

In small microwavable container, combine yogurt, flour and mustard. Microwave at Medium-High (70%) for 2 to 3 minutes or until sauce is thickened and bubbly. Serve over your choice of vegetable, sprinkled with cheese and paprika.

MAKES 1 CUP (250 ML) SAUCE, 2 TBSP (25 ML) PER SERVING.

THIS LIGHTER version of the traditional Easter Sunday beet recipe is wonderful served with roast chicken or pork.

1 tbsp	margarine OR butter	15 mL
2 tbsp	brown sugar	25 mL
2 tbsp	red wine vinegar	25 mL
1 ½ lb	small beets, cooked and peeled OR 2 cans (14 oz/398 mL) small beets, drained	750 g
½ cup	low-fat plain yogurt	125 mL
⅛ tsp	salt	0.5 mL
Pinch	freshly ground black pepper	Pinch

In large nonstick skillet, melt margarine over medium heat. Add sugar and vinegar; heat, stirring until sugar is dissolved. Stir in beets, tossing to coat well. Cover and heat to serving temperature.

Just before serving, stir in yogurt; sprinkle lightly with salt and pepper.

MAKES 6 SERVINGS.

NOTE:
Fresh beets were used in this analysis. If using canned beets, you may want to omit the salt as canned vegetables are higher in sodium.

NUTRIENT ANALYSIS
Per Serving

	Calories	80
g	Protein	2.3
g	Total Fat	2.2
g	Carbohydrate	13
g	Fibre	2.5
mg	Sodium	150
mg	Potassium	422
mg	Calcium	55
mg	Iron	0.8

 On the Canadian homestead, the year had five seasons; in addition to spring, summer, fall and winter, there was the preserving season, when canning, drying and pickling of beets as well as other fruits and vegetables were done to preserve the food supply for winter. *(The Canadian Prairie Homesteaders)*

Turnip Parsnip Gratin

ZESTY LEMON HOLLANDAISE SAUCE

This is another quick sauce that adds a piquant flavour to broccoli, cauliflower, or Brussels sprouts.

1 cup	low-fat plain yogurt	250 mL
2 tsp	all-purpose flour	10 mL
1	egg white	1
2 tsp	lemon juice	10 mL
1 tsp	Dijon mustard	5 mL
1 tsp	dried dill weed OR	5 mL
	2 tbsp (15 mL) fresh dill	
$\frac{1}{4}$ tsp	grated lemon rind	1 mL
$\frac{1}{4}$ tsp	garlic powder	1 mL
Pinch	white pepper	Pinch

In small microwavable container, whisk together yogurt, flour, egg white, juice, mustard, dill, rind, garlic powder and pepper. Microwave at Medium-High (70%) for 2 to 3 minutes or until sauce is thickened and bubbly; stir several times.

MAKES 1 ¼ CUPS (300 ML) SAUCE, 2 TBSP (25 ML) PER SERVING.

YELLOW TURNIPS, or swede turnips, are a close relative of the purple-topped white turnip. They are now more accurately known as rutabagas, from the Swedish word for turnip. They are wonderful combined with parsnips in this classic gratin. Traditionally, this dish has a rich sauce and is covered with breadcrumbs before browning in the oven or under a broiler. Our lighter version is similar and an excellent source of calcium as well.

1 cup	freshly grated Parmesan cheese, divided	250 mL
$\frac{1}{3}$ cup	all-purpose flour, divided	75 mL
3 cups	grated rutabaga (about $\frac{1}{2}$ lb/250 g)	750 mL
3 cups	grated parsnips (about $\frac{1}{2}$ lb/250 g)	750 mL
1 $\frac{1}{2}$ cups	low-fat milk	375 mL
$\frac{1}{2}$ tsp	ground nutmeg	2 mL
$\frac{1}{8}$ tsp	freshly ground black pepper	0.5 mL
$\frac{1}{4}$ cup	dried breadcrumbs	50 mL
2 tbsp	minced fresh parsley	25 mL

In 6-cup (1.5 L) casserole, mix $\frac{1}{2}$ cup (125 mL) cheese with 2 tbsp (25 mL) flour; stir in grated vegetables.

In small microwavable container, blend milk, remaining flour, nutmeg and pepper. Microwave at High (100%) for 5 minutes or until boiling; stir several times. Pour over vegetables.

Combine $\frac{1}{2}$ cup (125 mL) cheese, breadcrumbs and parsley; sprinkle over vegetables. Cover and bake in 350°F (180°C) oven for 1 hour or until vegetables are tender.

MAKES 6 SERVINGS.

NUTRIENT ANALYSIS
Per Serving

Calories		193
g	Protein	11
g	Total Fat	6.8
g	Carbohydrate	22
g	Fibre	1.2
mg	Sodium	391
mg	Potassium	405
mg	Calcium	348
mg	Iron	1.1

 The attics of early houses had strings of apples, onions, peaches, squash and pumpkins hanging from pegs to keep them over the long winter. Other vegetables such as turnips and carrots were buried in sand, covered with layers of straw, and topped with salt. *(A Cooking Legacy)*

Winter Vegetable Layers

ROOT-TYPE VEGETABLES get a lift from this recipe that's easy to prepare and a terrific addition to any warm meal during the cold winter months. For a change, use parsnips and red onions with the thinly sliced potatoes.

1 tbsp	margarine OR butter	15 mL
6	green onions, sliced	6
2	large potatoes, sliced	2
1 cup	sliced carrots	250 mL
1	medium beet, sliced	1
1 cup	sliced celery	250 mL
$\frac{1}{4}$ tsp	salt	1 mL
$\frac{1}{8}$ tsp	freshly ground black pepper	0.5 mL

In nonstick skillet, melt margarine over medium heat; cook onions for 5 minutes.

In 9-inch (23 cm) deep pie plate or quiche dish, layer potatoes, $\frac{1}{3}$ cooked onions, carrots, $\frac{1}{3}$ onions, beets, $\frac{1}{3}$ onions and celery. Sprinkle each layer very lightly with salt and pepper.

Cover and bake in 375°F (190°C) oven for about 1 hour or until vegetables are tender.

MAKES 6 SERVINGS.

SUMMER VEGETABLE LAYERS

Similar concept, different season. Typical Italian flavours blend to make this tasty side dish, which uses some of the faster cooking summer vegetables and is a good source of calcium.

4	medium potatoes, thinly sliced	4
1	medium onion, thinly sliced	1
1	small zucchini, thinly sliced	1
$\frac{1}{4}$ tsp	dried oregano	1 mL
$\frac{1}{4}$ tsp	dried basil	1 mL
$\frac{1}{2}$ cup	freshly grated Parmesan cheese	125 mL
2	tomatoes, peeled and sliced	2

In greased 8-cup (2 L) shallow baking pan, arrange $\frac{1}{2}$ potatoes in an even layer. Layer onions and zucchini over potatoes; sprinkle with oregano and basil and $\frac{1}{2}$ the cheese. Make a final layer with remaining potatoes; top with tomato slices and remaining cheese.

Bake, uncovered, in 425°F (220°C) oven for 40 minutes or until potatoes are tender.

MAKES 4 SERVINGS.

NUTRIENT ANALYSIS		
Per Serving		
Calories		*80*
g	Protein	1.8
g	Total Fat	2.0
g	Carbohydrate	14
g	Fibre	1.7
mg	Sodium	173
mg	Potassium	483
mg	Calcium	25
mg	Iron	0.8

 Probably one of the more unhealthy habits of the pioneers was the practice of keeping peas green until Christmas. After washing and drying them, they were placed in bottles covered with soft mutton fat or suet. The bottles were then corked and pieces of bladder and leather were tied over them before they were stored in a cold cellar. (*The First American Cookbook*) Modern freezing and canning techniques have certainly provided us with healthier methods for preserving peas and other vegetables.

Garlic Scalloped Potatoes

PARMESAN CHEESE and garlic lend a marvellous Caesar flavour to these scalloped potatoes. Using unpeeled red potatoes adds interest as well as fibre. An extra bonus — this dish is also a good source of calcium.

1 tbsp	margarine OR butter	15 mL
1	large onion, chopped	1
4	large cloves garlic, minced	4
2 tbsp	all-purpose flour	25 mL
2 cups	low-fat milk	500 mL
1/2 cup	freshly grated Parmesan cheese	125 mL
2 tsp	Dijon mustard	10 mL
1/4 tsp	salt	1 mL
1/4 tsp	freshly ground black pepper	1 mL
4 cups	sliced, unpeeled red potatoes	1 L
1/4 cup	chopped Italian parsley	50 mL

In large nonstick skillet, melt margarine over medium heat; cook onion and garlic for 5 minutes or until tender. Add flour and cook for 2 minutes; stir well.

Gradually add milk; cook, stirring constantly, until thickened. Stir in cheese and seasonings; add potatoes.

Turn into lightly greased 8-cup (2 L) casserole. Bake in 350°F (180°C) oven for about 1 hour or until potatoes are tender. Garnish with parsley and serve.

MAKES 6 SERVINGS.

NUTRIENT ANALYSIS		
Per Serving		
Calories		204
g	Protein	9.4
g	Total Fat	6.3
g	Carbohydrate	28
g	Fibre	2.3
mg	Sodium	368
mg	Potassium	769
mg	Calcium	241
mg	Iron	1.3

 In early kitchens, cooked foods to be stored were "potted": packed tightly, forced into earthenware pots and sealed with clarified butter. Foods could only be stored for very short periods until the principle of refrigeration revolutionized North American eating habits. *(A Cooking Legacy)*. Refrigeration has extended our storage times, relieving us from having to use such high-fat methods for preserving foods.

Vegetables and a Garden of Herbs

BASIL—OREGANO—DILL—TARRAGON—
MINT—CHIVES—THYME—ROSEMARY—
PARSLEY—CILANTRO

AN EASY WAY to add enjoyment to your meals
is to enhance your vegetables with a variety of
herbs. Herbs are the aromatic leaves (and a
few flowers) of plants grown in temperate
climates. For those interested in lowering
their salt intake, a knowledgable use of herbs adds
taste to a wide variety of foods.

Fresh herbs are wonderful and frequently available. Store them
in dry paper towelling in the refrigerator or stand them upright in a
glass of water. Better yet, plant some in your garden or in small pots
in a sunny window to be snipped when needed. To replace dried
herbs with fresh use approximately 1 tbsp (15 mL) minced fresh for
1 tsp (5 mL) dried.

Store valuable dried herbs in tightly closed containers away
from heat, light and moisture. Buy only small amounts so that they
are used within six months for best flavour.

Try these herbs on your vegetables to replace butter or margarine:

Asparagus: basil, chives, tarragon, thyme
Beans: basil, dill, parsley, rosemary, tarragon, thyme
Beets: basil, dill, parsley, tarragon, thyme
Broccoli: basil
Cabbage: basil, dill, parsley, rosemary
Carrots: basil, chives, dill, parsley, oregano, tarragon, thyme
Cauliflower: chives, dill, parsley
Celery: basil, dill, parsley, oregano, rosemary
Corn: chives, cilantro
Eggplant: basil, parsley, tarragon
Mushrooms: chives, parsley, oregano
Onions: basil, chives, oregano, parsley, rosemary, thyme
Peas: basil, chives, dill, mint, rosemary
Potatoes: basil, chives, dill, parsley, tarragon, thyme
Spinach: basil, chives, mint
Tomatoes: chives, cilantro, mint, oregano, parsley
Zucchini: basil, cilantro, oregano, tarragon

6 Rice, Pasta and Grains

Raves for Rice *Why not explore the wide range of different rices now available? White and brown, long-grain, short-grain, basmati, wahini, arborio and pecan are just a few. In fact, there are reputedly more than 7,000 different types of rice!* ◆ *Rice is low in both fat and calories, is cholesterol-free and high in complex carbohydrates. Brown rices retain the several layers of nutrient-rich bran that surrounds the edible rice kernel. This layer is removed in white rice. Rice labelled parboiled or converted has been pressure-steamed before the bran is removed to infuse some of the nutrients into the grain.* ◆ *Prepackaged seasoned rice mixes are not only expensive, they are also high in salt and additives. Look for our Rice and Lentil Pilaf Mix (page 76). The price is right and you control what goes into it.*

Pasta the Good *Pastas are great for meal planning. Budget-friendly, they reduce the initial cost and extend more expensive foods. Replacing fats in your diet with pasta allows you to decrease fat consumption and increase consumption of complex carbohydrates, starches and fibre. With the exception of egg noodles, pasta is a low-fat, cholesterol-free food.* ◆ *A 2-cup (500 mL) serving of pasta provides up to 14 grams of incomplete protein, about one-third of the daily requirement. Adding cheese, meat, peas or beans will complete the protein.*

Great Grains *We are now hearing much more about such grains as quinoa, barley, couscous and kasha. Water is the easiest liquid in which to cook these grains, but stock, wine and tomato juice are all possible alternatives.* ◆ *All quinoa needs is a fast shower under warm running water and a short simmer before adding it to a wide choice of other foods such as sun-dried tomatoes, shredded vegetables, nuts, raisins or currants. Barley is considered the oldest of all cultivated cereal grains and is rich in protein, thiamin and potassium. Couscous is a convenience grain and cooks as quickly as instant rice. Kasha is another quick-cooking grain that is high in protein and low in fat and calories. Grains are full of exciting flavours, and they make wonderful side dishes.*

Spiced Basmati Rice

BASMATI RICE is much valued in Indian and Middle Eastern kitchens for its fragrant aroma and nut-like flavour. This variation is a wonderful side dish for barbecued meat.

2 tsp	vegetable oil	10 mL
2	cinnamon sticks	2
4	whole cloves	4
1	bay leaf	1
1 cup	chopped onion	250 mL
1 tbsp	finely chopped gingerroot	15 mL
2	large cloves garlic, crushed	2
Pinch	turmeric	Pinch
1 cup	basmati rice	250 mL
2 1/2 cups	chicken stock	625 mL
1/2 cup	water	125 mL

In microwavable 8-cup (2 L) covered casserole, combine oil, cinnamon, cloves and bay leaf; microwave at High (100%) for 2 minutes. Add onion, gingerroot, garlic and turmeric; microwave at High for 3 minutes or until onion is soft.

Stir in rice, stock, and water. Cover and microwave at High for 8 minutes or until boiling; stir. Microwave at Medium-High (70%) for 20 minutes or until liquid is absorbed and rice is tender; stir twice.

Allow rice to stand, covered, for 10 minutes. Remove cinnamon sticks, cloves and bay leaf before serving.

MAKES 6 SERVINGS.

NUTRIENT ANALYSIS		
Per Serving		
Calories		150
g	Protein	3.2
g	Total Fat	2.3
g	Carbohydrate	28
g	Fibre	0.8
mg	Sodium	363
mg	Potassium	98
mg	Calcium	22
mg	Iron	0.4

Risotto Primavera

ARBORIO is the Italian short-grain rice with the ability to absorb great quantities of flavourful broth. Slow simmering with constant stirring produces a marvellous creamy risotto, a dish that is becoming increasingly popular in North America.

2 tsp	olive oil, divided	10 mL
$\frac{1}{2}$ cup	chopped onion	125 mL
1 cup	arborio rice	250 mL
$\frac{1}{3}$ cup	dry white wine OR chicken stock	75 mL
1 cup	chicken stock	250 mL
3 cups	water	750 mL
1 $\frac{1}{2}$ cups	sliced mushrooms	375 mL
$\frac{1}{2}$	medium sweet red pepper, sliced	$\frac{1}{2}$
1 cup	frozen peas	250 mL
$\frac{1}{4}$ cup	freshly grated Parmesan cheese	50 mL
Pinch	freshly ground black pepper	Pinch
Pinch	ground nutmeg	Pinch

In large nonstick saucepan, heat 1 tsp (5 mL) oil over medium heat; cook onion for 5 minutes or until soft. Stir in rice and cook for 3 minutes (do not allow rice to brown). Add wine; cook until wine is absorbed. Stir in stock and cook until stock is absorbed.

Continue stirring, adding water, $\frac{1}{2}$ cup (125 mL) at a time, until all water has been used and rice is tender and creamy; stir frequently. (This will take about 20 minutes.)

Meanwhile, in nonstick skillet, heat remaining oil over medium heat; sauté mushrooms and red pepper for 5 minutes or until soft. Stir in peas.

Stir vegetable mixture, cheese, pepper and nutmeg into cooked rice.

MAKES 6 SERVINGS.

NUTRIENT ANALYSIS		
Per Serving		
Calories		*197*
g	Protein	6.0
g	Total Fat	3.4
g	Carbohydrate	33
g	Fibre	1.6
mg	Sodium	252
mg	Potassium	180
mg	Calcium	73
mg	Iron	1.0

Rice and Lentil Pilaf Mix

THE PRICES ASKED for fancy rice mixes made us wish we could make our own. So, we set about to develop this one. Stored in a tightly sealed container, the mix will keep for several months.

2 cups	brown rice	500 mL
1 cup	dried red lentils, washed	250 mL
1 cup	wild rice, washed	250 mL
1 cup	barley	250 mL
$\frac{1}{3}$ cup	low-sodium chicken bouillon powder	75 mL
$\frac{1}{4}$ cup	dried onion flakes	50 mL
$\frac{1}{4}$ cup	dried parsley	50 mL
2 tbsp	Italian seasoning	25 mL
2 tsp	garlic powder	10 mL
1 tsp	paprika	5 mL
$\frac{1}{2}$ tsp	celery seed	2 mL
$\frac{1}{2}$ tsp	chili powder	2 mL
$\frac{1}{4}$ tsp	dry mustard	1 mL

VARIATIONS:

Add $\frac{1}{4}$ cup (50 mL) chopped dried mushrooms or assorted chopped dried vegetables to mix after baking.

Spread brown rice, lentils and wild rice on large baking sheet. Bake in 300°F (150°C) oven for 20 minutes; stir once. Remove from oven and cool.

In large bowl, combine rice mixture, barley, bouillon powder, onion, parsley and seasonings. Store in tightly sealed container at room temperature.

MAKES ABOUT 7 CUPS (1.75 L) MIX.

Cooking Directions:

1 cup	Rice and Lentil Pilaf Mix	250 mL
2 $\frac{1}{2}$ cups	water	625 mL

In medium saucepan, combine mix and water. Cover and bring to a boil; reduce heat and simmer for about 45 minutes or until all water has been absorbed and rice is tender.

MAKES 4 SERVINGS COOKED RICE AND LENTIL PILAF, 1 CUP (250 mL) EACH.

NUTRIENT ANALYSIS		
Per Serving		
Calories		*127*
g	Protein	5.0
g	Total Fat	0.8
g	Carbohydrate	26
g	Fibre	2.7
mg	Sodium	124
mg	Potassium	170
mg	Calcium	19
mg	Iron	1.4

Pasta with Goat Cheese and Tomatoes

WHEN AVAILABLE, use fresh plum tomatoes in this marvellous sauce. For best results, we suggest seeding the tomatoes. Fresh goat cheese is lower in fat and sodium than ripened goat cheeses. It combines with the pasta to make a main dish that is a good source of iron.

10	ripe plum tomatoes (about 1 $\frac{1}{2}$ lb/750 g)	10
$\frac{1}{4}$ cup	loosely packed fresh basil leaves OR 1 tbsp (15 mL) dried	50 mL
2 tbsp	chopped ripe olives	25 mL
1 tbsp	olive oil	15 mL
1 tbsp	lemon juice	15 mL
1 tbsp	grated lemon rind	15 mL
2	small cloves garlic, crushed	2
$\frac{1}{4}$ tsp	freshly ground black pepper	1 mL
$\frac{1}{2}$ lb	fresh goat cheese, crumbled	250 g
$\frac{1}{3}$ cup	freshly grated Parmesan cheese	75 mL
4 cups	dry penne or medium shell pasta (about 300 g)	1 L

Cut each tomato in half crosswise. Hold each half over a bowl and gently squeeze. Strain juice, discard seeds and reserve juice. Coarsely chop tomatoes. (It's unnecessary to peel them.)

In large bowl, stir together chopped tomatoes, reserved tomato juice, basil, olives, oil, lemon juice and rind, garlic, pepper and cheeses; set aside.

In large amount of boiling water, cook pasta according to package directions, or until tender but firm; drain well.

Lightly toss cooked pasta with tomato mixture. Serve immediately.

MAKES 6 SERVINGS.

NUTRIENT ANALYSIS		
Per Serving		
Calories		347
g	Protein	14
g	Total Fat	13
g	Carbohydrate	45
g	Fibre	2.8
mg	Sodium	336
mg	Potassium	363
mg	Calcium	145
mg	Iron	3.2

Bow-Tie Pasta with Zucchini and Peppers

FARFALLE, or bow-tie pasta, is becoming more readily available in our stores. With zucchini and sweet red, green, yellow or orange pepper strips, it becomes a superbly colourful vegetable dish that is an excellent source of iron. Don't be alarmed about the amount of garlic—it gives a lovely flavour to the dish and is not at all overpowering.

4 cups	farfalle/bow-tie pasta (about 250 g)	1 L
1 tbsp	olive oil	15 mL
5	cloves garlic, coarsely chopped	5
1	large zucchini, cut into julienne strips	1
1	sweet orange pepper, thinly sliced	1
2 tbsp	chopped fresh parsley	25 mL
$\frac{1}{4}$ tsp	salt	1 mL
$\frac{1}{8}$ tsp	freshly ground black pepper	0.5 mL
3 tbsp	freshly grated Parmesan cheese	45 mL

In large amount of boiling water, cook pasta according to package directions, or until tender but firm; drain and return to pot. Meanwhile, in large nonstick skillet, heat oil over medium-high heat; cook garlic for 1 minute. Add zucchini and pepper; cook for 4 minutes or until just tender. Stir in parsley and seasonings.

Lightly toss cooked pasta with vegetable mixture; sprinkle with cheese and serve immediately.

MAKES 4 SERVINGS.

NUTRIENT ANALYSIS		
Per Serving		
Calories		*301*
g	Protein	11
g	Total Fat	5.7
g	Carbohydrate	52
g	Fibre	2.9
mg	Sodium	249
mg	Potassium	343
mg	Calcium	87
mg	Iron	3.6

 In early kitchens, macaroni was often served as a sweet dish by boiling 2 ounces of macaroni in a pint of milk, a bit of lemon peel and cinnamon. It was cooked until the "pipes" were swelled to their utmost size without breaking. They were then put on a dish with a custard poured over top. *(Out of Old Ontario Kitchens)*

Fettuccine with Herbed Cheese Sauce

PASTA AND NOODLES

Almost every country has a form of pasta or noodles: spaetzle in Germany, pierogi in Poland, cellophane noodles in China. In Italian, the word pasta means paste and refers to dough made by combining durum wheat flour, called semolina, with a liquid. Pasta is a term generally used to describe a wide variety of shapes made from this type of dough. Egg may be added, but dough containing a lot of egg is usually called noodles. Pasta comes in many shapes often referred to by a specific name: farfalle (bows), fusilli (spiralled spaghetti) and penne (large, straight tubes cut on the diagonal).

COOKING TIPS:

When it comes to saucing pasta, a general rule is to use light sauces for stuffed pastas like ravioli and heavier, richer sauces for spaghetti-type pastas.

THIS MAIN COURSE pasta dish is perfect for supper or a fast meal and it is a good source of calcium and iron. Without the ham, it is a creamy side dish for six people. As well as being perfect for fettuccine, try the sauce over cooked red-skinned potatoes or as a topping for baked potatoes.

$3/4$ lb	dry fettuccine	375 g
2 tsp	olive oil	10 mL
1	large onion, chopped	1
1 cup	sliced mushrooms	250 mL
2	cloves garlic, minced	2
2 cups	low-fat cottage cheese	500 mL
1 cup	low-fat milk	250 mL
$1/3$ cup	freshly grated Parmesan cheese	75 mL
$1/4$ tsp	white pepper	1 mL
$1/4$ cup	chopped fresh basil leaves OR 1 tbsp (15 mL) dried	50 mL
1 cup	low-fat ham, cut into thin strips	250 mL

In large amount of boiling water, cook fettuccine according to package directions, or until tender but firm; drain and return to pot.

Meanwhile, in large nonstick skillet, heat oil over medium-high heat; cook onion, mushrooms and garlic for 5 minutes or until soft.

In food processor or blender container, process cottage cheese until smooth. Add milk, Parmesan cheese and pepper; blend well. Stir cheese mixture, basil and ham into onion-mushroom mixture.

Combine with fettuccine and serve immediately.

MAKES 6 SERVINGS.

NUTRIENT ANALYSIS
Per Serving

Calories		382
g	Protein	27
g	Total Fat	7.1
g	Carbohydrate	51
g	Fibre	2.1
mg	Sodium	816
mg	Potassium	430
mg	Calcium	208
mg	Iron	3.4

Pesto Pasta Sauces

THE WONDERFUL FLAVOUR of these pasta sauces is marvellous on hot cooked pasta and a novel change from traditional basil pesto. The olive oil used in the more traditional pesto sauce is replaced with plain yogurt to give an excellent source of calcium to these two versions.

FRESH TOMATO PESTO SAUCE

1 cup	fresh basil leaves OR	250 mL
	$\frac{1}{4}$ cup (50 mL) dried	
3	medium ripe tomatoes, peeled and chopped	3
1	large clove garlic	1
$\frac{1}{2}$ cup	low-fat plain yogurt	125 mL
$\frac{1}{2}$ cup	freshly grated Parmesan cheese	125 mL
$\frac{1}{4}$ tsp	freshly ground black pepper	1 mL
$\frac{1}{4}$ tsp	hot pepper sauce	1 mL

In food processor or blender container, process basil, tomatoes and garlic until coarsely chopped. Add yogurt, cheese and seasonings; purée until smooth. Remove and refrigerate or freeze until ready to use.

MAKES 2 $\frac{1}{4}$ CUPS (550 mL) SAUCE, SUFFICIENT FOR 4 SERVINGS OF COOKED PASTA.

LIGHT PESTO SAUCE

1 cup	fresh basil leaves OR	250 mL
	$\frac{1}{4}$ cup (50 mL) dried	
1	medium sweet red OR green pepper, cubed	1
2	cloves garlic	2
$\frac{1}{2}$ cup	low-fat plain yogurt	125 mL
$\frac{1}{2}$ cup	freshly grated Parmesan cheese	125 mL
1 tbsp	lemon juice	15 mL
Pinch	cayenne pepper	Pinch

In food processor or blender container, process basil, red pepper and garlic until coarsely chopped. Add yogurt, cheese, juice and cayenne; purée until smooth. Remove and refrigerate or freeze until ready to use.

MAKES 1 $\frac{1}{3}$ CUPS (325 mL) SAUCE, SUFFICIENT FOR 3 SERVINGS OF COOKED PASTA.

VARIATION:

For a tasty dip, replace plain yogurt in Fresh Tomato Pesto Sauce with light mayonnaise or light sour cream. Serve with raw vegetables, bread sticks or corn tortillas as dippers.

NUTRIENT ANALYSIS

Tomato Pesto
Per Serving

Calories		105
g	Protein	8.1
g	Total Fat	4.7
g	Carbohydrate	8.8
g	Fibre	1.6
mg	Sodium	267
mg	Potassium	377
mg	Calcium	288
mg	Iron	1.6

Light Pesto
Per Serving

Calories		122
g	Protein	10
g	Total Fat	5.9
g	Carbohydrate	8.0
g	Fibre	0.6
mg	Sodium	347
mg	Potassium	278
mg	Calcium	381
mg	Iron	1.6

Kasha Pilaf with Leeks

VARIATIONS:

- Sauté 1 cup (250 mL) sliced mushrooms, diced zucchini, chopped broccoli or frozen mixed vegetables with the leeks.
- Replace leeks with 1 cup (250 mL) frozen peas and 3 green onions, sliced.

KASHA

Kasha is made from buckwheat, which is native to Russia. When the triangular seeds of this plant are hulled and roasted, they are called kasha. Kasha is available in coarse, medium and fine grinds, as well as whole, and can be cooked the same way as rice. To keep kasha fluffy, it is important to mix it first with beaten egg or egg white. Then toast the kernels for several minutes before adding the liquid.

The seeds are also used to make buckwheat flour — wonderful for pancakes.

KASHA IS NUTTY-flavoured buckwheat kernels that have been hulled and roasted. It makes a filling side dish that is a change from rice and potatoes and a good source of iron and complex carbohydrates. It is especially good when cooked in beef stock and combined with leeks.

2	leeks	2
1	egg white, beaten	1
3/4 cup	kasha	175 mL
1 1/2 cups	chicken OR beef stock	375 mL
1/2 tsp	dried thyme	2 mL
1 tsp	olive oil	5 mL
1/2 cup	chopped sweet red OR green pepper	125 mL
1 tbsp	chopped fresh parsley	15 mL
1/8 tsp	freshly ground black pepper	0.5 mL

Thinly slice, wash and separate white part of leeks; set aside.

In large saucepan, thoroughly combine egg white and kasha. Over high heat, cook kasha for 2 to 3 minutes or until grains are dry and separate; stir constantly.

Add stock and thyme. Cover and bring to a boil; reduce heat and simmer for 10 minutes if using fine-ground kasha and 15 minutes if using whole or coarse-ground kasha, or until all liquid is absorbed.

Meanwhile, in large nonstick skillet, heat oil over medium heat; cook leeks and red pepper for 3 to 4 minutes or until tender. Fluff kasha with a fork; stir in leek mixture, parsley and pepper.

MAKES 4 SERVINGS.

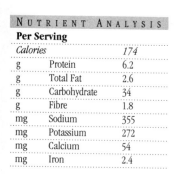

Barley Bake with Tomatoes and Mushrooms

BARLEY

Barley is a very tough little grain. Each kernel has three layers of protection, all of which are very fibrous. The refining process removes these husks, leaving only the endosperm, which we know as pot barley. If the barley is further steamed and polished, it is known as pearl barley. Hulled barley with only the outer husk removed is by far the most nutritious form of the grain, but the fibrous texture and long cooking reduces its appeal to all but the most dedicated fibre seeker.

THIS IS ONE of those fabulous recipes you'll keep on hand and make for buffet or pot-luck dinners. It freezes well and is great as a high-fibre replacement for rice and potatoes.

2 tsp	vegetable oil	10 mL
2 cups	sliced mushrooms	500 mL
1	large onion, chopped	1
1	large carrot, chopped	1
1	stalk celery, chopped	1
1 cup	barley	250 mL
1 cup	boiling water	250 mL
3	large tomatoes, peeled and chopped	3
1/4 cup	dry white wine or chicken stock	50 mL
2 tbsp	tomato paste	25 mL
1 tsp	salt	5 mL
1 tsp	dried thyme	5 mL
1/4 tsp	freshly ground black pepper	1 mL
	Garnish: Chopped fresh parsley	

In large nonstick skillet, heat oil over medium-high heat; cook mushrooms, onion, carrot and celery for 10 minutes or until softened.

Rinse barley under cold running water; drain. In bowl, combine barley, water, tomatoes, wine, tomato paste, seasonings and onion mixture; stir well. Turn into 8-cup (2 L) casserole and bake in 350°F (180°C) oven for about 1 hour or until barley is tender.

Serve sprinkled with parsley.

MAKES 8 SERVINGS.

NUTRIENT ANALYSIS

Per Serving

Calories		134
g	Protein	4.4
g	Total Fat	2.1
g	Carbohydrate	25
g	Fibre	5.9
mg	Sodium	360
mg	Potassium	440
mg	Calcium	28
mg	Iron	1.7

Quinoa with Sun-Dried Tomatoes

SUN-DRIED TOMATOES enhance the nutty flavour of the Peruvian grain quinoa in this delicious dish, an excellent source of iron.

1 cup	quinoa	250 mL
2 tbsp	chopped sun-dried tomatoes	25 mL
1 tsp	margarine OR butter	5 mL
2	green onions, sliced	2
2	small cloves garlic, minced	2
2 cups	chicken stock	500 mL
$1/4$ tsp	freshly ground black pepper	1 mL
Dash	hot pepper sauce	Dash
	Garnish: Chopped cilantro	

Wash quinoa thoroughly in a fine sieve; set aside.

Soak tomatoes for a few minutes in a small amount of boiling water; drain well.

In medium saucepan, melt margarine over low heat; sauté drained tomatoes, onions and garlic for 3 minutes. Add stock, seasonings and quinoa. Cover and bring to a boil; reduce heat and simmer for 25 to 30 minutes or until all liquid is absorbed.

Serve sprinkled with cilantro.

MAKES 4 SERVINGS.

Saffron Couscous

THIS STAPLE of North African cooking is traditionally cooked by steaming it over a pot of simmering stew. An easier method and just as good is to let it steep in boiling liquid for several minutes. We like serving it with grilled or roasted meats.

1 tsp	olive oil	5 mL
2	dry shallots OR small onions, minced	2
1	clove garlic, minced	1
$1\,1/2$ cups	chicken stock	375 mL
$1/8$ tsp	crushed saffron threads	0.5 mL
1 cup	couscous	250 mL
2 tbsp	currants	25 mL
1 tbsp	chopped fresh parsley	15 mL
Pinch	ground white pepper	Pinch

In large saucepan, heat oil over medium heat; cook shallots and garlic for 2 minutes, stirring constantly.

Add stock and saffron. Bring to a boil and stir in couscous; remove from heat, cover and let stand for 5 minutes.

Stir in currants, parsley and pepper.

MAKES 4 SERVINGS.

NUTRIENT ANALYSIS

Quinoa
Per Serving

Calories		191
g	Protein	6.8
g	Total Fat	4.1
g	Carbohydrate	33
g	Fibre	2.5
mg	Sodium	456
mg	Potassium	415
mg	Calcium	41
mg	Iron	4.3

Saffron Couscous
Per Serving

Calories		210
g	Protein	6.8
g	Total Fat	1.9
g	Carbohydrate	41
g	Fibre	1.3
mg	Sodium	330
mg	Potassium	142
mg	Calcium	25
mg	Iron	0.8

Southwest Millet and Rice

A less expensive and common substitute for saffron is turmeric. However, don't expect the same flavour delivery. Turmeric provides the golden-yellow colour, but not the traditional flavour of saffron. In pioneer days, marigold petals were dried and powdered to be used as a replacement for saffron.

For a nutty flavour, toast millet in dry nonstick skillet over medium heat for about 5 minutes or until the grain becomes a light brown and the millet begins to pop. Then soften it in boiling water before cooking.

MILLET HAS BEEN GROWN since prehistoric times. It is one of many species of grain-bearing grasses and is high in fibre. The variety introduced into North America is yellow in colour and is sometimes referred to as golden millet.

3/4 cup	dried millet	175 mL
1 tbsp	olive oil	15 mL
2	large onions, chopped	2
2	large cloves garlic, minced	2
1 cup	packed cilantro leaves, chopped	250 mL
1/2	small jalapeño pepper, finely chopped	1/2
2 1/4 cups	chicken stock	550 mL
3/4 cup	long-grain white rice	175 mL
1/4 cup	white wine OR chicken stock	50 mL
1 tsp	ground cumin	5 mL
1/2 tsp	turmeric	2 mL
Pinch	cayenne	Pinch
1 cup	cooked OR frozen corn kernels	250 mL
1	sweet green pepper, sliced	1
1	large tomato, chopped	1
	Garnish: Chopped cilantro	

In large bowl, cover millet with 3 cups (750 mL) boiling water; let stand for 5 minutes; drain.

Meanwhile, in large nonstick skillet, heat oil over medium-high heat; cook onions, garlic, cilantro and jalapeño for 5 minutes or until softened. Add stock, rice, wine, millet and seasonings. Cover and bring to a boil; reduce heat and simmer for 20 minutes or until rice and millet are tender and liquid is absorbed.

Add corn, green pepper and tomato and heat on low just until warm. Serve sprinkled with chopped cilantro.

MAKES 6 SERVINGS.

NUTRIENT ANALYSIS

Per Serving

Calories		282
g	Protein	7.2
g	Total Fat	4.5
g	Carbohydrate	53
g	Fibre	4.4
mg	Sodium	335
mg	Potassium	381
mg	Calcium	42
mg	Iron	1.9

7

Meats and Poultry

Meat

- ◆ Ginger Beef with Spinach Stir-Fry
- ◆ Down Under Beef with Kiwifruit
- ◆ Half-Hour Spicy Beef
- ◆ Baked Autumn Ratatouille and Beef
- ◆ Moroccan Lamb Patties with Goat Cheese
- ◆ Lamb Tajine
- ◆ Veal Scaloppine with Fennel and Mushrooms
- ◆ Fruited Mandarin Pork Chops
- ◆ Lemon 'n' Herb Pork Kebabs
- ◆ Country Pork Stew

Poultry

- ◆ Baked Lemon Garlic Chicken Breasts
- ◆ Mandarin Chicken Bundles
- ◆ Spicy Chicken Stir-Fry
- ◆ Chicken Legs with Wine and Sweet Potatoes
- ◆ Tomato Chicken Pilaf
- ◆ Middle Eastern Chicken, Rice and Lentil Stew
- ◆ Crusty Spiced Turkey Thighs
- ◆ Turkey and Eggplant Roll-ups
- ◆ Turkey Pita Pockets al Greco
- ◆ Rock Cornish Hens with Provençal-Style Stuffing

Meats and poultry have a significant place in a healthy meal plan because they are the main source of complete proteins. The most important function of protein is to build and repair body tissue.

◆ *Protein is an essential nutrient, but protein sources are often high in fat. Improved breeding and feeding have resulted in today's beef being 50% leaner than it was 20 years ago. These days, lean beef is comparable to chicken. The pork industry has also developed a leaner product that is currently 23% lower in fat and 26% lower in cholesterol than the pork of 10 years ago. Trimming away any visible fat also helps reduce the fat from your meat cuts. Our recipes for meats and poultry are tested using low-fat cooking techniques.* ◆ *Since half the fat in poultry is found both in and underneath the skin, remove the skin to further lower the calorie and fat content. And you can do even better than that—choose white meat, which is lower in fat, over dark.* ◆ *Ground turkey and chicken are becoming increasingly popular. In fact, recipes for both products are as plentiful as those for ground beef have been over the years. Be aware, however, that at the time of writing, ground poultry — unlike ground beef — is not regulated for fat level.*

Ginger Beef with Spinach Stir-Fry

STIR-FRYING is a fast cooking method for the busy cook. Cut up meat and vegetables, then stir-fry in a wok or skillet to serve an attractive meal in minutes. Fresh green spinach gives a bright colour to this dish, which provides an excellent source of iron.

1 lb	flank steak	500 g
Marinade:		
3 tbsp	light soy sauce	45 mL
1 tbsp	cornstarch	15 mL
1 tbsp	dry sherry	15 mL
1 tsp	granulated sugar	5 mL
1 tbsp	vegetable oil	15 mL
1/2 tsp	sesame oil	2 mL
1 tbsp	minced gingerroot	15 mL
1	clove garlic, minced	1
1 cup	sliced green onions	250 mL
1/2 lb	mushrooms, sliced	250 g
1	pkg (10 oz/284 g) fresh spinach, stemmed and cut into large pieces	1
1/4 tsp	freshly ground black pepper	1 mL
3 cups	hot cooked rice (1 cup/250 mL raw)	750 mL

Thinly slice steak.

Marinade: In bowl or plastic bag, combine soy sauce, cornstarch, sherry and sugar. Place steak strips in marinade; refrigerate for 1 hour or longer.

In wok or large nonstick skillet, heat vegetable and sesame oils over high heat; stir-fry gingerroot and garlic for 30 seconds.

Add beef and marinade; stir-fry for about 2 minutes or just until beef begins to brown.

Add onions and mushrooms; stir-fry for 2 minutes or until onions begin to soften.

Add spinach and pepper; stir-fry for 1 minute. Serve over hot cooked rice.

MAKES 5 SERVINGS.

NUTRIENT ANALYSIS		
Per Serving		
Calories		*345*
g	Protein	26
g	Total Fat	11
g	Carbohydrate	35
g	Fibre	3.0
mg	Sodium	401
mg	Potassium	982
mg	Calcium	96
mg	Iron	4.3

Down Under Beef with Kiwifruit

Marinating meats, particularly in acid mixtures such as wine, vinegar and lemon juice, both tenderizes them and enhances their flavour. Herbs and spices are often included. Certain beef cuts can be made much more tender after several hours in a flavourful marinade — cross rib, sirloin tip and rump roasts, blade and flank steaks, and inside (top) round are all cuts that benefit from a tenderization treatment. The length of time required to marinate will depend on the toughness of the meat. Chicken and pork require no tenderizing, so marinades are used only to add flavour.

Papain is an enzyme extracted from papaya and found in commercial meat tenderizers. When using commercial tenderizers, follow directions on the label; don't use more and don't leave it on longer than recommended, or meat surface will become mushy. Kiwifruits and pineapple also contain this enzyme, which acts to tenderize meat.

In addition, marinades act to moisten the surface of meat and prevent drying out during cooking, especially when barbecuing.

WE HAVE EACH recently visited the land "down under" and loved this marinade, ideal for less tender, but very lean, cuts of beef. Each serving provides an excellent source of iron.

1 lb	round or sirloin tip steak	500 g
Marinade:		
2	ripe kiwifruit, peeled and mashed	2
1/4 cup	lime juice	50 mL
1/4 cup	water	50 mL
2 tsp	granulated sugar	10 mL
2	cloves garlic, crushed	2
1 tbsp	finely chopped gingerroot	15 mL
1 tsp	dried marjoram	5 mL
1/2 tsp	freshly ground black pepper	2 mL
2 cups	shell pasta	500 mL
	Garnish: Sliced kiwifruit	

Trim all visible fat from steak and discard.

Marinade: In bowl or plastic bag, combine kiwifruit, juice, water, sugar, garlic, gingerroot and seasonings. Place steak in marinade; refrigerate for about 4 hours to tenderize beef.

Remove meat; reserve marinade. Preheat barbecue or broiler on high. Just before cooking brush grill lightly with oil. Broil or barbecue meat 4 inches (10 cm) from heat for about 5 minutes per side, to desired degree of doneness.

Meanwhile, in large pot of boiling water, cook pasta according to package directions or until tender but firm; drain well and place in serving dish; keep warm.

Slice steak in thin strips. Heat reserved marinade to boiling and pour over cooked pasta. Top with steak strips and serve with kiwifruit garnish.

MAKES 5 SERVINGS.

Per Serving

Calories		256
g	Protein	23
g	Total Fat	3.0
g	Carbohydrate	34
g	Fibre	2.0
mg	Sodium	35
mg	Potassium	425
mg	Calcium	24
mg	Iron	3.6

Half-Hour Spicy Beef

THIRTY MINUTES is all you need — 20 minutes to marinate the beef for superb flavour and 10 minutes to cook the meat and vegetables. Allow 5 minutes of this cooking time for the noodles. Presto! Everything is ready for a relaxed dinner.

1 lb	round steak	500 g
Marinade:		
2 tbsp	light soy sauce	25 mL
2 tbsp	ketchup	25 mL
2 tbsp	dry sherry OR apple juice	25 mL
2 tsp	minced gingerroot	10 mL
1 tsp	horseradish	5 mL
1 tbsp	vegetable oil, divided	15 mL
2	medium onions, cut into eighths	2
1 cup	cauliflower florets	250 mL
1 cup	broccoli florets	250 mL
3	celery stalks, sliced	3
1	medium zucchini, sliced	1
$\frac{1}{2}$ cup	carrot coins	125 mL
$\frac{1}{2}$ tsp	celery seeds	2 mL
$\frac{1}{2}$ lb	Chinese rice OR other noodles	250 g
$\frac{1}{3}$ cup	low-fat plain yogurt	75 mL

Remove all visible fat from beef and discard; cut beef into thin 2-inch (5 cm) strips.

Marinade: In bowl or plastic bag, combine soy sauce, ketchup, sherry, gingerroot and horseradish. Place beef strips in marinade; marinate at room temperature for 20 minutes.

In large nonstick skillet, heat 1 tsp (5 mL) oil over medium-high heat; stir-fry onions, cauliflower, broccoli, celery, zucchini, carrot and celery seeds for 6 minutes or until tender-crisp; remove vegetables.

Remove beef from marinade; reserve marinade. Add remaining 2 tsp (10 mL) oil to skillet and stir-fry beef for about 3 minutes or until no longer pink. Return vegetables to skillet.

Meanwhile, soak rice noodles in boiling water for about 5 minutes (or cook other noodles according to package directions). Drain. Add yogurt to reserved marinade; stir into beef-vegetable mixture and heat briefly. Serve over noodles.

MAKES 6 SERVINGS.

NUTRIENT ANALYSIS

Per Serving

Calories		299
g	Protein	26
g	Total Fat	4.7
g	Carbohydrate	40
g	Fibre	2.5
mg	Sodium	615
mg	Potassium	856
mg	Calcium	84
mg	Iron	3.4

Baked Autumn Ratatouille and Beef

COOKING TIPS:
For a ratatouille side dish, omit beef crust, chop tomatoes and cook with the other vegetables. Serve sprinkled with cheese.

RATATOUILLE from Provence combines the wonderful summer vegetables of eggplant, tomatoes, onions, green peppers, zucchini, garlic and herbs. This version with its ground beef crust is a complete meal that provides a good source of iron.

Meat Crust:

1 lb	lean ground beef	500 g
½ cup	chopped onion	125 mL
¼ cup	dried breadcrumbs	50 mL
1 tsp	seasoned salt	5 mL
1 tsp	dried oregano	5 mL
¼ tsp	freshly ground black pepper	1 mL

Ratatouille:

1 tbsp	vegetable oil	15 mL
1	medium eggplant, peeled and chopped	1
1	medium zucchini, chopped	1
2 cups	sliced mushrooms	500 mL
½ cup	chopped sweet green pepper	125 mL
¼ cup	chopped onion	50 mL
2	large cloves garlic, minced	2
1 tsp	dried basil OR	5 mL
	1 tbsp (15 mL) fresh	
¼ tsp	freshly ground black pepper	1 mL
2	large tomatoes, sliced	2
½ cup	freshly grated Parmesan cheese	125 mL

Meat Crust: In large bowl, lightly combine beef, onion, breadcrumbs and seasonings. Press into bottom of 13 x 9-inch (3.5 L) baking dish; set aside.

Ratatouille: In large nonstick skillet, heat oil over medium-high heat; cook eggplant, zucchini, mushrooms, green pepper, onion and garlic for 10 minutes or until all liquid has evaporated and mixture is reduced to about ½; stir frequently. Stir in basil and pepper; cook for 2 minutes.

Spoon vegetables over meat crust. Bake in 350°F (180°C) oven for 25 minutes or until meat is cooked. Top with tomato slices, sprinkle with cheese and bake for about 5 minutes more to warm tomatoes and melt cheese. To serve, cut into squares.

MAKES 6 SERVINGS.

NUTRIENT ANALYSIS
Per Serving

Calories		*253*
g	Protein	20
g	Total Fat	14
g	Carbohydrate	13
g	Fibre	2.7
mg	Sodium	445
mg	Potassium	545
mg	Calcium	153
mg	Iron	2.6

Moroccan Lamb Patties with Goat Cheese

NORTH AFRICAN flavours add interest to grilled lamb burgers and melted goat cheese makes a wonderful topping. They provide a good source of iron, and grilling the burgers helps reduce the amount of fat.

GOAT CHEESE

Goat cheese, also known as chèvre, from the French word for goat, has a wonderful tart flavour. Some cheeses are softer than others, so choose one soft enough for spreading on Moroccan Lamb Patties. Fresh goat cheese is the same as unripened.

1 lb	lean ground lamb	500 g
2	cloves garlic, minced	2
2 tbsp	minced fresh cilantro	25 mL
$1/2$ tsp	ground cumin	2 mL
$1/4$ tsp	red pepper flakes	1 mL
$1/4$ tsp	salt	1 mL
$1/8$ tsp	freshly ground black pepper	0.5 mL
2 tbsp	fresh goat cheese	2 tbsp
5	whole wheat buns	5
	Garnish: Alfalfa sprouts, chopped green onions, chopped sweet red pepper	

In bowl, combine lamb, garlic, cilantro and seasonings. Shape into 5 patties.

Preheat barbecue or broiler on high. Just before cooking, brush grill lightly with oil. Broil or barbecue patties 4 inches (10 cm) from heat for about 6 minutes or until lightly browned on one side. Turn and cook for 4 minutes or until starting to brown on second side. Top each patty with cheese; cook for 2 to 3 minutes or until second side is light brown and cheese has melted. (Lamb may be served rare to well done, depending on each person's individual preference.)

Serve patties in whole wheat buns with choice of garnishes.

MAKES 5 SERVINGS.

NUTRIENT ANALYSIS

Per Serving

Calories		283
g	Protein	20
g	Total Fat	14
g	Carbohydrate	19
g	Fibre	2.1
mg	Sodium	405
mg	Potassium	327
mg	Calcium	63
mg	Iron	2.2

Lamb Tajine

TAJINE is a classic North African stew named for the dish in which it is cooked — an earthenware casserole with a cone-shaped lid. A 10-cup (2.5 L) covered casserole will replace a tajine dish for simmering the shoulder lamb chops in this deliciously spiced dish, which is a good source of iron.

CILANTRO

In North America, fresh coriander leaves are usually known as cilantro. Cilantro, the Spanish word for coriander, is considered to be one of the most widely used herbs in the world, but its pungent flavour makes it an acquired taste for most Canadians. Cilantro adds its distinctive flavour most notably to Mexican and Asian cuisine.

4	lamb shoulder chops (about 1 lb/500g)	4
1 tsp	vegetable oil	5 mL
2	medium onions, sliced	2
2	cloves garlic, minced	2
2 tsp	minced gingerroot	10 mL
1/2 tsp	ground coriander	2 mL
1/4 tsp	ground cumin	1 mL
1/4 tsp	paprika	1 mL
1/4 tsp	salt	1 mL
1/8 tsp	crushed saffron threads	0.5 mL
1	can (14 oz/398 mL) tomatoes	1
1/4 cup	chopped fresh parsley	50 mL
1/4 cup	pimiento-stuffed olives	50 mL
3 cups	hot cooked rice (about 1 cup/250 mL raw)	750 mL

Remove all visible fat from chops and discard; set aside.

In nonstick skillet, heat oil over medium heat; cook onions, garlic, gingerroot and seasonings for about 5 minutes or until onions are soft, stirring frequently. Place onion mixture in 10-cup (2.5 L) casserole.

In nonstick skillet, brown chops on both sides; place over onions and top with tomatoes. Cover and bake in 325°F (160°C) oven for 1 1/2 hours or until chops are very tender. Remove meat from chops; discard bone and return meat to casserole. Stir in parsley and olives and serve over rice.

MAKES 4 SERVINGS.

NUTRIENT ANALYSIS
Per Serving

Calories		348
g	Protein	19
g	Total Fat	10
g	Carbohydrate	45
g	Fibre	3.6
mg	Sodium	600
mg	Potassium	545
mg	Calcium	96
mg	Iron	2.7

Veal Scaloppine with Fennel and Mushrooms

FENNEL, sometimes called anise, is a popular vegetable in Italian cuisine. Eaten raw, it has a flavour resembling licorice. When cooked, the flavour becomes very subtle and the vegetable develops a tender texture. This quick and easy dish is delightful to serve to friends or family.

1 lb	veal scaloppine	500 g
1 tsp	olive oil	5 mL
4	fresh mushrooms, sliced (use wild mushrooms such as shiitake, chanterelles OR oyster, if available)	4
1	fennel bulb, cored and thinly sliced	1
$\frac{1}{2}$ cup	chicken stock	125 mL
1 tsp	fresh thyme OR $\frac{1}{4}$ tsp (1 mL) dried	5 mL
1 tsp	cornstarch	5 mL
1 tbsp	cold water	15 mL
	Garnish: Chopped fresh parsley	

With a meat mallet, pound veal between pieces of waxed paper to an even thickness ($\frac{1}{8}$ inch /3 mm).

In nonstick skillet, heat oil over medium-high heat; sauté a few pieces of veal at a time, turning quickly. Remove to a serving platter and keep warm. Repeat until all veal is cooked. (Be careful not to overcook veal or it will become tough.)

In same skillet, cook mushrooms and fennel slices for 5 minutes or until fennel is tender; stir frequently. Add stock and thyme; simmer, uncovered, for about 3 minutes.

Combine cornstarch and water; stir into vegetables and cook until thickened, stirring constantly. Serve vegetables over veal and sprinkle with parsley.

MAKES 6 SERVINGS.

NUTRIENT ANALYSIS		
Per Serving		
Calories		112
g	Protein	16
g	Total Fat	3.5
g	Carbohydrate	3.1
g	Fibre	0.2
mg	Sodium	209
mg	Potassium	292
mg	Calcium	15
mg	Iron	0.8

Fruited Mandarin Pork Chops

FRUIT AND PORK are excellent company for each other. The chops and rice can be kept warm in the oven until you are ready to serve, allowing time to enjoy an appetizer with your family or guests.

6	loin pork chops (about 1 ½ lb/750 g)	6
1 tbsp	vegetable oil	15 mL
½ cup	chicken stock	125 mL
1	can (8 oz/227 mL) crushed pineapple, with juice	1
1	can (10 oz/284 mL) mandarin oranges, drained	1
2 tbsp	cornstarch	25 mL
1 tbsp	lime juice	15 mL
1 tbsp	tomato paste	15 mL
1 tsp	grated lime rind	5 mL
4 cups	hot cooked rice (about 1 ¼ cups/300 mL raw)	1 L

Remove all visible fat from chops and discard. In large nonstick skillet, heat oil over medium-high heat; brown chops on each side. Remove to shallow casserole dish.

In same skillet, stir together stock, pineapple, oranges, cornstarch, lime juice, tomato paste and lime rind. Cook over medium heat until slightly thickened; pour over chops.

Cover dish and bake in 350°F (180°C) oven for 45 minutes or until meat is tender.

Serve over cooked rice.

MAKES 6 SERVINGS.

 When an early prairie homesteader butchered a pig, everything but the squeal was used:
• the ham, back and hocks were cured in a brine barrel.
• some of the meat was sliced, cooked and packed into crocks and covered with hot fat to seal it.
• trimmings were ground, spiced and stuffed into casings for sausages.
• fat was cut into chunks and baked slowly to rend out the lard.

(Canadian Prairie Homesteaders)

Today, with leaner pork and improved slaughtering and curing techniques, we can be assured of lower-fat meats.

Lemon 'N' Herb Pork Kebabs

LEAN PORK CUBES, marinated in lemon juice and herbs, are wonderful barbecued or broiled. For a complete meal, thread onion wedges, pineapple cubes, green or yellow pepper chunks and parboiled red potato pieces on separate skewers and cook with the meat.

1 ½ lb	pork tenderloin (2 small)	750 g
Marinade:		
2 tbsp	chopped onion	25 mL
1	clove garlic, crushed	1
¼ cup	chicken stock	50 mL
2 tbsp	lemon juice	25 mL
1 tbsp	vegetable oil	15 mL
1 tbsp	chopped fresh parsley	15 mL
1 tbsp	chopped fresh rosemary OR	15 mL
	1 tsp (5 mL) dried	
2 tsp	lemon rind	10 mL

Cut pork into large cubes.

Marinade: In plastic bag, combine onion, garlic, stock, juice, oil, parsley, rosemary and rind. Place pork in marinade; refrigerate for several hours for flavour to develop.

Remove pork from marinade; reserve marinade. Thread pork on skewers. Preheat barbecue or broiler on high. Just before cooking, brush grill lightly with oil. Broil or barbecue pork 4 inches (10 cm) from heat for about 15 minutes or until meat is cooked; brush frequently with reserved marinade.

MAKES 8 SERVINGS.

TARRAGON MUSTARD

Fancy homemade mustards enhance the flavour of roast pork and other meats. We like to make them during the holidays to use as small gifts.

In food processor or blender container, process ½ cup (125 mL) dry mustard, ¼ cup (50 mL) each of sugar and white vinegar, 1 tbsp (15 mL) dried tarragon, ⅛ tsp (0.5 mL) each of salt and freshly ground black pepper. With machine running, slowly add 2 tbsp (25 mL) olive oil. Blend until mixture resembles smooth mayonnaise. Pour into clean jar and refrigerate. If too thick at serving time, add water to thin to desired consistency.

MAKES ¾ CUP (175 mL).

Variations:

- Replace tarragon with mustard seeds, poppy seeds or caraway seeds.

- Replace tarragon with ¼ cup (50 mL) dry sherry.

- Replace tarragon with frozen raspberry concentrate. Add ¼ tsp (1 mL) turmeric and a pinch of dried rosemary.

NUTRIENT ANALYSIS

Per Serving

Calories		115
g	Protein	18
g	Total Fat	3.9
g	Carbohydrate	0.9
g	Fibre	0.1
mg	Sodium	69
mg	Potassium	324
mg	Calcium	11
mg	Iron	1.2

Country Pork Stew

WELCOME the family home with this fragrant pork stew. It is easy to prepare ahead and it freezes well, so why not double the recipe for busy days? This recipe, a good source of iron, is ideal for cooking in a slow pot cooker.

1 ½ lb	lean pork shoulder	750 g
1 tsp	vegetable oil	5 mL
1	large onion, sliced	1
1	large cooking apple, cored and chopped	1
4	medium tomatoes, chopped	4
½ cup	dry white wine OR apple juice	125 mL
½ cup	water	125 mL
1 tsp	salt	5 mL
1 tsp	curry powder	5 mL
¼ tsp	freshly ground black pepper	1 mL
1	bay leaf	1
4 cups	hot cooked rice (about 1 ¼ cups/300 mL raw)	1 L

Trim all visible fat from meat and discard; cut pork into cubes.

In large nonstick skillet, heat oil over medium-high heat; brown pork and onion for about 10 minutes or until golden. Add apple, tomatoes, wine and seasonings; cover, reduce heat and simmer for about 1 ½ hours or until meat is tender. Remove bay leaf and serve over rice.

MAKES 6 SERVINGS.

NUTRIENT ANALYSIS

Per Serving

Calories		401
g	Protein	30
g	Total Fat	11
g	Carbohydrate	40
g	Fibre	2.6
mg	Sodium	483
mg	Potassium	723
mg	Calcium	52
mg	Iron	2.3

Baked Lemon Garlic Chicken Breasts

LOOK NO FURTHER. Here is a fast-baked chicken recipe that is perfect when there is little time for preparing supper. For an easy side dish, cook rice in chicken bouillon with some dried vegetable flakes while the chicken bakes. All you need add for a well-balanced meal are a green vegetable and a simple salad.

1/4 cup	fine dried breadcrumbs	50 mL
3	cloves garlic, minced	3
1 tbsp	finely minced fresh parsley	15 mL
1 tsp	dried thyme	5 mL
1/4 tsp	paprika	1 mL
2 tbsp	lemon juice	25 mL
1 tsp	vegetable oil	10 mL
4	boneless, skinless chicken breast halves (about 1 lb/500 g)	4

In plastic bag, toss together breadcrumbs, garlic, parsley, thyme and paprika.

In shallow bowl, combine lemon juice and oil. With pastry brush, spread mixture over chicken breasts. Shake breasts, 1 at a time, in crumb mixture to coat well.

Arrange chicken in single layer on nonstick or lightly greased baking pan. Press any remaining crumbs onto top of chicken. Bake in 375°F (190°C) oven for 30 minutes or until chicken is no longer pink inside and juices run clear.

MAKES 4 SERVINGS.

NOTE:
This dish cooks in approximately 1/2 the time in a combination microwave-convection oven. Follow the manufacturer's directions for cooking poultry.

BAKED DIJON CHICKEN

Combine 1/3 cup (75 mL) low-fat plain yogurt, 1 tbsp (15 mL) Dijon mustard and several drops hot pepper sauce. Use to coat 4 boneless, skinless chicken breast halves. Sprinkle with 1/2 cup (125 mL) fresh whole wheat breadcrumbs and 2 tbsp (25 mL) freshly grated Parmesan cheese. Bake in 450°F (230°C) oven for 20 minutes or until chicken is no longer pink and juices run clear.

MAKES 4 SERVINGS.

NUTRIENT ANALYSIS		
Per Serving		
Calories		185
g	Protein	28
g	Total Fat	4.6
g	Carbohydrate	6.5
g	Fibre	0.2
mg	Sodium	117
mg	Potassium	254
mg	Calcium	31
mg	Iron	1.5

 An 1833 cookbook "dedicated to those who are not ashamed of economy" tells of various ways to decide about the age of poultry: If the bottom of the breastbone is soft and gives easily, it is a sign of youth; if stiff, the poultry is old. If young, the legs are lighter, and the feet do not look so hard, stiff and worn. (*The American Frugal Housewife*)

Mandarin Chicken Bundles

A CLASSIC Oriental-style main course, these bundles are excellent served cold for a buffet. Either prepare ahead or allow guests to prepare them as required.

Mandarin Sauce:

1/2 cup	chicken stock	125 mL
1 tsp	minced gingerroot	5 mL
1	large clove garlic, crushed	1
2 tsp	chili powder	10 mL
1 1/2 tsp	cornstarch	7 mL
1/2 tsp	dry mustard	2 mL
1	head iceberg lettuce	1
4	boneless, skinless chicken breast halves (about 1 lb/500 g)	4
3 tbsp	light soy sauce	45 mL
1/2 tsp	ground ginger	2 mL
1 tsp	vegetable oil	5 mL
1	can (10 oz/284 mL) water chestnuts, drained and chopped	1
1 cup	chopped celery	250 mL
1 cup	chopped mushrooms	250 mL
3	green onions, chopped	
	Garnish: Lemon wedges	

Mandarin Sauce: Combine stock, gingerroot, garlic, chili powder, cornstarch and mustard; set aside.

Core, rinse and thoroughly drain lettuce; chill to crisp.

Chop chicken finely. In plastic bag, combine chicken, soy sauce and ginger; refrigerate for 30 minutes to develop flavour.

Remove chicken from marinade. In large nonstick skillet, heat oil over medium-high heat; cook chicken for 10 minutes or until meat loses pink colour. Add water chestnuts, celery, mushrooms and onions; stir-fry for about 2 minutes.

Stir in Mandarin Sauce; cook and stir for 1 to 2 minutes or until liquid is thickened and slightly reduced; remove from heat and chill.

Separate crisp lettuce cups; place in serving bowl. Serve chicken mixture in separate bowl.

To serve, spoon about 1/3 cup (75 mL) chicken mixture into each lettuce cup; fold over for eating. Serve with lemon wedges.

MAKES 4 SERVINGS.

NUTRIENT ANALYSIS

Per Serving

Calories		207
g	Protein	31
g	Total Fat	3.5
g	Carbohydrate	13
g	Fibre	2.0
mg	Sodium	608
mg	Potassium	752
mg	Calcium	63
mg	Iron	2.7

Spicy Chicken Stir-Fry

THIS IS ONE of our favourite recipes for midweek entertaining. Black bean sauce and ginger add some bite to this easy stir-fry. Serve over hot cooked rice for a fast meal when time is short.

³/₄ lb	boneless, skinless chicken breasts	375 g
1 tsp	cornstarch	5 mL
¹/₄ tsp	white pepper	2 mL
¹/₈ tsp	salt	0.5 mL
1	stalk broccoli	1
5	stalks celery, sliced	5
3	green onions, cut into 1-inch (2.5 cm) pieces	3
1	sweet red pepper, thinly sliced	1
2 tsp	vegetable oil	10 mL
1 tbsp	minced gingerroot	15 mL
1	clove garlic, minced	1
1 tbsp	black bean sauce	15 mL
1	fresh jalapeño pepper, seeded and very thinly sliced	1
3 cups	hot cooked rice (1 cup/250 mL raw)	750 mL

BLACK BEAN SAUCE

Black bean sauce is available in the Chinese section of most grocery stores. It is a thick, salty sauce with a pungent spicy flavour. Dark soy sauce is fine as a substitute.

Cut chicken into cubes. In small bowl, combine cornstarch, pepper and salt; stir in chicken and set aside.

Remove florets from broccoli; cut into small pieces. Peel stem and cut into 2-inch (5 cm) lengths; cut each length into 4 strips.

In microwavable container, cover and microwave broccoli, celery, onions and pepper with 1 tsp (5 mL) water, at High (100%) for 3 minutes or until vegetables are slightly tender.

In wok or nonstick skillet, heat oil over medium-high heat. Stir-fry gingerroot, garlic and bean sauce for 10 to 20 seconds. Add chicken and stir-fry until all pink has disappeared.

Add broccoli mixture and jalapeño pepper. Stir-fry for 1 minute or until vegetables are just tender.

Serve over hot cooked rice.

MAKES 4 SERVINGS.

NUTRIENT ANALYSIS

Per Serving

Calories		311
g	Protein	25
g	Total Fat	4.2
g	Carbohydrate	42
g	Fibre	2.6
mg	Sodium	385
mg	Potassium	624
mg	Calcium	82
mg	Iron	1.7

Chicken Legs with Wine and Sweet Potatoes

SIMMER this delicious one-dish meal all afternoon if time permits; it can be ready sooner, if required. Chicken legs become more tender with longer cooking, whereas chicken breasts tend to become stringy.

4	chicken legs	4
1/2 tsp	vegetable oil	2 mL
1	medium onion, chopped	1
4	shallots, peeled	4
8	whole mushrooms	8
4	cloves garlic, minced	4
1 tbsp	minced gingerroot	15 mL
2	sweet potatoes, peeled and sliced	2
1/2 cup	pitted prunes	125 mL
1/4 cup	raisins	50 mL
1 cup	dry white wine OR apple juice	250 mL
1/2 tsp	ground cumin	2 mL
1/4 tsp	salt	1 mL
1/8 tsp	ground cinnamon	0.5 mL
Pinch	freshly ground black pepper	Pinch
	Garnish: Chopped fresh parsley	

Remove skin and fat from chicken and discard.

In large nonstick skillet, heat oil over medium heat; brown chicken on all sides. Add onion and shallots; cook for 1 to 2 minutes.

Add mushrooms, garlic, gingerroot, sweet potatoes, prunes, raisins, wine and seasonings. Cover and bring to a boil; reduce heat and simmer for 25 to 30 minutes or until chicken is cooked and sweet potato is tender.

Serve sprinkled with parsley.

MAKES 4 SERVINGS.

COOKING TIPS:
Chicken combines well with many flavours, including wine, herbs, yogurt, sour cream, juice, bouillon, fruits and most vegetables. Remember that dark meat is somewhat higher in fat. A chicken breast weighing 86 grams has 3 grams of fat, whereas a drumstick of similar weight has 5 grams of fat.

NUTRIENT ANALYSIS
Per Serving

Calories		468
g	Protein	31
g	Total Fat	9.5
g	Carbohydrate	57
g	Fibre	6.4
mg	Sodium	274
mg	Potassium	958
mg	Calcium	83
mg	Iron	4.0

Tomato Chicken Pilaf

WE ARE CONVINCED that the 1990s will be remembered for introducing ground chicken and turkey into our menus. The source of the "hidden" fibre in this recipe may surprise you.

1 tsp	vegetable oil	5 mL
³⁄₄ lb	ground chicken	375 g
1 cup	sliced mushrooms	250 mL
1	small onion, chopped	1
1	clove garlic, minced	1
1 ¹⁄₂ cups	tomato juice	375 mL
¹⁄₂ cup	water	125 mL
¹⁄₄ tsp	dried thyme	1 mL
¹⁄₄ tsp	salt	1 mL
Pinch	freshly ground black pepper	Pinch
¹⁄₃ cup	high-fibre bran cereal	75 mL
¹⁄₃ cup	long-grain brown rice	75 mL
	Garnish: Chopped fresh parsley	

In large nonstick skillet, heat oil over medium-high heat; cook chicken, mushrooms, onion and garlic for 5 minutes or until meat is no longer pink.

Add tomato juice, water and seasonings. Bring to a boil; add cereal and rice. Cover, reduce heat and simmer for about 35 minutes or until rice is tender.

Serve sprinkled with parsley.

MAKES 4 SERVINGS, 1 CUP (250 mL) EACH.

COOKING TIPS:

Pilaf is a highly seasoned rice dish originating in India and its neighbouring countries. Rice is the most common grain used but other grains such as bulgur make for interesting variations. The grains are first browned with onions, garlic or other vegetables, then spices are added with the liquid—in India, pilafs are highly spiced with curry. When poultry or other meat is added, it becomes a satisfying main dish high in complex carbohydrates.

NUTRIENT ANALYSIS		
Per Serving		
Calories		*233*
g	Protein	18
g	Total Fat	8.3
g	Carbohydrate	23
g	Fibre	3.7
mg	Sodium	628
mg	Potassium	599
mg	Calcium	37
mg	Iron	2.9

Middle Eastern Chicken, Rice and Lentil Stew

MIDDLE EASTERN foods frequently use cinnamon and garlic in combination with meat. We find they give a delightful flavour to this chicken and lentil stew, which is a high source of fibre and an excellent source of iron. Our only regret: taking so long to discover some marvellous food flavour experiences.

1 lb	lean ground chicken	500 g
1 cup	chopped onion	250 mL
2	large cloves garlic, minced	2
1 tbsp	dried mint OR	15 mL
	3 tbsp (45 mL) chopped fresh	
1 1/2 tsp	ground cinnamon	7 mL
1/4 tsp	freshly ground black pepper	1 mL
1 cup	dried brown lentils, washed	250 mL
3/4 cup	long-grain rice	175 mL
1 1/2 cups	chicken stock	375 mL
1/2 cup	dry red wine OR chicken stock	125 mL
1/2 cup	tomato sauce	125 mL

Garnish:

1/2 cup	crumbled feta cheese	125 mL
1	large firm tomato, chopped	1
1 tsp	dried mint OR	5 mL
	1 tbsp (15 mL) chopped fresh	

In large nonstick skillet, cook chicken over medium heat for 5 minutes or until all pink colour has disappeared, stirring to break up; drain fat. Add onion and garlic; cook for 5 minutes or until tender. Add seasonings; cook for 2 minutes.

Add lentils, rice, stock, wine and tomato sauce. Cover, bring to a boil, reduce heat and simmer for about 25 minutes or until rice is cooked.

Combine cheese, tomato and mint; use to garnish each serving.

MAKES 6 SERVINGS.

COOKING TIPS:

Canned lentils may replace dried. In this recipe, drain and wash them to remove excess salt; add them to stew about 10 minutes before cooking is complete.

NUTRIENT ANALYSIS

Per Serving

Calories		370
g	Protein	27
g	Total Fat	8.5
g	Carbohydrate	44
g	Fibre	4.3
mg	Sodium	521
mg	Potassium	704
mg	Calcium	101
mg	Iron	4.8

Crusty Spiced Turkey Thighs

A PUNGENT BLEND of spices enhances the flavour of turkey thighs. Removing the bone is not hard and makes serving the meat very easy.

1	small leek	1
2	medium turkey thighs (about 1 $\frac{1}{2}$ lb/750 g)	2
1 tsp	vegetable oil	5 mL
$\frac{1}{2}$ tsp	lemon juice	2 mL
$\frac{1}{2}$ tsp	ground cumin	2 mL
$\frac{1}{2}$ tsp	dried coriander	2 mL
$\frac{1}{2}$ tsp	paprika	2 mL
$\frac{1}{4}$ tsp	freshly ground black pepper	1 mL
$\frac{1}{4}$ tsp	ground cardamom	1 mL
$\frac{1}{8}$ tsp	cayenne pepper	0.5 mL

COOKING TIPS:

Cut up a whole turkey to provide several different meals. Roast the breast whole; bake the thighs for another meal; use the wings and back to make broth (see Homemade Chicken Stock, page 38) and cook the legs in some of the stock for turkey and noodles. Remember, freeze raw turkey if you are not able to use it within 2 days.

Cut white part of leek into 2 pieces (each about 2 inches/5 cm long). Remove skin from each turkey thigh and discard; with sharp knife, cut out bone, leaving meat in one piece. Place 1 piece of leek in cavity of each thigh and wrap meat around it to form a small roll.

In bowl, blend oil, juice and spices to form a paste. Rub into surface of turkey.

Place rolls on nonstick or lightly greased baking pan. Bake in 350°F (180°C) oven for 40 to 45 minutes or until meat is no longer pink and juices run clear. To serve, cut thighs into slices.

MAKES 4 SERVINGS.

NUTRIENT ANALYSIS		
Per Serving		
Calories		*185*
g	Protein	24
g	Total Fat	7.3
g	Carbohydrate	4.9
g	Fibre	0.7
mg	Sodium	72
mg	Potassium	312
mg	Calcium	50
mg	Iron	2.9

Turkey and Eggplant Roll-ups

EGG ROLL WRAPPERS are excellent for wrapping around the turkey and eggplant filling. The wrappers cook in a tomato sauce and are more delicate than commercial noodles. You can substitute ground chicken, if you like.

1	small eggplant, peeled	1
³⁄₄ lb	lean ground turkey	375 g
¹⁄₂	medium onion, chopped	¹⁄₂
1	clove garlic, minced	1
¹⁄₂ cup	diced celery	125 mL
¹⁄₈ tsp	salt	0.5 mL
1	can (28 oz/796 mL) diced tomatoes	1
¹⁄₄ cup	red wine OR water	50 mL
1 ¹⁄₂ tsp	minced fresh thyme OR	7 mL
	¹⁄₂ tsp (2 mL) dried	
8	egg roll wrappers	8
1 cup	shredded part-skim mozzarella cheese	250 mL

Cut 8 slices, crosswise, ¹⁄₄-inch (5 mm) thick, from eggplant. Chop remaining eggplant; there should be about 2 cups (500 mL).

In large nonstick skillet, cook turkey, onion, garlic, celery, salt and chopped eggplant over medium heat for 10 minutes or until turkey is no longer pink and vegetables are tender.

Combine tomatoes, wine and thyme. Stir 1 cup (250 mL) into turkey mixture. Spread ¹⁄₂ cup (125 mL) in bottom of 13 x 9-inch (3.5 L) baking dish.

Spread about ¹⁄₂ cup (125 mL) turkey mixture on each egg roll wrapper. Roll up and place in centre of baking dish.

Arrange eggplant circles around edge of dish, overlapping slices, if necessary. Spoon remaining sauce over rolls and eggplant slices.

Cover and bake in 375°F (190°C) oven for 35 minutes or until eggplant is tender and rolls are heated through. Sprinkle cheese over top and broil under pre-heated broiler until brown.

MAKES 4 SERVINGS.

NUTRIENT ANALYSIS

Per Serving

Calories		439
g	Protein	31
g	Total Fat	14
g	Carbohydrate	46
g	Fibre	4.9
mg	Sodium	663
mg	Potassium	1007
mg	Calcium	327
mg	Iron	4.3

 The first Canadian reference to turkey has been documented between the years 1759 and 1796. Old Fort Niagara's archaeologists have found 22 turkey bones in their excavations, providing evidence of the use of turkey at Niagara and on the Great Lakes–St. Lawrence frontier. British soldiers obtained turkey by trading with the Indians. *(The King's Bread, 2nd Rising)*

Turkey Pita Pockets al Greco

GREAT for a Saturday night dinner and a nice change from hamburgers. Our families love them!

1 tsp	vegetable oil	5 mL
1 lb	lean ground turkey	500 g
½ cup	chopped onion	125 mL
1	clove garlic, minced	1
1 tbsp	dried mint OR	
	3 tbsp (45 mL) fresh	15 mL
1 tsp	dried oregano	5 mL
½ tsp	salt	2 mL
¼ tsp	freshly ground black pepper	1 mL
½ cup	water	125 mL
½ cup	white wine OR apple juice	125 mL
6	whole wheat pita breads (7 inches/18 cm)	6

Garnishes:

1 cup	chopped tomato	250 mL
1 cup	chopped cucumber	250 mL
½ cup	crumbled feta cheese	125 mL
½ cup	low-fat plain yogurt	125 mL

In large nonstick skillet, heat oil over medium-high heat; add turkey, onion and garlic; cook for about 5 minutes or until meat loses its pink colour; drain fat. Stir in seasonings, water and wine; cook, uncovered, for 5 minutes or until all liquid has evaporated.

Cut pita breads in half and warm. Spoon turkey mixture into each pita half. Add as much tomato, cucumber, cheese and yogurt as desired for garnish.

MAKES 6 SERVINGS.

 Turkey is native to North America, where it was probably first domesticated in Mexico. In the early 16th century, the Spanish took the Mexican species back with them to Europe, where it was called turkey since it resembled the turkey-cock or guinea fowl. *(Encyclopaedia Britannica)*

Rock Cornish Hens with Provençal-Style Stuffing

THIS STUFFING is also wonderful in broiler-fryer chickens, pork chop pockets or with pork spareribs.

2	Rock Cornish hens (about 1 lb/500 g each, thaw if frozen)	2
1 tsp	margarine OR butter	5 mL
1 $\frac{1}{2}$ cups	chopped mushrooms	375 mL
$\frac{1}{2}$ cup	chopped onion	125 mL
1	clove garlic, minced	1
2	large tomatoes, diced	2
$\frac{1}{4}$ cup	dried breadcrumbs	50 mL
2 tbsp	chopped fresh parsley	25 mL
2 tsp	dried tarragon	10 mL
$\frac{1}{2}$ tsp	dried thyme	2 mL
$\frac{1}{8}$ tsp	salt	0.5 mL
$\frac{1}{8}$ tsp	freshly ground black pepper	0.5 mL

COOKING TIPS:

Because of the delicate flavour of Rock Cornish hens, it is important to season them with care. Garnishes do not need to be elaborate to be attractive. Clusters of green grapes and prunes with some mint leaves look wonderful. Or prepare green onion fans by cutting onions in short lengths. Snip both ends in thin strips about 1-inch (2.5 cm) long and place them in ice water to curl.

Wash and dry hens; remove fat and discard.

In nonstick skillet, melt margarine over medium heat; cook mushrooms, onion, garlic and tomatoes for 8 to 10 minutes or until slightly thickened. Stir in breadcrumbs and seasonings; cool slightly.

Spoon stuffing into cavity of each hen; truss with skewers and kitchen cord.

Roast in 350°F (180°C) oven for 45 to 50 minutes or until juices run clear; or place on barbecue rotisserie and cook until done.

To serve, cut each hen in half.

MAKES 4 SERVINGS.

NUTRIENT ANALYSIS

Per Serving

Calories		374
g	Protein	47
g	Total Fat	14
g	Carbohydrate	13
g	Fibre	2.0
mg	Sodium	284
mg	Potassium	741
mg	Calcium	51
mg	Iron	3.0

8

Fish

Fishing for Facts *Fish is a nutritious and low-fat protein alternative to meat. And its fat content is of the omega-3 fatty acid type, which plays a role in reducing blood cholesterol levels.* ◆ *Choosing and preparing fresh or frozen fish is often considered one of the mysteries of the deep. For many people, fish is canned tuna and salmon. But today, more than 100 varieties of fresh and frozen fish are available in Canada. The quick processing most frozen fish now receives preserves its flavour and freshness. However, the flavour of truly fresh fish is still unmatched by the frozen product (There is also less variety in frozen fish).* ◆ *Those new to fresh fish may prefer to start with one of the mild-tasting ones, like halibut or sole. It should be cooked the day it's brought home to ensure the best flavour. If you have to keep the fish, freeze it for a brief time.*

How to Cook It *Correct cooking methods are important for fish, whether it is fresh or frozen. Barbecuing and grilling are suitable for fish with more fat, such as salmon, trout, char and swordfish. Fish with less fat, such as sole, perch, red snapper, pickerel and cod are best cooked in moist heat (microwaved or poached). Because of its high moisture level, fish can be cooked in a microwave oven with particularly good results.*

Fish Fillets Florentine with Red Peppers

KEEP FISH in mind when you're considering food that is low in calories and saturated fat. In this recipe, red pepper and green spinach provide great flavour and colour, help keep fat low, and can be used with a variety of fish fillets.

1	pkg (10 oz/284 g) fresh spinach	1
1	pkg (400 g) frozen fish fillets, thawed and separated (sole, haddock OR halibut)	1
1/2	medium sweet red pepper, cut into thin slices	1/2
1/2 tsp	olive oil	2 mL
1/2 cup	chicken stock	125 mL
2 tsp	cornstarch	10 mL
1/4 tsp	dried marjoram	1 mL

Wash and remove stems from spinach; shake dry. In shallow microwavable dish, cover and microwave spinach at High (100%) for 3 minutes or until wilted. Drain; press out excess water.

Wipe fish with paper towelling. Spread spinach evenly over bottom of dish; top with fish fillets. Cover and microwave at High for 6 minutes or until fish is opaque and flakes easily with a fork.

In small microwavable container, combine red pepper and olive oil. Microwave at High for 2 minutes or until pepper is soft. Combine stock, cornstarch and marjoram; stir into pepper. Microwave at High for 2 minutes or until mixture is thickened and bubbly; stir twice. Pour sauce over fish and serve.

MAKES 4 SERVINGS.

QUICK WAYS FOR FISH FILLETS

- Spoon a small amount of Light Pesto Sauce (page 80) on fillets and broil or microwave.
- Add 1 tbsp (15 mL) Tarragon Mustard (page 94) to 1/4 cup (50 mL) light mayonnaise. Spread on fillets and broil or microwave.
- Combine fruit chutney with low-fat plain yogurt; spoon over fish before cooking.

NUTRIENT ANALYSIS
Per Serving

Calories		118
g	Protein	21
g	Total Fat	1.7
g	Carbohydrate	4.5
g	Fibre	1.9
mg	Sodium	232
mg	Potassium	727
mg	Calcium	107
mg	Iron	3.1

Baked Fish with Mushroom and Rice Stuffing

Whole Fish: Make stuffing and carefully spoon into cavity of whole fish. Bake on foil-lined baking pan, uncovered, in 450°F (230°C) oven, allowing 10 minutes per 1-inch (2.5 cm) of thickness measured at thickest part of stuffed fish. Remove skin and cut into serving-sized pieces. Skin on bottom will generally stick to foil, allowing fish to be removed easily.

COOKING TIPS:

- Choose fish with firm flesh, fins in good condition, no odour and bright eyes, if the head is still attached.
- The lighter the colour of the meat, the lower the fat content.
- Allow 2 to 3 ounces (50 to 100 g) edible fish per serving.

RICE FILLING with mushrooms absorbs the wonderful fish flavours and may easily become a favourite stuffing for whole salmon, whitefish or rainbow trout as well as for other fish fillets. This recipe can easily be divided in half. When cooking one-half of a recipe in the microwave, shorten the cooking time by one-third.

1 tbsp	margarine OR butter	15 mL
1	small onion, chopped	1
2 cups	chopped mushrooms	500 mL
1 cup	chopped fresh spinach	250 mL
$\frac{1}{2}$ tsp	dried basil	2 mL
$\frac{1}{2}$ tsp	dried dill weed	2 mL
$\frac{1}{4}$ tsp	salt	1 mL
Pinch	freshly ground black pepper	Pinch
3 cups	hot cooked rice (1 cup/250 mL raw)	750 mL
1 $\frac{1}{2}$ lb	fish fillets (whitefish, salmon, sole, turbot OR whole fish)	750 g

In large nonstick skillet, heat margarine over medium-high heat; add onion, mushrooms and spinach; cook for 5 minutes or until softened and moisture has evaporated. Stir in seasonings and cooked rice.

Wipe fish with paper towelling and place half of fillets in 8 cup (2 L) microwavable casserole. Spoon rice stuffing over fish and top with remaining fillets. Cover and microwave at High (100%) for 12 to 15 minutes or until fish is opaque and flakes easily with a fork. If there is extra rice stuffing, place in small casserole, heat and serve with fish.

MAKES 8 SERVINGS.

NUTRIENT ANALYSIS
Per Serving

Calories		*214*
g	Protein	19
g	Total Fat	6.7
g	Carbohydrate	19
g	Fibre	1.0
mg	Sodium	154
mg	Potassium	424
mg	Calcium	49
mg	Iron	1.0

Tarragon Fish Provençal

CAPTURE the flavour and colour of French cooking in this easily prepared entrée for the after-5 host or hostess.

Fish lends itself well to garnishing, but people tend to think only of lemon as a garnish. For a change, try other citrus varieties such as spirals of orange or lime peel.

To microwave fish, allow 5 minutes per pound (500g) at High (100%) after fish is defrosted.

1 ½ cups	chicken stock	375 mL
¾ cup	long-grain white rice	175 mL
1 lb	fish fillets (sole, halibut OR haddock)	500 g
½ tsp	dried tarragon	2 mL
¼ tsp	dried thyme	1 mL
2	large tomatoes, chopped	2
1 cup	sliced mushrooms	250 mL
3	green onions, sliced	3
2	cloves garlic, minced	2
2 tbsp	white wine OR lemon juice	25 mL
1 cup	fresh whole wheat breadcrumbs	250 mL
1 tbsp	olive oil	15 mL

In medium saucepan, bring stock to a boil; add rice, reduce heat, cover, and simmer for 20 minutes or until stock has been absorbed. Spread in lightly greased shallow casserole. Wipe fish with paper towelling and arrange over rice; sprinkle with tarragon and thyme.

Combine tomatoes, mushrooms, onions, garlic and wine; spoon evenly over fish. Toss breadcrumbs with oil; spread over tomato mixture.

Bake in 450°F (230°C) oven for about 12 minutes or until fish is opaque and flakes easily with a fork.

MAKES 5 SERVINGS.

NUTRIENT ANALYSIS		
Per Serving		
Calories		*256*
g	Protein	21
g	Total Fat	4.9
g	Carbohydrate	29
g	Fibre	2.3
mg	Sodium	398
mg	Potassium	501
mg	Calcium	53
mg	Iron	1.4

Steamed Fish Rolls with Herbed Tomato Sauce

GOOD THINGS really do come in small packages. A hint of marjoram in this light tomato sauce enhances the delicate flavour of the salmon and sole.

12	large napa cabbage leaves OR 18 smaller leaves	12
1	can (7.5 oz/213 g) salmon, drained	1
1	pkg (400 g) frozen sole fillets, thawed	1
1 tsp	vegetable oil	5 mL
8	green onions, minced	8
4	fresh mushrooms, chopped	4
$\frac{1}{8}$ tsp	salt	0.5 mL

Sauce:

1 tsp	olive oil	5 mL
2	shallots, minced	2
1	clove garlic, minced	1
2 cups	diced peeled tomato	500 mL
2 tbsp	dry vermouth OR chicken stock	25 mL
$\frac{1}{2}$ tsp	dried marjoram	2 mL

COOKING TIPS:
Steaming fish wrapped in cabbage leaves, parchment paper or aluminum foil helps retain its natural moistness.

In large pot of boiling water, blanch cabbage leaves for 2 minutes; cool under running water, drain and set aside.

Break salmon into large chunks; cut sole fillets into $\frac{1}{2}$-inch (1 cm) cubes and combine with salmon.

In nonstick skillet, heat vegetable oil over medium heat; sauté onions and mushrooms until soft. Add salt and combine lightly with salmon and sole mixture.

Remove part of the heavy stem from each cabbage leaf. Place a mound of fish on stem end of each leaf; roll up bundles, tucking in sides. Place bundles on rack over boiling water. Cover and steam for 10 minutes or until filling is cooked.

Sauce: In small nonstick skillet, heat oil over low heat; cook shallots and garlic for about 4 minutes or until shallots are very soft. Add tomatoes, vermouth and marjoram; simmer for 10 minutes. Serve sauce over fish bundles.

MAKES 6 SERVINGS, 2 BUNDLES PER SERVING.

NUTRIENT ANALYSIS	
Per Serving	
Calories	167
g Protein	20
g Total Fat	6.2
g Carbohydrate	6.4
g Fibre	1.6
mg Sodium	271
mg Potassium	655
mg Calcium	119
mg Iron	1.3

Thai-Style Fish Stir-Fry

THAI CUISINE reflects both Chinese and Indian influences; the Chinese technique of stir-frying is happily combined with the brilliant use of spices and herbs found in Indian cooking. The wonderful flavour of Thai food comes from fish sauce, a clear brown extraction usually made from anchovies. It is used to season most meat and vegetable dishes, along with lots of garlic, shallots, limes and hot chilies. Try this delicious stir-fry with orange pepper to contrast beautifully with green snow peas. If you can't find fish sauce, use soy sauce instead.

Sauce:

	Juice of 1 lime	
½ cup	chicken stock	125 mL
2 tbsp	fish sauce OR soy sauce	25 mL
1 tsp	granulated sugar	5 mL
¼ tsp	white pepper	2 mL
⅛ tsp	crushed red chilies	0.5 mL
1 tbsp	cornstarch	15 mL
2 tbsp	water	25 mL

Stir-Fry:

1 tbsp	sesame oil	15 mL
2	cloves garlic, minced	2
2	dry shallots OR onions, sliced	2
1 tbsp	minced gingerroot	15 mL
¾ lb	firm-fleshed fish, cubed (bluefish OR grouper)	400 g
2	stalks celery, sliced	2
¼ lb	snow peas, trimmed	125 g
4	green onions, cut into 1-inch (2.5 cm) slices	4
1	sweet orange pepper, cut into thin slices	1
8	fresh shiitake OR white mushrooms, sliced	8

Sauce: In bowl, combine juice, stock, fish sauce, sugar, pepper and chilies; set aside. In second small bowl, combine cornstarch and water; set aside.

Stir-Fry: In large nonstick skillet or wok, heat oil over medium-high heat; stir-fry garlic, shallots and gingerroot for 30 seconds. Add fish cubes; stir-fry for about 4 minutes or until fish is opaque.

Add celery, peas, onions, pepper and mushrooms; stir-fry for 1 minute. Stir in sauce mixture. Cover and cook for 5 minutes or just until vegetables are starting to become tender. Stir in cornstarch mixture and cook until thickened, stirring constantly.

MAKES 4 SERVINGS.

NUTRIENT ANALYSIS		
Per Serving		
Calories		*220*
g	Protein	21
g	Total Fat	7.7
g	Carbohydrate	18
g	Fibre	3.0
mg	Sodium	604
mg	Potassium	768
mg	Calcium	56
mg	Iron	2.1

Middle Eastern Swordfish Steaks

SWORDFISH'S MEATY TEXTURE is ideal for grilling or barbecuing. The full-bodied, bold flavours of the marinade nicely complement this fish. If you don't want to use swordfish, salmon steaks are an excellent substitute.

2	swordfish steaks ($^1/_2$ lb/250 g each)	2
2 tbsp	chopped fresh parsley	25 mL
1	small jalapeño pepper, chopped	1
1 tbsp	vegetable oil	15 mL
3 tbsp	lemon juice	45 mL
1	clove garlic, minced	1
2 tsp	turmeric powder	10 mL
2 tsp	ground cinnamon	10 mL
2 tsp	ground cumin	10 mL
$^1/_4$ tsp	freshly ground black pepper	1 mL

COOKING TIPS:

A creative garnish for these steaks might be small bunches of purple grapes and lemon twists on a bed of endive.

Wipe fish with paper towelling and place in shallow baking dish. In small bowl, combine parsley, jalapeño pepper, oil, juice, garlic and seasonings. Spread mixture over each side of fish. Cover and refrigerate for several hours.

Preheat barbecue or broiler on high. Just before cooking, brush grill lightly with oil. Broil or barbecue steaks 4 inches (10 cm) from heat for 4 to 5 minutes per side or until fish is opaque and flakes easily with a fork.

MAKES 4 SERVINGS.

NUTRIENT ANALYSIS		
Per Serving		
Calories		188
g	Protein	23
g	Total Fat	8.5
g	Carbohydrate	4.4
g	Fibre	0.8
mg	Sodium	108
mg	Potassium	445
mg	Calcium	39
mg	Iron	2.9

Grilled Salmon with Fresh Tomato Salsa

MAKE THIS RECIPE when you are looking for a low-calorie entrée. Simple and elegant, it provides great flavour and superb appearance when entertaining.

Salsa:

1 cup	diced tomato (1 medium)	250 mL
¼ cup	finely chopped onion	50 mL
2 tbsp	chopped cilantro	25 mL
1 tbsp	lemon juice	15 mL
1 tbsp	tomato paste	15 mL
¼ tsp	garlic powder OR	1 mL
	1 small clove garlic, minced	
Dash	hot pepper sauce	Dash
Pinch	freshly ground black pepper	Pinch
	Lemon juice	
1 lb	salmon fillet	500 g
	Garnish: Curly endive, lemon twists	

OMEGA-3

Omega-3 fatty acids are polyunsaturated fatty acids, which have been identified as having a role in reducing the risk of heart disease. The main sources of these fatty acids are higher-fat fish such as salmon, sardines, mackerel and anchovies.

Salsa: In bowl, combine tomato, onion, cilantro, lemon juice, tomato paste and seasonings; set aside.

Sprinkle lemon juice over fish. Preheat grill or broiler on high. Just before cooking, brush grill lightly with oil. Barbecue or broil fish 4 inches (10 cm) from heat for 4 to 5 minutes per side or until fish is opaque and flakes easily with a fork.

Place fish on a platter, surround with curly endive and a few lemon twists, and top each fillet with a spoonful of salsa.

MAKES 5 SERVINGS.

NUTRIENT ANALYSIS		
Per Serving		
Calories		*166*
g	Protein	20
g	Total Fat	7.9
g	Carbohydrate	2.8
g	Fibre	0.6
mg	Sodium	52
mg	Potassium	372
mg	Calcium	10
mg	Iron	0.6

Salmon Cups with Lemon Chive Sauce

INTRODUCE your microwave oven to handy canned salmon to prepare this great-tasting and nutritious dinner for two in minutes. If there is any sauce left over, use it as a topping for vegetables.

Salmon Cups:

1	can (7.5 oz/213 g) salmon, drained	1
1/4 cup	chopped green onions	50 mL
1/4 cup	chopped mushrooms	50 mL
1/2 cup	fresh whole wheat breadcrumbs (1 slice)	125 mL
1	egg white	1
1 tbsp	chopped fresh parsley	15 mL
1/4 tsp	dried thyme	1 mL
1/8 tsp	salt	0.5 mL
1/8 tsp	freshly ground black pepper	0.5 mL

Lemon Chive Sauce:

1/2 cup	low-fat milk	125 mL
1 tbsp	all-purpose flour	15 mL
2 tbsp	minced chives	25 mL
2 tsp	lemon juice	10 mL
Pinch	white pepper	Pinch

Salmon Cups: Flake salmon and mash bones. Combine salmon with onions, mushrooms, breadcrumbs, egg white, parsley and seasonings.

Spoon into 2 small baking cups. Microwave at High (100%) for 3 minutes or until almost set. Let stand for 2 minutes to finish cooking.

Lemon Chive Sauce: In small microwavable container, whisk together milk, flour and chives. Microwave at High (100%) for 1 1/2 minutes or until mixture comes to a boil; stir once. Stir in lemon juice and pepper to taste. Serve sauce over salmon cups.

MAKES 2 SERVINGS.

COOKING TIPS:

An added benefit of canned salmon is the calcium contained in the bones, which become very soft during the canning process. Don't discard them, but crush and add them to the salmon for a dish that is an excellent source of calcium.

NUTRIENT ANALYSIS

Per Serving

Calories		*219*
g	Protein	25
g	Total Fat	6.5
g	Carbohydrate	15
g	Fibre	1.6
mg	Sodium	728
mg	Potassium	514
mg	Calcium	323
mg	Iron	1.9

Pasta with Fresh Tomato Tuna Sauce

WITH CANNED TUNA and some fresh vegetables, dinner can be on the table in minutes. This wonderful tuna sauce also goes very nicely over cooked rice or spaghetti squash. Each serving provides an excellent source of iron.

Sauce:

1 tbsp	margarine OR butter	15 mL
1/2 cup	chopped onion	125 mL
2	cloves garlic, minced	2
4	large tomatoes, peeled and chopped	4
1/2 cup	chopped celery	125 mL
1/2 cup	chopped zucchini	125 mL
1 tbsp	lemon juice	15 mL
1/2 tsp	granulated sugar	2 mL
1 tsp	dried basil OR 2 tbsp (25 mL) fresh	5 mL
1/2 tsp	dried oregano OR 2 tsp (10 mL) fresh	2 mL
1/4 tsp	salt	1 mL
1/4 tsp	freshly ground black pepper	1 mL
2	cans (6.5 oz/184 g each) solid tuna (packed in water)	2
1/2 lb	fettuccine or spaghetti	250 g

Sauce: In large nonstick skillet, heat margarine over medium heat; cook onion and garlic for 5 minutes or until tender. Add tomatoes, celery, zucchini, juice, sugar and seasonings. Cook, uncovered, over medium heat for 20 minutes or until liquid is thickened; stir occasionally.

Drain tuna, break into chunks; add to sauce and heat to serving temperature.

Meanwhile, in large pot of boiling water, cook fettuccine until tender but firm; drain and place in serving dish. Toss lightly with sauce.

MAKES 4 SERVINGS.

COOKING TIPS:

Open a can of tuna and what do you have?

- A fast meal by adding it to some stir-fried vegetables.
- A lunch by adding it to one of our low-fat salad dressings and serving over a lettuce wedge.
- A supper dish by adding it to chopped hard-cooked eggs and white sauce. Serve over noodles or multi-grain toast or fold into crepes.
- A fast main-course salad by adding it to cooked rice, light mayonnaise, chopped dill and celery, shredded carrot and zucchini.
- An anytime meal by adding it to sautéed green peppers and onions, chopped tomato and shredded light Cheddar cheese and served in taco shells.

NUTRIENT ANALYSIS
Per Serving

Calories		374
g	Protein	30
g	Total Fat	4.6
g	Carbohydrate	52
g	Fibre	3.7
mg	Sodium	486
mg	Potassium	716
mg	Calcium	47
mg	Iron	5.9

Gingered Lime Trout

The Canadian Department of Fisheries and Oceans has developed a foolproof cooking guide to help overcome hesitations about cooking fish: measure fish at its thickest part, then cook for 10 minutes per 1 inch (2.5 cm) of thickness. (If fish is frozen, double the cooking time.)

For example, a whole fish measuring 2 inches (5 cm) at the thickest part, or centre, would require 20 minutes cooking whether it is baked in a 450°F (230°C) oven, barbecued on high or poached in simmering water.

Fish steaks measuring ³⁄₄ inch (2 cm) at the thickest part would require 7 to 8 minutes baked in a 450°F (230°C) oven, barbecued or poached.

So, haul out the trusty kitchen ruler; whether it is metric or imperial, you will now be able to cook fish perfectly every time.

SERVE this elegant and simple entrée with whole wheat fettuccine noodles and a simple salad.

4	rainbow trout fillets (each 4 oz/125 g)	4
2 tbsp	lime juice	25 mL
1 tsp	grated lime rind	5 mL
1 tbsp	chopped gingerroot	15 mL
1 tbsp	chopped fresh dill OR	15 mL
	1 tsp (5 mL) dried	
¼ cup	sliced almonds	50 mL
1 tbsp	melted margarine OR butter	15 mL
Pinch	freshly ground black pepper	Pinch

Wipe fish with paper towelling. Place in lightly greased shallow baking pan.

Stir together juice, rind, gingerroot, dill and almonds. Spoon evenly over fish. Drizzle with margarine and sprinkle with pepper.

Cover with foil and bake in 450°F (230°C) oven for about 10 minutes or until fish is opaque and flakes easily with a fork.

MAKES 4 SERVINGS.

NUTRIENT ANALYSIS		
Per Serving		
Calories		*170*
g	Protein	19
g	Total Fat	9.2
g	Carbohydrate	2.3
g	Fibre	0.5
mg	Sodium	56
mg	Potassium	505
mg	Calcium	80
mg	Iron	2.0

9 Meat Alternatives

Meat Alternatives are protein-rich foods that generally have less fat than is associated with the traditional proteins of meats, fish and poultry. They are: dairy products, eggs, legumes, grains and nuts and seeds. These foods can provide variety in our diets, often at less cost. ◆ *Proteins provide us with the amino-acid building blocks we need for growth and repair of our bodies. Nine amino-acids are called essential; they must come from our daily diet because our bodies cannot make them. Animal sources of protein (milk, eggs, meat, fish and poultry), quinoa and soybeans are complete because they contain all of the essential amino-acids. Plant proteins, with the exception of soybeans, are not complete because they lack one or more of these essential amino-acids. Fortunately, we can make a complete protein by combining plant proteins with one another or with some animal protein. The other good news is that you don't have to combine complementary proteins at the same meal, as long as you are sure to eat a variety of sources over the day. A general guide is to combine grains or nuts and seeds with legumes or add some animal protein to plant (vegetable) proteins.*

Grains/Nuts and Seeds + Legumes

Animal Proteins + Vegetable Protein

◆ *Some great protein combinations are: Mexican Lentil and Rice Pizza (page 128), Vegetable Burritos (page 130), sunflower seeds added to Lentil and Brown Rice Salad (page 55), macaroni and cheese, pizza and peanut butter sandwiches.*

Chick-Pea Stir-Fry

CANNED CHICK-PEAS are available in all supermarkets to use for a fast meal. This recipe is served over cooked rice to provide a meatless meal with complementary proteins and a very high source of fibre and a good source of iron.

1 tbsp	olive oil	15 mL
1 tsp	sesame oil	5 mL
1	medium onion, sliced	1
2 cups	shredded Chinese cabbage	500 mL
$\frac{1}{2}$	sweet green pepper, chopped	$\frac{1}{2}$
4	green onions, sliced	4
2	cloves garlic, minced	2
1	can (19 oz/540 mL) chick-peas, drained and rinsed	1
$\frac{1}{2}$ cup	water	125 mL
2 tbsp	lime juice	25 mL
1 tbsp	grated lime rind	15 mL
1 tbsp	cornstarch	15 mL
$\frac{1}{2}$ tsp	ground ginger	2 mL
$\frac{1}{2}$ tsp	ground cumin	2 mL
$\frac{1}{2}$ tsp	chili powder	2 mL
4 cups	hot cooked rice (about 1 $\frac{1}{4}$ cups/300 mL raw)	1 L
	Garnish: Chopped fresh parsley	

In large nonstick skillet, heat olive and sesame oils over medium-high heat; cook onion, cabbage, pepper, green onions and garlic for about 5 minutes or until soft. Add chick-peas and heat through.

In small bowl, combine water, juice, rind, cornstarch and seasonings. Add to skillet; cook and stir for about 2 minutes or until slightly thickened. Serve over rice and sprinkle with parsley.

MAKES 4 SERVINGS.

COOKING TIPS:

When you are cooking rice for a meal, cook extra and freeze for recipes that require cooked rice, or to reheat in the microwave for a fast addition to a meal.

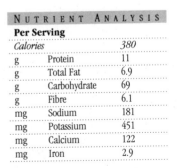

NUTRIENT ANALYSIS		
Per Serving		
Calories		*380*
g	Protein	11
g	Total Fat	6.9
g	Carbohydrate	69
g	Fibre	6.1
mg	Sodium	181
mg	Potassium	451
mg	Calcium	122
mg	Iron	2.9

NEXT PAGE: *Vegetable Burritos (page 130).*

Garbanzos with Vegetables

IN SPAIN, chick-peas are known as garbanzos. There, garbanzos are used extensively in stews, casseroles and salads. In this recipe, they provide protein and a very high source of fibre for a hearty and flavourful one-dish meal that is also a good source of iron and calcium.

1 tbsp	olive oil	15 mL
2	cloves garlic, minced	2
1	onion, chopped	1
2	carrots, sliced	2
2	stalks celery, sliced	2
2 cups	Homemade chicken stock (page 38)	500 mL
1	can (28 oz/796 mL) plum tomatoes	1
3/4 cup	long-grain white rice	175 mL
1 tsp	dried oregano	5 mL
1/8 tsp	red chili flakes	0.5 mL
1/8 tsp	freshly ground black pepper	0.5 mL
1	can (19 oz/540 mL) kidney beans, drained and rinsed	1
1	can (19 oz/540 mL) chick-peas, drained and rinsed	1
2	sprigs parsley OR cilantro, minced	2
1/2 cup	freshly grated Parmesan cheese	125 mL

COOKING TIPS:

Canned kidney beans and chick-peas are convenient, but if you have time, it is much less expensive to cook your own. Also, canned beans are often high in salt, which you may not want; rinsing before using helps reduce this salt. The extra time required to prepare dried beans will be justified if you cook extra beans and store them in the freezer to use as needed.

To cook beans, see Black Beans with Squash (page 132) for instructions. 1 cup (250 mL) dried beans or peas generally yields about 2 1/2 cups (625 mL) cooked.

In large saucepan, heat oil over medium heat; cook garlic, onion, carrots and celery for 5 minutes or until soft.

Add stock, tomatoes, rice and seasonings. Cover and bring to a boil; reduce heat and simmer for 20 minutes or until rice is cooked.

Add kidney beans, chick-peas and parsley; cook for 5 minutes or until serving temperature.

Sprinkle each serving with cheese.

MAKES 6 SERVINGS.

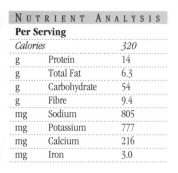

NUTRIENT ANALYSIS		
Per Serving		
Calories		*320*
g	Protein	14
g	Total Fat	6.3
g	Carbohydrate	54
g	Fibre	9.4
mg	Sodium	805
mg	Potassium	777
mg	Calcium	216
mg	Iron	3.0

PREVIOUS PAGE: *Plum Blueberry Crisp (page 146), Lemon Nut Biscotti (page 153), Naturally Sweet Soft Cookies (page 154), Microwave Maple Filled Pears (page 142).*

Falafel-Stuffed Pitas

LEGUMES

Legumes such as chick-peas, split peas, peanuts, and all kinds of beans (lima, kidney, pinto, white, black) are good protein sources and are rich in fibre and complex carbohydrates. Their protein is incomplete, which means they should be teamed up with grains or animal proteins such as cheese and yogurt. With the exception of peanuts and soybeans, legumes are much lower in fat than are animal proteins.

SPICES are added to ground chick-peas to form falafel—a Middle-Eastern food that has become popular with North Americans, especially when stuffed into these pocket breads. Not only are they tasty but together they are a high source of fibre and an excellent source of calcium and iron.

1 tsp	vegetable oil	5 mL
1/2 cup	chopped onion	125 mL
2	cloves garlic, minced	2
2 tbsp	sesame seeds	25 mL
1	can (14 oz/398 mL) chick-peas, drained and rinsed	1
1/2 cup	low-fat plain yogurt	125 mL
1/4 cup	chopped fresh parsley	50 mL
1/2 tsp	dried oregano	2 mL
1/2 tsp	paprika	2 mL
1/4 tsp	salt	1 mL
1/4 tsp	freshly ground black pepper	1 mL
1/8 tsp	ground allspice	0.5 mL
2 to 3	drops hot pepper sauce	2 to 3
4	whole wheat pita breads (7 inch/18 cm)	4
1/2 cup	shredded Monterey Jack OR other mild cheese	125 mL

Garnishes:

1 cup	shredded lettuce	250 mL
8	slices tomato	8
1/2 cup	chopped sweet green pepper	125 mL
1 cup	alfalfa sprouts	250 mL

In nonstick skillet, heat oil over medium heat; cook onion, garlic and sesame seeds for about 4 minutes or until onion is tender. Cool slightly.

In food processor container, process onion mixture, chick-peas, yogurt, parsley and seasonings until smooth.

Cut each pita bread in half. Spoon approximately 3 tbsp (45 mL) chick-pea mixture into each half; divide cheese over each. Place halves upright on microwavable baking dish. Microwave at High (100%) for 1 minute or until cheese begins to melt. Serve with choice of garnishes.

MAKES 4 SERVINGS.

NUTRIENT ANALYSIS
Per Serving

Calories		*377*
g	Protein	16
g	Total Fat	9.7
g	Carbohydrate	58
g	Fibre	5.2
mg	Sodium	668
mg	Potassium	519
mg	Calcium	293
mg	Iron	4.4

Tofu Lasagna

TOFU is an excellent source of protein. Its mildness blends nicely into this flavourful lasagna, making this recipe an excellent source of calcium and iron. The red lentils make a thick sauce and provide additional protein.

Sauce:

¹⁄₂ cup	dried red lentils, washed	125 mL
1 ¹⁄₂ cups	water	375 mL
1 tsp	vegetable oil	5 mL
¹⁄₂ cup	chopped onion	125 mL
2	cloves garlic, minced	2
1	can (28 oz/796 mL) tomatoes	1
1	can (5.5 oz/156 mL) tomato paste	1
2 tsp	dried oregano	10 mL
1 tsp	dried basil	5 mL
1 cup	low-fat cottage cheese	250 mL
1 cup	diced tofu (about 135 g)	250 mL
¹⁄₄ cup	freshly grated Parmesan cheese	50 mL
1	egg white	1
2 tbsp	chopped fresh parsley	25 mL
¹⁄₂ lb	shredded part-skim mozzarella cheese	250 g
9	oven-ready lasagna noodles	9
¹⁄₄ cup	freshly grated Parmesan cheese	50 mL

Sauce: In medium saucepan, bring lentils and water to a boil; reduce heat and simmer, covered, for 8 to 10 minutes or until soft. Set aside.

In large nonstick skillet, heat oil over medium heat; sauté onion and garlic for 2 to 3 minutes or until soft. Stir in tomatoes, tomato paste, oregano and basil. Cover and bring to a boil; reduce heat and simmer for 20 minutes. Stir in lentils.

In food processor or blender container, process cottage cheese, tofu, Parmesan cheese, egg white and parsley until smooth.

In lightly greased 9-inch (2 L) square baking pan, place ¹⁄₂ cup (125 mL) tomato sauce. Top with 3 noodles; cover with ¹⁄₂ cottage cheese mixture, ¹⁄₂ mozzarella cheese and ¹⁄₃ tomato sauce; repeat layers. Place remaining 3 noodles over top and cover with remaining sauce. Sprinkle with Parmesan cheese.

Cover and bake in 350°F (180°C) oven for 40 minutes. Let stand 15 minutes before cutting into squares.

MAKES 6 SERVINGS.

COOKING TIPS:
Tofu is a cheese-like cake made from liquid extracted from ground soybeans. The flavour of tofu is affected by the salt used to produce the curds. Try different brands until you find one you like. Tofu takes on the flavour of other ingredients, making it a versatile way to add protein to your diet. Use it to make Tofu Garden Quiche (page 124), a sandwich filling or salad dressing. If it is pressed on paper towels with weights, it becomes firmer and can be cut into small cubes to add to salads, soup, a stir-fry or casserole dish. Store tofu, covered with water, and change the water daily. Keep refrigerated or frozen. Freezing will change the texture, but it is a good way to store it when you have extra.

NUTRIENT ANALYSIS
Per Serving

Calories		*427*
g	Protein	33
g	Total Fat	13
g	Carbohydrate	48
g	Fibre	3.7
mg	Sodium	784
mg	Potassium	918
mg	Calcium	570
mg	Iron	6.3

Tofu Garden Quiche

SLIP TOFU, which is low in both fat and calories, into main course dishes, where it nicely absorbs the flavours of the other foods. Serve this crustless quiche, an excellent source of calcium and iron, either warm or cold with a green salad and hot rolls.

2 tsp	margarine OR butter	10 mL
½ cup	finely chopped onion	125 mL
2 cups	coarsely chopped vegetables (sweet red OR green pepper, green or yellow zucchini)	500 mL
2	eggs	2
1	pkg (19 oz/550 g) tofu, drained	1
2 tbsp	all-purpose flour	25 mL
1 tbsp	lemon juice	15 mL
1 tsp	dried oregano	5 mL
½ tsp	dried tarragon	2 mL
¼ tsp	salt	1 mL
Pinch	Each: garlic powder, ground nutmeg and freshly ground black pepper	Pinch
¼ cup	freshly grated Parmesan cheese	50 mL

EGGS

Eggs provide iron as well as other vitamins and minerals and are a complete source of protein. Each egg has 6 grams of total fat.

In large nonstick skillet, heat margarine over medium-high heat; cook onion and vegetables for about 10 minutes or until fairly dry; set aside.

In food processor or blender container, process eggs and tofu until smooth and creamy. Add flour, juice and seasonings; blend to combine.

Stir tofu mixture into reserved vegetables and pour into a lightly greased 10-inch (25 cm) quiche dish or deep pie plate. Sprinkle with cheese and bake in 350°F (180°C) oven for 50 minutes or until knife inserted in centre comes out clean. Let stand for 5 minutes. To serve, cut into 6 wedges.

MAKES 6 SERVINGS.

NUTRIENT ANALYSIS		
Per Serving		
Calories		*153*
g	Protein	12
g	Total Fat	8.8
g	Carbohydrate	8.3
g	Fibre	1.0
mg	Sodium	236
mg	Potassium	272
mg	Calcium	401
mg	Iron	5.6

Italian Vegetable Layers

COLOURFUL LAYERS of vegetables and ricotta cheese are sandwiched between lasagna noodles and slices of zucchini. The delicious result is an excellent source of calcium and a good source of iron.

6	lasagna noodles	6
2	medium carrots, shredded	2
1	medium onion, chopped	1
2 cups	chopped broccoli	500 mL
1	sweet red OR green pepper, cut into strips	1
2 tbsp	water	25 mL
1/4 tsp	salt	1 mL
1	container (300 g) part-skim ricotta cheese	1
1 1/2 cups	shredded part-skim mozzarella cheese	375 mL
3/4 cup	freshly grated Parmesan cheese, divided	175 mL
2	small zucchini, cut into 1/4-inch (5 mm) lengthwise strips	2
3	medium tomatoes, thinly sliced	3

In large amount of boiling water, cook lasagna noodles according to package directions, or until tender but firm; drain and set aside.

In 4-cup (1 L) microwavable container, cover and microwave carrots, onion, broccoli, red pepper and water at High (100%) for 5 minutes or until crisp-tender; drain and stir in salt.

In 11 x 7-inch (2 L) baking pan, arrange 3 noodles. Cover with 1/2 ricotta cheese, 1/2 vegetable mixture, 1/3 mozzarella cheese and 1/3 of Parmesan cheese. Arrange zucchini over cheeses. Cover with remaining ricotta cheese and vegetable mixture, 1/3 mozzarella cheese and 1/3 Parmesan cheese.

Place 3 lasagna noodles over top and sprinkle with remaining mozzarella cheese. Top with tomato slices and remaining Parmesan cheese.

Cover and bake in 350°F (180°C) oven for 1 hour or until vegetables are tender.

MAKES 6 SERVINGS.

DAIRY PRODUCTS

Dairy products provide complete protein and are important sources of calcium. They come in many forms: milk, yogurt, cottage, ricotta and a wide variety of other cheeses. Check the dairy section and experiment with something different the next time you shop.

NUTRIENT ANALYSIS

Per Serving

Calories		332
g	Protein	24
g	Total Fat	13
g	Carbohydrate	30
g	Fibre	3.8
mg	Sodium	586
mg	Potassium	635
mg	Calcium	557
mg	Iron	2.3

Crustless Cheese Pie

SPINACH and two kinds of cheese complement one another for a wonderful lunch or supper dish that provides an excellent source of calcium and a good source of iron. For a savory appetizer, bake in a flat square pan and cut into small pieces.

1	pkg (300 g) frozen chopped spinach, thawed	1
1	small onion, finely chopped	1
2	eggs	2
1 cup	low-fat cottage cheese	250 mL
1/2 cup	freshly grated Parmesan cheese	125 mL
1 tbsp	low-fat milk	15 mL
1 tbsp	whole wheat flour	15 mL
1/4 tsp	salt	1 mL
1	sweet red pepper, cut into rings	1

Drain spinach by pressing out moisture with slotted spoon. Spread 1/2 of spinach in bottom of lightly greased 9-inch (23 cm) pie plate or quiche dish; sprinkle with onion.

In large bowl, beat eggs, cottage and Parmesan cheeses, milk, flour and salt; stir in remaining spinach. Pour over spinach layer. Arrange red pepper rings on top.

Bake in 350°F (180°C) oven for 25 to 30 minutes or until knife inserted in centre comes out clean. Let stand for 5 minutes before cutting into wedges.

MAKES 4 SERVINGS.

COOKING TIPS:
Spinach came originally from Asia. It was the Dutch who introduced it to European cookery and the Spaniards who brought it to North America. During the 1920s, spinach went through an unpopular phase, which fortunately has passed. Its current popularity is recognized by the number of dishes one sees that are "Florentine," which means that spinach is an integral ingredient. Due to its high moisture content, it is preferable to thaw and drain frozen spinach before adding it to a recipe.

NUTRIENT ANALYSIS
Per Serving

	Calories	182
g	Protein	19
g	Total Fat	7.4
g	Carbohydrate	10
g	Fibre	3.0
mg	Sodium	756
mg	Potassium	427
mg	Calcium	322
mg	Iron	2.3

Lentil Chili

SOME FOODS are good for you, while others simply taste great! This chili recipe is a superb example of both good nutrition and great taste. Serve with fluffy cooked rice or toast for a complete protein meal that is very high in fibre and an excellent source of iron.

COOKING TIPS:

Red and brown or green lentils become very different products when they are cooked. Red lentils cook to a much softer texture and become mushy, whereas brown and green lentils keep their distinct shape. Use red lentils when making Bean and Lentil Pâté (page 26) or for pasta-type sauces such as the one for Mexican Lentil and Rice Pizza (page 128). Use the brown or green ones for combination dishes like this Lentil Chili.

2 cups	tomato juice	500 mL
2 cups	beef stock	500 mL
2 cups	diced raw potato	500 mL
1	can (19 oz/540 mL) chick-peas, drained and rinsed	1
1 cup	dried green OR brown lentils, washed	250 mL
2	small carrots, chopped	2
½ cup	chopped onion	125 mL
½	medium sweet green pepper, chopped	½
2	cloves garlic, minced	2
2 tbsp	chili powder	25 mL
1 tsp	dried basil	5 mL
¼ tsp	pepper	1 mL
½ cup	low-fat plain yogurt	125 mL

In large saucepan, combine tomato juice, stock, potato, chick-peas, lentils, carrots, onion, green pepper, garlic and seasonings. Cover, bring to a boil; reduce heat and simmer for about 30 minutes or until lentils are tender. Serve with yogurt.

MAKES 6 SERVINGS.

NUTRIENT ANALYSIS		
Per Serving		
Calories		276
g	Protein	16
g	Total Fat	2.0
g	Carbohydrate	52
g	Fibre	8.6
mg	Sodium	635
mg	Potassium	1076
mg	Calcium	108
mg	Iron	5.3

Mexican Lentil and Rice Pizza

COOKED RICE provides an interesting crust for this pizza. Adding lots of vegetables for toppings, a savory purée of cooked red lentils to replace the traditional tomato sauce, and using brown rice creates a dish that is high in fibre and packed with other nutrients.

Sauce:

²⁄₃ cup	dried red lentils, washed	150 mL
1 cup	water	250 mL
1	medium onion, chopped	1
1	small clove garlic, minced	1
2	bay leaves	2
Pinch	pepper	Pinch
2 cups	cooked brown OR white rice (²⁄₃ cup/150 mL raw)	500 mL
1	egg, beaten	1
¹⁄₂ cup	shredded part-skim mozzarella cheese	125 mL
1 tsp	chili powder	5 mL
¹⁄₄ tsp	dry mustard	1 mL
1 cup	shredded zucchini	250 mL
1 cup	small cauliflower florets	250 mL
1 cup	sliced mushrooms	250 mL
1	medium tomato, chopped	1
¹⁄₄ cup	chopped sweet green pepper	50 mL
¹⁄₂ cup	mild salsa	125 mL
1 cup	shredded part-skim mozzarella cheese	250 mL

Sauce: In large saucepan, combine lentils, water, onion, garlic, bay leaves and pepper. Cover and bring to a boil; reduce heat and simmer for 10 minutes or until tender. Remove bay leaves, mash and cool.

In medium bowl, combine rice, egg, cheese and seasonings. Press mixture into a lightly greased 9-inch (23 cm) pie plate. Bake in 400°F (200°C) oven for 10 minutes. Spread sauce over rice crust.

Place zucchini, cauliflower, mushrooms, tomato, green pepper and salsa over sauce. Return dish to oven and bake for 20 minutes; remove from oven and add cheese. Bake for 5 minutes more or until cheese is melted.

MAKES 6 SERVINGS.

NUTRIENT ANALYSIS

Per Serving

Calories		275
g	Protein	19
g	Total Fat	7.2
g	Carbohydrate	35
g	Fibre	5.4
mg	Sodium	187
mg	Potassium	645
mg	Calcium	259
mg	Iron	3.1

Tex-Mex Tortilla Pie

FLOUR TORTILLAS form the layers of this Mexican-inspired supper dish that is very high in fibre, as well as other nutrients. Using canned beans in the sauce to replace the traditional refried beans is a lower-fat choice.

1	can (14 oz/398 mL) beans in tomato sauce	1
1 tbsp	chili powder	15 mL
1/2 tsp	dried oregano	2 mL
1/2 tsp	ground cumin	2 mL
5	8-inch (20 cm) flour tortillas	5
2	fresh or canned jalapeño peppers, finely chopped	2
1 cup	shredded part-skim mozzarella cheese	250 mL
1/2 cup	shredded light Cheddar cheese	125 mL

Garnishes:

1/2 cup	mild salsa	125 mL
2	medium tomatoes, chopped	2
1/2 cup	shredded lettuce	125 mL

In food processor container, process beans and seasonings until smooth.

In 9-inch (23 cm) lightly greased baking dish, place 1 tortilla. Spread with 1/4 bean mixture, 1/4 peppers and 1/4 mozzarella. Repeat for 3 more layers. Place last tortilla on top; sprinkle with Cheddar.

Bake in 350°F (180°C) oven for 20 minutes or until cheese is melted and layers are heated through.

Cut into 4 wedges and serve with salsa, tomatoes and lettuce.

MAKES 4 SERVINGS.

NUTRIENT ANALYSIS

Per Serving

Calories		373
g	Protein	21
g	Total Fat	12
g	Carbohydrate	50
g	Fibre	10.4
mg	Sodium	889
mg	Potassium	828
mg	Calcium	441
mg	Iron	3.4

Vegetable Burritos

THESE BURRITOS are a marvellous last-minute meal for dinner or lunch and take only a few minutes to prepare in the microwave oven. Even better, they can be completely assembled and refrigerated until 5 minutes before serving.

1 cup	chopped zucchini	250 mL
$\frac{1}{2}$ cup	chopped onion	125 mL
2	small cloves garlic, crushed	2
2	plum tomatoes, chopped	2
1	medium carrot, thinly sliced	1
1	medium sweet green pepper, sliced	1
1 tsp	vegetable oil	5 mL
1 tsp	ground cumin	5 mL
$\frac{1}{2}$ tsp	dried basil	2 mL
$\frac{1}{2}$ tsp	dried oregano	2 mL
$\frac{1}{8}$ tsp	salt	0.5 mL
1	can (14 oz/398 mL) refried beans	1
8	8-inch (20 cm) flour tortillas	8
2 cups	shredded part-skim mozzarella OR light Cheddar cheese	500 mL

COOKING TIPS:

For lower-fat burritos, mash or purée 1 can beans in tomato sauce (kidney beans or pinto beans) in food processor to replace the refried beans.

In microwavable container, mix together zucchini, onion, garlic, tomatoes, carrot, green pepper, oil and seasonings. Cover and microwave at High (100%) for 6 minutes or until vegetables are tender. Stir several times.

Spoon refried beans down centre of each tortilla; top each with some of the vegetable mixture and $\frac{1}{4}$ cup (50 mL) cheese. Fold sides of each tortilla into the centre. Fold bottom over filling and roll up. Place on microwavable baking pan. Microwave at Medium-High (70%) for 5 minutes or until burritos are warm.

MAKES 8 BURRITOS.

NUTRIENT ANALYSIS		
Per Burrito		
Calories		*255*
g	Protein	14
g	Total Fat	8.6
g	Carbohydrate	31
g	Fibre	3.5
mg	Sodium	591
mg	Potassium	422
mg	Calcium	292
mg	Iron	2.9

Short-Cut Vegetarian Cassoulet

THIS IS our version of the classic French cassoulet, which traditionally consists of white beans and various meats and requires long cooking to develop its rich flavour. Using canned beans makes for a quick-cooking cassoulet that still has a wonderful flavour. How nice to know that it is very high in fibre and an excellent source of iron.

2 tsp	olive oil	10 mL
2	cloves garlic, minced	2
2	onions, minced	2
2	carrots, finely chopped	2
2	stalks celery, finely chopped	2
$\frac{1}{2}$ cup	dry vermouth OR beef stock	125 mL
$\frac{1}{2}$ cup	water	125 mL
$\frac{1}{4}$ cup	finely chopped fresh parsley	50 mL
2 tbsp	tomato paste	25 mL
$\frac{1}{2}$ tsp	dried thyme	2 mL
$\frac{1}{4}$ tsp	salt	1 mL
$\frac{1}{4}$ tsp	freshly ground black pepper	1 mL
1	can (19 oz/540 mL) white beans, drained and rinsed	1

In large nonstick skillet, heat oil over medium-high heat; sauté garlic and onions for 2 minutes. Add carrots and celery; cook for 2 minutes longer.

Add vermouth, water, parsley, tomato paste, thyme, salt and pepper. Cover and bring to a boil; reduce heat and simmer for 20 minutes. Add beans and simmer 10 minutes longer.

MAKES 4 SERVINGS.

COOKING TIPS:
For greater economy, replace canned beans with $\frac{1}{2}$ lb (250 g) dried beans. See page 132 for cooking directions.

CASSOULET
The traditional cassoulet is one of the finest of the French stews. Like so many French recipes, it is a dish that causes regional dispute, each district claiming it produces the very best cassoulet. A good cassoulet can be made by anyone with time and patience, for it requires long slow cooking to develop its rich and wonderful flavour.

NUTRIENT ANALYSIS		
Per Serving		
Calories		*238*
g	Protein	9.4
g	Total Fat	2.9
g	Carbohydrate	37
g	Fibre	6.1
mg	Sodium	218
mg	Potassium	902
mg	Calcium	125
mg	Iron	4.2

Black Beans with Squash

TEAMED WITH RICE, beans provide complex carbohydrates, vitamins and minerals. Yellow squash and other vegetables add colour and nutrients to this very high-fibre dish.

1 cup	dried black beans, washed	250 mL
3 cups	cubed yellow squash (acorn OR butternut)	750 mL
1 tsp	olive oil	5 mL
3	large onions, chopped	3
3	cloves garlic, minced	3
2	stalks celery, thinly sliced	2
1	large carrot, thinly sliced	1
1 tsp	minced gingerroot	5 mL
$^3/_4$ cup	chicken stock	175 mL
2 tsp	dried oregano	10 mL
2 tsp	ground cumin	10 mL
$^1/_4$ tsp	salt	1 mL
$^1/_4$ tsp	freshly ground black pepper	1 mL
$^1/_4$ cup	minced fresh cilantro	50 mL
3 cups	hot cooked rice (1 cup/250 mL raw)	750 mL

COOKING TIPS:

In our recipes we have used the "quick soak method" for cooking beans, which is preferred to the overnight soak method. Discarding the first soaking water helps to overcome some of the gas and bloating discomfort people associate with beans.

In large saucepan, combine beans with 3 cups (750 mL) cold water. Cover and bring to a boil; boil for 2 minutes. Remove from heat and let stand for 1 hour; drain. Cover beans with cold water and bring to a boil; reduce heat and simmer, covered, for 30 minutes or until beans are tender. Drain and set aside.

In steamer basket, over boiling water, steam squash, covered, for about 5 minutes or until just tender.

Meanwhile, in large nonstick skillet, heat oil over medium heat; cook onions, garlic, celery, carrot and gingerroot for 6 to 8 minutes or until soft; stir frequently. Add stock and seasonings. Cover and bring to a boil; reduce heat and simmer for 5 minutes. Add beans and squash and heat to serving temperature. Stir in cilantro and serve over rice.

MAKES 4 SERVINGS.

NUTRIENT ANALYSIS

Per Serving

Calories		*448*
g	Protein	18
g	Total Fat	3.2
g	Carbohydrate	90
g	Fibre	11.4
mg	Sodium	323
mg	Potassium	1525
mg	Calcium	184
mg	Iron	4.8

Cajun-Spiced Soybean Stew

CAJUN COOKING is a combination of French and Southern United States culinary traditions developed when the Acadians in Nova Scotia moved south. The vigorous, country-style dishes make generous use of green peppers, onions and celery. These flavours combine wonderfully with soybeans to provide a dish that is an excellent source of protein, a very high-fibre source, an excellent source of iron and a good source of calcium.

COOKING TIPS:

The soybean, a legume, is the only vegetable that provides complete protein. Use soybeans to replace kidney beans in your favourite chili recipe and either reduce or eliminate ground beef to cut down on saturated fat.

1 cup	dried soybeans, washed	250 mL
1 tsp	vegetable oil	5 mL
1	large onion, chopped	1
1	medium sweet green pepper, diced	1
1 cup	sliced celery	250 mL
2	cloves garlic, minced	2
1	can (28 oz/796 mL) diced tomatoes	1
3/4 cup	water	175 mL
1/2 cup	chopped celery leaves	125 mL
1/3 cup	long grain white rice	75 mL
1	bay leaf	1
1/2 tsp	dried basil	2 mL
1/2 tsp	salt	2 mL
1/4 tsp	freshly ground black pepper	1 mL
2 1/2 cups	chopped cabbage	625 mL

In large saucepan, combine beans with 3 cups (750 mL) cold water. Cover and bring to a boil; boil for 2 minutes. Remove from heat and let stand for 1 hour; drain. Cover beans with cold water and bring to a boil; reduce heat and simmer, covered, for 1 hour or until tender. (Soybeans will always be slightly crunchy.) Drain and set aside.

In large nonstick skillet, heat oil over medium heat; cook onion, green pepper, celery and garlic for about 10 minutes or until almost tender. Add tomatoes, water, celery, rice and seasonings. Cover and simmer for 10 minutes.

Add cabbage and soybeans and simmer for 15 minutes or until cabbage is tender and rice is cooked.

MAKES 4 SERVINGS.

NUTRIENT ANALYSIS		
Per Serving		
Calories		346
g	Protein	22
g	Total Fat	11
g	Carbohydrate	45
g	Fibre	10.0
mg	Sodium	707
mg	Potassium	1630
mg	Calcium	240
mg	Iron	9.4

Polenta Pie with Pesto

POLENTA is a traditional Italian porridge made from cornmeal and water and has many uses. This tasty version bakes it as a pie topped with Light Pesto Sauce, chopped tomatoes, broccoli florets and cheese. It is an excellent source of calcium.

2 cups	low-fat milk	500 mL
1 ½ cups	cornmeal	375 mL
¼ tsp	salt	1 mL
1 cup	chopped tomatoes	250 mL
1 cup	small broccoli florets	250 mL
¼ cup	chopped onion	50 mL
1 cup	Light Pesto Sauce (page 80)	250 mL
1 cup	shredded part-skim mozzarella OR light Cheddar cheese	250 mL

In large heavy saucepan, bring milk, cornmeal and salt slowly to a boil, stirring frequently; reduce heat and cook until thickened. Allow to cool and press into lightly greased 9-inch (23 cm) deep pie plate.

Arrange tomatoes, broccoli and onion on cornmeal crust. Top with Light Pesto Sauce and sprinkle with cheese. Bake in 350°F (180°C) oven for about 15 minutes or until vegetables are tender-crisp and cheese is melted. To serve, cut into 6 wedges.

MAKES 6 SERVINGS.

NUTRIENT ANALYSIS

Per Serving

Calories		*282*
g	Protein	15
g	Total Fat	7.8
g	Carbohydrate	38
g	Fibre	3.0
mg	Sodium	476
mg	Potassium	448
mg	Calcium	392
mg	Iron	1.4

Quinoa and Vegetable Stir-Fry

QUINOA (pronounced keen-wah) is a delicious nut-like grain that originates in Peru. When combined with lima beans, it is an excellent alternative to meat, high in fibre and an excellent source of iron.

1 cup	quinoa	250 mL
1 cup	water	250 mL
1 tsp	vegetable oil	5 mL
1/2 cup	chopped broccoli	125 mL
1/2 cup	diced zucchini	125 mL
1/4 cup	thinly sliced carrot	50 mL
1/2	pkg (350 g) frozen baby lima beans	1/2
1 tbsp	light soy sauce	15 mL
1	small tomato, diced	1

Wash quinoa until water is colourless; drain.

In medium saucepan, bring quinoa and water to a boil; reduce heat and simmer for 15 minutes or until tender; drain.

In nonstick skillet, heat oil over medium heat; cook broccoli, zucchini, carrot and lima beans for 5 minutes or until vegetables are tender, stirring frequently.

Stir vegetables, soy sauce and tomato into quinoa; heat to serving temperature.

MAKES 4 SERVINGS.

GRAINS

There is a great variety of grains available to add interest to your meals. Try some of the newer grains like quinoa and triticale. With the exception of quinoa, which is a complete protein (contains all nine essential amino-acids), grains are a source of incomplete protein and so are best matched up with legumes or dairy products. Think of grain products such as pasta as the main part of your meal with a small amount of meat or cheese for garnish and you will be following Canada's Food Guide to Healthy Eating.

NUTRIENT ANALYSIS		
Per Serving		
Calories		246
g	Protein	10
g	Total Fat	4.0
g	Carbohydrate	44
g	Fibre	4.9
mg	Sodium	163
mg	Potassium	691
mg	Calcium	53
mg	Iron	5.4

10 Desserts

Getting Our Just Desserts *We don't say "avoid dessert." What is important is to choose carefully from a variety of desserts, balancing dessert with other foods eaten during the day. With a little planning, dessert lovers can "have their cake and eat it too." Place emphasis on fruits if they have been light that day; choose a lower-fat dairy dessert if milk choices have been overlooked.* ◆ *The problem with desserts is their frequent high levels of sugar and fat. There are nine calories in each gram of fat and four calories in each gram of sugar. These calories become meaningful if fat and sugar represent a significant part of a dessert.* ◆ *The answer may be to choose lower-fat desserts like sherbet, frozen yogurt or Blueberry Ginger Sorbet (page 138) or one of the Fresh Fruit Dips (page 138). Our low-fat versions of some old favourites, Banana Yogurt Cake (page 150) or Harvest Date Squares (page 151), replace all of the fat with corn syrup and applesauce, banana or pumpkin. We believe the taste and texture are as good as those of the originals.* ◆ *Another day, if your meals have been lower in total fat, look up Apple Cranberry Clafouti (page 147) or Light Apricot Cheesecake (page 149). These desserts are relatively low in fat but will provide the necessary satisfaction we all seek from dessert-eating.* ◆ *Desserts can be healthy too! Flour in a dessert contributes complex carbohydrates, some fibre, protein, B vitamins, iron and even additional calcium. Common ingredients such as grated vegetables, fruit, grains like rolled oats and bran, eggs, milk and cheeses also add nutritive value.* ◆ *How active you are physically is a major factor in dessert selection. The more calories you burn up in physical activity, the more yummy dessert calories you can enjoy.*

Frozen Treats

FRESH FRUIT DIPS

Fresh fruit is one of the best desserts possible, especially when offered with one of the following fruit dips:

- Fresh pears or apples: In food processor or blender container, process $\frac{1}{2}$ (250 g) pkg light cream cheese, $\frac{1}{4}$ cup (50 mL) low-fat plain yogurt, 2 tsp (10 mL) grated gingerroot, and $\frac{1}{2}$ tsp (2 mL) grated lemon rind until smooth.

- Whole strawberries or melon wedges: Combine $\frac{1}{2}$ cup (125 mL) drained crushed pineapple, $\frac{1}{2}$ cup (125 mL) low-fat plain yogurt and $\frac{1}{4}$ tsp (1 mL) ground cinnamon.

- Banana or apple slices: Combine 3 tbsp (45 mL) frozen orange juice concentrate, 1 cup (250 mL) low-fat plain yogurt and $\frac{1}{8}$ tsp (0.5 mL) ground nutmeg.

- Pineapple chunks or spears, or melon wedges: In food processor or blender container, process 1 cup (250 mL) low-fat cottage cheese and 3 tbsp (45 mL) maple syrup until smooth. Remove and stir in 2 tbsp (25 mL) finely chopped walnuts or pecans.

FROZEN FOODS have long been considered a delicacy. They date back to the Romans and Chinese, who sent runners to the mountains for snow. Sorbets, sherbets and frozen yogurt make delicious desserts and are a much lower fat choice than is traditional ice cream. A sorbet, from the French word for sherbet, is a frozen mixture of sweetened fruit juice but unlike sherbet does not contain milk. These recipes are especially easy if you have an ice cream maker.

BLUEBERRY GINGER SORBET

SERVE THIS refreshing ice as a palate refresher between courses. The hint of ginger enhances the natural blueberry flavour.

2 cups	fresh OR frozen and thawed blueberries	500 mL
$\frac{1}{4}$ cup	lemon juice	50 mL
	Zest of 1 lemon	
2 tsp	minced gingerroot	10 mL
1 cup	granulated sugar	250 mL
$\frac{1}{2}$ cup	white wine OR apple juice	125 mL
$\frac{1}{2}$ cup	water	125 mL

In food processor or blender container, process blueberries, juice, zest, ginger, sugar, wine and water until smooth.

Freeze in ice cream maker according to manufacturer's directions, or pour into metal pan and leave in freezer until frozen around outside. Process in food processor or beat with electric mixer until smooth. Return to pan and freeze until firm.

MAKES 8 SERVINGS, ABOUT $\frac{1}{3}$ CUP (75 mL) EACH.

NUTRIENT ANALYSIS		
Per Serving		
Calories		*131*
g	Protein	0.3
g	Total Fat	0.2
g	Carbohydrate	31
g	Fibre	1.1
mg	Sodium	3
mg	Potassium	58
mg	Calcium	5
mg	Iron	0.2

PINEAPPLE BUTTERMILK SHERBET

BUTTERMILK combines nicely with pineapple for this deliciously smooth sherbet.

2 $\frac{1}{4}$ cups	buttermilk	550 mL
$\frac{1}{2}$ cup	granulated sugar	125 mL
1	unbeaten egg white	1
1	can (19 oz/540 mL) crushed pineapple in its own juice, drained	1

In large bowl, combine buttermilk, sugar and egg white. Stir in pineapple.

Freeze in ice cream maker according to manufacturer's directions, or pour into metal pan and leave in freezer until frozen around outside. Process in food processor or beat with electric mixer until smooth. Return to pan and freeze until firm.

MAKES 9 SERVINGS, $\frac{1}{2}$ CUP (125 mL) EACH.

FROZEN FRUIT YOGURT

FROZEN YOGURT makes a refreshing ending to a meal as well as being a good source of calcium.

$\frac{1}{2}$	pkg (10 oz/280 g) frozen unsweetened strawberries OR raspberries	$\frac{1}{2}$
$\frac{1}{2}$ cup	low-fat plain yogurt	125 mL
$\frac{1}{4}$ cup	dry skim milk powder	50 mL
$\frac{1}{4}$ cup	liquid honey	50 mL
1 cup	2% evaporated milk	250 mL

In food processor or blender container, process strawberries, yogurt, milk powder and honey until smooth. Blend in evaporated milk.

Freeze in ice cream maker according to manufacturer's directions, or pour into metal pan and leave in freezer until frozen around outside. Process in food processor or beat with electric mixer until smooth. Return to pan and freeze until firm.

MAKES 6 SERVINGS, ABOUT $\frac{1}{2}$ CUP (125 mL) EACH.

NUTRIENT ANALYSIS

Pineapple Buttermilk Sherbet
Per Serving

Calories		99
g	Protein	2.8
g	Total Fat	0.6
g	Carbohydrate	21
g	Fibre	0.4
mg	Sodium	79
mg	Potassium	163
mg	Calcium	87
mg	Iron	0.2

Frozen Fruit Yogurt
Per Serving

Calories		122
g	Protein	6.2
g	Total Fat	1.2
g	Carbohydrate	23
g	Fibre	0.4
mg	Sodium	90
mg	Potassium	319
mg	Calcium	224
mg	Iron	0.4

Tourte aux Pommes

A food processor is an asset to slice the apples evenly. Baking apples such as Cortland, Ida Red or Spy are essential for this tourte because the apple rings must keep their shape.

ESSENTIALLY an apple pie minus the crust, this recipe is great for apple pie lovers who don't want the work of making pastry or the calories in pie crust.

$\frac{1}{3}$ cup	red currant OR apple jelly	75 mL
$\frac{1}{4}$ cup	granulated sugar	50 mL
$\frac{1}{2}$ cup	water	125 mL
5	baking apples	5
$\frac{1}{2}$ cup	currants	125 mL
1 tsp	lemon juice	5 mL
	Grated rind of 1 lemon	

In large microwavable container, microwave jelly, sugar and water at High (100%) for 5 minutes.

Peel and core apples; slice very thinly, about $\frac{1}{8}$-inch (3 mm) thick. Add apples, currants, juice and rind to jelly mixture. Cover and microwave at High for 5 minutes. Stir gently and microwave, uncovered, at High for 7 minutes longer or until apples are translucent; stir twice.

Carefully remove apples from syrup; layer in lightly greased 10-inch (25 cm) quiche dish, pressing down to pack firmly. Microwave remaining syrup at High for about 5 minutes or until reduced to $\frac{1}{4}$ cup (50 mL). Pour over apples, cover and refrigerate for at least 8 hours or overnight. To serve, cut into wedges.

MAKES 6 SERVINGS.

NUTRIENT ANALYSIS

Per Serving

Calories		173
g	Protein	0.7
g	Total Fat	0.4
g	Carbohydrate	45
g	Fibre	3.0
mg	Sodium	4
mg	Potassium	241
mg	Calcium	19
mg	Iron	0.7

Lemon Mousse

THERE IS NOTHING like the flavour of fresh lemon. Serve this light and tangy dessert at the end of a particularly heavy meal.

$^1/_3$ cup	granulated sugar	75 mL
2	eggs, separated	2
	Grated rind of 1 lemon	
$^1/_4$ cup	lemon juice	50 mL
$^1/_2$ cup	water	125 mL
1 tsp	unflavoured gelatin	5 mL
2 tbsp	granulated sugar	25 mL

COOKING TIPS:

To get more juice from oranges, lemons and limes, microwave at High (100%) for 15 to 45 seconds before cutting.

In small microwavable container, combine sugar, egg yolks, rind, juice and water. Sprinkle gelatin over top; let stand for 1 minute to soften. Microwave at Medium (50%) for 4 to 5 minutes or until mixture is slightly thickened and gelatin is dissolved; stir frequently.

Transfer to metal bowl and freeze for 30 minutes or until mixture becomes thickened; stir several times.

Beat egg whites with 2 tbsp (25 mL) sugar until stiff peaks form. Fold into lemon mixture and pour into dessert dishes. Chill before serving.

MAKES 4 SERVINGS.

NOTE:

When using egg whites in a recipe where they will not be cooked, be sure to use fresh Grade A uncracked eggs that have just been taken from the refrigerator. Keep finished dish well chilled until it is served.

NUTRIENT ANALYSIS		
Per Serving		
Calories		*134*
g	Protein	3.9
g	Total Fat	2.5
g	Carbohydrate	25
g	Fibre	0.2
mg	Sodium	33
mg	Potassium	53
mg	Calcium	15
mg	Iron	0.4

 Eighteenth-century housewives were no different from modern cooks looking for quick tips on feeding unexpected company. One early cookbook urged the young housewife to keep a piece of calf's rennet soaking in wine. One glass of this wine added to a quart of sweetened milk made a cold custard that was ready in five minutes. (*The American Frugal Housewife*)

It's certainly not an idea that became very popular!

Microwave Maple-Filled Pears

VARIATIONS:

Try apricots with a filling of almonds and ground ginger; peaches with hazelnuts and ground mace; cored apples with walnuts and ground nutmeg.

OTHER FRUITS are excellent in this recipe as an alternative to pears: try peaches, pineapple slices, fresh apricots or apples with different spices and different nuts.

1/4 cup	chopped raisins	50 mL
2 tbsp	chopped pecans	25 mL
1/4 cup	maple syrup	50 mL
1/2 tsp	grated lemon rind	2 mL
1/2 tsp	ground cinnamon	2 mL
3	large pears, peeled, halved and cored	3

In small bowl, combine raisins, nuts, syrup, rind and cinnamon; set aside.

Microwave: In microwavable baking dish, place prepared pears, cut-side down. Cover and microwave at High (100%) for 5 minutes. Turn pears over; spoon maple mixture into centre of each pear. Cover and microwave at High for 3 to 4 minutes or until pears are tender.

Oven: In small baking pan, place pears, cut-side up, with 3 tbsp (45 mL) water; bake in 350°F (180°C) oven for 10 minutes. Fill centres with maple mixture and bake for 10 minutes. Serve warm.

MAKES 6 SERVINGS.

COOKING TIPS:

Pears are one of the few fruits that do not mature well if allowed to ripen on the tree. They are therefore picked in an unripened state, carefully packed, stored and shipped in that condition. For perfect eating, let them stand for a few days at room temperature. As they ripen, changes occur on the inside of the fruit that greatly increase the sugar and juice content. When they yield to gentle pressure at the stem end, they are ready for immediate use,

NUTRIENT ANALYSIS		
Per Serving		
Calories		121
g	Protein	0.8
g	Total Fat	2.0
g	Carbohydrate	27
g	Fibre	3.0
mg	Sodium	2
mg	Potassium	192
mg	Calcium	30
mg	Iron	0.6

Peach Melba Torte

Baked Pears and Cheese: Halve and core ripe pears. Top with a slice of Cheddar cheese or crumbly blue cheese. Bake in 400°F (200°C) oven for about 10 minutes or microwave at High (100%) until cheese has melted.

Pear-Cheese Crisp: Combine ¹⁄₂ cup (125 mL) shredded Cheddar cheese, ¹⁄₂ cup (125 mL) all-purpose flour, ¹⁄₂ cup (125 mL) quick-cooking rolled oats and 3 tbsp (45 mL) softened margarine or butter. Place 4 cups (1 L) peeled and sliced pears in 8-cup (2 L) round microwavable dish. Sprinkle oat mixture over top and microwave at High for 10 to 12 minutes or until pears are tender.

MAKES 6 SERVINGS.

MELBA is a French method of preparing a dessert originally created for the famous Australian opera singer. Peach Melba consists of a purée of raspberries poured over a poached ripe peach and served on vanilla ice cream. Ours is a frozen version.

Peach Sauce:

4	large ripe peaches, peeled and sliced OR	4
	1 can (28 oz/796 mL) peach slices, drained	
¹⁄₃ cup	granulated sugar	75 mL
¹⁄₄ cup	corn syrup	50 mL
1 tbsp	water	15 mL
4 tsp	cornstarch	20 mL

Raspberry Sauce:

2 cups	fresh OR frozen and thawed raspberries	500 mL
¹⁄₄ cup	granulated sugar	50 mL
¹⁄₄ cup	corn syrup	50 mL
¹⁄₄ cup	water	50 mL
1 tbsp	cornstarch	15 mL

Crust:

1 ¹⁄₂ cups	crushed vanilla wafer crumbs	375 mL
3 tbsp	melted margarine OR butter	45 mL
1	tub(1 L) vanilla frozen yogurt OR light ice cream	1
	Garnish: Fresh peach slices	

Peach Sauce: In food processor or blender container, purée peaches until smooth. In medium saucepan, combine peaches, sugar and corn syrup. Stir together water and cornstarch; stir into peach mixture. Cook over medium heat until thickened; stir frequently. Cool sauce.

Raspberry Sauce: In medium saucepan, combine raspberries, sugar and corn syrup. Stir together water and cornstarch; stir into raspberry mixture. Cook over medium heat until thickened; stir frequently. Press through a sieve to remove seeds; cool sauce.

Crust: Stir together crumbs and margarine. Set aside 2 tbsp (25 mL) crumbs. Press remainder into bottom of 10-inch (25 cm) springform pan.

Remove frozen yogurt from freezer and microwave at Low (30%) for 2 minutes to soften slightly. Spoon $\frac{1}{3}$ yogurt into crust. Spread with $\frac{3}{4}$ cup (175 mL) Peach Sauce and $\frac{1}{2}$ cup (125 mL) Raspberry Sauce.

Repeat layers, ending with yogurt. (There will be some Peach Sauce left to use when serving.) Sprinkle with reserved crumbs. Wrap securely and freeze until firm.

Before serving allow torte to stand at room temperature for 10 minutes or until slightly softened. Serve with remaining Peach Sauce and garnish with fresh peach slices.

MAKES 10 SERVINGS.

QUICK FRUIT DESSERTS

• Cut red or green grapes in half to make about 3 cups (750 mL), removing seeds, if necessary. Heat juice and rind from 1 lemon with $\frac{1}{2}$ cup (125 mL) honey for 5 minutes. Add grapes and warm. Ignite $\frac{1}{2}$ cup (125 mL) warm brandy and pour over grapes. Serve over light ice cream or frozen low-fat yogurt.

MAKES 6 SERVINGS.

• Lightly sprinkle washed strawberries with granulated sugar and balsamic vinegar. Stir gently and allow to stand for about 10 minutes for flavour to develop.

• Beat softened light cream cheese with enough low-fat milk to make spreading consistency. Add finely chopped candied ginger or dates and rum or brandy extract. Spread on graham wafers or digestive cookies. Top with slices of fresh fruit such as strawberries, kiwifruit or unpeeled apple.

 Coffee was not always available to the early prairie homesteaders. In Saskatchewan, the usual substitute was roasted wheat or barley kernels, or toasted bread crusts. Crumbled bran and syrup toasted in the oven made a drink similar to ones still available today. Other beverages were made from dried and roasted dandelion or chicory roots. *(Canadian Prairie Homesteaders)*

Light Crème Brûlée

MAKE THIS classic dessert in the microwave oven in one-quarter the time of the conventional oven method. Individual custard cups cook evenly and speed the cooking time for a tasty way to provide a good source of calcium.

$\frac{1}{2}$ cup	strong brewed coffee	125 mL
1	can (385 mL) 2% evaporated milk	1
$\frac{2}{3}$ cup	granulated sugar	175 mL
2	whole eggs	2
2	egg whites	2
1 tbsp	rum OR	15 mL
	1 tsp (5 mL) rum extract	
2 tbsp	brown sugar	25 mL
	Garnish: Sliced peaches, strawberries OR pears	

In microwavable bowl, combine coffee, milk and sugar. Microwave at High (100%) for 4 to 5 minutes or until hot. Stir to dissolve the sugar.

In large bowl, beat eggs, egg whites and rum until well blended. Stir in hot milk mixture and pour into six $\frac{1}{2}$ cup (125 mL) custard cups. Arrange cups in circle in microwave oven; microwave at Medium-High (70%) for 6 to 7 minutes. Remove each custard when it shows signs of bubbling. (Do not overcook—custards will still be slightly liquid). Chill until serving time.

Just before serving, sprinkle with brown sugar and place under broiler. Broil until sugar is melted and browned. Serve with fruit garnish.

MAKES 6 SERVINGS.

NUTRIENT ANALYSIS

Per Serving

Calories		200
g	Protein	8.3
g	Total Fat	3.0
g	Carbohydrate	34
g	Fibre	0
mg	Sodium	117
mg	Potassium	279
mg	Calcium	202
mg	Iron	0.5

Plum Blueberry Crisp

In 8-cup (2 L) round microwavable baking dish, place 5 large apples, peeled and sliced. Combine 1 cup (250 mL) Mixed Grain Granola (page 8), 1 tbsp (15 mL) all-purpose flour, 1 tbsp (15 mL) brown sugar and 1 tbsp (15 mL) soft margarine. Sprinkle over apples and microwave at High (100%) for 7 minutes or until apples are tender.

MAKES 6 SERVINGS.

PLUMS and blueberries are plentiful in the late summer and taste wonderful together. Surprise—there is no fat added to this crisp; it's the applesauce in the topping that helps bind it together.

4	red plums, sliced	4
3	large purple plums, sliced	3
1 cup	fresh OR frozen blueberries	250 mL
$\frac{1}{4}$ cup	maple syrup	50 mL
3 tbsp	brown sugar	45 mL
2 tbsp	cornstarch	25 mL
1 tbsp	lemon juice	15 mL
$\frac{2}{3}$ cup	brown sugar	150 mL
$\frac{2}{3}$ cup	quick-cooking rolled oats	150 mL
$\frac{2}{3}$ cup	all-purpose flour	150 mL
$\frac{1}{4}$ cup	unsweetened applesauce	50 mL
$\frac{1}{4}$ tsp	ground nutmeg	1 mL

Place plums and blueberries in 8-cup (2 L) baking pan. Combine syrup, 3 tbsp (45 mL) sugar, cornstarch and juice; mix into fruit.

In bowl, combine $\frac{2}{3}$ cup (150 mL) sugar, oats, flour, applesauce and nutmeg; mix well. Sprinkle over fruit. Bake in 400°F (200°C) oven for 25 minutes or until topping is browned and edges start to bubble.

MAKES 6 SERVINGS.

NUTRIENT ANALYSIS		
Per Serving		
Calories		287
g	Protein	3.7
g	Total Fat	1.3
g	Carbohydrate	67
g	Fibre	3.5
mg	Sodium	12
mg	Potassium	324
mg	Calcium	48
mg	Iron	1.8

Apple Cranberry Clafouti

CLAFOUTI, a specialty dessert of the Limousin region, in Central France, is made by pouring a thick batter over fresh fruit before baking. A warm piece of this delightfully simple dessert is sheer pleasure!

1 tbsp	margarine OR butter	15 mL
6 cups	sliced baking apples	1.5 L
½ cup	fresh OR frozen cranberries	125 mL
½ cup	low-fat milk	125 mL
⅓ cup	all-purpose flour	75 mL
⅓ cup	granulated sugar	75 mL
3	eggs	3
1 tbsp	rum or brandy OR	15 mL
	1 tsp (5 mL) rum or brandy extract	
¼ tsp	baking powder	1 mL
2 tbsp	granulated sugar	25 mL
1 tsp	ground cinnamon	5 mL

FRESH BERRIES IN RED WINE

Prepare a red wine syrup with 1 cup (250 mL) red wine, ½ cup (125 mL) granulated sugar and ¼ tsp (1 mL) vanilla extract. Simmer, covered, for about 5 minutes; cool. Refrigerate for up to 1 week. Just before serving, pour over fresh raspberries or strawberries in wine glasses and garnish with fresh mint.

MAKES ABOUT 1 ¼ CUPS (300 ML) SYRUP.

In large microwavable container, microwave margarine at High (100%) for 20 seconds or until melted. Stir in apples and microwave at High for 4 minutes or until apples are barely tender. Stir in cranberries; turn into 10-inch (25 cm) quiche dish.

In blender container or small bowl, blend milk, flour, ⅓ cup (75 mL) sugar, eggs, rum and baking powder until well combined. Pour over apple mixture.

Combine 2 tbsp (25 mL) sugar and cinnamon; sprinkle over top of clafouti. Bake in 350°F (180°C) oven for 45 minutes or until puffed and set. Cut into wedges and serve warm.

MAKES 6 SERVINGS.

NUTRIENT ANALYSIS
Per Serving

Calories		223
g	Protein	4.8
g	Total Fat	5.2
g	Carbohydrate	40
g	Fibre	2.8
mg	Sodium	75
mg	Potassium	205
mg	Calcium	54
mg	Iron	0.9

Rhubarb Cinnamon Dessert

RHUBARB HERALDS SPRING, so why not give it a welcome with this tangy rhubarb dessert. Like the Plum Blueberry Crisp, applesauce is used to replace some of the customary butter or margarine.

1 ¼ cups	cake and pastry flour, divided	300 mL
½ tsp	baking powder	2 mL
⅛ tsp	salt	0.5 mL
2 tbsp	margarine OR butter	25 mL
⅔ cup	unsweetened applesauce, divided	150 mL
1	egg, separated	1
4 cups	diced rhubarb	1 L
1 ⅛ cups	granulated sugar, divided	275 mL
1 tsp	vanilla extract	5 mL
2 tsp	ground cinnamon	10 mL

In food processor container or by hand, combine 1 cup (250 mL) flour, baking powder, salt, margarine, 2 tbsp (25 mL) applesauce and egg white until crumbly. Pat into bottom of 8-inch (2 L) square baking pan. Scatter rhubarb over base.

In small bowl, combine 1 cup (250 mL) sugar, ¼ cup (50 mL) flour, remaining applesauce, egg yolk and vanilla; spoon over rhubarb. Combine 2 tbsp (25 mL) sugar and cinnamon; sprinkle over top. Bake in 350°F (180°C) oven for 45 minutes or until bubbly around edges. Let cool before serving.

MAKES 9 SERVINGS.

COOKING TIPS:

Corn syrup, applesauce and pumpkin can act as replacements for shortening, butter, margarine and oil in baking. When using these fat replacements for cakes, it is important to use cake and pastry flour, which has a lower gluten content than does all-purpose flour. In a batter, mixing develops the gluten, which can make a cake tough. For the lightest cake, use a low gluten flour and be careful not to overmix.

NUTRIENT ANALYSIS		
Per Serving		
Calories		225
g	Protein	3.1
g	Total Fat	3.4
g	Carbohydrate	46
g	Fibre	0.9
mg	Sodium	92
mg	Potassium	202
mg	Calcium	67
mg	Iron	1.2

Light Apricot Cheesecake

APRICOTS add their rich flavour to this light cheesecake. The combination of low-fat cottage cheese and light cream cheese gives a richness to the cake, but still maintains a low-fat level.

Crust:

1 cup	graham wafer crumbs	250 mL
2 tbsp	corn syrup	25 mL
1 tbsp	margarine OR butter	15 mL

Filling:

$\frac{1}{2}$ lb	dried apricots	250 g
$\frac{1}{2}$ cup	water	125 mL
1	container (500 g) low-fat cottage cheese	1
1	pkg (250 g) light cream cheese	1
$\frac{1}{4}$ cup	all-purpose flour	50 mL
	Zest of 1 lemon	
3 tbsp	lemon juice, divided	45 mL
1	egg yolk	1
3	egg whites	3
$\frac{1}{3}$ cup	granulated sugar	75 mL
$\frac{1}{2}$ cup	water	125 mL
2 tbsp	granulated sugar	25 mL
1 tbsp	cornstarch	15 mL

COOKING TIPS:

This low-fat graham wafer crust can replace the higher-fat version used in many of your other recipes.

Crust: In food processor container or bowl, mix together graham crumbs, syrup and margarine. Press into bottom of 9-inch (23 cm) springform pan. Bake in 325°F (160°C) oven for 10 minutes or until lightly browned.

Filling: In microwavable container, microwave apricots and water at High (100%) for 4 minutes; cover and let stand for 10 minutes. In food processor or blender container, purée apricots until smooth. Remove purée and set aside.

In food processor, blend cottage cheese, cream cheese, flour, zest, 1 tbsp (15 mL) juice, egg yolk and $\frac{1}{2}$ cup (125 mL) of the apricot purée until smooth; set aside.

In large bowl, beat egg whites until frothy, gradually beat in $\frac{1}{3}$ cup (75 mL) sugar until stiff peaks form. Gently fold in cheese mixture. Carefully pour into prepared pan; smooth top. Bake in 325°F (160°C) oven for 45 minutes or until set around edges. Turn oven off and leave cake in oven for 20 minutes. Remove cake from oven and cool slightly.

Meanwhile, in microwavable container, stir together ½ cup (125 mL) water, 2 tbsp (25 mL) sugar, cornstarch and reserved puréed apricots. Microwave at High for 3 minutes or until mixture is thickened; stir several times. Stir in remaining juice. Spread over cheesecake and cool.

MAKES 12 SERVINGS.

Banana Yogurt Cake

THIS IS ANOTHER amazing dessert without shortening or oil. Banana and applesauce combine to give it a delicious flavour, and to keep it moist for several days.

2 cups	cake and pastry flour	500 mL
2 tsp	baking powder	10 mL
1 tsp	baking soda	5 mL
2	eggs	2
1 cup	granulated sugar	250 mL
½ cup	unsweetened applesauce	125 mL
1 cup	mashed banana (about 2 large bananas)	250 mL
⅔ cup	low-fat plain yogurt	150 mL

Lightly grease 13 x 9-inch (3.5 L) baking pan.

In bowl, combine flour, baking powder and baking soda.

In large bowl, beat eggs until frothy. Gradually beat in sugar until very thick. Stir in applesauce and banana. Add dry ingredients alternately with yogurt; stir after each addition.

Spread in prepared pan. Bake in 350°F (180°C) oven for 30 minutes or until centre is firm to touch. Cool completely on wire rack before cutting into squares.

MAKES 12 SERVINGS.

NUTRIENT ANALYSIS		
Per Serving		
Calories		175
g	Protein	3.5
g	Total Fat	1.3
g	Carbohydrate	38
g	Fibre	0.5
mg	Sodium	179
mg	Potassium	147
mg	Calcium	53
mg	Iron	1.4

Harvest Date Squares

THESE SUPER-MOIST cookie squares are almost fat-free. Eat them plain or sprinkled with icing sugar. Tuck one into brown bag lunches for a treat kids will love.

2 cups	cake and pastry flour	500 mL
2 tsp	baking powder	10 mL
1 tsp	baking soda	5 mL
1/2 tsp	ground cinnamon	2 mL
1/2 tsp	ground mace	2 mL
1/4 tsp	salt	1 mL
2	egg whites	2
3/4 cup	canned pumpkin	175 mL
1/2 cup	firmly packed brown sugar	125 mL
1/2 cup	orange juice	125 mL
1/2 cup	low-fat milk	125 mL
1/3 cup	corn syrup	75 mL
2 tsp	grated orange rind	10 mL
1 tsp	vanilla extract	5 mL
1/2 cup	chopped dates	125 mL
	Garnish: Icing sugar (optional)	

COOKING TIPS:

To cut up dates more easily, microwave at High (100%) for 1 to 2 minutes or until soft.

Lightly grease 9-inch (2.5 L) square baking pan.

In large bowl, combine flour, baking powder, baking soda and seasonings.

In second bowl, beat together egg whites, pumpkin, sugar, juice, milk, syrup, rind and vanilla. Stir into dry ingredients just until moistened. Stir in dates; spoon into prepared pan.

Bake in 350°F (180°C) oven for 35 to 40 minutes or until top springs back when lightly touched. Cool completely on wire rack before cutting into squares. Sprinkle with icing sugar, if desired.

MAKES 36 SQUARES.

NUTRIENT ANALYSIS		
Per Square		
Calories		55
g	Protein	0.9
g	Total Fat	0.2
g	Carbohydrate	13
g	Fibre	0.3
mg	Sodium	80
mg	Potassium	57
mg	Calcium	19
mg	Iron	0.7

 With our modern conveniences, baking a cake is a relative breeze. The early pioneers had to dry, pound and roll mounds of flour, sugar and spices before making a cake. Creaming butter and sugar together in a mixer for a few minutes is much easier on the arm than rubbing sugar, lard and butter for at least half an hour.

Gingerbread with Orange Sauce

MOIST AND SATISFYING, this quickly prepared dessert will become a family favourite. It is also good for you; each serving provides an excellent source of iron. Be sure to serve it warm with Orange Sauce.

Gingerbread:

³/₄ cup	all-purpose flour	175 mL
¹/₂ cup	whole wheat flour	125 mL
¹/₃ cup	firmly packed brown sugar	75 mL
³/₄ tsp	ground cinnamon	4 mL
¹/₂ tsp	ground ginger	2 mL
¹/₄ tsp	ground cloves	1 mL
¹/₂ tsp	baking soda	2 mL
¹/₄ tsp	salt	1 mL
¹/₃ cup	molasses	75 mL
¹/₄ cup	margarine OR butter	50 mL
¹/₄ cup	orange juice	50 mL
2	eggs	2
1 tsp	grated orange rind	5 mL

Orange Sauce:

1 cup	orange juice	250 mL
2 tbsp	firmly packed brown sugar	25 mL
1 tbsp	cornstarch	15 mL
¹/₂ tsp	grated orange rind	2 mL
¹/₄ tsp	ground cinnamon	1 mL

LET'S TALK MICROWAVE
A ring mould is the ideal shape for cooking food in the microwave oven. Microwave energy penetrates about 1-inch (2.5 cm) into the food, where it produces the heat that cooks the food. In a ring shape, the energy can enter from both the side and the centre, as well as the top and bottom to give very even cooking. For faster and more even cooking, food in the microwave oven should usually be covered to retain the heat and steam that is produced.

Gingerbread: Lightly grease 6-cup (1.5 L) microwavable ring mould.

In medium bowl, combine flours, sugar, seasonings, baking soda and salt. Add molasses, margarine, juice, eggs and rind. Beat with an electric mixer until well blended.

Pour batter into prepared mould; cover and microwave at Medium-High (70%) for 6 minutes or until top is no longer wet. Let stand on counter for 10 minutes before removing from pan.

Orange Sauce: In 2-cup (500 mL) glass measure, combine juice, sugar, cornstarch, rind and cinnamon; microwave, uncovered, at High (100%) for 3 to 4 minutes or until sauce comes to a boil and thickens. Stir after 2 minutes. Serve warm over gingerbread.

MAKES 8 SERVINGS, WITH 2 TBSP (25 ML) SAUCE EACH.

NUTRIENT ANALYSIS

Per Serving

Calories		*238*
g	Protein	4.2
g	Total Fat	7.2
g	Carbohydrate	40
g	Fibre	1.7
mg	Sodium	270
mg	Potassium	589
mg	Calcium	127
mg	Iron	3.6

NEXT PAGE: *Canada's Food Guide to Healthy Eating (side A).*

Healthy
Canada

■✦■ Health and Welfare   Santé et Bien-être social
Canada   Canada

CANADA'S
Food
Guide
TO HEALTHY EATING

Enjoy a variety
of foods from each
group every day.

Choose lower-
fat foods
more often.

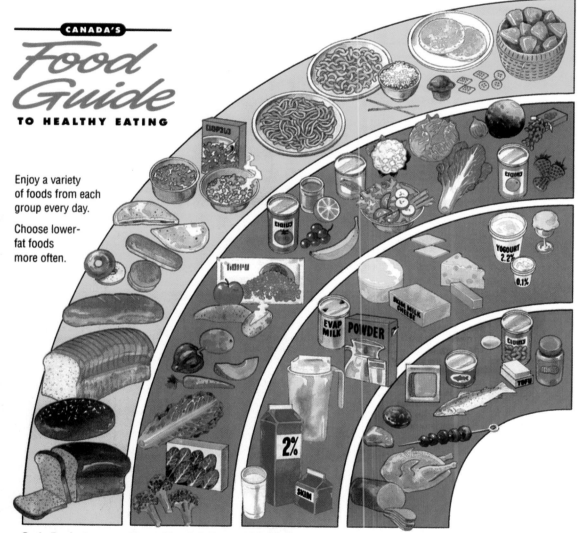

Grain Products
Choose whole grain
and enriched
products more
often.

Vegetables & Fruit
Choose dark green and
orange vegetables and
orange fruit more often.

Milk Products
Choose lower-fat
milk products more
often.

Meat & Alternatives
Choose leaner meats,
poultry and fish, as well
as dried peas, beans and
lentils more often.

Different People Need Different Amounts of Food

The amount of food you need every day from the 4 food groups and other foods depends on your age, body size, activity level, whether you are male or female and if you are pregnant or breast-feeding. That's why the Food Guide gives a lower and higher number of servings for each food group. For example, young children can choose the lower number of servings, while male teenagers can go to the higher number. Most other people can choose servings somewhere in between.

Grain Products
5-12
SERVINGS PER DAY

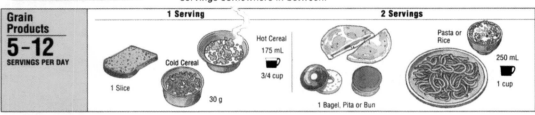

Vegetables & Fruit
5-10
SERVINGS PER DAY

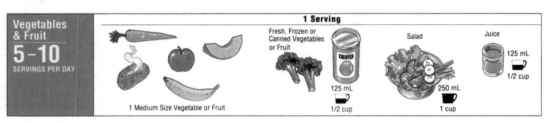

Milk Products
SERVINGS PER DAY
Children 4–9 years: 2–3
Youth 10–16 years: 3–4
Adults: 2–4
Pregnant & Breast-feeding
Women: 3–4

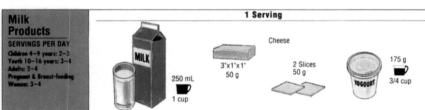

Other Foods

Taste and enjoyment can also come from other foods and beverages that are not part of the 4 food groups. Some of these foods are higher in fat or Calories, so use these foods in moderation.

Meat & Alternatives
2-3
SERVINGS PER DAY

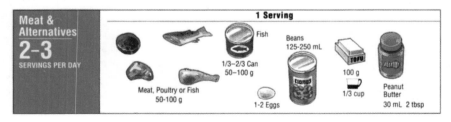

Enjoy eating well, being active and feeling good about yourself. That's VITALIT

© Minister of Supply and Services Canada 1992   Cat. No. H39-252/1992E   No changes permitted. Reprint permission not required.
ISBN 0-662-19648-1

Lemon Nut Biscotti

THESE TWICE-BAKED crunchy cookies are marvellous to serve with a cup of tea or a sweet wine.

$\frac{1}{4}$ cup	chopped hazelnuts OR almonds	50 mL
2 $\frac{1}{4}$ cups	all-purpose flour	550 mL
1 $\frac{1}{2}$ tsp	baking powder	7 mL
1 tsp	ground mace	5 mL
$\frac{1}{4}$ tsp	salt	1 mL
$\frac{3}{4}$ cup	granulated sugar	175 mL
$\frac{1}{3}$ cup	margarine OR butter	75 mL
3	egg whites	3
1 tsp	vanilla extract	5 mL
$\frac{1}{2}$ tsp	lemon extract	2 mL

COOKING TIPS:

Use your microwave oven to quickly toast chopped nuts or coconut. Place nuts or coconut in the centre of a microwave plate and microwave at High (100%) for several minutes until lightly browned. It is essential to stir every minute as they burn very quickly.

Roast nuts in shallow baking pan in 325°F (160°C) oven for 8 minutes or until toasted.

In bowl, combine flour, baking powder, mace and salt.

In large bowl, cream sugar and margarine until light and fluffy. Beat in egg whites and extracts. Stir in flour mixture; fold in toasted nuts.

Divide dough in half. Shape into 2 logs $\frac{3}{4}$-inch (2 cm) thick, 1 $\frac{1}{2}$-inches (4 cm) wide and 12-inches (30 cm) long; place on lightly greased baking sheet. Bake in 325°F (160°C) oven for 25 minutes or until golden brown. Remove to wire rack to cool for 5 minutes. Cut diagonally into slices about $\frac{1}{2}$-inch (1 cm) thick. Lay slices flat on baking sheet, return to oven and bake for 10 minutes to dry. Remove to wire rack to cool completely.

MAKES 42 BISCOTTI.

NUTRIENT ANALYSIS		
Per Biscotto		
Calories		58
g	Protein	1.1
g	Total Fat	1.9
g	Carbohydrate	9.0
g	Fibre	0.2
mg	Sodium	46
mg	Potassium	15
mg	Calcium	7
mg	Iron	0.3

 Modern-day cooking has become much more precise compared with cooking a century ago. Old recipes called for a heaping cup, a scant cup, spice to cover a silver dollar, a lump of butter the size of a black walnut. Baking was a real challenge as oven temperatures were often uneven and temperamental. A good cook was a marvel indeed. *(The Attic Cookbook)*

PREVIOUS PAGE: *Canada's Food Guide to Healthy Eating (side B).*

Naturally Sweet Soft Cookies

PEANUT BUTTER, used instead of other fats and oils, adds body, taste and texture to foods, while increasing their nutritive value.

½ cup	raisins	125 mL
½ cup	chopped dates	125 mL
1	medium ripe banana, mashed	1
⅓ cup	creamy peanut butter	75 mL
¼ cup	water	50 mL
1	egg	1
1 tsp	vanilla extract	5 mL
1 cup	quick-cooking rolled oats	250 mL
½ cup	all-purpose flour	125 mL
1 tsp	baking soda	5 mL

In medium bowl, combine raisins, dates, banana, peanut butter, water, egg and vanilla; stir well. Add oats, flour and baking soda; stir to blend well.

Drop by spoonfuls onto lightly greased or nonstick baking sheets; flatten with a fork. Bake in 350°F (180°C) oven for 10 minutes or until lightly browned. Cool completely on wire rack. Store in closed container.

MAKES 36 COOKIES.

 With few exceptions, no early cookbooks contained cookie recipes as we know them today. One had a recipe for Jackson Jumbles: "one cup of butter, one of cream, three of sugar, tea-spoonful of pearlash, two eggs, five cups of flour, to be dropped on a tin with a spoon to bake." *(The Cook Not Mad: or Rational Cookery)*

Oat Bran Pumpkin Loaf

NOURISHING oat bran in combination with pumpkin provides a healthy moist loaf—great for brown baggers or to serve with a cup of coffee or tea.

COOKING TIPS:

For added fibre in your diet, try some of the new flours. All-purpose wheat and oat flour and all-purpose flour with wheat bran can be used in place of all-purpose white flour in most recipes.

1 ¹/₃ cups	whole wheat flour	325 mL
¹/₂ cup	oat bran	125 mL
¹/₂ cup	firmly packed brown sugar	125 mL
2 tsp	baking powder	10 mL
¹/₂ tsp	baking soda	2 mL
¹/₂ tsp	ground allspice	2 mL
¹/₂ tsp	ground cinnamon	2 mL
¹/₂ tsp	ground ginger	2 mL
¹/₄ cup	vegetable oil	50 mL
1	egg, beaten	1
1 cup	canned pumpkin	250 mL
¹/₂ cup	raisins	125 mL

Lightly grease 8 x 4-inch (1.5 L) loaf pan.

In large bowl, stir together flour, bran, sugar, baking powder, baking soda and spices.

In second bowl, combine oil, egg and pumpkin. Stir in raisins. Add to dry ingredients, stirring just until moistened. Spoon into prepared loaf pan.

Bake in 350°F (180°C) oven for 45 minutes or until tester inserted in centre comes out clean. Cool for 10 minutes before removing from pan to wire rack to cool completely.

MAKES 16 SLICES.

NUTRIENT ANALYSIS
Per Slice

Calories		*132*
g	Protein	2.9
g	Total Fat	4.4
g	Carbohydrate	22
g	Fibre	2.4
mg	Sodium	84
mg	Potassium	166
mg	Calcium	37
mg	Iron	1.3

Quick breads have one distinctive ingredient: baking powder. But until the end of the 18th century, lightness in baking could be achieved only by laboriously beating air into dough along with eggs, or by adding yeast or spirits. In the 1790s, pearlash—a refined form of potash that produces carbon dioxide in baking methods—was discovered in the United States. It transformed baking methods and 8,000 tons of it were exported to Europe in 1792. It was not until the 1850s that baking powder, as we know it today, became commercially available. *(The American Heritage Cookbook)*

11

Canadiana

We want this section to give our readers a feeling for Canada's rich cooking heritage. In addition, it provides our home economics/family studies classrooms with a Canadian cooking resource. ◆ *Home economists from Canada's 10 provinces and the Yukon and Northwest Territories have provided the recipes, all of which follow Canada's Food Guide to Healthy Eating. Each represents the eating traditions of the province or territory of origin. This short section is, of course, just a sampling of the wide variety of foods available from coast to coast in this country.* ◆ *Our book is not the first to be written on a Canadian theme by members of The Canadian Home Economics Association. The well-known* Laura Secord Canadian Cook Book *was first published in 1966 and is still in print. In 1981,* A Collage of Canadian Cooking *was published to introduce Canadian consumers to metric cooking.*

Newfoundland/Labrador Baked Codfish au Gratin

CODFISH has been a staple food of Newfoundland and Labrador for centuries. Dried salt cod provided food during the long winter months. The Grand Banks fishing ground, where it is found, was one of the major attractions for Europeans arriving on Canada's shores in the early years. This dish, with its milk and cheese, provides an excellent source of calcium.

1	pkg (14 oz/400 g) frozen codfish	1
1 1/2 cups	low-fat milk	375 mL
3 tbsp	all-purpose flour	45 mL
1/4 cup	finely chopped green onion	50 mL
1/2 tsp	salt	2 mL
1/4 tsp	freshly ground black pepper	1 mL
1 cup	shredded light Cheddar cheese, divided	250 mL

Place fish on flat microwavable dish. Cover and defrost for 11 minutes on defrost program or until fish is defrosted. Separate fillets, cover and microwave at High (100%) for 5 minutes or until fish is opaque and flakes easily with a fork; set aside.

In large microwavable container, whisk milk and flour until blended. Microwave at High for about 5 minutes or until boiling; stir several times. Add onion, salt and pepper.

Lightly grease 8-cup (2 L) baking pan. Pour in 1/4 cup (50 mL) sauce; cover with 1/2 of fish and 1/2 of cheese. Pour 1/2 cup (125 mL) sauce over and layer with remaining fish. Pour remaining sauce over fish; sprinkle with remaining cheese. Bake in 350°F (180°C) oven for 30 minutes or until top is browned.

MAKES 4 SERVINGS.

Recipe adapted from one submitted by the Newfoundland Home Economics Association.

NUTRIENT ANALYSIS

Per Serving

Calories		239
g	Protein	30
g	Total Fat	8.2
g	Carbohydrate	9.9
g	Fibre	0.4
mg	Sodium	625
mg	Potassium	387
mg	Calcium	339
mg	Iron	1.0

 "For dressing codfish: put the fish first into cold water and wash it, then hang it over the fire and soak it six hours in scalding water, then shift it into clean water and let it scald one hour, it will be much better than to boil." *(The Cook Not Mad: or Rational Cookery)*

Prince Edward Island Potato Carrot Muffins

PRINCE EDWARD ISLAND is famous for potatoes, one of the world's most versatile foods. In this recipe, they are combined with carrots for a delicious moist muffin.

3/4 cup	whole wheat flour	175 mL
3/4 cup	all-purpose flour	175 mL
3/4 cup	granulated sugar	175 mL
2 tsp	baking powder	10 mL
1 tsp	baking soda	5 mL
1 tsp	ground cinnamon	5 mL
1/2 tsp	salt	2 mL
1/4 cup	vegetable oil	50 mL
1/4 cup	low-fat milk	50 mL
1	egg	1
1 cup	grated carrots	250 mL
1 cup	grated potatoes	250 mL
1/2 cup	raisins	125 mL

In large bowl, combine flours, sugar, baking powder, baking soda, cinnamon and salt.

In second bowl, combine oil, milk and egg. Add to dry ingredients along with carrots, potatoes and raisins, stirring just until moistened; do not overmix.

Spoon into 12 medium paper-lined or nonstick muffin cups, filling 3/4 full. Bake in 350°F (180°C) oven for about 20 minutes or until muffins are lightly browned and firm to the touch.

MAKES 12 MUFFINS.

Recipe adapted from one submitted by the Prince Edward Island Home Economics Association.

NUTRIENT ANALYSIS
Per Muffin

Calories		188
g	Protein	3.1
g	Total Fat	5.4
g	Carbohydrate	33
g	Fibre	1.9
mg	Sodium	284
mg	Potassium	195
mg	Calcium	41
mg	Iron	1.1

 Root cellars, or cold rooms, were an important part of pioneer houses. It was common to place carrots and other root vegetables in boxes of sand to be stored in a place where they would not freeze. They were then used in countless ways—carrot cake, carrot salad, baked carrots, boiled carrots, carrot pudding and even carrot pie.

Nova Scotia Festive Seafood Chowder

MANY KINDS of seafood are found off Nova Scotia's shores. When you want to serve something exceptional for a casual get-together, a bowl of this delicious chowder would be a perfect supper dish. It is a good source of calcium and iron.

2 tbsp	margarine OR butter	25 mL
1	onion, chopped	1
1 cup	water	250 mL
2 cups	diced potatoes	500 mL
1/2 lb	boneless fish fillets, cut into bite-sized pieces	250 g
1/2 lb	scallops	250 g
5 cups	low-fat milk	1.25 L
1/4 cup	all-purpose flour	50 mL
1/2 tsp	salt	2 mL
Pinch	freshly ground black pepper	Pinch
1 cup	lobster meat, diced	250 mL
1/2 lb	mussels OR clams, steamed and shucked	250 g
	Garnish: Chopped fresh parsley	

In large saucepan, melt margarine over medium heat; sauté onion until soft. Add water and potatoes. Cover and bring to a boil; reduce heat and simmer for about 7 minutes or until almost tender.

Add fish and scallops; simmer for 5 minutes or until fish is opaque and flakes easily with a fork.

Whisk together milk, flour, salt and pepper. Add to pan, return to the boil, stirring constantly; reduce heat and simmer for 1 minute. Stir in lobster and mussels. Heat over medium heat until heated through. Sprinkle a little parsley over each serving.

MAKES 8 SERVINGS, 1 1/4 CUPS (300 mL) EACH.

Recipe adapted from one submitted by the Nova Scotia Home Economics Association.

NUTRIENT ANALYSIS		
Per Serving		
Calories		*270*
g	Protein	27
g	Total Fat	7.7
g	Carbohydrate	22
g	Fibre	1.0
mg	Sodium	522
mg	Potassium	801
mg	Calcium	234
mg	Iron	2.9

 The first settlers from England arrived in Acadia in 1749. Soups, chowders and stews were the most common foods due to the need to cook in large iron kettles over the open hearth. Later, inns and coffee houses were established featuring hot mutton pies, beef soup and mutton broth. *(Out of Old Nova Scotia Kitchens)*

New Brunswick Yogurt Blueberry Muffins

BLUEBERRIES have become a favourite fruit throughout Canada, but nowhere are they as well known as in New Brunswick. These muffins are so delicious you will want to keep a good supply in the freezer.

2 ½ cups	whole wheat flour	625 mL
½ cup	granulated sugar	125 mL
¼ cup	wheat germ	50 mL
2 tsp	baking powder	10 mL
1 tsp	baking soda	5 mL
½ tsp	salt	2 mL
⅓ cup	soft margarine OR butter	75 mL
1 ¼ cups	low-fat plain yogurt	300 mL
2	eggs	2
	Grated rind of 1 orange	
1 ¼ cups	blueberries	300 mL

In large bowl, stir together flour, sugar, wheat germ, baking powder, baking soda and salt.

In second bowl, combine margarine, yogurt, eggs and rind. Stir in blueberries. Add to dry ingredients, stirring just until moistened; do not overmix.

Spoon into 18 large paper-lined or nonstick muffin cups, filling ¾ full. Bake in 400°F (200°C) oven for about 20 minutes or until muffins are lightly browned and firm to the touch.

MAKES 18 MUFFINS.

Recipe adapted from one submitted by the New Brunswick Home Economics Association.

NUTRIENT ANALYSIS

Per Muffin

Calories		*141*
g	Protein	4.4
g	Total Fat	4.8
g	Carbohydrate	22
g	Fibre	2.7
mg	Sodium	242
mg	Potassium	143
mg	Calcium	56
mg	Iron	0.9

 Our Maritime provinces have always enjoyed a recipe called Blueberry Grunt, a steamed dessert with dumplings and blueberries. The odd name is said to come from the noises made by the fruit as it steams under a cover of dumplings.

Quebec Maple Syrup Cake

ENJOY this delicately flavoured cake, which contains only a small amount of fat. Be sure to use pure maple syrup to capture the true maple flavour.

2 ¼ cups	cake and pastry flour	550 mL
2 tsp	baking powder	10 mL
2	egg whites	2
½ cup	granulated sugar, divided	125 mL
¼ cup	margarine OR butter	50 mL
1 cup	maple syrup, divided	250 mL
½ cup	low-fat milk	125 mL
2 tbsp	finely chopped walnuts	25 mL

Mix together flour and baking powder.

In small bowl, beat egg whites until frothy; gradually beat in ¼ cup (50 mL) sugar until stiff peaks form; set aside.

In large bowl, cream margarine and remaining sugar. Stir in ½ of flour mixture, ¾ cup (175 mL) maple syrup, then remaining flour mixture. Stir in milk; gently fold in beaten egg whites.

Pour batter into lightly greased 8-inch (2 L) square baking pan*; sprinkle with walnuts.

Bake in 350°F (180°C) oven for 30 minutes or until top springs back when lightly touched. Let cake cool for 5 minutes; brush top with remaining maple syrup.

MAKES 16 SMALL SERVINGS.

NOTE:
If you are baking in a nonstick or glass pan, reduce oven temperature to 325°F (160°C).

Recipe adapted from one submitted by the Quebec Home Economics Association.

COOKING TIPS:

Look for the words Pure Maple Syrup on the label when buying syrup. Maple syrup is available in different grades, based on colour. The colour is related to the intensity of the flavour. For cooking, choose the stronger flavoured grade of syrup called Medium, or Amber. For serving over ice cream, puddings or pancakes, choose the lighter, more delicate grades called Light and Extra Light.

Maple syrup is one of nature's delicacies and we are indebted to Canada's native peoples for revealing the secret of the maple tree. Early French settlers learned from the Ojibwa about "sugaring off" and the period called "the maple moon," or "sugar month." Maple sugar was more commonly used than cane sugar, which arrived from the West Indies in barrels. An Iroquois legend tells of piercing the bark of the maple tree and the use of the "sweet water" to cook venison, thus establishing the culinary tradition of maple-cured meat.

NUTRIENT ANALYSIS

Per Serving

Calories		*168*
g	Protein	2.1
g	Total Fat	3.7
g	Carbohydrate	32
g	Fibre	0.1
mg	Sodium	79
mg	Potassium	76
mg	Calcium	49
mg	Iron	1.3

Ontario Cheddar Cheese Bites

ONTARIO is famous for its Cheddar cheese. These easy appetizer bites, a new twist to traditional cheese tartlets, are best served slightly warm.

2	egg whites	2
¼ tsp	lemon juice	1 mL
1 cup	finely shredded light old Cheddar cheese	250 mL
2 tsp	finely minced onion	10 mL
1 tsp	Worcestershire sauce	5 mL
½ tsp	paprika	2 mL
½ tsp	dry mustard	2 mL

In small bowl, beat egg whites and juice just until stiff peaks form. Gently fold in cheese, onion, Worcestershire, paprika and mustard.

On nonstick baking sheet, drop by teaspoonful, making 24 small mounds. Bake in 450°F (230°C) oven for 8 minutes or until well browned. Cool on rack. Serve slightly warm.

MAKES 24 APPETIZER BITES.

Recipe adapted from one submitted by the Ontario Home Economics Association.

NUTRIENT ANALYSIS		
Per Appetizer		
Calories		*17*
g	Protein	1.7
g	Total Fat	1.0
g	Carbohydrate	0.2
g	Fibre	0
mg	Sodium	37
mg	Potassium	11
mg	Calcium	35
mg	Iron	0.1

 In 1893, a 22,000-pound cheese was sent as part of the Canadian exhibition to the World's Columbian Exposition in Chicago. Made in Perth, Ontario, it required one day's milk from 10,000 cows. It was the world's largest cheese until 1963, when an even larger one was made in Wisconsin.

Manitoba Curried Wild Rice Walnut Salad

COMPARED with white rice, wild rice is relatively expensive. We stretch it by adding several vegetables and apple to this salad. Also, remember 1 part wild rice swells to 4 parts after cooking, compared with 3 parts for white rice.

$^2/_3$ cup	wild rice	150 mL
$^1/_4$ tsp	salt	1 mL
$^1/_2$ cup	sliced green onions	125 mL
$^1/_2$ cup	grated carrot	125 mL
2 tbsp	finely chopped fresh parsley	25 mL

Curry Lemon Dressing:

2 tbsp	lemon juice	25 mL
1 tbsp	vegetable oil	15 mL
1 tbsp	water	15 mL
1 tbsp	light salad dressing OR mayonnaise	15 mL
$^1/_2$ tbsp	granulated sugar	7 mL
1	small clove garlic, minced	1
$^1/_4$ tsp	curry powder	1 mL
1	tart firm apple, cored and diced	1
$^1/_4$ cup	coarsely chopped walnuts	50 mL

Wash wild rice well under cold running water; drain. In medium saucepan bring 2 cups (500 mL) water to a boil. Add rice and salt, reduce heat, cover, and simmer for 40 minutes or until rice is tender; drain. Stir in onions, carrot and parsley.

Dressing: In small bowl, whisk together juice, oil, water, salad dressing, sugar, garlic and curry powder. Pour dressing over rice mixture. Cover and refrigerate for 1 to 2 hours.

Just before serving stir in apple and walnuts.

MAKES 6 SERVINGS, $^3/_4$ CUP (175 mL) EACH.

Recipe adapted from one submitted by the Manitoba Association of Home Economists.

NUTRIENT ANALYSIS		
Per Serving		
Calories		*151*
g	Protein	3.8
g	Total Fat	6.5
g	Carbohydrate	21
g	Fibre	2.1
mg	Sodium	139
mg	Potassium	198
mg	Calcium	22
mg	Iron	0.8

 Wild rice is really not a rice but the grain from a marsh grass native to the northern Great Lakes area. Grown abundantly in marshlands in Manitoba, it was an important food for the Indians and was sold by them to the settlers when they arrived in Canada.

Saskatchewan Spicy Hot Yellow Split Peas

THE SASKATCHEWAN PRAIRIE has an ideal climate for growing grains and pulses such as yellow split peas. They are an excellent meat alternative providing high fibre and an excellent source of iron and protein. Make and freeze extra servings of this flavourful supper dish for busy days.

2 cups	dried yellow split peas, washed	500 mL
1/3 cup	liquid honey	75 mL
1/4 cup	light soy sauce	50 mL
2 tsp	cornstarch	10 mL
1 tbsp	sesame oil	15 mL
10	cloves garlic, minced	10
4	dried chilies, seeded and crushed	4
2 tsp	minced gingerroot	10 mL
1/2	sweet red pepper, diced	1/2
1/2 cup	currants	125 mL
6 cups	cooked white rice (2 cups/500 mL raw)	1.5 L
	Garnish: Chopped fresh parsley	

COOKING TIPS:

Pulses are the dried seeds of any of several legumes, including beans, peas and lentils. Yellow split peas resemble chick-peas in flavour, whereas green split peas taste more like green peas. When yellow ones are cooked, they can be used to replace puréed chick-peas in a dish such as hummus.

In large saucepan, combine peas and 4 cups (1 L) water; bring to a boil. Cover, reduce heat and simmer for 25 minutes or until peas are soft; drain.

In small bowl, whisk together honey, soy sauce, 2 tbsp (25 mL) water and cornstarch; set aside.

In large nonstick skillet, heat oil over medium heat; sauté garlic, chilies and gingerroot for 1 to 2 minutes. Stir in red pepper, currants and peas; sauté for about 5 minutes, stirring frequently. Add honey mixture and cook until thickened and bubbly, stirring constantly. Serve over rice; garnish with parsley.

MAKES 6 SERVINGS.

Recipe adapted from one submitted by the Association of Saskatchewan Home Economists.

NUTRIENT ANALYSIS		
Per Serving		
Calories		567
g	Protein	22
g	Total Fat	3.7
g	Carbohydrate	114
g	Fibre	5.5
mg	Sodium	346
mg	Potassium	914
mg	Calcium	94
mg	Iron	4.2

Alberta Beef Stew

ALBERTA is known for its excellent beef. This recipe combines a lean cut, round steak, with assorted vegetables for a good old-fashioned stew. Research into early heritage recipes reveals the surprising use of allspice, cinnamon or mace as a seasoning in beef stews.

1 ½ lb	lean boneless round steak OR stewing beef	750 g
¼ cup	all-purpose flour	50 mL
½ tsp	salt	2 mL
¼ tsp	pepper	1 mL
1	large clove garlic, chopped	1
1 cup	beef stock	250 mL
1 cup	tomato juice	250 mL
1 tbsp	tomato paste	15 mL
1 tbsp	lemon juice	15 mL
1 tsp	Worcestershire sauce	5 mL
1 tsp	paprika	5 mL
½ tsp	ground allspice	2 mL
½ tsp	ground cinnamon	2 mL

Vegetables:

4	small onions, halved	4
3	medium carrots, cut into large chunks	3
4	medium potatoes, cut into large chunks	4
2 cups	cubed turnip	500 mL
1 cup	green beans, trimmed and cut in half	250 mL

Trim all visible fat from beef and discard; cut meat into large cubes. Combine flour, salt and pepper. Toss beef in flour mixture. Add beef and garlic to Dutch oven or large casserole. Cover and bake in 400°F (200°C) oven for 30 minutes.

Reduce heat to 300°F (150°C); add stock, tomato juice, tomato paste, lemon juice, Worcestershire and seasonings. Cover and bake for 1 hour. Add vegetables and bake for about 1 hour longer or until vegetables are tender.

MAKES 8 SERVINGS.

Recipe adapted from one submitted by the Alberta Home Economics Association.

 Recipes from the 18th and 19th centuries use many interesting descriptive terms. For example, instructions calling for "a wine glass of...," "two porringers of...," "as much mace as needed," "boil at 2 or 3 wallops." Of course, we all know that "butter the size of an egg" is about ¼ cup, although this depends on the size of the egg. What is equal to 2 tbsp — "the size of a walnut"?

Nutrient Analysis		
Per Serving		
Calories		*214*
g	Protein	20
g	Total Fat	3.7
g	Carbohydrate	26
g	Fibre	3.8
mg	Sodium	455
mg	Potassium	837
mg	Calcium	50
mg	Iron	3.3

British Columbia Barbecued Salmon

SALMON is highly prized for its delicious flavour and versatility as a main course, salad or spread.

2	salmon fillets, about 1 lb/500 g each	2
¼ cup	dry white wine OR apple juice	50 mL
1 tbsp	Dijon mustard	15 mL
1 tbsp	horseradish	15 mL
1 tbsp	oyster sauce	15 mL
1 tbsp	chili sauce	15 mL
1 tbsp	light soy sauce	15 mL
2	green onions, finely chopped	2

COOKING TIPS:

The easiest way to barbecue fish is with a fish basket. This eliminates the difficulty of turning fish on the grill. There are also some excellent nonstick barbecue grill racks available. These have holes that allow fish to develop barbecue flavours without being directly on the grill.

In shallow baking dish, place fillets. Combine wine, mustard, horseradish, oyster and chili sauce, soy sauce and onions; pour over fish. Cover and refrigerate to marinate for 8 to 10 hours.

Remove fish from marinade. Preheat broiler or barbecue on high. Just before cooking, brush grill lightly with oil. Broil or barbecue fish 4 inches (10 cm) from heat for 4 to 5 minutes per side or until fish is opaque and flakes easily with a fork or bake in 450°F (230°C) oven for 10 minutes per 1-inch (2.5 cm) of thickness.

MAKES 8 SERVINGS.

Recipe adapted from one submitted by the British Columbia Home Economics Association.

NUTRIENT ANALYSIS		
Per Serving		
Calories		204
g	Protein	25
g	Total Fat	9.9
g	Carbohydrate	1.0
g	Fibre	0.1
mg	Sodium	237
mg	Potassium	380
mg	Calcium	13
mg	Iron	0.7

Yukon/Northwest Territories Cranberry Orange Muffins

COOKING TIPS:

Cranberries are native to the marshy areas of northern and eastern Canada. Their tart flavour combines well with other fruits and makes delicious relishes, cobblers, pies and other desserts.

Cranberries resist rapid deterioration due to their high benzoic acid content and can be stored for up to 2 months or frozen for up to a year.

The Northwest Territories have a food guide developed for First Nations people. In it, references for food are slightly different than the national Food Guide. Bannock is included in the Bread and Cereal group; birds are in the Protein group; berries and wild greens are in the Fruit and Vegetable group, making it more adaptable to their daily diet.

FOR MOST Yukon families, fall is the time to gather the usually abundant crop of low-bush cranberries. This recipe is from a home economist in the Yukon, who told us that it is her favourite cranberry muffin recipe, made special by the little hands that help her pick them.

1 ½ cups	fresh or frozen and thawed cranberries	375 mL
1 ½ cups	all-purpose flour	375 mL
1 cup	whole wheat flour	250 mL
1 cup	granulated sugar	250 mL
2 tsp	baking powder	10 mL
1 tsp	baking soda	5 mL
½ tsp	salt	2 mL
½ cup	orange juice	125 mL
½ cup	low-fat milk	125 mL
3 tbsp	vegetable oil	45 mL
1	egg	1
	Grated rind of 1 orange	

Finely chop cranberries; set aside.

In large bowl, combine flours, sugar, baking powder, baking soda and salt.

In second bowl, combine juice, milk, oil, egg and rind. Stir in cranberries. Add to dry ingredients, stirring just until moistened. Spoon into 18 large paper-lined or nonstick muffin cups, filling ¾ full. Bake in 375°F (190°C) oven for 20 minutes or until muffins are lightly browned and firm to the touch. Remove from pan.

MAKES 18 MUFFINS.

Recipe adapted from one submitted by the Yukon Home Economics Association.

12

Fun For Kids

This part of the book is for you, kids. Maybe you're just beginning to be interested in the idea of making some great dishes to serve to your friends or your family. You can have lots of fun making one of the After-School Treats (pages 170 and 171) with a friend or the Upside-Down Pizza (page 173) for your dinner. You are never too young to get started on good eating habits that will help keep you healthy for the rest of your life. For example, being sure you get enough fruits, vegetables, cereals and breads, not too many fats and enough fibre, will provide you with a start towards a healthy lifestyle.

Smart Snack Attacks *A snack food should have enough nutrients to justify its calories. When you choose snack foods from the four food groups, you know you are "eating smart."* ◆ *Choose from: Breads and cereals; Fruits and vegetables, possibly spread with cheese or peanut butter; Quick snacks of milk, juice, cheese and yogurt; Some meats, tuna and salmon.*

Smart Lunch for the Bunch *Try some different things to pack in your lunch. Wrap a tortilla around some cooked meat or spread it with peanut butter. Stuff a pita bread with sandwich meat or hard-cooked egg slices. There are many kinds of bread now available, so try a different one for a regular sandwich. Fill celery strips with cheese or peanut butter. Find a big red apple, orange or other fruit that you like. Tuck in some raisins or a Brownie (page174) to satisfy your sweet tooth. Lunch should give you lots of energy to get you through the afternoon.*

Make sure you don't forget about exercise. Get up and move...turn off that tube! Remember what fun it is to play tag, ride your bicycle, fly a kite? Or have you forgotten how much fun it is to play ball, build a snowman, jump in the leaves. Go for it...call up a friend and start doing it!

After-School Treats

FOR HIGH ENERGY, kids need foods to help tide them over from one
activity to another. These snacks will do just that.

CRISPY SQUARES

6 cups	crispy-type cereal	1.5 L
1 cup	raisins	250 mL
1 cup	corn syrup	250 mL
³/₄ cup	chocolate hazelnut spread	175 mL

In large bowl, stir together cereal and raisins.

In 2-cup (500 mL) microwavable container, combine syrup and
chocolate spread; microwave at High (100%) for 2 minutes or until
hot. Stir into cereal mixture until well mixed. Pat into 13 x 9-inch
(3.5 L) pan. (Use a little oil to grease your hands if the cereal sticks
to them.) Cool in pan and cut into squares.

MAKES 48 SQUARES.

GRANOLA FRUIT MUNCHIES

2 cups	high-fibre bran cereal	500 mL
1 cup	raisins	250 mL
¹/₂ cup	cut-up dried apricots	125 mL
¹/₂ cup	flaked coconut	125 mL
¹/₂ cup	liquid honey	125 mL
¹/₃ cup	all-purpose flour	75 mL
¹/₄ cup	low-fat milk	50 mL
2 tbsp	vegetable oil	25 mL
1	egg, slightly beaten	1

In large bowl, combine cereal, raisins, apricots, coconut, honey,
flour, milk, oil and egg; stir to blend.

Press firmly into lightly greased 8-inch (20 cm) square
baking pan. Bake in 325°F (160°C) oven for about 35
minutes or until firm in centre. Cool in pan and cut
into squares.

MAKES 25 SQUARES.

POWER BARS

VARIATIONS:

Add other ingredients of your choice to the fruit snack: chopped apricots, sunflower seeds, coconut flakes, banana chips, popped popcorn, Chinese noodles, chocolate chips.

$\frac{1}{2}$ cup	liquid honey	125 mL
$\frac{1}{2}$ cup	chunky peanut butter	125 mL
1 tbsp	vegetable oil	15 mL
1	large banana, mashed	1
2 cups	quick-cooking rolled oats	500 mL
$\frac{1}{2}$ cup	natural wheat bran	125 mL
$\frac{1}{4}$ cup	wheat germ	50 mL
$\frac{1}{4}$ cup	sunflower seeds	50 mL
$\frac{1}{2}$ tsp	ground cinnamon	2 mL

In microwavable 2 cup (500 mL) container, combine honey, peanut butter and oil; microwave at High (100%) for 1 $\frac{1}{2}$ minutes or until mixture becomes liquid. Stir in banana.

In large bowl, combine oats, bran, wheat germ, sunflower seeds and cinnamon. Stir in banana mixture.

Press firmly into lightly greased 13 x 9-inch (3.5 L) baking pan. Bake in 325°F (160°C) oven for about 20 minutes or until golden brown. Cut into bars and cool. Store in tightly sealed container.

MAKES 35 BARS.

NUTTY FRUIT SNACK

2 tbsp	margarine OR butter	25 mL
3 cups	O-shaped oat cereal	750 mL
2 cups	pretzels	500 mL
1 cup	salted peanuts	250 mL
1 cup	raisins	250 mL

In large nonstick skillet, melt margarine over medium-low heat. Stir in cereal and cook for 5 minutes or until cereal is lightly toasted; stir all the time. Remove from heat and cool. Stir in pretzels, peanuts and raisins. Store in an airtight container.

MAKES 14 SERVINGS, $\frac{1}{2}$ CUP (125 mL) EACH.

NUTRIENT ANALYSIS

Power Bars

Per Bar

Calories		72
g	Protein	2.3
g	Total Fat	3.2
g	Carbohydrate	9.9
g	Fibre	1.4
mg	Sodium	19
mg	Potassium	85
mg	Calcium	7
mg	Iron	0.5

Nutty Fruit Snack

Per Serving

Calories		157
g	Protein	4.5
g	Total Fat	7.4
g	Carbohydrate	20
g	Fibre	1.7
mg	Sodium	219
mg	Potassium	191
mg	Calcium	25
mg	Iron	1.2

Make-Ahead Cheese Sandwich

LET'S TALK MICROWAVE

It's easy to cook with the microwave oven providing you remember a few tips.

- Do not place any metal in the microwave oven. Ask your parents which dishes are allowed.
- Wear oven mitts when removing foods from the microwave oven.
- Watch for steam escaping when you open packages of microwave popcorn or other foods you have cooked in the microwave oven. The steam that escapes can scald.
- Sometimes foods cooked in the microwave oven develop "hot spots." Stir foods well before eating.
- To avoid overcooking, check food for doneness before suggested cooking time is finished.
- Ask for help if a dish is too heavy.

EITHER MOM OR KIDS can get this quick lunch ready in the morning when it is convenient to make extra toast. Then, at noon, pop it into the microwave oven for a speedy and tasty lunch that is high in fibre, an excellent source of calcium and a good source of iron. Serve with assorted raw vegetables.

4	slices whole wheat bread, toasted	4
8	small slices light Cheddar cheese (2 oz/60 g cheese)	8
1	egg, lightly beaten	1
$\frac{1}{3}$ cup	low-fat milk	75 mL
1 tbsp	tomato ketchup	15 mL
1 tsp	prepared mustard	5 mL
$\frac{1}{4}$ tsp	dried basil	1 mL

Place 2 toast slices in 11 x 7-inch (2 L) baking pan. Top with cheese slices, then remaining 2 toast slices.

Combine egg, milk, ketchup, mustard and basil; pour over toast. Cover and refrigerate for 2 to 3 hours.

With cover on, microwave at Medium (50%) for 3 minutes; rotate and microwave for 2 to 3 minutes more or until sandwiches are no longer soft and moist.

MAKES 2 SERVINGS.

NUTRIENT ANALYSIS

Per Serving

Calories		298
g	Protein	19
g	Total Fat	11
g	Carbohydrate	33
g	Fibre	5.7
mg	Sodium	681
mg	Potassium	318
mg	Calcium	333
mg	Iron	2.5

 The Canadian Home Economics Association was an early advocate of good lunches for children. In 1944, CHEA urged provincial departments of education to stress school lunch programs. They were much needed, if reports of early school lunches are typical: "In the early Canadian prairie schools, the lunch pail was usually an empty syrup pail or a five-pound lard pail with a wire handle and a metal cover. Inside were sandwiches of jam, syrup or brown sugar. Sometimes there would be a left-over chicken leg or a hard-boiled egg. Some of the children brought sandwiches of lard, with a bit of salt or cocoa sprinkled on the lard. The children who brought cakes and cookies every day were envied by the rest of us." (*Canadian Prairie Homesteaders*)

Upsidᵉ-Down Pizza

THIS RECIPE IS A FAVOURITE of our families. It's also easy to adapt to whatever ingredients you have on hand. We check out the refrigerator and use any vegetables we see in the crisper and use Cheddar cheese in place of mozzarella—you get the idea. Whichever cheese or vegetables you find, this pizza is an excellent source of calcium and a good source of iron.

SNACK ATTACK

Raw vegetable strips or pieces of fresh fruit make an easy snack. Creamy Low-Calorie Herb Dressing (page 49) is great as a dip for carrot and celery strips, green pepper and turnip pieces or mushrooms. One of the Fresh Fruit Dips (page 138) makes pieces of fresh fruit even more delicious.

1 lb	lean ground beef	500 g
1	large onion, chopped	1
1	jar (750 mL) spaghetti OR pizza sauce	1
3 cups	assorted chopped OR shredded vegetables (mushrooms, zucchini, sweet green OR red pepper, shredded carrot, broccoli florets, tomatoes)	750 mL
$1/2$ lb	shredded part-skim mozzarella cheese	250 g
2	eggs	2
1 cup	low-fat milk	250 mL
1 cup	all-purpose flour	250 mL
1 tbsp	vegetable oil	15 mL
$1/2$ tsp	dried oregano	2 mL
$1/4$ tsp	salt	1 mL
$1/2$ cup	freshly grated Parmesan cheese	125 mL

In large nonstick skillet, cook beef over medium heat for 5 minutes or until browned, stirring to break it up; drain off all fat. Add onion; cook for about 5 minutes or until onion is tender. Stir in sauce.

Pour mixture into lightly greased 13 x 9-inch (3.5 L) baking pan. Sprinkle with assorted vegetables and mozzarella cheese.

In medium bowl, beat together eggs, milk, flour, oil and seasonings; pour over meat mixture. Sprinkle with Parmesan cheese. Bake in 350°F (180°C) oven for 30 minutes or until topping is golden and vegetables are tender.

MAKES 8 SERVINGS.

NUTRIENT ANALYSIS

Per Serving

Calories		435
g	Protein	28
g	Total Fat	20
g	Carbohydrate	35
g	Fibre	1.7
mg	Sodium	910
mg	Potassium	789
mg	Calcium	386
mg	Iron	3.0

Brownies

IS IT POSSIBLE—brownies with no added fat? And only one bowl for mixing. No muss, no fuss. In our opinion, the perfect brownie!

³⁄₄ cup	cake and pastry flour	175 mL
³⁄₄ cup	granulated sugar	175 mL
¹⁄₃ cup	unsweetened cocoa	75 mL
¹⁄₂ tsp	baking powder	2 mL
¹⁄₂ tsp	salt	2 mL
¹⁄₄ cup	corn syrup	50 mL
¹⁄₄ cup	applesauce	50 mL
1	egg	1

In large bowl, stir together flour, sugar, cocoa, baking powder and salt.

Make a hole in the centre; stir in syrup, applesauce and egg. Spoon batter into lightly greased 8-inch (2 L) square baking pan. Bake in 350°F (180°C) oven for 25 to 30 minutes or until top springs back when lightly touched. Cool completely on wire rack before cutting into squares.

MAKES 16 SQUARES.

SNACK ATTACK

Next time, try this fruit shake using just a little peanut butter and the banana; or some ice cream for a special thick one; or a little chocolate syrup, or the straw-berry and raspberry frozen punches for extra flavour. Have fun making up your own flavour combos.

Fruit Smoothie

LIKE A MILK SHAKE, but even better. It is not nearly as high in fat, has high fibre and is a good source of calcium. Start with cold milk, fruit and yogurt if you can't wait to chill it.

1	large banana	1
1 cup	raspberries OR strawberries	250 mL
³⁄₄ cup	low-fat milk	175 mL
¹⁄₃ cup	low-fat plain yogurt	75 mL
1 tbsp	liquid honey	15 mL

In blender container, purée banana and berries until smooth. Add milk, yogurt and honey; blend for 1 minute or until smooth and frothy. Chill before serving or enjoy immediately.

MAKES 2 SERVINGS, ABOUT 1 CUP (250 mL) EACH.

NUTRIENT ANALYSIS		
Brownies		
Per Square		
Calories		*82*
g	Protein	1.1
g	Total Fat	0.8
g	Carbohydrate	19
g	Fibre	0.7
mg	Sodium	101
mg	Potassium	41
mg	Calcium	11
mg	Iron	0.8
Fruit Smoothie		
Per Serving		
Calories		*188*
g	Protein	6.5
g	Total Fat	3.0
g	Carbohydrate	37
g	Fibre	4.1
mg	Sodium	76
mg	Potassium	567
mg	Calcium	206
mg	Iron	0.7

Glossary of Cooking Terms

Kids, do you read a recipe and wonder what that word means? Here is a list to help you know what to do.

Bake.   To cook in an oven by dry heat. The oven does not need to be preheated (brought up to temperature before the food is put in) unless you are cooking something that depends on the hot air to make it rise such as popovers, souffles or angel cakes. Make sure that there is enough room around the food for the air to circulate.

Beat.   A fast circular motion with a whisk or spoon to make a mixture smooth and incorporate air.

Blanch.   To plunge food into boiling water for a very short time to loosen skins for peeling or to partially cook.

Blend.   To mix two or more ingredients together.

Boil.   To heat a liquid over high heat until rapid bubbles form.

Broil or Grill.   To cook under direct heat such as an oven broiler or a barbecue. The high heat can brown food without the use of fat, as in frying.

Chop, Dice, Mince.   To cut food into small pieces or cubes: chop means cut into large pieces (over ½ inch/1 cm square), dice means cut into medium-sized pieces (about ¼ inch/5 mm to ½ inch/1 cm square), and mince means cut into very fine pieces (less than ⅛ inch/3 mm square).

Cream.   To beat softened margarine, butter or shortening with sugar until very well mixed and fluffy.

Drain.   To remove the liquid from a food by pouring it into a strainer or colander.

Fold.   To blend one ingredient into another by gently turning one part over another with a rubber spatula and without stirring or beating.

Fry.   To cook a food in a hot skillet with fat over high heat.

Garnish.   To decorate food with colourful additions placed on or with it.

Grate.   To rub a solid food over a grater to make small shreds; or put through the grater blade of a food processor.

Julienne.   To cut food into thin strips the shape of a matchstick.

Knead. To fold a flour mixture over and onto itself with gentle stretching.

Melt. To change a solid food into a liquid by use of low heat or low microwave power.

Mix. To stir two or more ingredients together.

Poach. To cook a food in gently simmering water.

Process. To run a food processor with an on and off motion until the food is chopped to desired fineness.

Purée. To make solid food very smooth and almost liquid, generally by use of a food mill, blender or food processor.

Roast. To cook in an oven by dry heat with a bit of fat such as that on a roast, or potatoes.

Sauté. To cook small pieces of food very quickly in a skillet using a small amount of fat.

Simmer. To cook a food or a liquid over low heat so that there are small bubbles breaking on the surface (not boiling).

Steam. To cook food, placed on a rack, in the steam that rises from boiling water.

Stir. A circular motion used to combine ingredients, or to keep a product smooth.

Stir-fry. To cook food quickly in a skillet or wok with a little oil over high heat, stirring the food constantly.

Stuff. To fill the hollow of a food with a mixture of ingredients.

Toss. To gently mix together several ingredients using two forks or large spoons.

List of Resources

1. Beef Information Centre, 590 Keele St., Suite 422, Toronto, ON M6N 3E3
2. Canada Pork Inc., 125 Traders Blvd. E., Suite 2, Mississauga, ON L4Z 2E5
3. Canadian Chicken Marketing Agency, 377 Dalhousie St., Suite 300, Ottawa, ON, K1N 9N8
4. The Canadian Dietetic Association, 480 University Ave., Suite 601, Toronto, ON M5G 1V2
5. Canadian Egg Marketing Agency, 320 Queen St., Suite 1900, Place du Ville, Ottawa, ON K1R 5A3
6. Canadian Home Economics Association, 151 Slater St., Suite 901, Ottawa, ON K1P 5H3
7. Canadian Turkey Marketing Agency, 44 Peel Centre Dr., Suite 403, Brampton, ON L6T 4B5
8. Consumer and Corporate Affairs Canada, Food Division, Place du Portage, 50 Victoria St., Hull, PQ K1A 0C9
9. Consumers' Association of Canada, 307 Gilmour Street, Ottawa, ON K2P 0P7
10. Health and Welfare Canada, Health Services and Promotion Branch, Ottawa, ON K1A 1B4
11. National Institute of Nutrition, 265 Carling Ave., Suite 302, Ottawa, ON K1S 2E1

Bibliography

The American Heritage Cookbook. New York: American Heritage Publishing Co., Inc. (Charles Scribner's Sons), 1980.

Barss, B. M., and Sheila Kerr. *Canadian Prairie Home-steaders*. Calgary: Barker Publishing Ltd., 1979.

Bates, Christina. *Out of Old Ontario Kitchens*. Toronto: Pagurian Press Ltd., 1978.

Beeton, Mary Isabella. *Mrs. Beeton's Cookery and Household Management.* (new ed.) London: Ward, Lock, 1961.

Child, Lydia Marie. *The American Frugal Housewife*. Boston: Marsh & Capen and Carter & Hendee, 1829. Reprint of 12th edition, Old Sturbridge Village, a George Dawson Bk., Cambridge, Mass: Applewood Books, 1833.

The Cook Not Mad: or Rational Cookery. Kingston, U. C.: James Macfarlane, 1831; Toronto: R.A. Abramson, 1972.

Elverson, Virginia T., and Mary Ann McLanahan. *A Cooking Legacy*. New York: Cornerstone Library, 1975.

Encyclopaedia Britannica (Micropaedia) vols. IX and X, 15th ed., 1975.

Farmer, Dennis and Carol. *The King's Bread, 2nd Rising: Cooking at Niagara 1726-1815*. Youngstown, N.Y.: Old Fort Niagara Association, Inc., 1989.

Jones, Evan. *American Food, The Gastronomic Story*. New York: P. Dutton & Co., Inc., 1975.

McCormick, Veronica. *A Hundred Years in the Dairy Industry*. Ottawa: Dairy Farmers of Canada, 1967.

Nightingale, Marie. *Out of Old Nova Scotia Kitchens*. Toronto: Pagurian Press Ltd., 1971.

Raffald, Elizabeth. *The Experienced English Housekeeper*. 2d ed. London: R. Baldwin, 1771. Reprint. London: E & W Books, 1970.

Randolph, Mrs. Mary. *The Virginia Housewife*. Washington: Thompson & Homans, 1831. Edited by Karen Hess. Columbia, S.C.: University of South Carolina Press, 1984.

Scaragall, Jeanne. *Pioneer Potpourri*. Methuen: Toronto, 1974.

Simmons, Amelia. *The First American Cookbook*. New York: Dover Publications Inc., 1958.

Wilkinson, Gertrude. *The Attic Cookbook*. Baltimore, Md.: Penguin Books Inc., 1972.

Index

Common Core Standards Practice and Review

Progress Monitoring Assessments

PEARSON

Boston, Massachusetts   Chandler, Arizona   Glenview, Illinois   Upper Saddle River, New Jersey

ISBN-13: 978-0-13-318597-3
ISBN-10:   0-13-318597-4

5 6 7 8 9 10 V069 15 14 13

PEARSON

Table of Contents

Summative Assessments, Form K

Common Core End-of-Course Assessment

Common Core Performance-Based Assessment

Introduction

SAT/ACT Preparation

Common Core Standards Practice Answers

Answers

Common Core Performance-Based Assessment Scoring Rubrics

SAT/ACT Practice Test Answers

Student Answer Sheets

To the Teacher

Pearson is pleased to offer you *Common Core Standards Practice and Review • Progress Monitoring Assessments*, a comprehensive resource of assessments that you can use to monitor your students' progress throughout the school year and to help them prepare for high-stakes Common Core assessments. These assessments can be used to inform instruction (formative) or to evaluate student learning (summative).

Screening Test

Before launching into the curriculum, you may want to gather information on how proficient your students are with the pre-requisite concepts and skills that will allow them to be successful in the course. Use the Screening Test to measure your students' readiness for this course. The Screening Test Report, which lists all of the skills assessed on the test, can be used to isolate areas of weakness students may have.

Common Core Standards Practice and Teacher Notes

Starting on page 1, these 30 pages offer students weekly practice on targeted Common Core Standards. The assessment items follow the progression of concepts and skills found in Pearson's *Geometry Common Core* and focus in particular on the standards that are considered major content emphases. Students will encounter assessment items that are representative of the kinds of items they will find on the upcoming assessments from PARCC and SBAC. Each weekly practice has a Teacher Notes page that helps you see how to use the practice page in class. The notes will include correlation to Common Core State Standards and Mathematical Practices.

Common Core Readiness Assessments

Each of the five (5) Common Core Readiness Assessments focuses on the concepts and skills that students are expected to master in 2-, or 3-chapter increments. The Common Core Readiness Assessments Reports, found after each Common Core Readiness Assessments, identify the standard(s) that each item assesses and provides lesson references where student can gain more practice with the concept or skill, as needed.

Summative Assessments

These assessments can be used to evaluate student learning at specified intervals. There are four (4) Quarter Tests, a Mid-Course Test, and a cumulative Final Test. All of these are available at two levels, G and K. The Form G tests are designed to measure students' mastery of content with the rigor presented in the lessons and exercises of the Student Edition while the Form K tests assess the same content, but are more appropriate for less proficient readers, English Language Learners (ELLs), and struggling students.

End-of-Course Assessment

The End-of-Course Assessment provides practice for the Common Core End-of-Course Assessments currently under development by the two assessment consortia, the Partnership for the Assessment of Readiness for College and Career (PARCC) and Smarter Balanced Assessment Consortium (SBAC). Students will encounter innovative assessment items. The assessment items focus on the major content emphases of both PARCC and SBAC assessments, while still including assessment of the supporting and additional content emphases. The End-of-Course Report can be used to evaluate students' mastery of these content emphases and to identify areas of potential weakness on the high-stakes assessments.

Performance-Based Assessments

The four (4) Performance-Based Assessments offer students rich and complex, multi-part, real-world tasks to help them prepare for the Performance-Based Assessment or Performance Tasks that they will be expected to complete as part of the PARCC or SBAC assessment. In the Answers section, you will find a scoring rubric to evaluate student work on these tasks.

SAT and ACT Practice

These pages can acquaint students with topics and question formats that they are likely to find on the SAT or ACT. The information provided on pages 115 through 121 can help students feel less anxious when they take these high-stakes assessments, and the practice test provides them with familiarity about the format and content of the assessment items.

Screening Test

Choose the best answer for the problems.

1. Which is the place value of the underlined digit?

8,1<u>4</u>7,456,748

  A hundred thousands
  B millions
  C ten millions
  D ten thousands

2. Which is the value of the underlined digit?

<u>7</u>28,426

  F   7000
  G   70,000
  H   700,000
  J 7,000,000

3. Which number does the shaded part of the model represent?

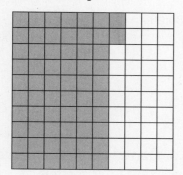

  A 0.75
  B 0.62
  C 0.38
  D 0.22

4. Which number is modeled below?

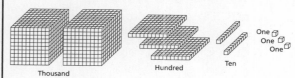

  F   123
  G   2023
  H   2323
  J 11,323

5. Which fraction is represented by the shaded area below?

  A $\frac{1}{2}$
  B $\frac{3}{4}$
  C $1\frac{1}{2}$
  D $2\frac{1}{6}$

6. A retail company charted their monthly sales shown in the table below. During which month were sales the greatest?

Retail Sales	
Month	**Sales**
January	$2,072,146
February	$2,126,341
March	$2,824,271
April	$2,842,126

  F January
  G February
  H March
  J April

7. Which statement is false?

A $0.8 = \dfrac{3}{5}$

B $\dfrac{2}{3} > 0.34$

C $2.375 > 2\dfrac{1}{4}$

D $3\dfrac{8}{11} < 3\dfrac{12}{13}$

8. Find the sum.
$$\begin{array}{r} 167,654 \\ +\ 98,786 \end{array}$$

F 266,440

G 275,330

H 276,540

J 286,330

9. Find the difference.
$$\begin{array}{r} 80,092 \\ -10,063 \end{array}$$

A 70,411

B 70,310

C 70,029

D 60,029

10. Find the sum. $\dfrac{16}{31} + \dfrac{17}{31}$

F $\dfrac{1}{31}$

G $1\dfrac{2}{31}$

H $1\dfrac{3}{31}$

J $2\dfrac{1}{31}$

11. Find the difference. $\dfrac{34}{45} - \dfrac{9}{45}$

A $\dfrac{7}{15}$

B $\dfrac{24}{45}$

C $\dfrac{5}{9}$

D $\dfrac{15}{9}$

12. Add.
$$\begin{array}{r} 121.347 \\ +\ 28.821 \end{array}$$

F 150.168

G 149.168

H 142.168

J 50.168

13. Multiply. 3240×720

A 23,332,900

B 2,332,800

C 2,132,900

D 1,332,802

14. Divide. $88,868 \div 26$

F 3510

G 3510 R21

H 3418

J 3418 R21

15. A bakery produces 1450 muffins per day. About how many dozen muffins are produced in a 5-day work week?

A about 7250 dozen

B about 1450 dozen

C about 604 dozen

D about 506 dozen

16. Which proportion could be used to solve the following problem?

The scale on a map is 1 inch = 50 miles. The distance between two cities is 425 miles. What is the distance on the map?

F $\dfrac{425}{x} = \dfrac{1}{50}$

G $\dfrac{50}{x} = \dfrac{1}{425}$

H $\dfrac{50}{1} = \dfrac{x}{425}$

J $\dfrac{1}{50} = \dfrac{x}{425}$

17. Which number is odd?

A 372,244
B 460,320
C 760,216
D 820,371

18. What is the prime factorization of 300?

F $2^2 \cdot 5^3$
G $2^2 \cdot 3 \cdot 5^3$
H $2^2 \cdot 3 \cdot 5^2$
J $2 \cdot 3 \cdot 5^3$

19. Simplify. $\dfrac{8(7-4)^2 + 3 \cdot 2 \cdot 5}{2}$

A 39
B 51
C 255
D 750

20. You need to control the growing temperature for your bean plants. Which unit of measurement would you use?

F meters
G liters
H grams
J degrees

21. When you measure the temperature of your bean plants (from Question 20) which instrument should you use?

A micrometer
B stick
C thermometer
D ruler

22. How many feet of fencing is needed to fence in a 130 feet by 225 feet area?

F 355 feet
G 385 feet
H 710 feet
J 29,250 feet

23. A recreation park measures 560 meters long by 700 meters wide. A 250-meter by 150-meter area of the park is used for soccer and baseball fields. How much of the area remains?

A 37,500 square meters
B 80,000 square meters
C 354,500 square meters
D 392,000 square meters

24. A painter plans to paint the walls of a living room. In order to help estimate how many cans of paint are needed, what needs to be determined?

F the perimeter of the living room
G the total area of the living room
H the volume of the living room
J the area of the living room walls

25. What is the best geometric description of the figure shown?

A circle
B cylinder
C hemisphere
D sphere

26. What is the approximate measure of the angle shown below?

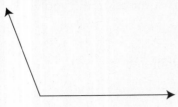

   F   60°
   G 90°
   H 100°
   J 175°

27. I have 6 faces, 8 vertices, and 12 edges. Which figure am I?

   A triangular prism
   B square pyramid
   C cylinder
   D cube

28. Which solid figure can be constructed using the following shapes?

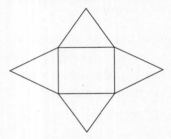

   F square prism
   G square pyramid
   H rectangular prism
   J cube

29. Which shapes make up the bases of the following figure?

   A rectangles
   B triangles
   C squares
   D circles

30. The table shows the number of students who traveled to Florida cities for vacation.

Florida Vacations	
City	Number of Students
Orlando	180
Miami	160
Fort Myers	130
Tallahassee	50

Which pictograph best represents the information in the table?

F

Florida Vacations	
City	Number of Students
Orlando	✿✿✿✿✿✿✿✿✿
Miami	✿✿✿✿✿✿✿✿
Fort Myers	✿✿✿✿✿✿◖
Tallahassee	✿✿◖

each ✿ = 20

G

Florida Vacations	
City	Number of Students
Orlando	✿✿✿✿✿✿✿✿✿
Miami	✿✿✿✿✿✿✿✿
Fort Myers	✿✿✿✿✿✿◖
Tallahassee	✿✿◖

each ✿ = 25

H

Florida Vacations	
City	Number of Students
Orlando	✿✿✿✿✿✿✿✿✿
Miami	✿✿✿✿✿✿✿✿
Fort Myers	✿✿✿✿✿✿◖
Tallahassee	✿✿◖

each ✿ = 50

J

Florida Vacations	
City	Number of Students
Orlando	✿✿✿✿✿✿✿✿✿
Miami	✿✿✿✿✿✿✿✿
Fort Myers	✿✿✿✿✿✿◖
Tallahassee	✿✿◖

each ✿ = 100

Name ____________________ Class __________ Date __________

31. The table shows the number of different colors of marbles a student found when he opened a bag.

Marble Colors	
Color	**Number**
Red	15
Purple	18
Yellow	12
Orange	16
Green	15

What is the probability that he will randomly pick up a yellow marble?

A 25%
B 20%
C 16%
D 12%

32. A spinner is spun and the results are shown in the table below.

Color	Tally
Silver	~~IIII~~ ~~IIII~~ IIII
Gold	I

What is the probability of spinning silver?

F likely
G unlikely
H certain
J impossible

33. Your friend is making sandwiches for lunch. She has the choices of turkey, roast beef, or ham, wheat or white bread, and American, Swiss, or Colby cheese. How many different sandwiches can she make?

A 3
B 8
C 18
D 20

34. What is the probability of spinning a letter B on Spinner 1 and the number 1 on Spinner 2?

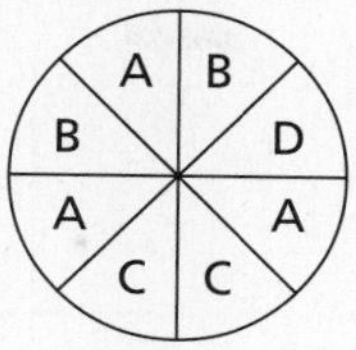

Spinner 1

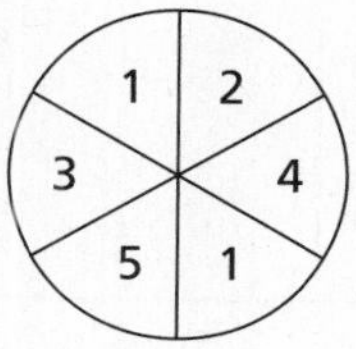

Spinner 2

F $\frac{3}{4}$
G $\frac{1}{2}$
H $\frac{1}{3}$
J $\frac{1}{12}$

35. Which number replaces the question mark in the number pattern shown below?

0, 2, 2, 4, ?, 10, 16, 26, . . .

A 4
B 5
C 6
D 8

36. Which rule describes the pattern?

x	y
5	14
3	10
1	6
	2

F Divide x by 4 and add 3.
G Multiply x by 2 and add 4.
H Add 9 to x.
J Multiply by 6.

37. What are the coordinates of point A?

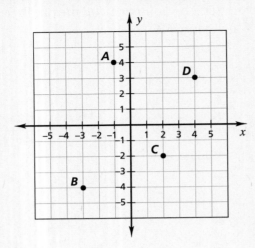

    A $(-3, -4)$
    B $(4, 3)$
    C $(-2, 2)$
    D $(-1, 4)$

38. Evaluate $5(x + y)^2$ when $x = 3$ and $y = 9$.

    F 720
    G 149
    H 120
    J 60

39. Which of the following is the algebraic sentence for "twice a number decreased by 8 is 112"?

    A $2x + 8 = 112$
    B $2x - 8 = 112$
    C $8x = 112$
    D $\dfrac{x}{8} - 2 = 112$

40. Solve.

    $2y + 35 = -7$

    F $y = 14$
    G $y = 21$
    H $y = -14$
    J $y = -21$

41. Solve.

    $6x - 4 = 68$

    A $x = 455$
    B $x = 20$
    C $x = 12$
    D $x = 6$

42. Solve. $\dfrac{m}{9} + 7 = 15$

    F $m = \dfrac{8}{9}$
    G $m = 17$
    H $m = 27$
    J $m = 72$

Name _____ Class _____ Date _____

Screening Test Report

Mathematics Concepts	Test Item(s)	Proficient? Yes or No
Identify the place value and actual value of digits in whole numbers.	1, 2	
Connect model, number word, or number using various models and representations for whole numbers, fractions, and decimals.	3, 4, 5	
Order or compare whole numbers, decimals, or fractions.	6, 7	
Add and subtract: whole numbers.	8, 9	
Add and subtract: fractions with like denominators.	10, 11	
Add and subtract: decimals through ten-thousandths.	12	
Multiply whole numbers: no larger than six-digit by three-digit.	13	
Divide whole numbers: up to six-digit by three-digit.	14	
Solve application problems involving decimal operations.	15	
Use simple ratios to describe problem situations.	16	
Identify odd and even numbers.	17	
Identify factors of whole numbers.	18	
Apply basic properties of operations.	19	
Identify the attribute that is appropriate to measure in a given situation.	20	
Select or use appropriate measurement instruments such as ruler, meter stick, clock, thermometer, or other scaled instruments.	21	
Solve problems involving perimeter of plane figures, providing the formula as part of the problem.	22	
Solve problems involving area of rectangles, providing the formula as part of the problem.	23	
Select or use appropriate type of unit for the attribute being measured such as length, time, or temperature.	24	
Describe (informally) real world objects using simple plane and simple solid figures.	25	
Identify or draw angles and other geometric figures in the plane.	26	
Describe attributes of two- and three-dimensional shapes.	27	
Assemble simple plane shapes to construct a given shape.	28	
Recognize two-dimensional faces of three-dimensional shapes.	29	

Mathematics Concepts	Test Item(s)	Proficient? Yes or No
Pictograms, bar graphs, circle graphs, line graphs, line plots, tables, and tallies.	30	
Read or interpret a single set of data. Use informal probabilistic thinking to describe chance events (i.e., likely and unlikely, certain and impossible).	31, 32	
List all possible outcomes of a given situation or event.	33	
Represent the probability of a given outcome from pictures of spinners and other devices.	34	
Recognize, describe, or extend numerical patterns.	35	
Translate between the different forms of representations (symbolic, numerical, verbal, or pictorial) of whole-number relationships (such as from a written description to an equation or from a function table to a written description).	36	
Graph or interpret points with whole-number or letter coordinates on grids or in the first quadrant of the coordinate plane.	37	
Use letters and symbols to represent an unknown quantity in a simple mathematical expression.	38	
Express simple mathematical relationships using number sentences.	39	
Find the value of the unknown in a whole-number sentence.	40, 41, 42	

Student Comments:

_____

_____

_____

_____

Parent Comments:

_____

_____

_____

_____

Teacher Comments:

_____

_____

_____

_____

Weekly Practice Overview

OVERVIEW

Looking Back	Mathematics of the Week	Looking Ahead
Students have previously examined the basic concepts of points, lines, and angles (G.CO.A.1). In Algebra 1, students learned how to solve linear equations (A.REI.B.3).	Students should understand the basic tools of geometry: points, lines, planes, and angles. They should also be able to measure and calculate the measure of segments and angles.	Later this chapter, students will further explore measuring line segments as they study distance in the coordinate plane (G.GPE.B.6, G.GPE.B.7).

COMMON CORE CONTENT STANDARDS

G.CO.A.1 Know precise definitions of angle,…, based on the undefined notions of point, line, distance along a line,…

G.GPE.B.6 Find the point on a directed line segment between two given points that partitions the segment in a given ratio.

Mathematical Practice Standards: 1, 2, 5, 6
Materials: Ruler

TEACHING NOTES

Selected Response

1. *Error Analysis*: Students show understanding of the basic elements of plane geometry. If a student chooses A or B, he or she is confusing the relationships between lines, segments, and rays. Review the definitions of these terms by drawing examples of each on the board for students to identify. If a student chooses C, he or she does not understand that there is an infinite number of lines in a plane.

Constructed Response

2. Students calculate distance between two points given other distances. If students have trouble starting the problem, suggest they begin by labeling point 0. Ask them how they will determine the position of the points on the line. Students may first wish to determine the position of points M and L by using the given length for ML. Once students have plotted these points, they may use point L and the length of KL to find point K. They can then use the same reasoning to find the position of point J.

Extended Response

3. Students calculate the value of a pair of angles using basic algebra. Remind students that when two angles form a linear pair, they are supplementary, which means the angles add up to 180°. If students have difficulty solving for x, guide them to substitute the expressions they know in the equation $m\angle ABC + m\angle CBD = 180$. Once students determine the value of x, they can substitute that value to find the angle measurements.

Common Core Standards Practice

Week 1

Selected Response

1. Which of the following statements is true?

   A A line is part of a segment.
   B A line is part of a ray.
   C A plane contains a finite number of lines.
   D A line extends in two opposite directions without end.

Constructed Response

2. Points M, K, L, and J lie on a line.

   a. Label points on the line so that J is between M and L, $ML = 11$, $KL = 14$, and $KJ = 9$.

   b. What is MJ?

Extended Response

3. $\angle ABC$ and $\angle CBD$ form a linear pair. $m\angle ABC = 3x + 10$ and $m\angle CBD = 22x + 45$.

   a. Find x.

   b. Find $m\angle ABC$ and $m\angle CBD$.

   c. Show how you can check your answer.

OVERVIEW

Looking Back	Mathematics of the Week	Looking Ahead
Students in previous grades have worked with finding the distance between two points on a coordinate plane (8.G.B.8).	Students perform basic geometric constructions. They also determine the distance between two points, often assisted through values on the coordinate plane.	In Chapters 4 and 6, students will examine the dimensions of polygons plotted on a coordinate plane (G.GPE.B.7, G.SRT.B.5).

COMMON CORE CONTENT STANDARDS

G.CO.D.12 Make formal geometric constructions with a variety of tools and methods (compass and straightedge, . . .).

G.GPE.B.6 Find the point on a directed line segment between two given points that partitions the segment in a given ratio.

Mathematical Practice Standards: 1, 2, 5
Materials: Compass and straightedge

TEACHING NOTES

Selected Response

1. *Error Analysis*: Students calculate the midpoint when given the coordinates of the endpoints of a line segment. If a student selects answer choice A, he or she found the correct y-coordinate but made a mistake finding the proper x-coordinate of the midpoint, most likely by not accounting for the negative sign in –2. If a student selects answer choice C, he or she added the two given y-coordinates but did not find the average. If a student selects answer choice D, he or she may have subtracted the two given y-coordinates instead of finding the average.

Constructed Response

2. Students use given line segments to construct another line segment of a given length. Ask students to describe their plan for constructing segment *AB*. Students should indicate that they need to draw a straight line segment using a straightedge, and then construct each of the two given line segments *FG* and *JK* end-to-end. Ask students how the construction of line segment *AB* is similar to adding two digits to find a sum.

Extended Response

3. Students calculate the distance between points on a coordinate plane. Remind students of the Distance Formula and how it is used to find the length of a line segment. Remind them to work carefully when subtracting with negative numbers. If time permits, suggest that students first plot the four points on a coordinate grid. Have students use their diagrams to check whether or not their results make sense.

Common Core Standards Practice

Week 2

Selected Response

1. What is the midpoint of the line segment connecting $(-2, 7)$ and $(4, 15)$?

A $(3, 11)$

B $(1, 11)$

C $(1, 22)$

D $(1, 8)$

Constructed Response

2. Construct $\overline{AB}$ so that $FG + JK = AB$.

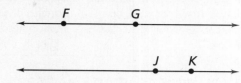

Extended Response

3. a. Consider the points $A(2, 8)$, $B(5, 4)$, $C(-1, 4)$, $D(-4, 0)$. Find AB, AC, AD, BC, BD, and CD.

b. Write the names of the segments in the correct cell of the table.

Length of Segment = 5	Length of Segment ≠ 5

OVERVIEW

Looking Back	Mathematics of the Week	Looking Ahead
Students have used logical reasoning to arrive at valid conclusions when solving problems (A.REI.A.1).	Students should arrive at conclusions through logical reasoning and understand and logically construct proofs.	Throughout the Geometry course, students will prove various theorems (G.CO.C.9, G.CO.C.10, G.CO.C.11).

COMMON CORE CONTENT STANDARDS

F.IF.A.3 Recognize that sequences are functions, sometimes defined recursively, whose domain is a subset of the integers;

G.CO.C.9 Prove theorems about lines and angles.

G.CO.C.10 Prove theorems about triangles.

G.CO.C.11 Prove theorems about parallelograms.

Mathematical Practice Standards: 1, 2, 3, 6, 7

TEACHING NOTES

Selected Response

1. *Error Analysis*: Students show understanding of the term counterexample. If a student selects answer choice A, he or she has not judged the conditional correctly and has not found a counterexample. If the student answers B or C, he or she is not choosing a valid counterexample, since both 4 and 15 are not prime numbers.

2. *Error Analysis*: Students continue a pattern of letters. If a student selects answer choices B, C, or D, he or she has not found the correct alphabetical sequence. Have students write out the first 15 letters of the alphabet and circle the letters in the question to help them derive a pattern.

Constructed Response

3. Students show their understanding of logic. Ask students to identify the hypothesis and conclusion of the conditional. Make sure students know that the second statement is a subset of the conditional's conclusion, and not a subset of the hypothesis. Remind students that the Law of Detachment requires that the second statement must match the hypothesis of the conditional in order to make a valid conclusion.

Extended Response

4. Students match the reasons for each statement in a proof. Keep in mind that this chapter will be the first formal introduction to constructing proofs for most students. Before they begin the problem, read aloud each reason in the proof to the class. As you read, ask for volunteers to define or explain each reason. Remind students that as they solve problems, they are often using logic based on the reasons found in proofs.

Common Core Standards Practice

Week 3

Selected Response

1. Is the following statement true? If it is false, choose a correct counterexample.

    If a number is prime, then it is odd.

A True
B False; 4 is even.
C False; 15 is odd.
D False; 2 is even.

2. What are the next two terms in the sequence?

        a, d, g, j, m,…

A p, s
B n, o
C n, q
D m, p

Constructed Response

3. Use the Law of Detachment to draw a conclusion. If it is not possible, then state why.

    If you get in your car, then you will drive to the store.

    You are seen shopping at the store.

Extended Response

4. The points *J*, *K*, and *L* are arranged on the line as shown below. $JK = KL$, $JK = 3x + 9$, $JL = 45$. Prove that $x = 4.5$. Fill in the blanks using the following reasons: Transitive Property of Equality, Given, Substitution, Division Property of Equality.

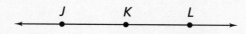

Statements	Reasons
1) $JK = KL$	1) Given
2) $JK = 3x + 9$	2) Given
3) $KL = 3x + 9$	3) _____
4) $JL = JK + KL$	4) Segment Addition Postulate
5) $JL = 3x + 9 + 3x + 9$	5) _____
6) $JL = 6x + 18$	6) Combining Like Terms
7) $JL = 45$	7) _____
8) $6x + 18 = 45$	8) Transitive Property of Equality
9) $6x = 27$	9) Subtraction Property of Equality
10) $x = 4.5$	10) _____

OVERVIEW

Looking Back	Mathematics of the Week	Looking Ahead
Students have worked with slopes of parallel lines in Algebra 1 (G.GPE.B.5).	Students should understand the properties of parallel lines, including how angles made by them and a transversal are related.	In Chapter 6 students will apply the properties of parallel lines when studying parallelograms (G.CO.C.11).

COMMON CORE CONTENT STANDARDS

G.CO.C.9 Prove theorems about lines and angles.

Mathematical Practice Standards: 1, 2, 3

TEACHING NOTES

Selected Response

1. *Error Analysis*: Students calculate the measure of one angle given the measure of another angle in a figure. If a student selects answer choice A, he or she is likely subtracting 90 from the given angle measure of 131. If a student selects answer choice B, he or she is finding the measure of the supplementary angle to $\angle 3$, and not the measure of the congruent $\angle 6$. If a student selects answer choice D, he or she may be subtracting the measure of $\angle 3$ from 360.

Constructed Response

2. Students use theorems about parallel lines to find the measure of an angle. Ask students to draw or describe how to draw the situation described in the exercise. Tell them to keep in mind that the measure of $\angle B$ is 89. Remind students of the Alternate Interior Angles Theorem. Encourage students to draw the situation for the problem. It may help to make angle B have a smaller acute measure. Ask them to first determine if $\angle A$ is congruent or supplementary to $\angle B$. Make sure students set $4x - 7$ equal to 89 when solving the exercise.

Extended Response

3. Students match reasons to statements in an incomplete proof. Remind students that they have already proved that if $r \parallel s$ then $\angle 1$ and $\angle 7$ are supplementary. Now, they will prove that if $\angle 1$ and $\angle 7$ are supplementary, then $r \parallel s$. Briefly review which angles in the figure are congruent. As the angles are discussed, make two lists showing congruent groups of angles. Ask volunteers to offer pairs of supplementary angles, making a third list as pairs are offered. Make sure the angle pair 1 and 7 are listed. Ask volunteers to state the definitions of the Substitution Property, the Converse of the Same Side Interior Angles Postulate, and the Vertical Angles Theorem before beginning the exercise.

Common Core Standards Practice   Week 4

Selected Response

1. If $m\angle 3 = 131$, what is $m\angle 6$?

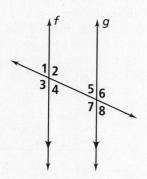

A 41
B 49
C 131
D 229

Constructed Response

2. $\angle A$ and $\angle B$ are alternate interior angles formed by two parallel lines and a transversal. $m\angle A = 4x - 7$ and $m\angle B = 89$. Find x.

Extended Response

3. Prove that $r \parallel s$ if $\angle 1$ and $\angle 7$ are supplementary by writing the correct reason in the appropriate place.

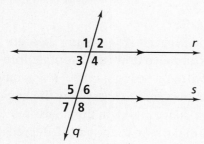

Fill in the blanks using the following reasons:
- Substitution Property
- Converse of the Same-Side Interior Angles Postulate
- Vertical Angles Theorem

Statements	Reasons
1) $\angle 1$ and $\angle 7$ are supplementary.	**1)** Given
2) $\angle 1 \cong \angle 4$	**2)** Vertical Angles Theorem
3) $\angle 4$ and $\angle 7$ are supplementary.	**3)** _____
4) $\angle 7 \cong \angle 6$	**4)** _____
5) $\angle 4$ and $\angle 6$ are supplementary.	**5)** Substitution Property
6) $r \parallel s$	**6)** _____

OVERVIEW

Looking Back	Mathematics of the Week	Looking Ahead
In Algebra 1 students learned the relationship between slopes of parallel lines and the relationship between slopes of perpendicular lines (G.GPE.B.5). Students have also previously studied the relationship of angles within triangles (G.CO.C.10).	Students should understand the differences between parallel and perpendicular lines. They also should understand the nature of the interior and exterior angles of a triangle.	In Algebra 2 students will review the relationships between parallel and perpendicular lines and will use interior angles of triangles with trigonometric equations (G.GPE.B.5, G.CO.C.10).

COMMON CORE CONTENT STANDARDS

G.CO.C.10 Prove theorems about triangles...measures of interior angles of a triangle sum to 180°...

G.MG.A.3 Apply geometric methods to solve design problems.

Mathematical Practice Standards: 1, 2, 3, 4

TEACHING NOTES

Selected Response

1. *Error Analysis*: Students show understanding of parallel and perpendicular lines in a plane. If a student selects answer choice B, he or she is likely missing or misinterpreting one step of the exercise. If a student selects answer choices C or D, he or she does not understand the facts stated in the exercise.

Constructed Response

2. Students calculate angle measures in a triangle using the Triangle Angle-Sum Theorem. Review the Triangle Angle-Sum Theorem with students and also how the Alternate Interior Angles Theorem proves that the sum of the angles within a triangle is 180. Then, have students draw an illustration of triangle *ABC* and an auxiliary line to show how the angles add up to 180. Students should label the angles at the auxiliary line with the measures given in the exercise. When students solve the exercise, make sure they use 180 degrees as the sum of the angles.

Extended Response

3. Students match reasons to statements in an incomplete proof. Review the listed theorems and definitions. Suggest to students that they make a drawing to better visualize the situation to use as they complete the proof. The drawing should show triangle *ABC*, the angles *A*, *B*, and *C*, and the exterior angles 1, 2, and 3, labeled according to the exercise. If students have difficulty with Step 10, remind them to combine what they know from Step 8 and Step 9.

Common Core Standards Practice

Week 5

Selected Response

1. Lines *a*, *b*, and *c* exist in the same coordinate plane. $a \perp b$ and $b \perp c$. Which of the following statements is true?

   A $a \parallel c$
   B $a \perp c$
   C $b \parallel c$
   D $a \parallel b$

Constructed Response

2. In $\triangle ABC$, $m\angle A = 24$, $m\angle B = x$ and $m\angle C = 2x$. Find $m\angle B$ and $m\angle C$.

Extended Response

3. Consider $\triangle ABC$. The exterior angles of $\triangle ABC$ are $\angle 1$, $\angle 2$, and $\angle 3$, respectively. Prove that the sum of the measures of the exterior angles of the triangle is 360. Use the reasons below to complete the proof. Some reasons may be used more than once.

   - Angles that form a linear pair are supplementary.
   - Triangle Angle-Sum Theorem
   - Definition of supplementary angles

   - Subtraction Property of Equality
   - Addition Property of Equality
   - Substitution Property

Statements	Reasons
1) *ABC* is a triangle with exterior angles 1, 2, and 3.	1) Given
2) $\angle 1$ and $\angle A$ are supplementary.	2) Angles that form a linear pair are supplementary.
3) $m\angle 1 + m\angle A = 180$	3) _____
4) $\angle 2$ and $\angle B$ are supplementary.	4) Angles that form a linear pair are supplementary.
5) $m\angle 2 + m\angle B = 180$	5) _____
6) $\angle 3$ and $\angle C$ are supplementary.	6) Angles that form a linear pair are supplementary.
7) $m\angle 3 + m\angle C = 180$	7) _____
8) $m\angle 1 + m\angle A + m\angle 2 + m\angle B + m\angle 3 + m\angle C = 540$	8) _____
9) $m\angle A + m\angle B + m\angle C = 180$	9) _____
10) $m\angle 1 + m\angle 2 + m\angle 3 + 180 = 540$	10) _____
11) $m\angle 1 + m\angle 2 + m\angle 3 = 360$	11) _____

OVERVIEW

Looking Back	Mathematics of the Week	Looking Ahead
In Chapter 1 students learned how to make some basic constructions (G.CO.D.12). In Algebra 1 students learned about slopes of lines including parallel and perpendicular lines (G.GPE.B.5).	Students need to be able to construct parallel lines. They also need to understand parallel and perpendicular lines in the context of linear equations.	In Chapter 12 students will construct perpendicular lines to find the center of a circle (G.CO.D.12). In Algebra 2, students will work more with linear equations (A.CED.A.2, F.IF.B.4).

COMMON CORE CONTENT STANDARDS

G.CO.D.12 Make formal geometric constructions with a variety of tools and methods…constructing a line parallel to a given line through a point not on the line…

G.GPE.B.5 Prove the slope criteria for parallel and perpendicular lines and use them to solve geometric problems.

Mathematical Practice Standards: 1, 4, 5, 6, 7, 8
Materials: Compass and straightedge

TEACHING NOTES

Selected Response

1. *Error Analysis*: Students show understanding of the equations of vertical lines. If the student answers B, he or she is likely confusing vertical and horizontal, or parallel and perpendicular. If the student answers C or D, he or she does not understand how the slope of a line relates to its equation.

Constructed Response

2. Students construct a parallel line. If students have difficulty remembering how to construct a parallel line, suggest they draw the line DG, and consider it to be a transversal between line GH and the new line that will be parallel to line GH. Remind them that corresponding angles are congruent, and ask how they could construct congruent corresponding angles.

Extended Response

3. Students determine the slope of lines perpendicular to a given line. Remind students that when an equation is in the form $y = mx + b$, the slope of the line is equal to m. Practice rewriting linear equations in two variables so that they are in the form, $y = mx + b$. Students should know that the product of the slopes of two perpendicular lines is –1.

Common Core Standards Practice

Week 6

Selected Response

1. Which equation when graphed is parallel to any vertical line?

   A $x = 3$
   B $y = 4$
   C $x = y$
   D $y = x + 8$

Constructed Response

2. Construct a line through point D that is parallel to $\overline{GH}$.

Extended Response

3. **a.** Find the slope of each line represented by an equation below.

   b. Which of the following equations represent lines that are perpendicular to the line with equation $y = 3(x - 1)$? Write each equation in the appropriate box.

   $$y = 3x + 8$$ $$5x + 15y = 1$$

   $$y = -3x + 10$$ $$y = -\frac{1}{3}x - 5$$

   $$3x - 9y = 14$$

Perpendicular to $y = 3(x-1)$	Not Perpendicular to $y = 3(x-1)$

Common Core Standards Practice

For use after Lessons 4-1 through 4-4

OVERVIEW

Looking Back	Mathematics of the Week	Looking Ahead
In previous grades students have worked with similar triangles in a variety of ways (8.G.A.4, 8.G.A.5).	Students should understand the properties of congruent triangles, how to determine whether triangles are congruent, and how to use congruent triangles to solve problems.	In Chapter 9, students will revisit congruent triangles when working with congruence transformations (G.CO.B.7).

COMMON CORE CONTENT STANDARDS

G.CO.C.10 Prove theorems about triangles.

G.SRT.B.5 Use congruence and similarity criteria for triangles to solve problems and to prove relationships in geometric figures.

Mathematical Practice Standards: 1, 2, 3, 6

TEACHING NOTES

Selected Response

1. *Error Analysis*: Students show understanding of the definition of congruent triangles. If a student answers B, C, or D, he or she is confusing the order of the vertices and is not matching corresponding parts of congruent triangles.

Constructed Response

2. Students use the Distance Formula to compare triangles. Discuss with students triangle congruence by the SSS Postulate. Using the two given triangles, have volunteers describe corresponding angles and sides. Ask students how they will know which postulate to use in this exercise. Then ask them to describe a plan of how they will solve the exercise. As students work, make sure they compare the correct corresponding sides as they find the lengths of the sides.

Extended Response

3. Students show understanding of the triangle congruence postulates. Remind students that congruent figures have the same size and shape. If time permits, work through an example of constructing a congruent triangle to a shape you create, similar to the exercise. When you present your example, make sure to include two to three restrictions similar to those in the exercise. As you complete the example for students, note the steps you take to make sure all restrictions are met. As students begin the exercise, ask them to consider a plan when constructing the congruent triangle. When students explain the postulate that proves the triangles are congruent, make sure the postulate corresponds to the reasoning they present.

Common Core Standards Practice   Week 7

Selected Response

1. If $\triangle ABC \cong \triangle DEF$, which of the following statements is true?

    A $\overline{CB} \cong \overline{FE}$

    B $\overline{AC} \cong \overline{DE}$

    C $\overline{AC} \cong \overline{EF}$

    D $\overline{BC} \cong \overline{DE}$

Constructed Response

2. Consider the points $J(2, 3)$, $K(5, 7)$, $L(8, 3)$, $M(-2, 1)$, $N(1, 5)$, $O(4, 1)$. Is $\triangle JKL \cong \triangle MNO$? Justify your answer.

Extended Response

3. a. Construct a triangle that is congruent to the triangle shown below. The entire triangle must be in the first quadrant, $m\angle B = 90$, and one vertex must be at $(1, 1)$.

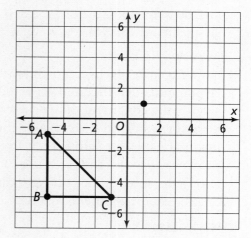

    b. Which postulate proves that the triangles are congruent? Explain.

Common Core Standards Practice

OVERVIEW

Looking Back	Mathematics of the Week	Looking Ahead
Earlier in Chapter 4 students proved that triangles are congruent using various methods (G.SRT.B.5, G.CO.C.10).	Students should be able to work with congruent triangles to solve problems and prove relationships in these triangles.	In Chapter 9, students will revisit congruent triangles when working with congruence transformations (G.CO.B.7).

COMMON CORE CONTENT STANDARDS

G.SRT.B.5 Use congruence and similarity criteria for triangles to solve problems and to prove relationships in geometric figures.

Mathematical Practice Standards: 1, 2, 3

TEACHING NOTES

Selected Response

1. *Error Analysis*: Students use understanding of vocabulary about triangles to find the measure of an angle. If a student selects answer choice A, he or she has likely made an error considering the angle measures of equilateral triangles. If a student selects answer choice C, he or she is likely giving the measure of an angle in an equilateral triangle instead of the measure of ∠DCB. If a student selects answer choice D, he or she is likely giving the measure of ∠ADC or ∠BDC.

Constructed Response

2. Students solve algebraic equations they set up using congruence statements. Review the Hypotenuse-Leg Theorem with students. Then have students identify the corresponding sides in the congruent triangles. When solving the problem, some students may find it helpful to label the diagram with the given information. As students work to solve for x, make sure they are setting the correct corresponding parts equal to each other. Students should realize that they only need to solve for x using either the corresponding hypotenuse measures or the corresponding leg measures, but not both. They can check their answer using the other equation.

Extended Response

3. Students match the reasons to the correct statements to complete the proof. Revisit the Vertical Angles Theorem, the SAS Postulate, and the definition of equilateral triangles with students. Then ask volunteers to point out the corresponding parts of triangles *MLR* and *PNR*. If students have difficulty when working with the potential reasons, invite them to label the diagram by adding congruence marks to better keep track of what they know. Point out to students that while the figure appears to be a rectangle they cannot assume that it is as they solve it. Instead they should use the given statements to prove the triangles congruent.

Common Core Standards Practice   **Week 8**

Selected Response

1. $\triangle ABC$ is an equilateral triangle.
$\triangle ACD \cong \triangle BCD$; $\overline{CD}$ bisects $\angle ACB$.
What is $m\angle DCB$?

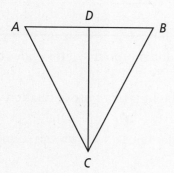

    A 15
    B 30
    C 60
    D 90

Constructed Response

2. Given:
   $AB = 12, BC = 2x + 3,$
   $DF = 13, FH = 6x - 18$
For what value of x are the triangles congruent by the Hypotenuse-Leg Theorem?

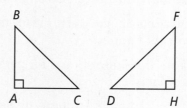

Extended Response

3. Given: $\triangle LRN$ is equilateral; $\overline{MR} \cong \overline{PR}$
   Prove: $\triangle MLR \cong \triangle PNR$

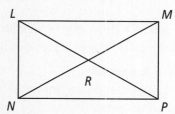

Rearrange the potential reasons to align properly with the corresponding statements. Write them in order in the middle column of the table.

Statements	Reasons	Potential Reasons
1) $\triangle LRN$ is equilateral; $\overline{MR} \cong \overline{PR}$	1) _____	Vertical Angles Theorem
		SAS Postulate
2) $\overline{LR} \cong \overline{NR}$	2) _____	Given
3) $\angle LRM \cong \angle NRP$	3) _____	Definition of equilateral $\triangle$
4) $\triangle MLR \cong \triangle PNR$	4) _____	

Common Core Standards Practice

For use after Lessons 5-1

OVERVIEW

Looking Back	Mathematics of the Week	Looking Ahead
In Chapter 1, students solved problems involving the midpoints of line segments (G.GPE.B.6).	Students use the properties and relationships of midsegments of triangles to solve problems.	In Chapter 6, students will use midsegments when exploring trapezoids (G.SRT.B.5).

COMMON CORE CONTENT STANDARDS

G.CO.C.10 Prove theorems about triangles...the segment joining midpoints of two sides of a triangle is parallel to the third side and half the length....

G.SRT.B.5 Use congruence...criteria for triangles to solve problems and to prove relationships in geometric figures.

G.GPE.B.5 Prove the slope criteria for parallel and perpendicular lines and use them to solve geometric problems.

G.GPE.B.7 Use coordinates to compute perimeters of polygons and areas of triangles and rectangles, e.g., using the distance formula.

Mathematical Practice Standards: 1, 2, 3, 4

TEACHING NOTES

Selected Response

1. *Error Analysis*: Students show understanding of the Midsegment Theorem. If a student selects answer choice A, he or she is dividing by 2 instead of multiplying by 2. If a student selects answer choice B, he or she did not understand the question. If a student selects answer choice D, he or she is miscalculating or not using the correct ratio of the midsegment of a triangle and the third side of the triangle.

Constructed Response

2. Students use the Midsegment Theorem to solve an algebraic equation. Remind students that the information needed to solve a problem may be in the drawing as it is here. Ask what is the significance of the line segment drawn between the two congruent pairs of line segments. Make sure students realize this is the midsegment of the triangle. Ask a volunteer to explain the relationship between the midsegment and the third side of the triangle. As students solve for x, make sure they set the length of the third side to two times the length of the midsegment.

Extended Response

3. Students will informally prove two statements using points on a coordinate plane. Review with students how to find the slope of a line using the coordinates of two points on the line, and that parallel lines have the same slope. Also review the Distance Formula with students. Students may prove the lines are parallel by finding the slopes and prove $AB = \left(\dfrac{1}{2}\right)DF$ with the actual calculations.

Common Core Standards Practice

Week 9

Selected Response

1. D is the midpoint of $\overline{AB}$. G is the midpoint of $\overline{BC}$. $DG = 5$. What is AC?

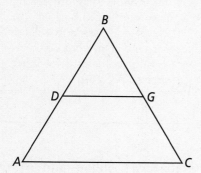

A 2.5
B 5
C 10
D 15

Constructed Response

2. What is the value of x?

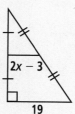

Extended Response

3. a. Prove $\overline{AB} \parallel \overline{DF}$ using the slope formula.

b. Prove $AB = \dfrac{1}{2}$ using the Distance Formula.

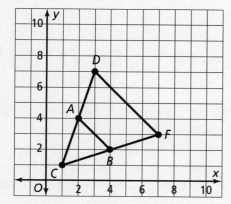

OVERVIEW

Looking Back	Mathematics of the Week	Looking Ahead
In Chapter 1, students worked with perpendicular bisectors and angle bisectors, including how to construct bisectors (G.CO.A.1, G.CO.D.12).	Students should understand perpendicular bisectors and angle bisectors, and their properties. Students also need to use relationships from triangles formed using these bisectors.	In Chapter 7, students will apply angle bisectors to the Triangle-Angle-Bisector Theorem (G.SRT.B.4). In Chapter 12, students will use perpendicular lines when solving problems involving circles (G.C.A.2).

COMMON CORE CONTENT STANDARDS

G.CO.D.10 Prove theorems about triangles.

G.SRT.B.5 Use congruence and similarity criteria for triangles to solve problems and to prove relationships in geometric figures.

Mathematical Practice Standards: 1, 2, 3

TEACHING NOTES

Selected Response

1. *Error Analysis*: Students use understanding of isosceles triangles to solve this problem. If a student selects answer choices A or C, he or she has likely miscalculated the proportion of the angle bisector. If a student selects answer choice D, he or she is giving the given measure of *RS* instead of the measure of *WS*.

Constructed Response

2. Students write and solve an algebraic equation that matches the measures of the sides shown in this problem. Remind students of the Perpendicular Bisector Theorem by asking a volunteer to restate the theorem. Since *S* is a point on the bisector, tell students that points *W* and *T* are equidistant from *S*, and that line segments *WS* and *ST* are congruent to each other. Make sure students set the measures of these two line segments equal to each other when solving for *x*.

Extended Response

3. Students prove statements using coordinates of a figure. Review the Distance Formula with students. Tell students that, although the relationship shown is about an angle, here they will be using the Distance Formula and Slope Formula. Students will prove that $AD = DB$ with calculations. As students prepare for the second part of the exercise, ask them to speculate how the information they just proved will assist them in proving that $\overline{CD}$ is the perpendicular bisector of $\overline{DF}$. Tell students that they may use the coordinate grid to help find slopes of lines and lengths of line segments. Students may be aware that they will be showing the Converse of the Perpendicular Bisector Theorem with this proof.

Common Core Standards Practice   Week 10

Selected Response

1. $\overline{WT}$ is the angle bisector of $\angle STR$.
If $m\angle S = m\angle R$ and $RS = 8$, what is WS?

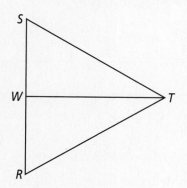

A 2
B 4
C 6
D 8

Constructed Response

2. $\overline{RS}$ is the perpendicular bisector of $\overline{WT}$. $WS = 7x + 4$ and $ST = 53$. Find x.

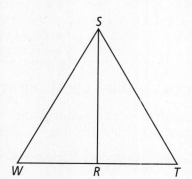

Extended Response

3. $\overline{CD}$ is the angle bisector of $\angle ACB$.
  a. Using the Distance Formula, prove that $AD = DB$.

  b. Prove that $\overline{CD}$ is the perpendicular bisector of $\overline{AB}$.

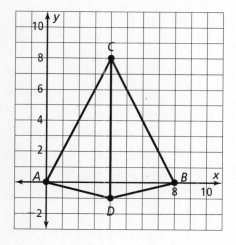

Common Core Standards Practice

Week 11

OVERVIEW

Looking Back	Mathematics of the Week	Looking Ahead
In Chapter 1 students learned about perpendicular bisectors and angle bisectors, including how to construct these bisectors (G.CO.A.1, G.CO.D.12).	Students use their understanding of circumcenters and inscribed and circumscribed circles of triangles. They also use the properties of midsegments to solve problems.	In Chapter 12, students will study inscribed angles within circles (G.C.A.2).

COMMON CORE MATHEMATICAL CONTENT STANDARDS

G.CO.C.10 Prove theorems about triangles...the segment joining midpoints of two sides of a triangle is parallel to the third side and half the length....

G.CO.D.12 Make formal geometric constructions with a variety of tools and methods.

G.SRT.B.5 Use congruence...criteria for triangles to solve problems and to prove relationships in geometric figures.

G.C.A.2 Identify and describe relationships among inscribed angles, radii, and chords.

G.C.A.3 Construct the inscribed and circumscribed circles of a triangle....

Common Core Mathematical Practice Standards: 1, 2, 5, 6
Materials: Compass and straightedge

TEACHING NOTES

Selected Response

1. *Error Analysis*: Students find the coordinates for the circumcenter of a triangle given the coordinates of the vertices. If a student selects answer choice A or B, he or she is likely confusing the order of the coordinates. If a student selects answer choice B or C, he or she is likely making an error in the sign when finding the midpoints.

Constructed Response

2. Students use the properties of midsegments to find their lengths. Ask students to reiterate what they know about the length of midsegments of triangles. Tell them to consider this knowledge when setting the two statements equal to each other. Make sure students set the length of segment *AB* equal to 2 times the length of segment *DE*.

Extended Response

3. Students construct a triangle along with the inscribed and circumscribed circle. Review the definitions of inscribed and circumscribed circles, relative to triangles. Remind students that to draw each type, they will need to construct bisectors. Ask which type of bisector will be needed to draw the inscribed circle. Then ask which type of bisector will be needed to draw the circumscribed circle. Make sure students understand that the center of an inscribed circle will always be inside the triangle.

Common Core Standards Practice   Week 11

Selected Response

1. What are the coordinates of the circumcenter for $\triangle ABC$?

$A(0, 5), B(-4, 5), C(-4, -3)$

A $(-1, 2)$
B $(1, -2)$
C $(2, -1)$
D $(-2, 1)$

Constructed Response

2. Find the value of x.

$DE = 6x$

$AB = 4x + 32$

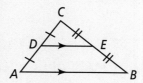

Extended Response

3. a. Draw an obtuse triangle and construct the inscribed and circumscribed circle.

b. Describe your method.

OVERVIEW

Looking Back	Mathematics of the Week	Looking Ahead
In previous grades, students worked with parallelograms (G.GPE.B.7). In Algebra 1, students learned how to solve linear equations (A.REI.B.3).	Students find the sum of the angle measures in a polygon. They also apply properties of parallelograms.	In Chapter 10 students will continue to work with parallelograms (G.GPE.B.7). Throughout Geometry, students will prove various theorems (G.CO.C.9, G.CO.C.10, G.CO.C.11).

COMMON CORE MATHEMATICAL CONTENT STANDARDS

G.CO.C.11 Prove theorems about parallelograms.

G.SRT.B.5 Use congruence . . . criteria for triangles to solve problems and to prove relationships in geometric figures.

Common Core Mathematical Practice Standards: 1, 2, 3, 7

TEACHING NOTES

Selected Response

1. *Error Analysis*: Students find the sum of the angle measures of a polygon with 10 sides. If the student selects answer choice A, he or she is likely applying the formula incorrectly and multiplying 180 by n instead of $(n - 2)$. If a student selects answer choice C, he or she probably does not understand the concept and is giving the sum of the angle measures of a triangle or simply giving part of the formula. If a student selects answer choice D, he or she computes an answer that is off by a factor of 10.

Constructed Response

2. Students use the properties of a parallelogram to find the lengths of parts of the diagonals. Although there are two variables in the figure, in this exercise students are solving two single-variable equations. Review general properties of parallelograms with students. Then ask them how to use the relationships among diagonals of parallelograms to solve this exercise. As students work through the exercise, make sure they are setting the correct pairs of congruent segments equal, and that they realize not all four segments will necessarily be equal to each other.

Extended Response

3. Students prove that a figure is a parallelogram given that its diagonals bisect each other. Review the various ways to determine whether a figure is a parallelogram. Then ask students to state what they know from the given information. Tell students that they may work backwards, and find ways to prove the statement. Have them look for ways they can use the givens to get the desired conclusion. If students have difficulty getting started, suggest they write the ways they can prove a quadrilateral is a parallelogram and use this as a guide as they manipulate the given information.

Common Core Standards Practice

Week 12

Selected Response

1. What is the sum of the angle measures of a decagon?

   A 1800

   B 1440

   C 180

   D 144

Constructed Response

2. Solve to find the values of *x* and *y* in the parallelogram.

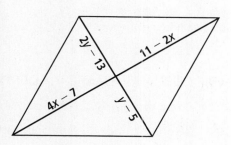

Extended Response

3. $\overline{LN}$ and $\overline{MO}$ bisect each other at *P*. Prove that *LMNO* is a parallelogram.

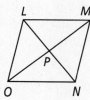

OVERVIEW

Looking Back	Mathematics of the Week	Looking Ahead
In previous grades, students worked with parallelograms and rectangles (G.GPE.B.7). In Algebra 1, students learned how to solve linear equations (A.REI.B.3).	Students work with the properties of parallelograms, rectangles, and trapezoids.	In Chapter 10, students will continue to work with parallelograms (G.GPE.B.7). They will also learn how to find the area of trapezoids (G.MG.A.1).

COMMON CORE MATHEMATICAL CONTENT STANDARDS

G.CO.C.11 Prove theorems about parallelograms.

G.SRT.B.5 Use congruence ... criteria for triangles to solve problems and to prove relationships in geometric figures.

Mathematical Practice Standards: 1, 2, 3

TEACHING NOTES

Selected Response

1. *Error Analysis*: Students find the length of a diagonal of a rectangle given two equations for their lengths. If a student selects answer choice A, he or she is likely subtracting 12 from 15, instead of adding 12 and 15, when solving for x. If a student selects answer choice B, he or she is stating the value of x instead of substituting and finding the length of the diagonal. If a student selects answer choice C, he or she may be substituting the value of x into the expression for AC without adding 15, or is making another computational error.

Constructed Response

2. Students find the missing measures of the angles of a quadrilateral given a description of the quadrilateral and one angle measure. Remind students of the definition of isosceles trapezoid. You may wish to have a volunteer label for the class a sample isosceles trapezoid, showing congruent angles, congruent sides, and parallel sides. Remind students that in *WXYZ*, two angles that share a leg are supplementary.

Extended Response

3. Students prove that a diagonal bisects an angle of a parallelogram. Explain to students that they will use properties of parallelograms to prove the desired conclusion. Review the properties of parallelograms and of angles formed by a set of parallel lines intersected by a transversal. Remind students that it is important to consider the given information in order to find the direction for starting a proof. Ask students to consider how the given "line segment *AC* bisects angle *DAB*" might be used to find the direction for proving the conclusion "line segment *AC* bisects angle *DCB*." Encourage students to realize that they may need to investigate the relationship between angles in the parallelograms to prove the desired conclusion.

Common Core Standards Practice   Week 13

Selected Response

1. In rectangle $ABCD$, $AC = 2x + 15$ and $DB = 5x - 12$. What is the length of a diagonal?

A 1
B 9
C 18
D 33

Constructed Response

2. Quadrilateral $WXYZ$ is an isosceles trapezoid and $m\angle Z = 74$. What are $m\angle W$, $m\angle X$, and $m\angle Y$?

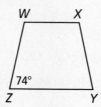

Extended Response

3. **Given:** $ABCD$ is a parallelogram.
$\overline{AC}$ bisects $\angle DAB$.
Prove: $\overline{AC}$ bisects $\angle DCB$.

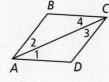

Common Core Standards Practice

OVERVIEW

Looking Back	Mathematics of the Week	Looking Ahead
In Chapter 1, students used the coordinate plane to find distance (G.GPE.B.7). In Algebra 1, students reviewed graphing in the coordinate plane (A.CED.A.2).	Students use the coordinate plane to classify polygons. They also use coordinate geometry to determine relationships involving lines, angles, and figures.	In Chapter 12, students will continue to work with the coordinate plane to find the equation, center, and radius of a circle (G.GPE.A.1).

COMMON CORE MATHEMATICAL CONTENT STANDARDS

G.GPE.A.4 Use coordinates to prove simple geometric theorems algebraically.

G.SRT.A.5 Use coordinates to compute perimeters of polygons....

Common Core Mathematical Practice Standards: 1, 2, 3, 6

TEACHING NOTES

Selected Response

1. *Error Analysis*: Students choose the most precise name for a quadrilateral given the coordinates of the vertices. If a student selects answer choice A, he or she is likely confusing which two pairs of sides of the quadrilateral are congruent. If a student selects answer choice B, he or she does not realize there are no right angles in the quadrilateral. If a student selects answer choice C, he or she does not realize there are two pairs of parallel sides.

Constructed Response

2. Students will name a quadrilateral using its points on a coordinate plane. Remind students that in mathematics, they are often called upon to provide clear explanations and arguments to prove conclusions. Have a brief discussion about suggestions for how to provide clear explanations. Ask students which type of quadrilateral they will try to prove for the given points. Have volunteers name which properties they might need to determine and which formulas they might use to prove *ABCD* is a rectangle.

Extended Response

3. Students will use coordinate geometry to determine if the relationships involving lines, angles, and figures can be made using coordinate geometry. Point out that this exercise provides conclusions that may or may not be reached, without using the coordinates of figures. Tell students that they may be able to use theorems to determine whether or not a conclusion can be generally made. If students have difficulty, suggest they draw sample diagrams and use variables for coordinates to better see if a conclusion can be reached using only coordinate geometry.

Common Core Standards Practice   Week 14

Selected Response

1. What is the most precise name for the quadrilateral defined by the following points in the coordinate plane?

$A(1, -4), B(1, 1), C(-2, 2), D(-2, -3)$

A kite
B rectangle
C isosceles trapezoid
D parallelogram

Constructed Response

2. Quadrilateral $ABCD$ has vertices $A(0, 1), B(-1, 4), C(2, 5),$ and $D(3, 2)$.
  a. Plot the points.

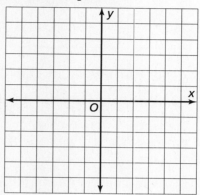

  b. Is quadrilateral $ABCD$ a rectangle? Explain.

Extended Response

3. Use the table to categorize which of the following conclusions can be reached using coordinate geometry.

$\overline{XY} \cong \overline{ST}$ $\overline{JK}$ bisects $\overline{MN}$. $\angle P \cong \angle O$ $\triangle ABC$ is a right triangle.
   $\overline{RS} \parallel \overline{TU}$ $\overline{WX} \perp \overline{YZ}$ $m\angle K + m\angle L = 180$

Can Be Reached	Cannot Be Reached

OVERVIEW

Looking Back	Mathematics of the Week	Looking Ahead
In Algebra 1, students used similar figures to solve problems (A.CED.A.1, A.REI.B.3).	Students identify and work with similar figures and understand how they can be used to solve problems.	In Chapter 10, students will find the perimeter and area of similar figures (G.GMD.A.3). In Chapter 11, students will compare similar solids (G.MG.A.1, G.MG.A.2).

COMMON CORE MATHEMATICAL CONTENT STANDARDS

G.SRT.B.5 Use ... similarity criteria for triangles to solve problems and to prove relationships in geometric figures.

G.GPE.A.5 Prove the slope criteria for parallel and perpendicular lines and use them to solve geometric problems.

G.GPE.A.7 Use coordinates to compute perimeters of polygons....

Common Core Mathematical Practice Standards: 1, 2, 3, 6

TEACHING NOTES

Selected Response

1. *Error Analysis*: Students determine whether two triangles are similar. If a student selects answer choice B, he or she is misinterpreting the Angle-Angle Postulate, as only one angle can be proved congruent. If a student selects answer choice C, he or she is misinterpreting the Side-Side-Side Theorem, as corresponding sides are not all in the same ratio. If a student selects answer choice D, he or she is misinterpreting the Side-Angle-Side Theorem, as the corresponding sides are not proportional.

Constructed Response

2. Students explain why two triangles are similar. Review the ways to prove that two triangles are similar. Then ask students to look at the given information. Ask volunteers to name corresponding congruent angles and any corresponding sides that establish a proportion. Make sure that students understand that the vertical angles are congruent, even though they are not marked accordingly. Once students have determined the similarity, they should use a proportion to solve for *x*.

Extended Response

3. Students plot and name a quadrilateral given its vertices. Review how the coordinate plane can be used to classify quadrilaterals. Remind students of the properties and formulas that can be used to confirm the classification of a quadrilateral. Ask volunteers to list the hierarchy of the various quadrilaterals to help provide a guideline for this exercise. If students have difficulty finding the correct classification, remind them that drawing diagonals may help.

Common Core Standards Practice   **Week 15**

Selected Response

1. Are the triangles similar? If so, choose the reasoning.

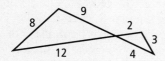

   A No, corresponding sides are not proportional.
   B Yes, Angle-Angle Similarity
   C Yes, Side-Side-Side Similarity
   D Yes, Side-Angle-Side Similarity

Constructed Response

2. **a.** Explain why the triangles are similar.
   b. Solve for the value of *x*.

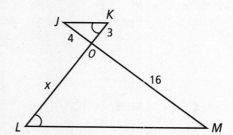

Extended Response

3. Quadrilateral *ABCD* has vertices $A(1, 1)$, $B(5, 3)$, $C(3, -1)$, and $D(-1, -3)$.
   a. Plot the points and draw diagonals.
   b. What is the best classification for the quadrilateral? Explain your reasoning.

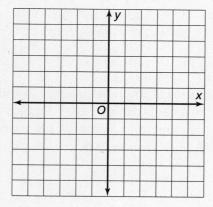

OVERVIEW

Looking Back	Mathematics of the Week	Looking Ahead
In Chapter 4, students worked with congruent triangles (G.SRT.B.5). In Algebra 1, students worked with similar figures (A.CED.A.1, A.REI.B.3).	Students will construct triangles to help solve problems and prove theorems about triangles and side and angle relationships.	In Chapter 8, students will work specifically with right triangles (G.SRT.C.6, G.SRT.C.8). In Chapter 9, students will learn how transformations affect congruence and similarity (G.CO.B.6, G.SRT.A.3).

COMMON CORE MATHEMATICAL CONTENT STANDARDS

G.CO.D.12 Make formal geometric constructions with a variety of tools...constructing perpendicular lines, including the perpendicular bisector of a line segment....

G.SRT.B.4 Prove theorems about triangles. Theorems include: a line parallel to one side of a triangle divides the other two proportionally and conversely....

Common Core Mathematical Practice Standards: 1, 2, 3, 4, 5, 6

TEACHING NOTES

Selected Response

1. *Error Analysis*: Students show understanding of how to prove that the sides of a triangle can be divided proportionally. If a student selects answer choice B, have them review the theorems in Lessons 7-3. If a student selects answer choice D, he or she should review the basic facts of the Pythagorean Theorem and how it relates to only right triangles.

Constructed Response

2. Students diagram and solve a real-world problem involving the length of a shadow. Students should begin the problem by converting all measurements to the same units. Their diagrams should help them realize that they do not need to use the Pythagorean Theorem to solve for the height of the utility pole.

Extended Response

3. Students prove certain segments of a triangle are proportional when the triangle is split with a line parallel to one side. Writing formal geometric proofs can be very difficult for some students. Have students start by identifying the corresponding angles that are congruent. They should be able to prove that the two triangles are similar, by using the triangle similarity theorems.

Common Core Standards Pracitce

Week 16

Selected Response

1. Which of the following reason(s) help(s) prove $\dfrac{ME}{ED} = \dfrac{NF}{FD}$?

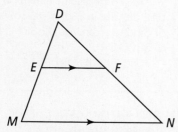

   A Angle-Angle Similarity
   B Side-Angle-Side Theorem
   C Side-Splitter Theorem
   D Pythagorean Theorem

Constructed Response

2. A yardstick that is perpendicular to the ground casts a 5-ft shadow. At the same time, a utility pole casts a shadow that is 6 yd long.

   a. Draw a diagram of this scenario.

   b. How tall is the utility pole?

Extended Response

3. Prove $\dfrac{VS}{VT} = \dfrac{WU}{WT}$.

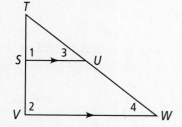

OVERVIEW

Looking Back	Mathematics of the Week	Looking Ahead
In Chapter 1, students learned the basic tools of geometry, including right angles (G.CO.A.1). In Lesson 4-6, students were introduced to right triangles (G.SRT.B.5).	Students solve problems using trigonometric ratios.	Later in Chapter 8, students extend their knowledge of relationships in right triangles to work with angles of elevation and depression, and the Laws of Sine and Cosine (G.SRT.C.8, G.SRT.D.11).

COMMON CORE MATHEMATICAL CONTENT STANDARDS

G.SRT.C.6 Understand that by similarity, side ratios in right triangles are properties of the angles in the triangle, leading to definitions of trigonometric ratios for acute angles.

G.SRT.C.7 Explain and use the relationship between the sine and cosine of complementary angles.

G.SRT.C.8 Use trigonometric ratios and the Pythagorean Theorem to solve right triangles in applied problems.

G.MG.A.1 Use geometric shapes, their measures, and their properties to describe objects.

Common Core Mathematical Practice Standards: 1, 2, 3, 4, 5, 6

TEACHING NOTES

Selected Response
1. *Error Analysis*: Students use the 45°-45°-90° triangle to find the length of the legs of a triangle. If a student selects answer choices A, B, or D, he or she does likely not understand that this is a 45°-45°-90° triangle or does not understand how to use the special relationship between the sides of a 45°-45°-90° triangle.

Constructed Response
2. Students use trigonometric ratios to find a missing side length and a missing angle measure of two adjacent triangles. Students should recognize that the missing side length and angle measure can be found by using the sine and cosine ratios.

Extended Response
3. Students are faced with a real-world problem involving the use of trigonometric ratios. The first part of the question asks students to sketch the scenario, which will help visual learners solve the problem. Students should use the sine function to determine the answer. Remind students to round their answer to the nearest foot.

Name _____ Class _____ Date _____

Common Core Standards Practice   **Week 17**

Selected Response

1. What is the value of x?

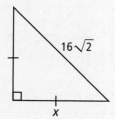

    A 8
    B $8\sqrt{2}$
    C 16
    D $16\sqrt{2}$

Constructed Response

2. Find the values of w and x to the nearest degree.

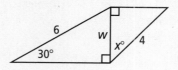

Extended Response

3. To hang a 9-ft hammock from a tree, you first tie one end to the trunk of the tree. When the hammock is tied on one end, it makes a 20° angle with the ground.

    a. Use a compass and protractor to model this scenario.

    b. How far up the tree is the hammock tied on? Round your answer to the nearest foot.

OVERVIEW

Looking Back	Mathematics of the Week	Looking Ahead
Students were introduced to trigonometric ratios in Lesson 8-3 (G.SRT.D.11). In Chapter 7, students modeled situations with triangles (G.SRT.C.8).	Students use the Law of Sines and the Law of Cosines to solve problems.	In Algebra 2, students will extend their knowledge of the Law of Sines and the Law of Cosines to find the area of a triangle and missing angle measures (G.SRT.C.9)

COMMON CORE MATHEMATICAL CONTENT STANDARDS

G.SRT.C.8 Use trigonometric ratios and the Pythagorean Theorem to solve right triangles in applied problems.

G.SRT.D.11 Understand and apply the Law of Sines and the Law of Cosines to find unknown measurements in right and non-right triangles (e.g., surveying problems, resultant forces).

Common Core Mathematical Practice Standards: 1, 2, 4

TEACHING NOTES

Selected Response

1. *Error Analysis*: Students solve a problem that requires the use of the Law of Sines. If a student selects answer choice A, he or she may have forgotten to take the inverse sine after solving for the sine of angle *C*. If a student selects answer choices B or D, he or she may not have used the Law of Sines correctly.

Constructed Response

2. Students solve a real-world problem that requires the use of the Law of Cosines. Students should notice this is not a right triangle, but that the three side lengths are given and the unknown is an angle measure. This should lead students to use the Law of Cosines to determine the missing angle measure.

Extended Response

3. Students draw a diagram and solve a real-world problem involving angles and distances between three points. Sketching this situation is required because it will lead students into finding the third angle measure and use the Law of Sines to find the ship's distance from the port. Make sure students set up their proportions correctly.

Common Core Standards Practice

Week 18

Selected Response

1. In $\triangle ABC$, $AB = 24$, $BC = 36$, and $m\angle A = 118$. What is $m\angle C$?

   A about 1

   B about 21

   C about 36

   D about 54

Constructed Response

2. A center fielder catches a fly ball in the outfield. Her distance to the shortstop is 80 ft, as shown in the figure. If she is 135 ft away from first base, what is the value of x?

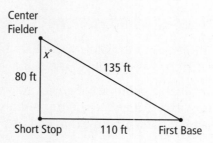

Center
Fielder

$x°$

80 ft

135 ft

Short Stop   110 ft   First Base

Extended Response

3. A cruise ship has sailed 1130 mi from the port in Alaska. From the ship, the captain records an angle measurement between the port in Alaska and the port in Canada as 53°. He knows the angle from the port in Alaska between the ship and the port in Canada is 88°.

   a. Draw a diagram of the ship's position.

   b. To the nearest mile, how far is the ship from the port in Canada? Explain how you know

OVERVIEW

Looking Back	Mathematics of the Week	Looking Ahead
Students learned how to translate in the coordinate plane in Algebra 1 (F.BF.B.3).	Students perform translations, reflections, and rotations in the coordinate plane.	Later in Chapter 9, students will work with congruence transformations (G.CO.B.7) and similarity transformations (G.SRT.A.2).

COMMON CORE MATHEMATICAL CONTENT STANDARDS

G.CO.A.2 Represent transformations in the plane using... compare transformations that preserve distance and angle to those that do not.

G.CO.A.5 Given a geometric figure and a rotation, reflection, or translation, draw the transformed figure using, e.g., graph paper, tracing paper, or geometry software. Specify a sequence of transformations that will carry a given figure onto another.

G.CO.B.6 Use geometric descriptions of rigid motions to transform figures and to predict the effect of a given rigid motion on a given figure....

Common Core Mathematical Practice Standards: 1, 2, 4, 5

TEACHING NOTES

Selected Response

1. *Error Analysis*: Students find a reflection image given the coordinates of the point. If a student selects answer choice A, he or she may have mistaken the reflection to be over the line $y = x$, instead of over the x-axis. If a student selects answer choice B, he or she may have found the image after a 180 degree rotation around the origin. If a student selects answer choice C, he or she may have thought the reflection was over the y-axis.

Constructed Response

2. Students find the image of a translation of a square given a graph of the preimage. Some students may write the coordinates of the preimage on their paper and perform the subtraction needed to find the coordinates of the image. Other students may find the coordinates of the image on the graph by moving the points 3 units to the left and 5 units down, and then listing the coordinates of the image second.

Extended Response

3. Students plot the given points of a triangle, find and graph a glide reflection image, and find a different transformation that will result in the same image. Students may have trouble interpreting the notation in the problem. Clarify that the 180° rotation is performed first, and the reflection over the x-axis is the second step.

Common Core Standards Practice   Week 19

Selected Response

1. Find the coordinates of the image.

$R_{x\text{-axis}}(7, -2)$

  A $(-2, 7)$
  B $(-7, -2)$
  C $(-7, 2)$
  D $(7, 2)$

Constructed Response

2. a. What are the vertices of $T_{<-3, -5>}(ABCD)$?

  b. Graph the image of $ABCD$.

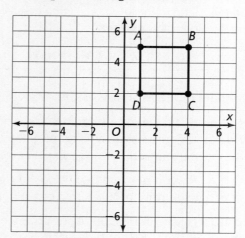

Extended Response

3. a. Plot the points $A(-3, 2)$, $B(-1, 3)$, $C(-1, 1)$.

  b. Graph the image of $\triangle ABC$ after the given transformation.

  $(R_{x\text{-axis}} \circ r_{(180°, o)})(\triangle ABC)$

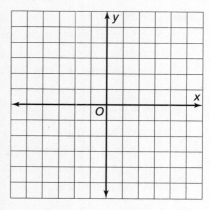

  c. Describe another transformation that will make the same image.

Common Core Standards Practice

Week 20

OVERVIEW

Looking Back	Mathematics of the Week	Looking Ahead
In Chapter 4, students used triangle congruence theorems and postulates (G.SRT.B.5). Earlier in Chapter 9, students worked with isometries (G.CO.A.2, G.CO.A.4, G.CO.A.5, G.CO.B.6).	Students find congruence transformations given the coordinates of the preimage and the image.	Later in Chapter 9, students will work with dilations (G.SRT.A.1a) and similarity transformations (G.SRT.A.2).

COMMON CORE MATHEMATICAL CONTENT STANDARDS

G.CO.A.5 Given a geometric figure and a rotation, reflection, or translation, draw the transformed figure using, e.g., graph paper, tracing paper, or geometry software. Specify a sequence of transformations that will carry a given figure onto another.

G.CO.B.6 Use geometric descriptions of rigid motions to transform figures and to predict the effect of a given rigid motion on a given figure....

G.CO.B.7 Use the definition of congruence in terms of rigid motions to show that two triangles are congruent if and only if corresponding pairs of sides and corresponding pairs of angles are congruent.

G.CO.B.8 Explain how the criteria for triangle congruence (ASA, SAS, and SSS) follow from the definition of congruence in terms of rigid motions.

Common Core Mathematical Practice Standards: 1, 2, 3, 4, 5

TEACHING NOTES

Selected Response

1. *Error Analysis*: Students are given a coordinate plane showing two congruent triangles and are asked to choose which congruence transformation maps one onto the other. If a student selects answer choice B, he or she chose the correct order of the transformations, but selected the wrong reflection axis as well as an incorrect translation. If a student selects answer choices C or D, the student should review rotations about the origin.

Constructed Response

2. Students are given two congruent rectangles on a coordinate grid and are asked to find four different isometries that could map one onto the other. Students should start with the translations, and should then use reflections and rotations for the isometries.

Extended Response

3. Students verify the Angle-Side-Angle Postulate for congruence. Students should describe each step as an isometry to move one triangle on to the other. Students should find and record a series of isometries that maps $\triangle ABC$ to $\triangle XYZ$.

Common Core Standards Practice

Week 20

Selected Response

1. In the diagram below, $\triangle ABC \cong \triangle XYZ$. What is a congruence transformation that maps $\triangle ABC$ onto $\triangle XYZ$?

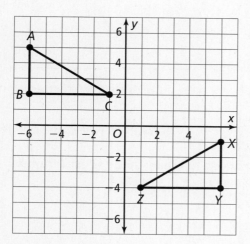

A $R_{y\text{-axis}} \circ T_{<-6,\,0>}$
B $R_{x\text{-axis}} \circ T_{<6,\,0>}$
C $r_{(180°,\,O)} \circ T_{<0,\,-1>}$
D $R_{x\text{-axis}} \circ r_{(180°,\,O)}$

Constructed Response

2. The figure below shows two congruent rectangles. What are four different isometries that map the top rectangle onto the bottom rectangle?

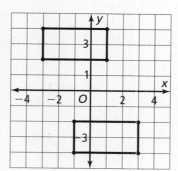

Extended Response

3. Verify the ASA postulate for triangle congruence by using congruence transformations.

Given: $\overline{AB} \cong \overline{XY}$, $\angle A \cong \angle X$, $\angle B \cong \angle Y$

Prove: $\triangle XYZ \cong \triangle ABC$

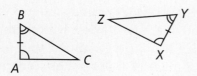

OVERVIEW

Looking Back	Mathematics of the Week	Looking Ahead
In Chapter 7, students explored ratios and proportions, as well as similar polygons and proportions in triangles (G.SRT.B.5, G.SRT.B.4).	Students work with dilations of figures and scale factors. They also perform similarity transformations and use these transformations to verify similarity.	In Chapters 10 and 11, students will continue to work with similar figures, proportions, and scale factors (G.GMD.A.3, G.MG.A.1).

COMMON CORE MATHEMATICAL CONTENT STANDARDS

G.SRT.A.1.b The dilation of a line segment is longer or shorter in the ratio given by the scale factor.

G.SRT.A.2 Given two figures, use the definition of similarity in terms of similarity transformations to decide if they are similar. . . .

G.SRT.A.3 Use the properties of similarity transformations to establish the AA criterion for two triangles to be similar.

Also **G.SRT.A.1.a**.

Common Core Mathematical Practice Standards: 1, 2, 3, 6

TEACHING NOTES

Selected Response

1. *Error Analysis*: Students determine a scale factor and dilation of a given figure. If a student selects answer choice B, he or she placed the image measurement $A'C'$ in the denominator. If a student selects answer choices C or D, he or she may have confused the image and pre-image points or may not understand the difference between reduction and enlargement.

Constructed Response

2. Students graph a quadrilateral given its points and perform a given dilation. Remind students that a center of dilation at the origin allows the image to be found by multiplying the original coordinates by the scale factor. Ask students if the image will be an enlargement or a reduction.

Extended Response

3. Students apply a similarity transformation to a real-world context. Remind students that similar figures are the compositions of rigid motions and dilations. Review with them the ways triangles can be proved similar: the Angle-Angle Similarity Postulate, the Side-Angle-Side Similarity Theorem, and the Side-Side-Side Similarity Theorem. As students find the distance across the drop zone, make sure they are using the ratio between corresponding sides, or a scale factor of 4.25, to find the distance.

Common Core Standards Practice

Week 21

Selected Response

1. Is $D_{(n, A)}(\triangle ABC) = \triangle A'B'C'$ an enlargement or a reduction? What is the scale factor n of the dilation?

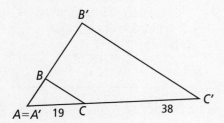

    A enlargement; $n = 3$

    B enlargement; $n = \dfrac{1}{3}$

    C reduction; $n = 3$

    D reduction; $n = \dfrac{1}{3}$

Constructed Response

2. $ABCD$ has vertices $A(1, 3)$, $B(-2, 3)$, $C(-4, -3)$, $D(-1, -3)$.
    a. Graph $ABCD$.
    b. Graph $A'B'C'D'$, the image of $ABCD$ after a dilation with center $(0, 0)$ and a scale factor of 3.

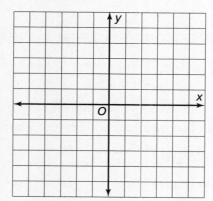

Extended Response

3. An army captain wants to use similar triangles to determine the distance d across the drop zone shown below.

    a. Are the two triangles similar? Explain your reasoning.

    b. What is the distance across the drop zone?

OVERVIEW

Looking Back	Mathematics of the Week	Looking Ahead
In Chapter 1, students found the perimeter and area of triangles and rectangles (N.Q.A.1). In Algebra 1, students worked with formulas to find perimeters and areas of plane figures (A.CED.A.4, A.REI.B.3).	Students find the areas of regular polygons, including the areas of triangles. They also find the perimeters and areas of similar figures.	In Algebra 2, students will use determinants of matrices to find areas of polygons (N.VM.C.10). They will also find the area of triangles using the sine of an angle (G.SRT.D.9).

COMMON CORE MATHEMATICAL CONTENT STANDARDS

G.SRT.A.9 Derive the formula $A = 1/2\, ab \sin(C)$ for the area of a triangle....

G.GPE.B.7 Use coordinates to compute...areas of triangles and rectangles.

G.MG.A.1 Use geometric shapes, their measures,...to describe objects.

Common Core Mathematical Practice Standards: 1, 2, 6, 7

TEACHING NOTES

Selected Response

1. *Error Analysis*: Students find the area of a triangle given two sides and an included angle. If a student selects answer choice A, he or she is likely using the cosine function, instead of the sine function. If a student selects answer choice C, he or she forgot to divide by 2. If a student selects answer choice D, he or she multiplied by 2 instead of dividing by 2 in the formula.

Constructed Response

2. Students use the given areas of two similar figures to compare their side lengths and perimeters. Review with students the relationship between the perimeters of similar figures and the relationship between the areas of similar figures. Remind them that the ratio of the areas is ratio of the squares of the side lengths. Tell students that although a visual representation of a figure is often helpful when working with a geometric situation, in this case a specific figure is not needed.

Extended Response

3. Students describe two methods for finding the area of a hexagon. Invite a brief class discussion to review how to provide clear explanations. Elicit from the class the importance of using precise mathematical terminology and, if necessary, the value of writing step-by-step instructions. Students should use the formula for area given the perimeter. If students have difficulty seeing the second method of using the area of one equilateral triangle and multiplying it by 6, remind them that they may find a hint by studying the drawing. If students use the first method, make sure they first find the perimeter instead of simply substituting the length of one side in the formula.

Common Core Standards Practice   Week 22

Selected Response

1. Find the area of the triangle to the nearest square inch.

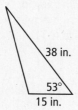

38 in.

53°

15 in.

A 171 in.^{2}

B 228 in.^{2}

C 455 in.^{2}

D 910 in.^{2}

Constructed Response

2. Two similar trapezoids have areas 98 in.^{2} and 242 in.^{2}.

a. What is the scale factor?

b. What is the ratio of their perimeters?

Extended Response

3. a. Describe two different methods for finding the area of the floor of a stage that is shaped like the regular hexagon *ABCDEF*.

b. What is the area?

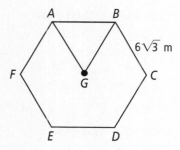

OVERVIEW

Looking Back	Mathematics of the Week	Looking Ahead
In Chapter 1, students found the circumferences and areas of circles (N.Q.A.1). In Algebra 1, students worked with formulas to find the area and circumferences of circles (A.CED.A.4, A.CED.A.1, A.REI.A.1, A.REI.B.3).	Students find measures of central angles and arcs, circumference and arc length, and areas of circles. They also work with sectors and segments of circles and should be able to find the areas of these sectors and segments.	In Chapter 12, students will extend their knowledge of circles, including using tangents and graphing circles (G.C.A.2, G.GPE.A.1).

COMMON CORE MATHEMATICAL CONTENT STANDARDS

G.C.A.2 Identify and describe relationships among inscribed angles, radii....

G.C.B.5 Derive...the formula for the area of a sector.

Also **G.CO.A.1, G.GMD.A.1**.

Common Core Mathematical Practice Standards: 1, 2, 4, 5, 6

TEACHING NOTES

Selected Response

1. *Error Analysis*: Students find the area of a sector of a circle. If a student selects answer choice A or B, he or she solved for the area of the entire circle *B*. If a student selects answer choice C or D, he or she forgot to multiply by π.

Constructed Response

2. Students find the length of a minor arc of a circle. Review with students the formulas for the circumference of a circle in terms of the radius and the diameter, the formula for arc length, and the definitions of minor and major arc. Ask a volunteer what steps should be taken to find the angle measure associated with minor arc *AB*. Make sure students use the correct measurement when finding the circumference of the circle.

Extended Response

3. Students draw two circles given two parameters, and then find the area of the intersecting region. Remind students that often the best way to find the area of a figure is to subtract from the whole the area a part that is easily calculated. Make sure students' drawings are correct before they begin part (b). If students have difficulty with part (b), direct them to draw lines connecting the two points where the circles intersect to the centers of the circles to clarify how they may work the problem. If necessary, tell students to use trigonometric ratios to help find the measure of the central angle. Make sure students find the area of the entire region contained by both circles and only count each part once.

Common Core Standards Practice

Week 23

Selected Response

1. What is the area of sector *ABC*?

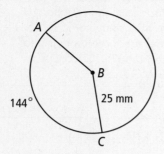

A 625π mm^2

B 625 mm^2

C 250π mm^2

D 250 mm^2

Constructed Response

2. Find the length of minor arc *AB*.

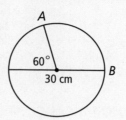

Extended Response

3. Circles *A* and *B* each have a radius of 10 and *AB* = 10.

    a. Draw a diagram that shows both circles.

    b. Find the area of the region that is contained by both circles.

OVERVIEW

Looking Back	Mathematics of the Week	Looking Ahead
In Chapter 1, students reviewed working with nets (G.CO.A.1). In previous grades, students also used nets to describe three-dimensional objects (G.GMD.B.4).	Students draw and use nets to visualize three-dimensional objects and find the surface areas of three-dimensional objects.	Students will use this type of visualization in Algebra 2 as they study conic sections and use three-dimensional coordinates (G.GMD.B.4, G.MG.A.1).

COMMON CORE MATHEMATICAL CONTENT STANDARDS

G.GMD.B.4 Identify the shapes of two-dimensional cross-sections of three-dimensional objects....

G.MG.A.1 Use geometric shapes, their measures, and their properties to describe objects.

Common Core Mathematical Practice Standards: 1, 2, 4, 5, 6, 7

TEACHING NOTES

Selected Response

1. *Error Analysis*: Students visualize the shape of a cross section of a triangular pyramid. If a student selects answer choice A, he or she is not visualizing the correct figure. If a student selects answer choice B, he or she is likely confusing the horizontal cross section of a triangular pyramid with that of a rectangular pyramid. If a student selects answer choice C, he or she is likely confusing the horizontal cross section of a triangular pyramid with that of a square pyramid.

Constructed Response

2. Students sketch a polyhedron with rectangular faces and then sketch two different nets for the figure. Review with students a basic net for a rectangular prism. If time permits, construct a sample prism and put an asymmetrical letter or symbol on each side. Ask the class to draw a net for this prism. Then take the prism apart and have students check to see if they drew the letters or symbols in the proper position and orientation on the net. As students complete the exercise, make sure they draw a polyhedron with faces that are all rectangles, and that they do not make the common mistake of drawing a rectangular prism with square faces on the end.

Extended Response

3. Students draw the nets of three figures. Remind students of what is meant by *regular polyhedron* in terms of these figures. Ask volunteers to list the number of faces, edges, and vertices for each polyhedron. If space permits, and if students have difficulty with the nets, you may wish to establish a station for students to construct paper nets to test their drawings.

Common Core Standards Practice

Week 24

Selected Response

1. What shape is formed by the cross section of a triangular pyramid with a horizontal plane?

   A pentagon
   B rectangle
   C square
   D triangle

Constructed Response

2. **a.** Sketch a polyhedron with faces that are all rectangles.

   b. Draw two different nets for the polyhedron.

Extended Response

3. Draw the net of each regular polyhedron.

a.

b.

c.

OVERVIEW

Looking Back	Mathematics of the Week	Looking Ahead
In Algebra 1, students worked with the surface areas and volumes of prisms, cylinders, cones, and spheres (G.GMD.A.3).	Students find surface areas and volumes of geometric figures, including prisms, cylinders, pyramids, cones, and spheres.	Students will use their knowledge of surface areas and volumes of geometric figures to solve problems in Algebra 2 (G.GMD.A.3).

COMMON CORE MATHEMATICAL CONTENT STANDARDS

G.GMD.A.1 Give an informal argument for the formulas for...volume of a cylinder....

G.GMD.A.3 Use volume formulas for cylinders, pyramids, cones, and spheres to solve problems.

G.MG.A.1 Use geometric shapes, their measures, and their properties to describe objects.

Common Core Mathematical Practice Standards: 1, 2, 3, 6

TEACHING NOTES

Selected Response

1. *Error Analysis*: Students find the volume of a cylinder. If a student selects answer choice A, he or she is likely multiplying the diameter by the height, while ignoring the value of π. If a student selects answer choice C, he or she is likely taking the square of the diameter and then multiplying it by the height, while ignoring the value of π. If a student selects answer choice D, he or she is likely taking the square of the height and then multiplying it by the diameter while ignoring the value of π.

Constructed Response

2. Students find the volume of a conference center given the base length and the height. Sketch a square pyramid for the class. Remind students that a square pyramid is defined as having a square for a base. Review the formula for the volume of a square pyramid, and write it below the drawing. Ask a volunteer to label the measurements given in the exercise. Make sure students multiply the height by the area of the base, and not by the base length.

Extended Response

3. Students solve a real-world problem about three-dimensional figures. Ask students whether they will need to find surface area, volume, or both to solve this exercise. Then ask students what measurements they will need to find in order to answer this exercise. Tell students that it is not enough to simply find out whether the melted yogurt will overflow the cone; they must also explain the answer. Remind students that their explanations should be clear and logical.

Common Core Standards Practice

Week 25

Selected Response

1. What is the volume of a cylinder with a diameter of 4 in. and a height of 10 in.? Round your answer to the nearest cubic inch.

   A 40 in.^3
   B 126 in.^3
   C 160 in.^3
   D 400 in.^3

Constructed Response

2. A conference center is in the shape of a square pyramid with a base length of 219.8 m and a height of 174.34 m. To the nearest cubic meter, what is the approximate volume of the conference center?

Extended Response

3. A vendor presses a full scoop of frozen yogurt into a cone. The frozen yogurt has a diameter of 7 cm. The cone has a height of 14 cm and a base diameter the width of the frozen yogurt. If the frozen yogurt melts into the cone, will the cone overflow? Explain.

OVERVIEW

Looking Back	Mathematics of the Week	Looking Ahead
In Algebra 1, students worked with surface areas and volumes of prisms, cylinders, cones, and spheres (G.GMD.A.3). They also worked with similar figures and proportions (A.CED.A.1, A.REI.B.3).	Students find surface areas and volumes of geometric figures, including prisms, cylinders, pyramids, cones, and spheres. They will also apply this information to find surface areas and volumes of similar solids.	Students will use their knowledge of surface areas and volumes of geometric figures in everyday activities throughout their lives (G.GMD.A.3).

COMMON CORE MATHEMATICAL CONTENT STANDARDS

G.GMD.A.3 Use volume formulas for cylinders, pyramids, cones, and spheres to solve problems.

Also **G.MG.A.1, G.MG.A.2**.

Common Core Mathematical Practice Standards: 1, 2, 4, 6

TEACHING NOTES

Selected Response

1. *Error Analysis*: Students find the volume of a pyramid given two similar pyramids: one with a given volume and a scale factor for the sides and base edge of the other. If a student selects answer choice A, he or she is likely multiplying only by the scale factor instead of the cube of the scale factor. If a student selects answer choice B, he or she is likely making a computational error, possibly first multiplying the original volume by 2 and then multiplying by the square of the scale factor. If a student selects answer choice C, he or she is likely multiplying by the square of the scale factor, as would be done when comparing surface areas of the pyramids.

Constructed Response

2. Students find the volume of a balloon given that its radius is quadrupled from the given information. Remind students that, when working with the volumes of similar three-dimensional figures, it is not necessary to recalculate the volume of the second figure from scratch when the scale factor is available. Although the scale factor is not given directly, students can figure it out from the information in the exercise. As students complete the exercise, make sure they do not simply find the cube of the scale factor but that they multiply the cube of the scale factor by the volume of the original balloon, to find the volume of the new balloon.

Extended Response

3. Students are given a list of objects and their measurements and have to order the volumes from least to greatest. Review with students the formulas for the volume of a cube, cylinder, pyramid, cone, and prism. Remind students that when comparing measurements of any sort, including volume, it is critical that all measurements use the same unit. In this case, all measurements are in centimeters, so a comparison will work without any modification.

Common Core Standards Practice

Week 26

Selected Response

1. A pyramid has a volume of 108 m³. A similar pyramid has base edges and a height that are $\frac{1}{3}$ of the length of those in the original pyramid. What is the volume of the smaller pyramid?

   A 36 m³
   B 24 m³
   C 12 m³
   D 4 m³

Constructed Response

2. A spherical balloon can hold a volume of 2 cm³ of helium. If the radius of the balloon is quadrupled, how much helium can the new balloon hold?

Extended Response

3. List these solids in order from the one with the least volume to the one with the greatest volume.

   A a cube with edge 5 cm
   B a cylinder with radius 4 cm and height 4 cm
   C a square pyramid with base edges 6 cm and height 6 cm
   D a cone with radius 4 cm and height 9 cm
   E a rectangular prism with base 5 cm-by-5 cm and height 6 cm

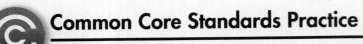

OVERVIEW

Looking Back	Mathematics of the Week	Looking Ahead
In Chapter 1, students learned how to make basic constructions (G.CO.D.12). In Chapter 10, students learned about circles, central angles, and arcs (G.CO.A.1).	Students work with tangents, chords, arcs, and perpendicular bisectors to chords, and how they relate to circles. They also need to find the measure of central angles and inscribed angles of a circle.	In Algebra 2, students will work with central angles and intercepted arcs in circles when they study radian measure (F.TF.A.1).

COMMON CORE MATHEMATICAL CONTENT STANDARDS

G.C.A.2 Identify and describe relationships among . . . radii, and chords . . . the radius of a circle is perpendicular to the tangent where the radius intersects the circle.

> **Common Core Mathematical Practice Standards:** 1, 2, 5, 6
> **Materials:** Compass and straightedge

TEACHING NOTES

Selected Response

1. *Error Analysis*: Students find the radius of a circle. If a student selects answer choice A, he or she is likely uses the wrong middle term for the square of the hypotenuse, and arrives at the term $88x$ instead of $44x$. If a student selects answer choice C, he or she likely solved for the length of the hypotenuse. If a student selects answer choice D, he or she is likely making multiple errors including not taking the square root.

Constructed Response

2. Students are given an arc and are instructed to find the center of the circle that contains the arc, and explain their steps. Start by reading Theorem 12-10 to students: In a circle, the perpendicular bisector of a chord contains the center of the circle. Remind them that two diameters of a circle intersect at the circle's center. If necessary, review with students the steps in constructing a perpendicular bisector. As students work, make sure they draw two chords on the arc to find the center of the circle. Tell students they may check their drawings by using the center they find to construct the complete circle that contains the given arc.

Extended Response

3. Students classify inscribed angles, central angles, and arcs by their measure. Review the Inscribed Angle Theorem and its corollaries. Tell them that they will use these to help find the measures of angles and intercepted arcs shown in this exercise. Before beginning the exercise, briefly discuss the examples with students.

Common Core Standards Practice   Week 27

Selected Response

1. What is the value of x to the nearest tenth?

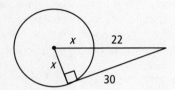

A 4.8 units
B 9.5 units
C 31.5 units
D 372 units

Constructed Response

2. Use the arc below to find the center of the circle that contains the arc. Explain the process.

Extended Response

3. Classify each angle/arc measure as greater than 90, less than 90, or equal to 90.

Greater than 90	Less than 90	Equal to 90

OVERVIEW

Looking Back	Mathematics of the Week	Looking Ahead
In Chapter 10, students studied center and radius in regards to circles (G.C.A.1). In Chapter 6, students worked with polygons in the coordinate plane (G.CO.A.1).	Students write an equation for a circle using the coordinate plane and find the center and radius of a circle. Students also draw and describe a locus, including a locus that has two conditions.	In Algebra 2, students will continue working with circles in the coordinate plane, including finding the center, radius, and equation, through calculations and graphing. (G.GPE.A.1).

COMMON CORE MATHEMATICAL CONTENT STANDARDS

G.GPE.A.1 Derive the equation of a circle of given center and radius using the Pythagorean Theorem.

Common Core Mathematical Practice Standards: 1, 2, 4

TEACHING NOTES

Selected Response

1. *Error Analysis*: Students find the center and radius of a circle given its equation. If a student selects answer choices B, C, or D, he or she is may have misinterpreted the sign when using the equation to find the center of a circle. If a student selects answer choice F, he or she did not take the square root when using the equation to find the center of a circle.

Constructed Response

2. Students write an equation for a circle. Remind students that the definition of a locus is a set of points that meet a certain condition or set of conditions. Ask students to state the conditions that are given in this exercise. Tell them that they may choose to graph some examples of points that fit the conditions to generate a pattern. Some students may recognize the definition of a circle without plotting examples of points. Ask students to think about the significance of the point (0, –8).

Extended Response

3. Students solve a real-world problem using a circle and its equation. Tell students that the equator, or cross section, is not only a circle but is known as a great circle since the center of the circle is also the center of the sphere. Make sure students use the radius and not the diameter when writing the equation in part (a). Students may use one of two methods to find the circumference in part (c): multiply the 1-degree arc length found in part (b) by 360, or use the formula for the circumference of a circle. Make sure students remember to divide the circumference by the speed to find the time it will take the rover to travel the distance.

Common Core Standards Practice   Week 28

Selected Response

1. Which of the following describe the circle represented by the following equation?

$$(x + 17)^2 + (y - 14)^2 = 196$$

A center $(-17, 14)$
B center $(17, 14)$
C center $(-17, -14)$
D center $(17, -14)$
E radius 14
F radius 196

Constructed Response

2. Write an equation for the locus of points in the coordinate plane that are 11 units from $(0, -8)$.

Extended Response

3. The diameter of Mars is about 6792 km.

    a. Write an equation that represents the equator on the surface of Mars with the center of Mars as the origin.

    b. Find the length of a 1-degree arc on the equator of Mars to the nearest tenth of a kilometer.

    c. If it takes a Mars rover 1 hr to navigate 3 km on the surface of Mars, estimate how long it will take the rover to circumnavigate Mars.

OVERVIEW

Looking Back	Mathematics of the Week	Looking Ahead
In Algebra 1, students worked with experimental and theoretical probability, surveys and samples, and permutations and combinations (S.IC.B.3, S.CP.A.1, S.CP.B.9)	Students find theoretical probability. Students also make conjectures about a population based on a survey. Finally, students work with permutations and combinations.	Later in Chapter 13, students will work with probability models (S.CP.A.4) and conditional probability (S.CP.A.3).

COMMON CORE MATHEMATICAL CONTENT STANDARDS

S.CP.A.5 Recognize and explain the concepts of conditional probability and independence in everyday language and everyday situations.

S.CP.B.6 Find the conditional probability of *A* given *B* as the fraction of *B*'s outcomes that also belong to *A*, and interpret the answer in terms of the model.

S.CP.B.9 Use permutations and combinations to compute probabilities of compound events and solve problems.

Also, **S.CP.A.4**.

Common Core Mathematical Practice Standards: 1, 2, 3, 4, 5, 6

TEACHING NOTES

Selected Response

1. *Error Analysis*: Students find the probability of not winning a game given the conditional that a number greater than four must be rolled in order to win. If a student selects answer choice A, he or she may have found the probability of 8 favorable outcomes over 12 possible outcomes. If a student selects answer choice B, he or she may have found the complement of the probability 8 favorable outcomes over 12 possible outcomes. If a student selects answer choice C, he or she may have not understood the problem.

Constructed Response

2. Students use the results of a survey to make predictions about a population. For part (a), students should know that a probability distribution shows the probability of each possible outcome. For parts (b) and (c), students should base their predictions using their probability distributions from part (a).

Extended Response

3. Students correct the error in a statement about the number of possible outcomes in a real-world situation. If students are struggling, ask if the order of the songs is important. Since the order of the songs is not important, this is an example of a combination, rather than a permutation.

Common Core Standards Practice

Week 29

Selected Response

1. You are playing a board game with two standard number cubes. It is your last turn and if the sum of the numbers you roll is greater than 4, you will win the game. What is the probability that you will NOT win the game?

   A $\dfrac{2}{3}$

   B $\dfrac{1}{3}$

   C $\dfrac{1}{4}$

   D $\dfrac{1}{6}$

Constructed Response

2. The results from a survey of 150 students from Central High are shown below.

   a. Make a probability distribution table of the number of children in the families of Central High students.

   b. If Central High has 953 students, predict the number of families that will have exactly 3 children.

   c. How many families will have either two or three children?

Number of Children in Family	Frequency
1	38
2	42
3	30
4	27
More than 4	13

Extended Response

3. A member of a band told the band that there are 3,991,680 different ways to choose 7 out of 12 songs that the band wants to play at the upcoming show. Explain the error in his statement and find the correct answer.

Common Core Standards Practice

Week 30

OVERVIEW

Looking Back	Mathematics of the Week	Looking Ahead
Earlier in Chapter 13, students worked with experimental and theoretical probability (S.CP.A.1).	Students use conditional probability to solve problems.	Students will extend their work with probability in Algebra 2 (S.CP.A.2, S.CP.B.3, S.CP.B.4, S.CP.A.5, S.CP.B.6, S.CP.B.7).

COMMON CORE MATHEMATICAL CONTENT STANDARDS

S.CP.A.2 Understand that two events A and B are independent if the probability of A and B occurring together is the product of their probabilities, and use this characterization to determine if they are independent.

S.CP.A.3 Understand the conditional probability of A given B as $P(A$ and $B)/P(B)$, and interpret independence of A and B as saying that the conditional probability of A given B is the same as the probability of A, and the conditional probability of B given A is the same as the probability of B.

S.CP.A.5 Recognize and explain the concepts of conditional probability and independence in everyday language and everyday situations.

S.CP.B.6 Find the conditional probability of A given B as the fraction of B's outcomes that also belong to A, and interpret the answer in terms of the model.

Also **S.MD.B.6, S.MD.B.7**.

Common Core Mathematical Practice Standards: 1, 2, 5, 6

TEACHING NOTES

Selected Response

1. *Error Analysis*: Students solve a real-world problem involving conditional probabilities. If student selects answer choice A, he or she did not calculate the probabilities correctly. If a student selects answer choice C, he or she did calculations to find the complement of the event. If a student selects answer choice D, he or she found a complement of the event.

Constructed Response

2. Students find the probability of two particular events occurring based on given conditions. For part (a), have students start by making a tree diagram to organize the information in the problem. Then have them find the probabilities in pieces.

Extended Response

3. Students solve a real-world problem involving conditional probabilities. If students are struggling with part (b), have them repeat the steps performed in part (a) using the probability of the field being muddy of 40%. However, students should be able to extrapolate from the problem that since the team wins more games on muddy fields, if the chance of a muddy field decreases, then the chances of winning also decrease.

Common Core Standards Practice

Week 30

Selected Response

1. A particular basketball team has a 75% chance of winning a tournament if its star player is able to play. Otherwise, the team has a 40% chance of winning. The doctor says that the star player has a 60% chance of being able to play. What is the probability that the team will win the tournament?

   A 67%

   B 61%

   C 55%

   D 48%

Constructed Response

2. In a survey of shoppers, 54% use coupons, 36% belong to shoppers clubs, and 18% use coupons and belong to shoppers clubs.

   a. What is the conditional probability that a shopper uses coupons given that he or she belongs to shoppers clubs?

   b. What is the conditional probability that a shopper belongs to shoppers clubs given that he or she uses coupons?

Extended Response

3. A soccer team wins 65% of its games on muddy fields and 30% of its games on dry fields. The probability of the field being muddy for its next game is 70%.

   a. What is the probability that the team will win its next game?

   b. If the probability of the field being muddy decreases, how will that influence the probability of the team winning its next game?

Common Core Readiness Assessment 1

1. A frame is 45 in. by 32 in. How many square feet are in the area of this frame?

A 120 ft^2
B 100 ft^2
C 10 ft^2
D 12 ft^2

2. The circumference of circle P is 800 mm, the circumference of circle Q is 200 cm, and the circumference of circle R is 4 m. What is the sum of the distances around each circle?

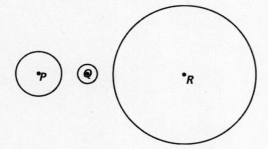

F 24.2 m
G 7.5 m
H 6.8 m
J 31.4 m

3. A plot of land is about 13,000 ft by 8000 ft. Approximately how many square miles is this? Round to the nearest whole number.

A 1040 mi^2
B 4 mi^2
C 3939 mi^2
D $19,697 \text{ mi}^2$

4. The proof that vertical angles 1 and 3 are congruent is started below.

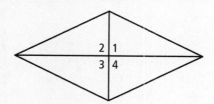

Statement	Reason
$m\angle 1 + m\angle 2 = 180$	Angles 1 and 2 are supplementary angles.
$m\angle 2 + m\angle 3 = 180$	Angles 2 and 3 are supplementary angles.

Which statement should be next?

F $m\angle 1 + m\angle 2 = m\angle 2 + m\angle 3$
G $m\angle 3 + m\angle 4 = 180$
H $m\angle 1 + m\angle 2 = m\angle 2 + m\angle 1$
J $m\angle 2 + m\angle 4 = 180$

5. What could also be proved true from the diagram in Exercise 4?

   A $m\angle 1 = m\angle 2$

   B $m\angle 3 = m\angle 4$

   C $m\angle 2 = m\angle 3$

   D $m\angle 2 = m\angle 4$

6. Given the diagram below, which of the following statements is NOT true?

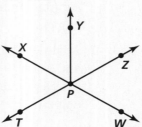

   F $\overleftrightarrow{PR}$ and $\overleftrightarrow{SQ}$ intersect in point T.

   G $\overrightarrow{PT}$ and $\overleftrightarrow{TQ}$ are both rays.

   H $\overleftrightarrow{ST}$ and $\overline{PR}$ are both segments.

   J $\overrightarrow{PT}$ and $\overleftrightarrow{QT}$ are opposite rays.

7. In the figure below, you cannot assume that ___?___ .

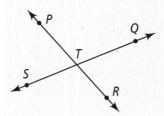

   A $\angle XPT$ and $\angle ZPW$ are vertical angles.

   B $m\angle YPW = 110$

   C Points T, P, and Z are collinear.

   D $\overleftrightarrow{XW}$ and $\overleftrightarrow{TZ}$ intersect in point P.

8. Which figure below shows a pair of supplementary angles that are NOT adjacent?

F

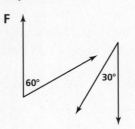

G

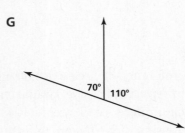

H

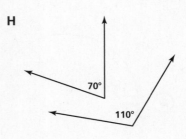

J

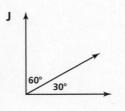

9. $\angle TUV$ and $\angle VUW$ are adjacent complementary angles. If $m\angle TUV = 80$, what is $m\angle VUW$?

    A 10

    B 90

    C 70

    D 170

10. Which item is never used to make constructions?

    F straightedge

    G measurement markings on a ruler

    H compass

    J pencil

11. Which diagram shows the construction of an angle bisector?

A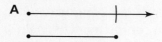

B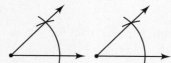

C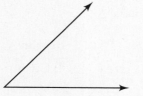

D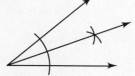

12. What is being constructed?

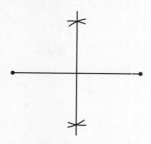

    F perpendicular bisector

    G parallel lines

    H circle

    J copy of an angle

13. What is the distance between points $A(1, 9)$ and $B(4, -2)$?

    A $\sqrt{58}$ **C** $\sqrt{130}$

    B 58   **D** 130

14. $\overline{AB}$ has endpoints $A(2, 4)$ and $B(8, y)$. If AB is 10, what is the value of y?

    F 8   **H** 64

    G 12   **J** 100

15. Q is the midpoint of $\overline{PR}$. What are the coordinates of point R?

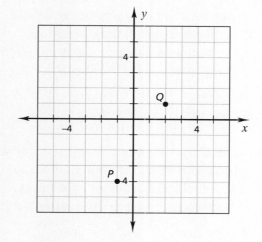

    A $(6, 5)$ **B** $(5, 6)$

    C $(4, 5)$ **D** $(2, 5)$

16. A rectangular picture has an area of 30 square inches. The length of the picture is 1 inch more than the width. What is the perimeter of the picture?

F 5 in.   **H** 11 in.
G 6 in.   **J** 22 in.

17. Given that the figure below is a quarter of a circle, which of the formulas could be used to find the length of the curved part?

A $\dfrac{\pi r}{4}$ **C** πr

B $\dfrac{\pi r}{2}$ **D** $\dfrac{\pi r^2}{2}$

18. The perimeter of a rectangle is 100 yd. If its width is four times its length, what is the area?

F 625 yd^2 **H** 400 yd^2
G 525 yd^2 **J** 225 yd^2

19. A regular postage stamp is approximately 2 centimeters wide and 3 centimeters tall. If there are 5 rows of 6 stamps on a sheet, what is the approximate area of the sheet?

A 54 cm   **C** 180 cm
B 54 cm^2 **D** 180 cm^2

20. What is the difference between the areas of a square with a side length of 4 units and a circle with a diameter of 4 units? Round your answer to the nearest tenth.

F π units   **H** 3.4 units
G 3.4 units^2 **J** 0 units^2

21. What is proven below?

Statement	Reason
1. $m\angle 1 + m\angle 2 = 90$	**1.** Given
2. $m\angle 2 + m\angle 3 = 90$	**2.** Given
3. $m\angle 1 + m\angle 2 = m\angle 2 + m\angle 3$	**3.** Transitive Property of Equality
4. $m\angle 1 = m\angle 3$	**4.** Subtraction Property of Equality
5. $\angle 1 \cong \angle 3$	**5.** Angles with the same measure are congruent.

A Angles 1 and 3 are congruent when angle 2 is a complement of both angles 1 and 3.
B Angles 1 and 3 are congruent when angle 2 is a complement of angle 1.
C Angles 1 and 3 are congruent when angle 2 is a complement of angle 3.
D Angles 1, 2, and 3 are right angles.

22. In the proof below, what reason is missing?

Given: $\angle 1$ and $\angle 2$ are right angles.
Prove: $\angle 1 \cong \angle 2$

Statement	Reason
1. $\angle 1$ and $\angle 2$ are right angles.	**1.** Given
2. $m\angle 1 = 90$ and $m\angle 2 = 90$	**2.** Definition of a right angle.
3. $m\angle 1 = m\angle 2$	**3.** ?
4. $\angle 1 \cong \angle 2$	**4.** Angles with the same measure are congruent.

F Subtraction Property of Equality
G Addition Property of Equality
H Transitive Property of Equality
J Angles with the same measure are congruent.

23. If $\overline{AQ}$ is a perpendicular bisector of $\overline{CB}$, the distance from A to C is the same as the distance from A to B. The proof is started below.

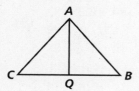

Statement	Reason
1. $\overline{AQ}$ is a perpendicular bisector of $\overline{CB}$.	**1.** Given
2. $\overline{AQ} \perp \overline{CB}$	**2.** Definition of perpendicular bisector.
3. $\overline{CQ} \cong \overline{QB}$	**3.** Definition of perpendicular bisector.
4. $\overline{AQ} \cong \overline{AQ}$	**4.** _?_

What property justifies the last statement?

A Symmetric
B Transitive
C Reflexive
D Substitution

24. What construction is being performed based on what is shown?

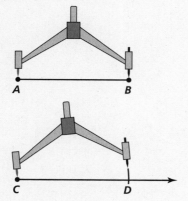

F Bisecting a segment
G Drawing a parallel line
H Copying a segment
J Drawing a perpendicular bisector

25. Which construction is shown in the diagram below?

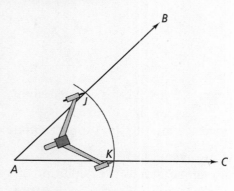

A Bisecting $\angle BAC$
B Copying $\angle BAC$
C Copying $\overline{JK}$
D Bisecting $\overline{JK}$

26. To construct the perpendicular bisector of $\overline{PQ}$, what is the correct first step?

F Put the compass point on point P and draw a long arc. Be sure the opening is equal to $\frac{1}{2}AB$.

G Put the compass point on point P and draw a short arc. Be sure the opening is equal to $\frac{1}{2}AB$.

H Put the compass point on point P and draw a long arc. Be sure the opening is greater than $\frac{1}{2}AB$.

J Put the compass point on point P and draw a short arc. Be sure the opening is greater than $\frac{1}{2}AB$.

27. Which statement and reason should go next in the following paragraph proof?

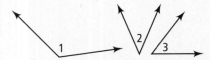

Given: $\angle 1$ and $\angle 2$ are supplementary.
$\qquad m\angle 2 = m\angle 3$
Prove: $\angle 1$ and $\angle 3$ are supplementary.

We are given that $\angle 1$ and $\angle 2$ are supplementary. By the definition of supplementary, $m\angle 1 + m\angle 2 = 180$. $m\angle 2 = m\angle 3$ is given.

A $\angle 1$ and $\angle 3$ are supplementary by the definition of supplementary.

B $m\angle 1 + m\angle 3 = 180$ by the Substitution Property of Equality.

C $\angle 2$ and $\angle 3$ are not supplementary by the definition of supplementary.

D $m\angle 3 = m\angle 2$ by the Symmetric Property.

28. In the figure below, if $m\angle AXC = 10x$, then $m\angle BXD = $ __?__ .

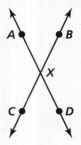

F $10x$ **H** $90 - 10x$
G $360 - 10x$ **J** $180 - 10x$

29. Find the value of x.

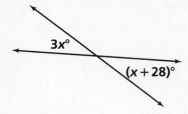

A $x = 7$
B $x = 14$
C $x = 9.3$
D $x = 4.7$

30. Name pairs of congruent angles in the figure.

I. $\angle EIF$ and $\angle GIH$
II. $\angle GIF$ and $\angle GIH$
III. $\angle EIF$ and $\angle GIF$
IV. $\angle EIG$ and $\angle FIH$

F I and IV
G II and III
H I and II
J I only

STOP

Name _____ Class _____ Date _____

Common Core Readiness Assessment 1 Report

Common Core State Standards	Test Items	Number Correct	Proficient? Yes or No	Geometry Student Edition Lesson(s)
Number and Quantity				
N.Q.A.1 Use units as a way to understand problems and to guide the solution of multi-step problems; choose and interpret units consistently in formulas; choose and interpret the scale and the origin in graphs and data displays.	1, 2, 3, 18, 19, 20			1-8
Geometry				
G.CO.A.1 Know precise definitions of angle, circle, perpendicular line, parallel line, and line segment, based on the undefined notions of point, line, distance along a line, and distance around a circular arc.	6, 7, 8, 9, 13, 14, 15, 16, 17, 27, 28, 29, 30			1-2, 1-3, 1-4, 1-6
G.CO.C.9 Prove theorems about lines and angles. *Theorems include: vertical angles are congruent; when a transversal crosses parallel lines, alternate interior angles are congruent and corresponding angles are congruent; points on a perpendicular bisector of a line segment are exactly those equidistant from the segment's endpoints.*	4, 5, 21, 22, 23			2-6
G.CO.D.12 Make formal geometric constructions with a variety of tools and methods (compass and straightedge, string, reflective devices, paper folding, dynamic geometric software, etc.). *Copying a segment; copying an angle; bisecting a segment; bisecting an angle; constructing perpendicular lines, including the perpendicular bisector of a line segment; and constructing a line parallel to a given line through a point not on the line.*	10, 11, 12, 24, 25, 26			1-6

Student Comments:

_____

_____

_____

_____

_____

_____

_____

Parent Comments:

_____

_____

_____

_____

_____

_____

_____

_____

_____

Teacher Comments:

_____

_____

_____

_____

_____

_____

_____

_____

_____

_____

Common Core Readiness Assessment 2

1. Use the diagram and the information given to complete the missing element of the two-column proof.

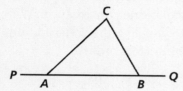

Given: $\angle CAP$ is an exterior angle of $\triangle CAB$.
Prove: $m\angle CAP = m\angle ABC + m\angle BCA$

Statements	Reasons
1. $\angle CAP$ is an exterior angle of $\triangle CAB$.	**1.** Given
2. $\angle CAP$ and $\angle CAB$ are supplementary.	**2.** Angles that form a straight angle are supplementary.
3. $m\angle CAP + m\angle CAB = 180$	**3.** Definition of supplementary angles
4. $m\angle ABC + m\angle BCA + m\angle CAB = 180$	**4.** Triangle Angle Sum Theorem
5. ?	**5.** Transitive Property of Equality
6. $m\angle CAP = m\angle ABC + m\angle BCA$	**6.** Subtraction Property of Equality

A $m\angle CBQ = 180 - m\angle ABC$
B $m\angle CAB = 180 - m\angle CAP$
C $m\angle CAP = 180 - m\angle CBQ$
D $m\angle CAP + m\angle CAB =$
$\quad m\angle ABC + m\angle BCA + m\angle CAB$

2. Use the diagram and the information given to complete the missing element of the two-column proof.

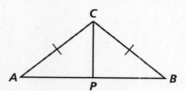

Given: Triangle ABC with $\overline{AC} \cong \overline{BC}$, $\overline{CP}$ bisects $\angle ACB$.
Prove: $\overline{CP} \perp \overline{AB}$

Statements	Reasons
1. $\overline{AC} \cong \overline{BC}$, $\overline{CP}$ bisects $\angle ACB$.	**1.** Given
2. $\angle ACP \cong \angle BCP$	**2.** Definition of angle bisector
3. $\overline{CP} \cong \overline{CP}$	**3.** Reflexive Property of congruent
4. $\triangle ACP \cong \triangle BCP$	**4.** SAS
5. $\angle CPA \cong \angle CPB$	**5.** Corresponding Parts of congruent Triangles are congruent
6. $\angle CPA$ and $\angle CPB$ are supplementary.	**6.** Angles that form a straight angle are supplementary.
7. $\angle CPA$ and $\angle CPB$ are right angles.	**7.** ?
8. $\overline{CP} \perp \overline{AB}$	**8.** Definition of perpendicular lines

F Angles opposite congruent sides of a triangle are congruent.
G Congruent supplementary angles are right angles.
H $\overline{CP} \perp \overline{PB}$
J Triangle Angle Sum Theorem

3. Find the value of x.

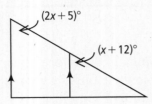

A $x = 3.5$
B $x = 7$
C $x = 8.5$
D $x = 17$

4. Classify the triangle produced by the following construction. Note that the final step is not shown.

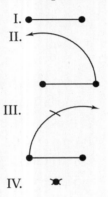

I.
II.
III.
IV.

F equilateral
G right
H right and isosceles
J obtuse and isosceles

5. Which line is perpendicular to the line $2x - 3y = 12$?

A $y = -\dfrac{2}{3}x + 12$
B $y = \dfrac{2}{3}x + 12$
C $y = -\dfrac{3}{2}x - 12$
D $y = \dfrac{3}{2}x - 12$

6. Which line is perpendicular to the line $x = \dfrac{1}{2}$?

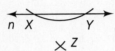

F $x = -2y$ **H** $x = -2$
G $y = -2x$ **J** $y = 2$

7. The diagrams below show steps for a perpendicular line construction. Which of the following lists the construction steps in the correct order?

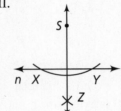

I.
II.
III.
IV.

A IV, II, I, III
B IV, II, III, I
C III, I, II, IV
D IV, I, II, III

8. What is the first step in constructing the perpendicular to line ℓ at point N?

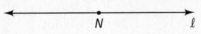

F Draw an arc above point N.
G Construct a 90° angle with vertex at point N.
H Mark two points on line l that are equidistant from N.
J With the compass at point N, draw a circle.

9. In the construction of a line parallel to line m though point P, what must be true about the construction of $\angle 1$ and $\angle PXY$?

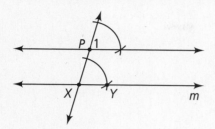

A $\angle 1$ and $\angle PXY$ must be acute.

B $\angle 1$ and $\angle PXY$ must be obtuse.

C $\angle 1$ and $\angle PXY$ must be congruent.

D $\angle 1$ and $\angle PXY$ must be supplementary.

10. Which of the following pairs of lines are not parallel?

F $y = -2, y = 4$

G $x + y = 3, x - y = 3$

H $y = \dfrac{1}{2}x + 5, y = \dfrac{1}{2}x - 4$

J $2x + y = -5, 6x + 3y = 9$

11. Which of the following lines is parallel to the line that passes through $(-1, -3)$ and $(5, 0)$?

A $y = \dfrac{1}{2}x + 9$

B $y = -\dfrac{1}{2}x - 3$

C $y = 2x + 5$

D $6x - 3y = -1$

12. What is the y-intercept of the line that is perpendicular to $y = -3x - 5$ and passes through the point $(-3, 7)$?

F 23   H 8

G $\dfrac{1}{3}$ J 10

13. Builders are replacing the congruent roofs on House A and House B. What is the measure of $\angle Z$ on House B?

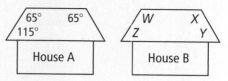

A 25°

B 65°

C 115°

D 180°

14. Engineers are planning a new cross street parallel to Elm St. What angle x should the new street make with Cedar Rd. so that it is parallel to Elm St?

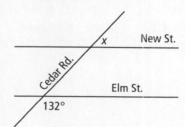

F 84°

G 132°

H 48°

J 42°

15. If these two triangular puzzle pieces are to be made congruent, what must be the measure of angle z?

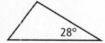

A 64°

B 116°

C 136°

D 26°

16. In the figure below, it is given that $\overline{BD} \cong \overline{CE}$. To prove $\triangle BCD \cong \triangle CBE$ by the SSS Congruence Theorem, what additional information is sufficient?

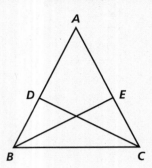

F $\angle A \cong \angle A$ **H** $\overline{AB} \cong \overline{AC}$
G $\overline{DC} \cong \overline{EB}$ **J** $\angle ADC \cong \angle AEB$

17. Given $\overline{AE}$ and $\overline{BD}$ bisect each other at point C, which congruence theorem would you use to prove $\triangle ABC \cong \triangle EDC$?

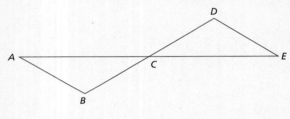

A HL   **C** SAS
B ASA   **D** SSS

18. For what values of x and y are the triangles congruent?

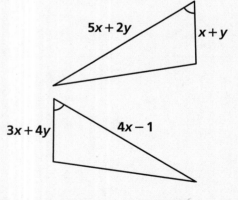

F $x = 2, y = -3$ **H** $x = 3, y = -2$
G $x = -2, y = 3$ **J** $x = -3, y = 2$

19. Under the conditions stated below, what postulate implies that $\triangle GHJ$ and $\triangle MHO$ are congruent?

$\overline{OH} \cong \overline{JH}, \angle O \cong \angle J$

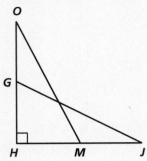

A ASA
B SAS
C SSS
D AAS

20. In the figure below, it is given that $\overline{AD} \cong \overline{AE}$. To prove $\triangle ADC \cong \triangle AEB$ by the ASA Congruence Theorem, what additional information is sufficient?

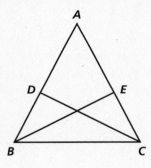

F $\overline{DC} \cong \overline{EB}$
G $\overline{AB} \cong \overline{AC}$
H $\angle ADC \cong \angle AEB$
J $\angle A \cong \angle A$

21. Use the diagram and the information given to complete the missing element of the two-column proof.

Given: $\overline{AB} \parallel \overline{XY}$
$\overline{AY}$ bisects $\overline{XB}$.
Prove: $\triangle AJB \cong \triangle YJX$.

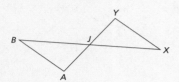

Statements	Reasons
1. $\overline{AB} \parallel \overline{XY}$	**1.** Given
2. $\angle B \cong \angle X$ $\angle A \cong \angle Y$	**2.** Converse of the Alternate Interior Angles Theorem then alt. int. $\angle$s are $\cong$.
3. $\overline{AY}$ bisects $\overline{XB}$.	**3.** Given
4. $\overline{JB} \cong \overline{JX}$	**4.** Definition of segment bisector
5. $\triangle AJB \cong \triangle YJX$	**5.** __?__

A ASA
B AAS
C SAS
D SSS

22. Given that $\overline{HF}$ is the bisector of $\angle EHG$ and $HE = HG$, which congruence statement can be used to prove that $\triangle EFH \cong \triangle GFH$?

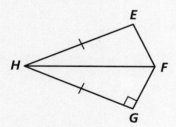

F ASA
G SAS
H HL
J SSS

23. In the figure, $\triangle PQR \cong \triangle RSP$ by SAS. What pair(s) of sides can you conclude are congruent by CPCTC?

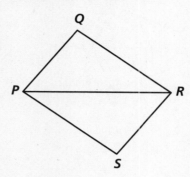

I. $\overline{QR} \cong \overline{SR}$
II. $\overline{QR} \cong \overline{SP}$
III. $\overline{QR} \cong \overline{PR}$

A I only
B I and II
C II only
D II and III

24. If $\triangle ABC \cong \triangle XYZ$ and $AB = 3$, $BC = 6$ and $AC = 4$, what is the length of $\overline{ZX}$?

F 3   H 5
G 4   J 60

25. Given $\triangle XYZ$ below, what is $m\angle XAY$?

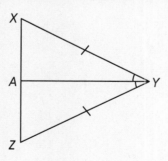

A 30°
B 60°
C 90°
D cannot be determined

Name _____ Class _____ Date _____

26. Which congruence statement can be used to prove that △EFH ≅ △GFH?

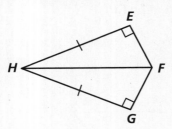

F HL
G SAS
H SSS
J ASA

27. The sails of two boats are pictured below. What is the value of y?

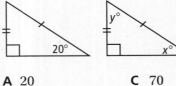

A 20   **C** 70
B 60   **D** 90

28. In the figure below, what is the measure of $\overline{GH}$?

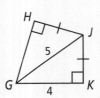

F 3   **H** 4
G 5   **J** 9

29. Under the conditions $\overline{JL} \cong \overline{NL}$ and $\overline{KL} \cong \overline{ML}$, what theorem or postulate implies △MJL ≅ △KNL?

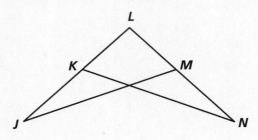

A SSS
B SAS
C ASA
D AAS

30. If $m\angle WYX = 35°$, what is $m\angle XZY$?

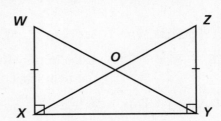

F 35°
G 145°
H 65°
J 55°

Common Core Readiness Assessment 2 Report

Common Core State Standards	Test Items	Number Correct	Proficient? Yes or No	Geometry Student Edition Lesson(s)
Geometry				
G.CO.C.9 Prove theorems about lines and angles. *Theorems include: vertical angles are congruent; when a transversal crosses parallel lines, alternate interior angles are congruent and corresponding angles are congruent; points on a perpendicular bisector of a line segment are exactly those equidistant from the segment's endpoints.*	1			3-2
G.CO.C.10 Prove theorems about triangles. *Theorems include: measures of interior angles of a triangle sum to 180°; base angles of isosceles triangles are congruent; the segment joining midpoints of two sides of a triangle is parallel to the third side and half the length; the medians of a triangle meet at a point.*	2			3-5, 4-5
G.CO.D.12 Make formal geometric constructions with a variety of tools and methods (compass and straightedge, string, reflective devices, paper folding, dynamic geometric software, etc.). *Copying a segment; copying an angle; bisecting a segment; bisecting an angle; constructing perpendicular lines, including the perpendicular bisector of a line segment; and constructing a line parallel to a given line through a point not on the line.*	7, 8, 9			3-6, 4-4, CB 3-2, CB 4-5
G.CO.D.13 Construct an equilateral triangle, a square, and a regular hexagon inscribed in a circle.	4			3-6, 4-5
G.SRT.B.5 Use congruence and similarity criteria for triangles to solve problems and to prove relationships in geometric figures.	3, 16–33			4-2, 4-3, 4-4, 4-5, 4-6, 4-7
G.GPE.B.5 Prove the slope criteria for parallel and perpendicular lines and use them to solve geometric problems (e.g., find the equation of a line parallel or perpendicular to a given line that passes through a given point).	5, 6, 10, 11, 12			3-8
G.MG.A.3 Apply geometric methods to solve design problems (e.g., designing an object or structure to satisfy physical constraints or minimize cost; working with typographic grid systems based on ratios).	13, 14, 15			3-4

Student Comments: _____

_____

_____

_____

_____

_____

Parent Comments: _____

_____

_____

_____

_____

_____

Teacher Comments: _____

_____

_____

_____

_____

_____

Common Core Readiness Assessment 3

1.

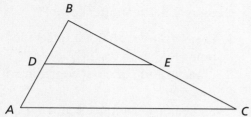

If you know that $\overline{DE} \parallel \overline{AC}$, and that D and E are midpoints, which of the following justifies that $AC = 2DE$?

A Triangle Midsegment Theorem
B Median-Altitude Theorem
C Corresp. parts of ≅ ⚠ are ≅
D Definition of triangle bisector

2. Find the measure of angle MNQ.

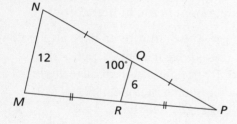

F 60
G 80
H 100
J 120

3. Find the value of x.

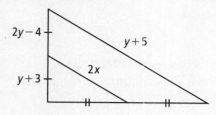

A 3
B 6
C 7
D 12

4. $\overline{SU}$, $\overline{RW}$, and $\overline{VT}$ are medians. Find the length of $\overline{XT}$.

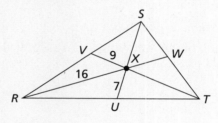

F 9   **H** 16
G 14   **J** 18

5. What is the point of concurrency of the lines containing the altitudes of a triangle?

A circumcenter
B incenter
C orthocenter
D centroid

6. Which of the following can be used to inscribe a circle in a triangle?

   F circumcenter
   G incenter
   H orthocenter
   J centroid

7. What is the center of a circle circumscribed about a triangle with vertices $(-2, 2)$ $(2, -2)$, and $(6, 2)$?

   A $(2, 2)$
   B $(2, 0)$
   C $(0, 2)$
   D $(0, 0)$

8. Suppose you are asked to complete the following indirect proof.

Given: n is negative.

Prove: n^2 is positive.

Which of the following is the assumption in the indirect proof?

   F n is positive.
   G n^2 is negative.
   H n is any real number.
   J n is neither positive nor negative.

9. Given: Lines m and n intersect in point P.

Prove: Lines m and n are coplanar.

Which of the following could be a statement in the indirect proof?

   A Lines m and n do not intersect in point P.
   B Lines m and n are not coplanar with point P.
   C Since lines m and n are not in the same plane, they do not share common points.
   D Since lines m and n do not share common points, they are not coplanar.

10. Given: $\triangle ABC$ is an isosceles triangle and $m\angle A = 90$.

Prove: $\angle A$ is the vertex angle.

Which of the following could be a statement in the indirect proof?

   F By the definition of base angles of an isosceles triangle, $\angle A \cong \angle B$.
   G By the definition of base angles of an isosceles triangle, $\angle B \cong \angle C$.
   H If $\angle A \cong \angle B$, then $m\angle A + m\angle B + m\angle C < 180$.
   J If $\angle A \cong \angle B$, then $m\angle A + m\angle B + m\angle C = 180$.

11. In a field, Raja, Mary, and Miguel are standing in the shape of a triangle. Raja is 128 feet from Mary, and Mary is 143 feet from Miguel. Which of the following is a possible distance between Raja and Miguel?

    A 153 feet

    B 271 feet

    C 288 feet

    D 307 feet

12. On a map, Meridian, Birmingham, and Montgomery form a triangle. Meridian is 109 miles from Birmingham and Birmingham is 91 miles from Montgomery. Which of the following is not a possible distance between Montgomery and Meridian?

    F 18 miles

    G 25 miles

    H 135 miles

    J 199 miles

13. The lengths of two sides of a triangle are 4 and 7. Give all possible lengths for the third side if the lengths of the sides are all integers.

    A 6, 7, 8, 9, 10, 11, 12

    B 3, 4, 5, 6, 7, 8

    C 5, 6, 7, 8

    D 4, 5, 6, 7, 8, 9, 10

14. What is the sum of the measures of the interior angles of the figure below?

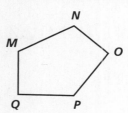

    F 900

    G 720

    H 540

    J 360

15. The measure of each interior angle of a regular 12-sided polygon is _?_ .

    A 148

    B 150

    C 152

    D 180

16. Figure *ABCDEF* is a regular hexagon. What is the measure of $\angle EFG$?

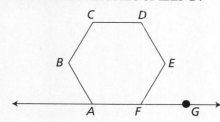

    F 40

    G 60

    H 90

    J 120

Name _____ Class _____ Date _____

Use the given coordinates to prove the most precise name for each quadrilateral.

17. $B(-3,1)$, $A(0,5)$, $L(4,2)$, $K(1,-2)$

    A square

    B parallelogram

    C rectangle

    D rhombus

18. $Q(1,1)$, $U(2,-4)$, $A(-3,-3)$, $D(-4,2)$

    F parallelogram

    G square

    H rhombus

    J rectangle

19. $C(4,-3)$, $D(0,-5)$, $E(-3,1)$, $F(1,3)$

    A parallelogram

    B square

    C rectangle

    D rhombus

20. Which of the following would prove that quadrilateral $QRST$ is a parallelogram?

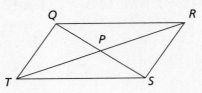

    F $\overline{QR} \cong \overline{ST}$

    G $\overline{QR} \parallel \overline{ST}$

    H $\overline{QP} \cong \overline{PS}$ and $\overline{TP} \cong \overline{PR}$

    J Two pairs of sides are congruent.

21. In $\triangle TRI$, M and D are midpoints of $\overline{IT}$ and $\overline{IR}$, respectively. Which can be proven true?

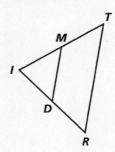

    A The measure of angle T is equal to the measure of angle R.

    B $MD = \left(\dfrac{1}{2}\right)TR$

    C $IM = \left(\dfrac{1}{2}\right)IR$

    D $\overline{IT} \cong \overline{IR}$

22. Which additional piece of information would prove that quadrilateral *WXYZ* shown below is a parallelogram?

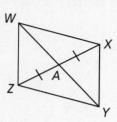

   F $\overline{WA} \cong \overline{AY}$
   G $\overline{WZ} \cong \overline{XY}$
   H $\angle WAX \cong \angle ZAY$
   J $m\angle WAX + m\angle YAX = 180$

23. The values for which ordered pair will show that *MATH* is a parallelogram?

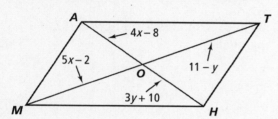

   A $\left(-6, \dfrac{1}{4}\right)$
   B $(1,1)$
   C $(4,-7)$
   D $(3,-2)$

24. Use the given coordinates to classify the triangle and find its perimeter *P*.
$S(1,-6), A(6,-6), U(3,-2)$

   F acute isosceles; $P = 15$
   G acute isosceles; $P = 10 + 2\sqrt{5}$
   H acute scalene; $P = 10 + 2\sqrt{5}$
   J acute scalene; $P = 15$

25. Arcs of congruent circles were constructed from the endpoints of $\overline{XY}$, intersecting at points *A* and *B* as shown. What is true about any point *P* on $\overleftrightarrow{AB}$ in this construction?

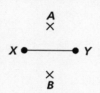

   A $\triangle PXY$ will be an acute isosceles triangle.
   B $\triangle PXY$ will be an equilateral triangle.
   C *P* will be on the perpendicular bisector of $\overline{XY}$.
   D *P* will be equidistant from *A* and *B*.

26. Which of the following statements is NOT true?

   F The diagonals of a rhombus are perpendicular to each other.
   G The diagonals of a kite are perpendicular to each other.
   H The diagonals of a kite bisect each other.
   J The diagonals of a parallelogram bisect each other.

27. The coordinates of three vertices of a parallelogram are $(0, 0)$, $(8, 5)$, and $(15, 7)$. Which of the following is a possible fourth vertex?

A $(-7, -2)$
B $(-3, -8)$
C $(23, 12)$
D $(7, 2)$

28. The figure shown is a kite. What is the x-coordinate of point P?

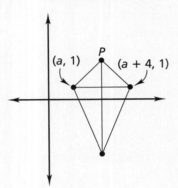

F $\dfrac{a}{2} + 4$

G $\dfrac{a + 4}{2}$

H $a + 2$

J $2a + 4$

29. Find the midpoint of the midsegment of the trapezoid if $A = (4s, 4t)$, $B = (4u, 4t)$, and $C = (4v, 0)$.

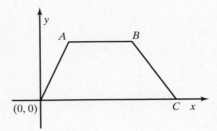

A $(t + u + v, t)$
B $(s + u + v, 2t)$
C $(u + 2v, 2t)$
D $(2s + 2u, 2t + 2t)$

30. Quadrilateral $JKLM$ has vertices $J(-4, -1)$, $K(-1, 2)$, and $L(6, 2)$. For what coordinates of point M is $JKLM$ a parallelogram?

F $(3, -2)$
G $(3, -1)$
H $(4, 0)$
J $(4, -1)$

Common Core Readiness Assessment 3 Report

Common Core State Standards	Test Items	Number Correct	Proficient? Yes or No	Geometry Student Edition Lesson(s)
Geometry				
G.CO.C.9 Prove theorems about lines and angles. *Theorems include: vertical angles are congruent; when a transversal crosses parallel lines, alternate interior angles are congruent and corresponding angles are congruent; points on a perpendicular bisector of a line segment are exactly those equidistant from the segment's endpoints.*	8, 9			5-2
G.CO.C.10 Prove theorems about triangles. *Theorems include: measures of interior angles of a triangle sum to 180°; base angles of isosceles triangles are congruent; the segment joining midpoints of two sides of a triangle is parallel to the third side and half the length; the medians of a triangle meet at a point.*	10, 21			5-1, 5-4
G.CO.C.11 Prove theorems about parallelograms. *Theorems include: opposite sides are congruent, opposite angles are congruent, the diagonals of a parallelogram bisect each other and its converse, rectangles are parallelograms with congruent diagonals.*	20, 22, 23, 26			6-2, 6-3, 6-4, 6-5
G.CO.D.12 Make formal geometric constructions with a variety of tools and methods (compass and straightedge, string, reflective devices, paper folding, dynamic geometric software, etc.). *Copying a segment; copying an angle; bisecting a segment; bisecting an angle; constructing perpendicular lines, including the perpendicular bisector of a line segment; and constructing a line parallel to a given line through a point not on the line.*	25			5-2, CB 6-9
G.SRT.B.5 Use congruence and similarity criteria for triangles to solve problems and to prove relationships in geometric figures.	1, 2, 3, 4, 11, 12, 13, 14, 15, 16			5-1, 5-2, 5-4, 6-1, 6-2, 6-3, 6-4, 6-5, 6-6
G.C.A.3 Construct the inscribed and circumscribed circles of a triangle, and prove properties of angles for a quadrilateral inscribed in a circle.	5, 6			5-3
G.GPE.B.4 Use coordinates to prove simple geometric theorems algebraically.	7, 17, 18, 19, 27, 28, 29, 30			6-9
G.GPE.B.7 Use coordinates to compute perimeters of polygons and areas of triangles and rectangles, e.g., using the distance formula.	24			6-7

Student Comments:

_____
_____
_____
_____
_____
_____
_____

Parent Comments:

_____
_____
_____
_____
_____
_____
_____
_____

Teacher Comments:

_____
_____
_____
_____
_____
_____
_____
_____

Common Core Readiness Assessment 4

1. Use the diagram and the information given to complete the missing element of the two-column proof.

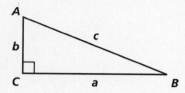

Given: $\triangle ABC$ with right angle C
Prove: $\sin A = \cos(\text{complement of } A)$

Statements	Reasons
1. $\triangle ABC$ is a right triangle.	**1.** Given
2. $\sin A = \dfrac{a}{c}$, $\cos B = \dfrac{a}{c}$	**2.** Definitions of sine and cosine ratios
3. _?_	**3.** Transitive Property of Equality
4. $\angle A, \angle B$ are complementary.	**4.** Acute angles of a right triangle are complementary.
5. $\sin A = \cos$ (complement of A)	**5.** Substitution Property of Equality

A $a^2 + b^2 = c^2$

B $\tan A = \dfrac{1}{\tan B}$

C $\sin A = \cos B$

D $\tan B = \dfrac{b}{a}$

2. $\triangle ABC \sim \triangle DEF$ and the similarity ratio of $\triangle ABC$ to $\triangle DEF$ is $\dfrac{4}{3}$. If $AB = 60$, what is DE?

F 80

G 45

H 15

J 180

3. Your parents are ordering your school pictures. They order one 8×10 (8 inches by 10 inches), two 5×7's, and 8 wallet size (2.5 inches by 3.25 inches). Which of the pictures are similar in dimension?

A wallet and 5×7

B wallet and 8×10

C 5×7 and 8×7

D none are similar

4. Which additional piece of information would be sufficient to prove $\triangle ABC \sim \triangle DEF$?

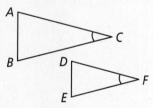

F $\angle A \cong \angle D$

G $\angle C \cong \angle E$

H $\angle A \cong \angle F$

J $\angle B \cong \angle F$

5. Given triangles I, II, and III below, which are similar?

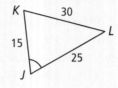
I

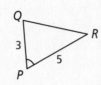
II   III

A I and II only
B II and III only
C I and III only
D I, II, and III

6. What is the perimeter of △ *PQR*?

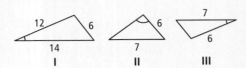

F 8
G 38
H 14
J 70

7. A young girl with a height of 124 centimeters casts a shadow that is 93 centimeters long. She is standing next to a tree that casts a shadow that is 13.5 meters long. How tall is the tree?

A 14 m
B 16 m
C 18 m
D 20 m

8. A 96-ft high transmission tower casts a 72-ft long shadow. An anchor wire runs from the top of the tower to the tip of the shadow. A ladder is set up vertically 66 feet from the base of the tower so the top of the ladder touches the wire. What is the height of the ladder?

F 6 ft
G 8 ft
H 10 ft
J 12 ft

9. A surveyor wants to find the distance *d* across a river. Using the measurements shown, what is a good estimate of *d*, in feet?

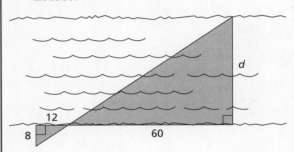

A 30 feet
B 40 feet
C 50 feet
D 60 feet

10. What is the height, *x*, in the triangle below?

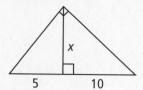

F $2\sqrt{5}$
G 5
H $5\sqrt{2}$
J 10

11. Find the height, *x*, of the triangle.

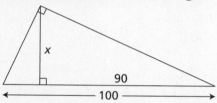

A 30
B 40
C 50
D 60

12. In $\triangle ABC$, $AC = 3$ and $CB = 4$. Which segment has a length of 1.8?

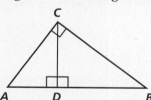

F $\overline{BC}$
G $\overline{DC}$
H $\overline{DB}$
J $\overline{DA}$

13. What is the value of *x* in the diagram below?

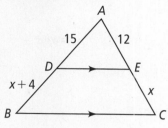

A 12
B 16
C 18
D 20

14. Given that $\triangle ABC$ is similar to $\triangle PQC$, explain why $\overleftrightarrow{AB}$ and $\overleftrightarrow{PQ}$ are parallel.

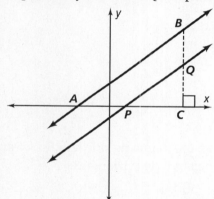

F Since Q is the midpoint of $\overline{BC}$, $\overleftrightarrow{AB}$ and $\overleftrightarrow{PQ}$ are parallel.

G Since $\triangle ABC$ and $\triangle PQC$ are right triangles, their hypotenuses are parallel.

H Since $\triangle ABC \sim \triangle PQC$, $\overline{AP} = \overline{BQ}$ and $\overline{PC} = \overline{QC}$. Therefore, $\overleftrightarrow{AB}$ and $\overleftrightarrow{PQ}$ are parallel.

J $\angle BAC \cong \angle QPC$ since they are corresponding angles of similar triangles. This pair of $\cong$ corresponding angles also makes $\overleftrightarrow{AB}$ and $\overleftrightarrow{PQ}$ parallel.

15. If $\triangle ABC$ is a triangle with $m\angle C = 90°$, which of the following must be true about angles A and B?

A $\dfrac{1}{\sin A} = \sin B$

B $\cos A = 1 - \cos B$

C $\tan A + \dfrac{1}{\tan B} = 1$

D $\sin A = \cos B$

16. What is the length of the hypotenuse of the triangle below to the nearest tenth?

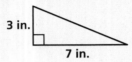

F 9.1 in.

G 8.6 in.

H 8.1 in.

J 7.6 in.

17. Given the following side lengths, which triangle is a right triangle?

A 10, 14, 24

B 10, 24, 26

C 13, 14, 28

D 14, 20, 26

18. What is the total perimeter of the two triangles shown below?

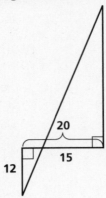

F 52 units

G 111 units

H 120 units

J 159 units

19. The length of one leg of a 45°-45°-90° triangle is 24. What is the perimeter of the triangle?

A $24\sqrt{2}$

B $24 + 24\sqrt{2}$

C $48 + 24\sqrt{2}$

D 96

20. Find the values of x and y.

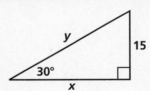

F $x = 15\sqrt{3}; y = 45$

G $x = 15\sqrt{2}; y = 30$

H $x = 30; y = 45$

J $x = 15\sqrt{3}; y = 30$

21. Find the value of *x*.

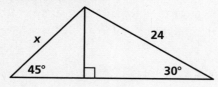

A $12\sqrt{2}$

B $24\sqrt{2}$

C 24

D 12

22. Choose the correct expression for tan *H*.

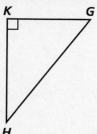

F $\dfrac{GK}{KH}$

G $\dfrac{GH}{KH}$

H $\dfrac{GK}{GH}$

J $\dfrac{KH}{KG}$

23. In △ *STU*, what is the sine ratio of ∠ *T* ?

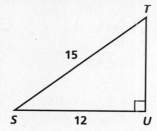

A $\dfrac{9}{15}$

B $\dfrac{12}{15}$

C $\dfrac{9}{12}$

D $\dfrac{15}{12}$

24. Find *x* to the nearest hundredth.

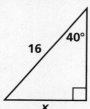

F *x* = 24.89

G *x* = 13.43

H *x* = 10.28

J *x* = 12.26

25. In △LMN, $m\angle L = 6°$, $m\angle N = 2°$, and MN = 16 in. Find LM. Round your answer to the nearest tenth.

  A 36.2 in.
  B 5.3 in.
  C 17.4 in.
  D 6.5 in.

26. In △XYZ, $m\angle Z = 34$, x = 61 cm, and z = 42 cm. Find $m\angle X$. Round your answer to the nearest tenth of a degree.

  F 54.3
  G 87.3
  H 22.6
  J 22.6 or 157.4

27. What is the area of △FGH to the nearest tenth of a square meter?

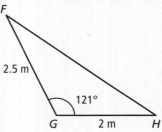

  A 4.3 m
  B 2.1 m
  C 2.5 m
  D 4.9 m

28. In △ABC, $m\angle B = 45$, a = 24 ft, and c = 30 ft. Find b. Round your answer to the nearest tenth.

  F 38.4 ft
  G 31.1 ft
  H 25.5 ft
  J 21.4 ft

29. In △DEF, d = 25 in., e = 28 in., and f = 20 in. Find $m\angle F$. Round your answer to the nearest tenth.

  A 43.9
  B 60.1
  C 76.1
  D 53.2

30. What is the measure of $\angle C$? Round your answer to the nearest tenth of a degree.

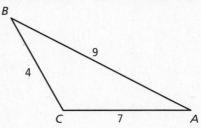

  F 73.4
  G 74.1
  H 106.6
  J 100.7

Common Core Readiness Assessment 4 Report

Common Core State Standards	Test Items	Number Correct	Proficient? Yes or No	Geometry Student Edition Lesson(s)
Geometry				
G.SRT.B.4 Prove theorems about triangles. *Theorems include: a line parallel to one side of a triangle divides the other two proportionally and its converse; the Pythagorean Theorem proved using triangle similarity.*	1			7-5, 8-1
G.SRT.B.5 Use congruence and similarity criteria for triangles to solve problems and to prove relationships in geometric figures.	2, 4, 5, 6, 10, 13			7-2, 7-3, 7-4
G.SRT.C.6 Understand that by similarity, side ratios in right triangles are properties of the angles in the triangle, leading to definitions of trigonometric ratios for acute angles.	11, 12, 22, 23			CB 8-3
G.SRT.C.7 Explain and use the relationship between the sine and cosine of complementary angles.	15			8-3
G.SRT.C.8 Use trigonometric ratios and the Pythagorean Theorem to solve right triangles in applied problems.	7, 8, 9,16, 17, 19, 21, 24			8-1, 8-2, 8-3, 8-4, CB 8-4
G.SRT.D.10 (+) Prove the Laws of Sines and Cosines and use them to solve problems.	18			8-5, 8-6
G.SRT.D.11 (+) Understand and apply the Law of Sines and the Law of Cosines to find unknown measurements in right and non-right triangles (e.g., surveying problems, resultant forces).	20, 25, 26, 27, 28, 29, 30			8-5, 8-6
G.GPE.B.5 Prove the slope criteria for parallel and perpendicular lines and use them to solve geometric problems (e.g., find the equation of a line parallel or perpendicular to a given line that passes through a given point).	14			7-3, 7-4
G.MG.A.1 Use geometric shapes, their measures, and their properties to describe objects (e.g., modeling a tree trunk or a human torso as a cylinder).	3			8-3

Student Comments:

_____

_____

_____

_____

_____

_____

_____

Parent Comments:

_____

_____

_____

_____

_____

_____

_____

Teacher Comments:

_____

_____

_____

_____

_____

_____

_____

Common Core Readiness Assessment 5

1. The vertices of $\triangle JKL$ are $J(-1, 8)$, $K(3, 5)$, and $L(6, -9)$. What are the vertices of the $T_{<4, -2>}(JKL)$?

  A $J'(-1, 8)$, $K'(3, 5)$, $L'(6, -9)$
  B $J'(4, -2)$, $K'(3, 5)$, $L'(6, -9)$
  C $J'(3, 6)$, $K'(7, 3)$, $L'(10, -11)$
  D $J'(-3, 12)$, $K'(1, 9)$, $L'(4, -5)$

2. Describe a single transformation of $\triangle ABC$ that is a composition of the following pair of transformations: $T_{<-5, -3>}(ABC)$ followed by $T_{<-4, -2>}(A'B'C')$.

  F $T_{<-1, -5>}(ABC)$
  G $T_{<-9, -5>}(ABC)$
  H $T_{<-9, -1>}(ABC)$
  J $T_{<-1, -1>}(ABC)$

3. $T_{<a, b>}(ABCD) = (A'B'C'D')$. If A is $(6, -8)$, A' is $(-2, 4)$, and B is $(4, -6)$, what are the coordinates of B'?

  A $(-4, -12)$
  B $(-8, -4)$
  C $(-4, 6)$
  D $(-2, -12)$

4. What are the coordinates of $R_{<y\text{-}axis>}(B)$?

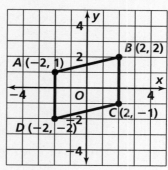

  F $(2, -2)$
  G $(-2, -2)$
  H $(-2, 2)$
  J $(2, 2)$

5. T' is the reflection of T across the line $x = 6$. If the coordinates of T' are $(-3, 7)$, what are the coordinates of T?

  A $(-3, -7)$
  B $(3, 7)$
  C $(7, 15)$
  D $(15, 7)$

6. What is the image of $E(3, 2)$ after being reflected across $x = -1$ and then being reflected across the x-axis?

  F $(-5, 2)$
  G $(-5, -2)$
  H $(5, 2)$
  J $(5, -2)$

7. If $\overline{AB}$ is rotated 90° about A the same way the hands of a clock move, what would be the coordinates of Point A'?

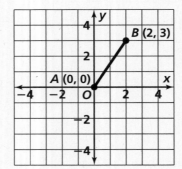

  A $(-1, 0)$
  B $(0, 0)$
  C $(0, -1)$
  D $(2, -1)$

8. Which of the following mappings of **OPEN** is NOT the result of just a single rotation?

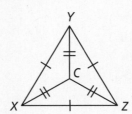

9. For $\triangle XYZ$, find the angle of rotation about point C that maps point X to point Z.

  A 30°
  B 60°
  C 120°
  D 180°

10. A dilation has center $(0, 0)$. What is the image of $H(-2, 4)$ for scale factor 1.5?

   F $H'(3, 6)$

   G $H'(-3, 6)$

   H $H'(-0.05, 5.5)$

   J $H'\left(-\dfrac{4}{3}, \dfrac{8}{3}\right)$

11. N-scale model trains have a scale factor 1 : 160. An N-scale model engine measures 3.75 in. What is the length of the actual engine?

   A 163.75 in.

   B 60 in.

   C $42\dfrac{2}{3}$ ft

   D 600 in.

12. $P'Q'R'S'$ is a dilation of $PQRS$. Describe the dilation.

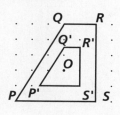

   F enlargement; center P; scale factor 2

   G enlargement; center O; scale factor 2

   H reduction; center P; scale factor $\dfrac{1}{2}$

   J reduction; center O; scale factor $\dfrac{1}{2}$

13. What is the area of △*TUV*?

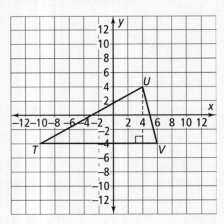

A 20 in.²

B 64 in.²

C 96 in.²

D 128 in.²

14. The area of parallelogram *MNOP* is 126 cm². The coordinates of *N* and *Q* are given. What is the length of $\overline{OP}$?

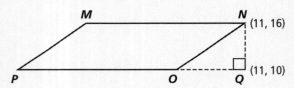

F 21 cm

G 42 cm

H 120 cm

J 756 cm

15. What is the area of the figure shown below?

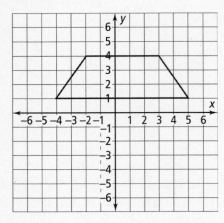

A 15 ft²

B 17 ft²

C 21 ft²

D 27 ft²

16. The area of two similar pentagons are 48 in.² and 75 in.² What is the ratio of their sides?

F 16 : 25

G 1 : 3

H 4 : 5

J 48 : 75

17. Circles C and C' with radii r and R are centered at the origin. C' is a dilation of C. What is the scale factor? What conclusion can be drawn from the fact that C' is a dilation of C?

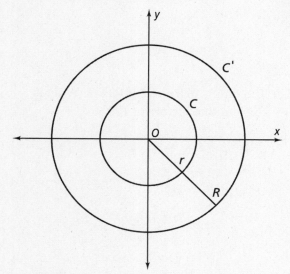

A $\dfrac{R}{r}$; C is similar to C'.

B $R + r$; C' has twice the circumference of C.

C $\dfrac{R}{r}$; C is a translation of C'.

D $R - r$; the ratio of the areas is $\dfrac{R}{r}$.

18. The two trapezoids below are similar. If the area of the small trapezoid is 70 ft², what is the area of the large trapezoid?

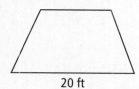

16 ft

20 ft

F 87.5 ft²
G 99.375 ft²
H 102.5 ft²
J 109.375 ft²

19. What is the area of the triangle below? Round your answer to the nearest tenth.

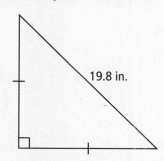

19.8 in.

A 49.0 in.²
B 98.0 in.²
C 138.6 in.²
D 196.0 in.²

20. What is the area of the regular pentagon?

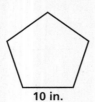

10 in.

   F about 345 in.^{2}
   G about 180 in.^{2}
   H about 172 in.^{2}
   J about 90 in.^{2}

21. What is the area of the regular dodecagon?

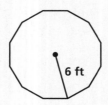

6 ft

   A about 53.9 ft^2
   B about 107.9 ft^2
   C about 139.2 ft^2
   D about 171.1 ft^2

22. The circumference of a circle is 15π mm. What is the radius of the circle?

   F 7.5 mm
   G 15 mm
   H 22.5 mm
   J 30 mm

23. The radius of a circle is 63 cm. What is the length of an arc of 120°?

   A 36.75π cm
   B 2315.35π cm
   C 73.5π cm
   D 42π cm

24. What is the length of $\overarc{MN}$? Round your answer to the nearest tenth.

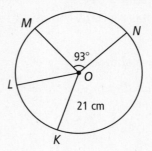

   F 17.0 cm
   G 30.5 cm
   H 85.4 cm
   J 131.9 cm

25. The diameter of a circle is 9 yd. What is the area of the circle?

    A 3π yd^2

    B 4.5π yd^2

    C 20.25π yd^2

    D 81π yd^2

26. Find the area of sector *TOP*. Round your answer to the nearest tenth.

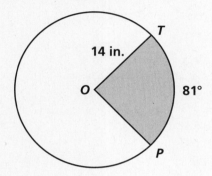

    F 19.8 in.^{2}

    G 138.5 in.^{2}

    H 9.9 in.^{2}

    J 277.1 in.^{2}

27. What is the area of the shaded segment? Round your answer to the nearest tenth.

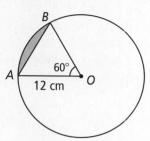

    A 13.0 cm^2

    B 44.2 cm^2

    C 62.4 cm^2

    D 75.4 cm^2

28. Assume that a dart you throw hits the dartboard shown and is equally likely to hit any spot on the board. Find the probability of hitting the shaded region.

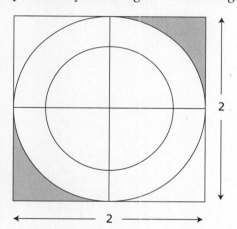

    F 10.7%

    G 21.5%

    H 42.9%

    J 78.5%

29. A square dart board at a carnival has a target that is shaped like a regular hexagon. Since few players were winning, the size of the target was increased as shown. What is the probability that a dart that hits the new board lands on the target?

Old Board

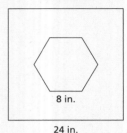

8 in.

24 in.

New Board

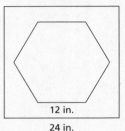

12 in.

24 in.

A 30%

B 43%

C 54%

D 65%

30. Four circles, each of radius 7 inches, are packed in a square as shown. If you throw a dart and hit the square target, what is the probability that your dart will land inside one of the circles? Express your answer as a percent to the nearest tenth.

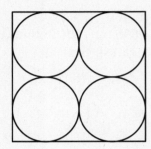

F 67.5%

G 78.5%

H 75.0%

J 50.0%

Common Core Readiness Assessment 5 Report

Common Core State Standards	Test Items	Number Correct	Proficient? Yes or No	Geometry Student Edition Lesson(s)
Geometry				
G.CO.A.1 Know precise definitions of angle, circle, perpendicular line, parallel line, and line segment, based on the undefined notions of point, line, distance along a line, and distance around a circular arc.	23, 24			10-6
G.CO.A.2 Represent transformations in the plane using, e.g., transparencies and geometry software; describe transformations as functions that take points in the plane as inputs and give other points as outputs. Compare transformations that preserve distance and angle to those that do not (e.g., translation versus horizontal stretch).	2, 5, 6			9-1, 9-2, 9-3, 9-4, 9-6 CB 9-1
G.CO.A.3 Given a rectangle, parallelogram, trapezoid, or regular polygon, describe the rotations and reflections that carry it onto itself.	3, 4, 9			CB 9-3
G.CO.A.4 Develop definitions of rotations, reflections, and translations in terms of angles, circles, perpendicular lines, parallel lines, and line segments.	8			9-1, 9-2, 9-3
G.CO.A.5 Given a geometric figure and a rotation, reflection, or translation, draw the transformed figure using, e.g., graph paper, tracing paper, or geometry software. Specify a sequence of transformations that will carry a given figure onto another.	1			9-1, 9-2, 9-3, 9-4 CB 9-2
G.CO.B.6 Use geometric descriptions of rigid motions to transform figures and to predict the effect of a given rigid motion on a given figure; given two figures, use the definition of congruence in terms of rigid motions to decide if they are congruent.	7			9-1, 9-2, 9-3, 9-4, 9-5
G.SRT.A.1.b The dilation of a line segment is longer or shorter in the ratio given by the scale factor.	10, 11			CB 9-6
G.SRT.A.2 Given two figures, use the definition of similarity in terms of similarity transformations to decide if they are similar; explain using similarity transformations the meaning of similarity for triangles as the equality of all corresponding pairs of angles and the proportionality of all corresponding pairs of sides.	12			9-7

Name _____ Class _____ Date _____

Common Core Readiness Assessment 5 Report

Common Core State Standards	Test Items	Number Correct	Proficient? Yes or No	Geometry Student Edition Lesson(s)
G.SRT.A.3 Use the properties of similarity transformations to establish the AA criterion for two triangles to be similar.	16, 18			9-7
G.SRT.D.9 (+) Derive the formula $A = 1/2\ ab$ sin(C) for the area of a triangle by drawing an auxiliary line from a vertex perpendicular to the opposite side.	19, 20, 21			10-5
G.C.A.1 Prove that all circles are similar.	17			10-6
G.C.A.2 Identify and describe relationships among inscribed angles, radii, and chords. *Include the relationship between central, inscribed, and circumscribed angles; inscribed angles on a diameter are right angles; the radius of a circle is perpendicular to the tangent where the radius intersects the circle.*	22, 25			10-6, CB 10-6
G.C.B.5 Derive using similarity the fact that the length of the arc intercepted by an angle is proportional to the radius, and define the radian measure of the angle as the constant of proportionality; derive the formula for the area of a sector.	26, 27			10-6, 10-7
G.GPE.B.7 Use coordinates to compute perimeters of polygons and areas of triangles and rectangles, e.g., using the distance formula.	13, 14, 15			10-1
S.CP.A.1 Describe events as subsets of a sample space (the set of outcomes) using characteristics (or categories) of the outcomes, or as unions, intersections, or complements of other events ("or", "and", "not").	28, 29, 30			10-8

Quarter 1 Test

Chapters 1–3

Form G

1. Find the value of x if $AC = 16$.

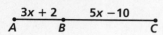

2. Find the value of x.

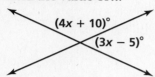

3. Construct the perpendicular bisector of $\overline{LM}$.

4. Construct a square with side length SQ.

5. What theorem justifies the following statement?

If $\angle 1$ and $\angle 2$ are complementary, and $\angle 1$ and $\angle 3$ are complementary, then $\angle 2 \cong \angle 3$.

6. Construct the bisector of $\angle STU$.

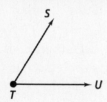

7. Line a is parallel to line b. Line a is also parallel to line c. How are lines b and c related? Explain.

8. Find the measure of $\angle TQM$.

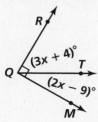

9. Reorder the reasons of the following proof to match the correct statements.

Given: $\overleftrightarrow{a}$ is parallel to $\overleftrightarrow{b}$.
Prove: $\angle 1$ is supplementary to $\angle 3$.

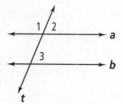

Statements	Reasons
1. $\overleftrightarrow{a}$ is parallel to $\overleftrightarrow{b}$.	a. Congruent Supplements Theorem
2. $\angle 1$ and $\angle 2$ are supplementary.	b. Corresponding Angles postulate
3. $\angle 2 \cong \angle 3$	c. Angles that form a straight angle are supplementary.
4. $\angle 1$ is supplementary to $\angle 3$.	d. Given

10. Find the intersection of planes ABC and LMO.

11. Find the circumference of a circle with area 36π m^2.

12. Given $K(-6, -2)$ and $M(2, 2)$, the midpoint of $\overline{KG}$, find the coordinates of G.

13. Construct a line that is perpendicular to ℓ at point P.

14. Find the coordinate of the midpoint of $\overline{TR}$ with $T(8, -3)$ and $R(-6, 8)$.

Quarter 1 Test (continued)

Form G

Chapters 1–3

15. Write an equation for the line parallel to $y = 3x + 4$ that contains $(3, 10)$.

16. What conditions in the figure below will prove $\ell \parallel m$?

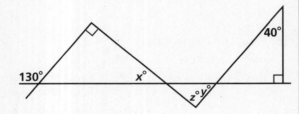

17. Find the length of $\overline{AB}$, given $A(5, -2)$ and $B(-3, -4)$.

18. What is the intersection of a plane and a line not contained in the plane?

19. Writing Explain why the following statement is incorrect:

If two lines do not intersect, then they are parallel.

Use the figure for Exercises 20–22.

20. Find the value of x.

21. Find the value of y.

22. Find the value of z.

23. Each face of a pyramid is an isosceles triangle with a vertex angle of $72°$. What is the measure of the base angles of each face?

24. Reorder the reasons of the following proof to match the correct statements.

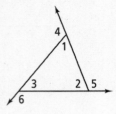

Given: triangle with one exterior angle at each vertex

Prove: $m\angle 4 + m\angle 5 + m\angle 6 = 360$

Statements	Reasons
1. $\angle 1$ and $\angle 4$ are supplementary. $\angle 2$ and $\angle 5$ are supplementary. $\angle 3$ and $\angle 6$ are supplementary.	**a.** Addition Property of Equality
2. $m\angle 1 + m\angle 4 = 180$ $m\angle 2 + m\angle 5 = 180$ $m\angle 3 + m\angle 6 = 180$	**b.** Subtraction Property of Equality
3. $m\angle 1 + m\angle 2 + m\angle 3 + m\angle 4 + m\angle 5 + m\angle 6 = 540$	**c.** Triangle Angle Sum Theorem
4. $m\angle 1 + m\angle 2 + m\angle 3 = 180$	**d.** Definition of supplementary angles
5. $m\angle 4 + m\angle 5 + m\angle 6 = 360$	**e.** Angles that form a straight angle are supplementary.

25. Main St. is parallel to Oak St. Main St. is parallel to Broad St. Fern St. is perpendicular to Oak St. What conclusion can you make about Fern St. and Broad St?

Quarter 2 Test

Chapters 4–6

Form G

1. $\triangle TLM \cong \triangle SQR$. What side is congruent to $\overline{MT}$?

2. Find the value of x.

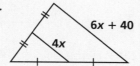

6x + 40

4x

3. Fill in the missing reasons for the proof below.

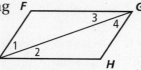

Given: paralellogram *FGHJ*

Prove: $\triangle JFG \cong \triangle GHJ$

Statements	Reasons
1. $\overline{FJ}\|\overline{GH}$ and $\overline{FG}\|\overline{JH}$	**1.** Definition of parallelogram
2. $\angle 1 \cong \angle 4$ and $\angle 2 \cong \angle 3$	**2.** If lines are ‖, then alt. int. $\angle s$ are $\cong$.
3. $\overline{GJ} \cong \overline{GJ}$	**3.** _?_
4. $\triangle JFG \cong \triangle GHJ$	**4.** _?_

4. Find $m\angle ABC$.

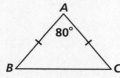

A

80°

B   C

For Exercises 6 and 7, state the postulate or theorem you could use to prove each pair of triangles congruent.

5. 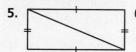   **6.**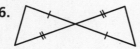

7. Give the coordinates of point *O* without using any new variables.

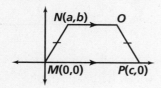

N(a,b)   O

M(0,0)   P(c,0)

8. Reorder reasons a through e of the proof to match the correct statements.

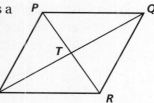

P   Q

T

S   R

Given: paralellogram *PQRS*, $\overline{PR} \perp \overline{QS}$

Prove: $\overline{QP} \cong \overline{QR}$

Statements	Reasons
1. $\overline{PR}$ and $\overline{QS}$ bisect each other at T.	**1.** *PQRS* is a parallelogram.
2. $\overline{PT} \cong \overline{TR}$	**a.** Reflexive Property of $\cong$
3. $\angle QTP \cong \angle QTR$	**b.** Corresp. Parts of $\cong \triangle s$ are $\cong$.
4. $\overline{QT} \cong \overline{QT}$	**c.** SAS
5. $\triangle QTP \cong \triangle QTR$	**d.** Both angles = 90° because $\overline{PR} \perp \overline{QS}$.
6. $\overline{QP} \cong \overline{QR}$	**e.** Definition of bisector

9. Construct $\triangle ABC$ with each side of length *AB*.

A ―――――― B

10. Given $\overline{GE} \cong \overline{EA}$ and $\angle A \cong \angle G$, find the value of x.

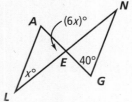

A   (6x)°   N

x°   E   40°

L   G

Quarter 2 Test (continued)   Form G

Chapters 4–6

11. What postulate or theorem can you use to prove the pair of triangles conguent? Name the congruence.

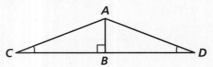

12. Given $\overline{RA} \cong \overline{TP}$, $\angle APT \cong \angle PAR$, $TA = 9x - 2$, and $PR = 6x + 7$, find the value of x.

13. Given the coordinates of the vertices for parallelogram $ABCD$, how can you use the coordinates to show that $ABCD$ is a rectangle?

14. Use the techniques of construction to find the circumcenter of $\triangle RST$.

15. Writing Explain two ways to show that a parallelogram is a rhombus.

16. Use the techniques of construction to find the incenter of $\triangle JKL$.

17. A triangle has vertices $(3, 0)$, and $(6, 4)$. One of its angles is bisected by the x axis. Find the perimeter and area of the triangle.

18. What postulate or theorem can you use to prove the pair of triangles congruent? Name the congruence.

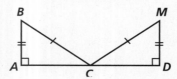

19. Find XY.

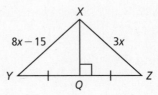

20. Writing Use indirect reasoning to show that there is only one right angle in a right triangle.

21. What is the most precise name for quadrilateral $ABCD$?

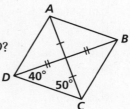

22. An isosceles triangle has angles measuring 65° and 50°. What is the measure of the third angle?

23. Reorder the reasons of the following proof to match the correct statements.

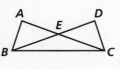

Given: $\overline{AB} \cong \overline{DC}$ $\angle ABC \cong \angle DCB$
Prove: $\overline{AC} \cong \overline{DB}$

Statements	Reasons
1. $\overline{AB} \cong \overline{DC}$	a. SAS Postulate
2. $\angle ABC \cong \angle DCB$	b. Reflexive Property
3. $\overline{BC} \cong \overline{CB}$	c. Given
4. $\triangle ABC \cong \triangle DCB$	d. CPCTC
5. $\overline{AC} \cong \overline{DB}$	e. Given

24. Is $\overline{AB}$ a midsegment? Explain.

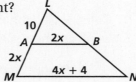

25. What is the most precise name for quadrilateral $ABCD$ with $A(-2, 0)$, $B(0, 3)$, $C(2, 0)$, and $D(0, -6)$?

Quarter 3 Test

Chapters 7–9

Form G

Determine whether the triangles are similar. If they are, write the similarity statement, and name the postulate or theorem that you can use to prove that they are similar. If not, write *not similar*.

1.

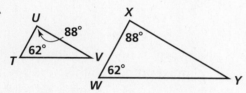

2.

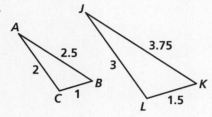

3. The lengths of three sides of a triangle are 7 cm, 11 cm, and 16 cm. Describe the triangle as acute, right, or obtuse.

Find the value of x. Round your answers to the nearest tenth.

4.

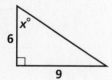

5.

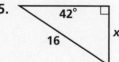

6. Express sin A, cos A, and tan A as ratios.

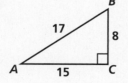

For Exercises 7–9, find the coordinates of the vertices of the image $ABCD$ for each transformation.

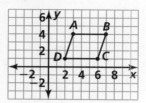

7. $T_{<4,-2>}(ABCD)$

8. $R_{x=-1}(ABCD)$

9. $r_{(180°, O)}(ABCD)$

10. What is the measure of x to the nearest tenth?

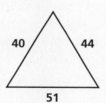

A 36.5° C 56.3°
B 49.1° D 74.6°

11. What is the image of $P(5, -1)$ for $T_{<-2, 4>}(P)$?

12. Which transformation is not an isometry?
A dilation   C rotation
B reflection   D glide reflection

13. A triangle has side lengths 6, $2\sqrt{13}$, and 4. Is the triangle a right triangle? Explain.

14. Find the value of x. Leave your answer in simplest radical form.

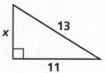

Quarter 3 Test (continued)   Form G

Chapters 7–9

Find the values of the variables for each pair of similar figures.

15.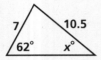

16.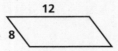

17. **Algebra** Find the measure of the acute angle that the line $y = \dfrac{1}{3}x + 4$ makes with a horizontal line. Round your answer to the nearest tenth.

18. The length of the sides of a triangular garden are 10 m, 11 m, and 13 m. Find the measure of the angle opposite the longest side to the nearest tenth of a degree.

19. In $\triangle PQR$, $p = 7$ ft, $q = 9$ ft, and $m\angle R = 55$. Find $m\angle Q$ to the nearest tenth of a degree.

20. $\triangle ABC$ has vertices $A(-1, 3)$, $B(0, 7)$, and $C(4, 2)$. Find the image of $\triangle ABC$ for a dilation with center $(0, 0)$ and a scale factor of 2.

21. Two trees are 100 ft apart. The height of the taller tree is 75 ft. The angle of depression from the top of the taller tree to the top of the shorter tree is 15°. Find the height of the shorter tree to the nearest foot.

Find the value of each variable. If your answer is not an integer, leave it in simplest radical form.

22.

23.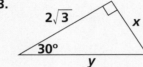

24. A photographic negative is 2 in. by 1.5 in. An enlarged print from this negative has a length of 9 in. as its shorter side. What is the length of its longer side?

25 . What is the value of x?

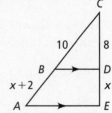

Quarter 4 Test

Form G

Chapters 10–13

1. Find the volume of the sphere to the nearest tenth.

8 cm

2. Find the area of the triangle. Round your answer to the nearest tenth.

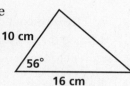

10 cm
56°
16 cm

Find the value of y.

3.

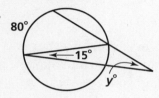

80°
←15°
y°

4.

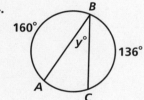

B
160°
y°
136°
A
C

5. **Writing** Explain how you can justify the formula for the area of a kite using the area of two triangles.

6. Find the area of the shaded region to the nearest hundredth.

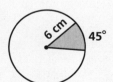

6 cm
45°

7. Find the value of x. Round your answer to the nearest tenth.

8
5
x

8. Describe the locus of points in a plane 5 units from $(-2, -3)$.

9. What is the volume of the cylinder in terms of π?

7 m
2 m

10. Find the area of the trapezoid.

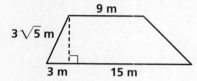

9 m
$3\sqrt{5}$ m
3 m   15 m

11. Find the number of vertices in a pyramid with six faces.

12. **Coordinate Geometry** Graph the circle $(x - 5)^2 + (y - 6)^2 = 16$. State the center and the radius of the circle.

Find $m\widehat{XY}$ to the nearest tenth.

13.

X
10
4
Y

14.

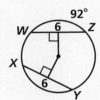

92°
W   6   Z
X
6
Y

15. Find the volume of the pyramid.

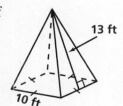

13 ft
10 ft

Quarter 4 Test (continued)   *Form G*

Chapters 10–13

16. The surface areas of two similar containers are 85 in² and 42 in². The volume of the smaller container is 57 in³. What is the volume of the larger container? Round your answer to the nearest whole number.

Find each measure in ⊙P.

17. $m\angle MPN$

18. $m\widehat{LM}$

19. $m\widehat{LQN}$

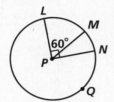

20. Find the area of a regular octagon with side length 8 in. and apothem 9.7 in.

21. Find the value of *x*.

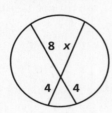

22. Write the equation of the circle.

23. Find the area of a regular decagon with radius 8 in. Round your answer to the nearest tenth.

24. Find the length of $\widehat{JK}$. Leave your answer in terms of π.

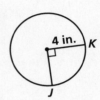

25. Find the area of a label on a soup can that has height 12.5 cm and diameter 7.25 cm. Round your answer to the nearest tenth.

Mid-Course Test

Form G

Chapters 1–6

1. Reorder the reasons of the following proof to match the correct statements.

Given: $\overline{XY} \cong \overline{XZ}$, and $\overline{XB}$ is the angle bisector of $\angle X$.
Prove: $\overline{XB} \perp \overline{YZ}$

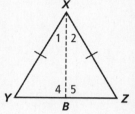

Statements	Reasons
1. $\overline{XY} \cong \overline{XZ}$	**1.** Given
2. $\angle 1 \cong \angle 2$	**a.** Reflexive Property of $\cong$
3. $\overline{XB} \cong \overline{XB}$	**b.** Corresp. Parts of $\cong \triangle$s are $\cong$.
4. $\triangle XYB \cong \triangle XZB$	**c.** Substitution Property of $\cong$
5. $\angle 4 \cong \angle 5$	**d.** Definition of $\angle$ bisector
6. $m\angle 4 + m\angle 5 = 180$	**e.** SAS
7. $2 \cdot m\angle 4 = 180$	**f.** Division Property of $=$
8. $m\angle 4 = 90$	**g.** $\angle$s that form a straight $\angle$ are supplementary.
9. $\overline{XB} \perp \overline{YZ}$	**9.** Definition of $\perp$

2. A carpenter adds a diagonal brace to a rectangular frame as shown. If the carpenter wants the triangles on either side of the brace to be congruent, what should be the measures of $\angle 1$, $\angle 2$, and $\angle 3$?

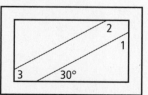

3. Find the length of $\overline{WZ}$.

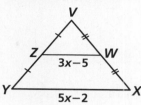

4. $\triangle ABC$ is similar to $\triangle PQR$. Find the value of x.

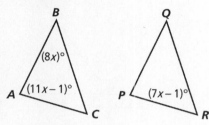

5. Graph quadrilateral $WXYZ$ with vertices $W(-3, 4)$, $X(2, 4)$, $Y(3, -1)$, and $Z(-2, -1)$ to determine its most precise name.

6. $FH = 56$. Find the value of x.

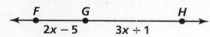

7. Find the values of the variables, given that $ABCDE$ is a regular pentagon.

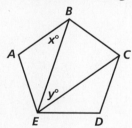

8. Write an equation for the line perpendicular to $y = \frac{2}{3}x + 1$ that contains $(0, 2)$.

Mid-Course Test (continued)   *Form G*

Chapters 1–6

9. Find the value of *x*.

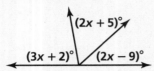

(2x + 5)°
(3x + 2)° (2x − 9)°

10. What is the measure of ∠*HKM*? Classify the angle as *acute, right, obtuse,* or *straight.*

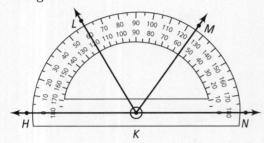

11. What is the measure of an exterior angle of a regular hexagon?

12. Name a pair of overlapping congruent triangles. State whether the triangles are congruent by SSS, SAS, ASA, AAS, or HL.

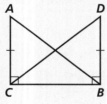

13. For isosceles trapezoid *PQRS*, give the coordinates of *R* without using any new variables.

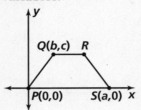

14. Refer to the diagram.
   a. Name a pair of same-side interior angles.
   b. Name a pair of corresponding angles.

15. Find *m*∠*MWT*.

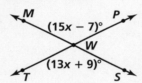

16. Find the measures of ∠1 and ∠2.

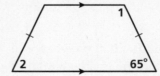

Mid-Course Test (continued)

Chapters 1–6

Form G

17. What is the circumcenter of a triangle?

18. What is the orthocenter of a triangle?

19. What conditions in the figure below will prove $\ell \parallel m$?

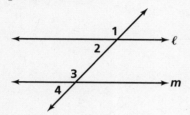

20. Line ℓ is perpendicular to line m. Line m is also perpendicular to line n. Line n is parallel to line p. How are lines ℓ and p related? Justify your answer.

21. If $\triangle ACB \cong \triangle CFD$, what are the congruent corresponding pairs?

22. Explain why a rectangle is always a parallelogram, but a parallelogram is not always a rectangle.

23. Relate side lengths AD and CD, given $\overline{AB} \cong \overline{CB}$ and $m\angle DBC < 90°$.

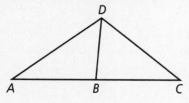

For Exercises 24–28, give *ABCD* the most precise name possible. Choose from *quadrilateral, parallelogram, rectangle, rhombus, kite, square,* and *trapezoid*.

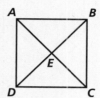

24. $ABCD$ is a parallelogram; $m\angle DEA = 90$.

25. $ABCD$ is a parallelogram; $AD = DC$; $AC = DB$.

26. $AE = CE$, $DE = BE$

27. $AE = BE = CE = DE$

28. $\overline{AB} \cong \overline{DC}$; $\overline{AD} \cong \overline{BC}$; $\overline{AC} \perp \overline{BD}$

29. Find x so D lies on the angle bisector of $\angle ABC$.

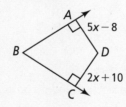

30. Find the measures of the numbered angles.

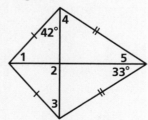

Mid-Course Test (continued)

Chapters 1–6

Form G

31. Find the values of the variables, given $\overline{BF} \parallel \overline{AH} \parallel \overline{IJ}$ and $\overline{IJ} \perp \overline{GI}$.

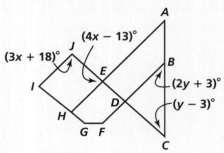

32. Find the midpoint of $\overline{AB}$ with $A(-1, 5)$ and $B(6, -3)$.

33. What can you conclude from the given true statements?

If it is raining, soccer practice will be canceled.
It is raining.

34. In parallelogram $RSTW$, find $m\angle 1$ and $m\angle 2$.

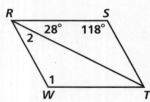

35. What is the distance between $(-2, 3)$ and $(4, -1)$? Round your answer to the nearest tenth.

36. A circle has radius 12 in. Find its area and circumference to the nearest tenth.

37. Find the value of x.

For each pair of triangles, state the postulate or theorem you can use to prove the triangles congruent. If the triangles cannot be proven congruent, write *not possible*.

38.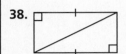

39.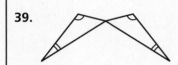

40.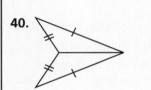

41.

42.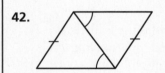

43.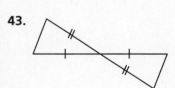

44.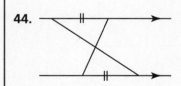

45.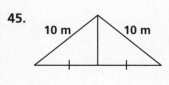

Final Test

Form G

Chapters 1–13

1. What is the measure of each exterior angle of a regular decagon?

2. Find the midpoint of $\overline{AB}$ with $A(-1, 5)$ and $B(6, -3)$.

3. Which lines or segments are parallel? Justify your answer.

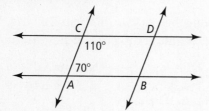

4. What postulate or theorem can you use to prove the pair of triangles congruent? Name the congruence.

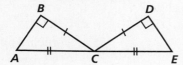

5. What is the image of $(-2, -5)$ reflected across $x = 2$?

6. Find the area of the trapezoid.

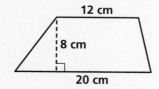

7. Find the area of a rhombus with sides of length 10 in. and longer diagonal of length 16 in.

8. Find the perimeter of the rectangle $TYOC$ with vertices $T(-6,6)$, $Y(2,10)$, $O(4,6)$, and $C(-4,2)$.

9. Find the area of the rectangle in Exercise #8.

10. Which of the following transformations are isometries?
   I. rotation II. glide reflection III. dilation

   A I only
   B I, II, and III
   C I and III only
   D I and II only

11. Find the length of $\overset{\frown}{AB}$. Round your answer to the nearest tenth.

12. Find the value of x. Round your answer to the nearest tenth.

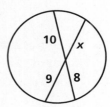

13. Find the area of a regular decagon if the distance from the center to a vertex is 4 cm. Round your answer to the nearest tenth.

14. Find the volume of a square pyramid with height 15 m and slant height 17 m.

15. Sketch and describe the locus of all points in a plane 3 units from the line $y = -2$.

16. Find the area of an equilateral triangle with sides of length 24 in.

17. Find the value of x. Round your answer to the nearest tenth.

Final Test (continued)

Form G

Chapters 1–13

18. Which is the equation of the circle with center $(-3, -2)$ passing through $(1, -5)$?

F $(x + 3)^2 + (y + 2)^2 = 25$
G $(x - 3)^2 + (y - 2)^2 = 5$
H $(x - 1)^2 + (y + 5)^2 = 5$
J $(x + 3)^2 + (y + 2)^2 = 5$

19. Find the value of x. Round your answer to the nearest tenth.

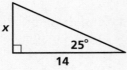

20. Find the value of x.

21. Two figures have a similarity ratio of $3 : 7$. If the area of the larger figure is 294 cm^2, what is the area of the smaller figure?

22. An observer at the top of a 50-m lighthouse sights a boat out at sea at an angle of depression of 15°. A short while later, the same boat is at an angle of depression of 22° along the same line of sight. To the nearest meter, how far did the boat travel?

23. The lengths of the sides of a triangle are 7.6 cm, 8.2 cm and 5.2 cm. Find the measure of the largest angle to the nearest tenth.

24. Find the value of x.

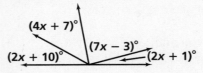

25. What is the image of $(2, -2)$ rotated 270° about the origin?

26. Reorder the reasons of the following proof to match the correct statements.

Given: $\overline{AB} \cong \overline{DC}$
$\angle A \cong \angle D$
Prove: $\overline{AE} \cong \overline{DE}$

Statements
1. $\overline{AB} \cong \overline{DC}$
2. $\angle A \cong \angle D$
3. $\angle AEB \cong \angle DEC$
4. $\triangle AEB \cong \triangle DEC$
5. $\overline{AE} \cong \overline{DE}$

Reasons
a. Given
b. AAS Theorem
c. Given
d. CPCTC
e. Vertical Angles Theorem

Final Test (continued)   Form G

Chapters 1–13

Complete each statement with the word always, sometimes, or never.

27. The vertices of a triangle are _?_ collinear.

28. If two lines are cut by a transversal, then alternate interior angles are _?_ congruent.

29. The diagonals of a rectangle are _?_ perpendicular.

30. What postulate or theorem can you use to prove the pair of triangles congruent? Name the congruence.

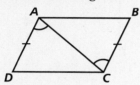

31. $\angle CBA \cong \angle CED$. Is $\overline{AB}$ a midsegment? Explain.

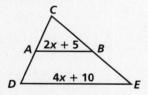

32. Suppose the two rectangles are similar and $x > 6$. Find x.

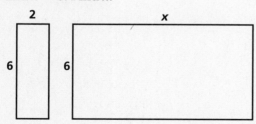

33. Find the value of x.

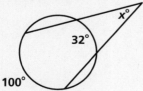

34. Find the area of the triangle. Round your answer to the nearest tenth.

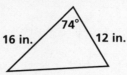

35. Find the measure of $\overarc{BC}$.

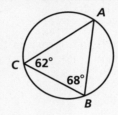

36. Find the volume of the cylinder in terms of π.

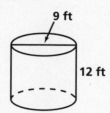

37. Find the area of the shaded region to the nearest tenth.

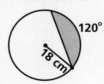

38. Find the value of x.

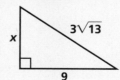

Final Test (continued)

Form G

Chapters 1–13

39. Identify the repeating figure that is translated to form the figure below.

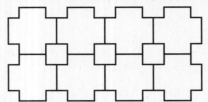

40. a. Find the surface area to the nearest tenth.
   b. Find the volume to the nearest tenth.

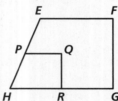

12 cm

41. *EFGH* ~ *PQRH*. Complete the proportion and the congruence statement.

a. $\dfrac{EF}{GH} = \dfrac{?}{RH}$

b. $\angle Q \cong$ ___?___

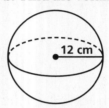

42. Find the value of *x*. Round your answer to the nearest tenth.

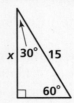

x | 30° \ 15

60°

43. Find the lengths of $\overline{MW}$ and $\overline{MX}$. Round your answers to the nearest tenth.

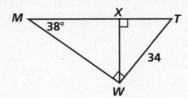

M — 38° — X — T

34

W

44. Find $m\angle ABC$.

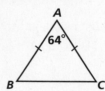

A

64°

B   C

45. What is the equation of the line perpendicular to $y = 3x - 7$ that contains $(6, 8)$?

Quarter 1 Test

Form K

Chapters 1–3

1. Find the value of x if $AC = 20$.

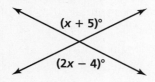

2. Find the value of x.

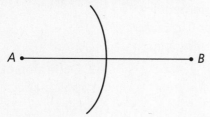

3. Complete the construction of the perpendicular bisector of $\overline{AB}$.

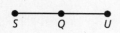

A •————————————————• B

4. Given $\overline{SU}$ with midpoint Q, construct a square with side length $\frac{1}{2}SU$.

S •———•———• U
      Q

5. What theorem justifies the following statement?

If $\angle 7$ and $\angle 8$ are supplementary, and $\angle 7$ and $\angle 9$ are supplementary, then $\angle 8 \cong \angle 9$.

6. Construct the bisector of right angle $\angle BIF$.

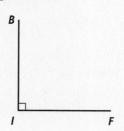

7. Line a is perpendicular to line c. Line b is also perpendicular to line c. How are lines a and b related? Explain.

8. Find $m\angle LBM$.

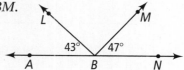

9. Reorder the reasons of the following proof to match the correct statements.

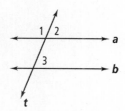

Given: $\angle 1$ is supplementary to $\angle 3$.
Prove: $\overleftrightarrow{a}$ is parallel to $\overleftrightarrow{b}$.

Statements	Reasons
1. $\angle 1$ is supplementary to $\angle 3$.	**a.** Angles that form a straight angle are supplementary.
2. $\angle 1$ is supplementary to $\angle 2$.	**b.** Converse of the Corresponding Angles postulate
3. $\angle 2 \cong \angle 3$	**c.** Given
4. $\overleftrightarrow{a}$ is parallel to $\overleftrightarrow{b}$.	**d.** Congruent Supplements Theorem

10. What is the intersection of planes $ABFE$ and $BCGF$?

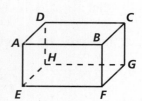

11. Find the circumference of a circle with area 25π m^2.

12. Given $L(2, 4)$ and $M(4, 8)$, the midpoint of $\overline{LG}$, find the coordinates of G.

Quarter 1 Test (continued)   Form K

Chapters 1–3

13. Construct a line through point *J* that is parallel to line ℓ.

J•

14. Find the coordinates of the midpoint of $(2, 3)$ and $(-6, 5)$.

15. Find the slope of a line parallel to the line $y = -3x + 5$.

16. What conditions in the figure below will *not* prove $a \parallel b$?

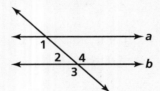

   F $\angle 1 \cong \angle 3$
   G $m\angle 2 + m\angle 4 = 180$
   H $\angle 1 \cong \angle 4$
   J $m\angle 1 + m\angle 2 = 180$

17. Find the length of $\overline{AB}$, given $A(-1, 6)$ and $B(3, 3)$.

18. What is the intersection of two distinct planes?

19. What are skew lines?

Use the figure for Exercises 25–27.

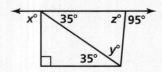

20. Find the value of *x*.

21. Find the value of *y*.

22. Find the value of *z*.

23. Each face of a pyramid is an isosceles triangle with a vertex angle of 70°. What is the measure of the base angles of each face?

24. List the missing reasons in the correct order to complete the proof.
Given: $m\angle 4 = m\angle 5 = 135$
Prove: $\angle 3$ is a right angle.

Statements	Reasons
1. $\angle 1$ and $\angle 4$ are supplementary. $\angle 2$ and $\angle 5$ are supplementary.	1. _?_
2. $m\angle 1 +$ $m\angle 4 = 180$ $m\angle 2 +$ $m\angle 5 = 180$	2. Definition of supplementary angles
3. $m\angle 4 = 135$ $m\angle 5 = 135$	3. _?_
4. $m\angle 1 = 45$ $m\angle 2 = 45$	4. Subtraction Property of Equality
5. $m\angle 1 + m\angle 2 +$ $m\angle 3 = 180$	5. Triangle Angle Sum Theorem
6. $m\angle 3 = 90$	6. _?_
7. $\angle 3$ is a right angle.	7. _?_

   a. Given
   b. Subtraction Property of Equality
   c. Angles that form a straight angle are supplementary.
   d. Definition of right angle

25. Dana St. is parallel to Gilman St., but not parallel to Wesley St. Pearl St. is perpendicular to Gilman St. What conclusion can you make about Pearl St. and Wesley St?

Quarter 2 Test

Chapters 4–6

Form K

1. $\triangle ABC \cong \triangle XYZ$. What side is congruent to $\overline{AC}$?

2. Find the value of x.

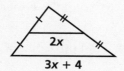
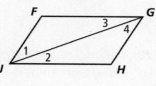

3. Reorder the reasons of the proof to match the correct statements.

Given: Parallelogram $FGHJ$
Prove: $\angle F \cong \angle H$

Statements	Reasons
1. $\overline{FJ} \| \overline{GH}$ and $\overline{FG} \| \overline{JH}$	**a.** If lines are ‖, then alt. int. $\angle s$ are $\cong$.
2. $\angle 1 \cong \angle 4$ and $\angle 2 \cong \angle 3$	**b.** Def. of parallelogram
3. $\overline{GJ} \cong \overline{GJ}$	**c.** ASA
4. $\triangle JFG \cong \triangle GHJ$	**d.** Reflexive Prop. of $\cong$

4. Find $m\angle YXZ$.

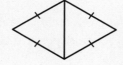

For Exercises 6 and 7, state the postulate or theorem you could use to prove each pair of triangles congruent.

5.

6.

8. Reorder reasons a, b, and c of the proof to match the correct statements.

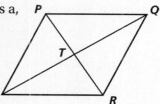

Given: parallelogram $PQRS$, $\overline{PR} \perp \overline{QS}$
Prove: $\overline{QP} \cong \overline{QR}$.

Statements	Reasons
1. $\overline{PR}$ and $\overline{QS}$ bisect each other at T.	1. Diagonals of a parallelogram bisect each other.
2. $\overline{PT} \cong \overline{TR}$	2. Def. of bisector
3. $\angle QTP \cong \angle QTR$	**a.** SAS
4. $\overline{QT} \cong \overline{QT}$	**b.** Reflexive Prop. of $\cong$
5. $\triangle QTP \cong \triangle QTR$	**c.** $\perp$ lines form $\cong$ right angles.
6. $\overline{QP} \cong \overline{QR}$	6. Corresp. Parts of $\cong \triangle s$ are $\cong$.

7. Give the coordinates of point O without using any new variables.

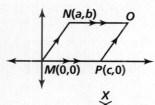

9. When constructing the equilateral triangle shown, the first two points drawn were _____ and _____, and the third point drawn was _____.

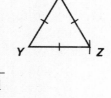

10. **Given:**
$\overline{GR} \cong \overline{MA}$;
$\overline{GM} \cong \overline{RA}$.
Find the value of x.

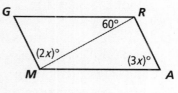

Quarter 2 Test (continued)   Form K

Chapters 4–6

11. What theorem or postulate can you use to prove the pair of triangles congruent?

12. Given $\overline{AP} \cong \overline{PB}$ and $\angle A \cong \angle B$, find the value of y.

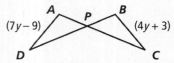

13. Given the coordinates of the vertices of parallelogram $ABCD$, how can you use the coordinates to show that $ABCD$ is a rhombus?

14. The circle centered at point O intersects the vertices of $\triangle RST$. Point O is located at the intersection of the _____ of the _____ of $\triangle RST$. Point O is called the _____ of $\triangle RST$.

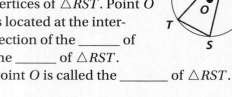

15. What is the most precise name for a quadrilateral with four right angles and four congruent sides?

   A parallelogram   C rhombus
   B rectangle   D square

16. The circle centered at point C intersects the sides of $\triangle JKL$ at points X, Y, and Z. Point C located at the intersection of the bisectors of the _____ of $\triangle JKL$. Point C is called the _____ of $\triangle JKL$.

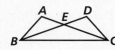

17. A triangle has vertices with coordinates $(0, 4)$ and $(3, 0)$. One side is on the x-axis and is bisected by the y-axis. Find the triangle's perimeter and area.

18. What theorem or postulate can you use to prove the pair of triangles congruent?

19. Find the value of x.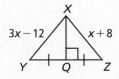

20. **Writing** Use indirect reasoning to show that there can be only one obtuse angle in a triangle.

21. What is the most precise name for quadrilateral $ABCD$?

22. An isosceles triangle has angles measuring 55° and 70°. What is the measure of the third angle?

23. Give the reason for the final statement to complete the following proof.

   Given: $\overline{AE} \cong \overline{DE}$
   $\angle EBC \cong \angle ECB$
   Prove: $\triangle AEB \cong \triangle DEC$

Statements	Reasons
1. $\overline{AE} \cong \overline{DE}$	1. Given
2. $\angle EBC \cong \angle ECB$	2. Given
3. $\overline{BE} \cong \overline{CE}$	3. Converse of Isosceles Triangle Theorem
4. $\angle AEB \cong \angle DEC$	4. Vertical angles
5. $\triangle AEB \cong \triangle DEC$	5. __?__

24. $\overline{AB} \parallel \overline{MN}$. Is $\overline{AB}$ a midsegment? Explain.

25. What is the most precise name for quadrilateral $ABCD$ with $A(4, 0)$, $B(6, 3)$, $C(2, 3)$, and $D(0, 0)$?

Quarter 3 Test

Form K

Chapters 7–9

Determine whether the triangles are similar. If they are, write the similarity statement and name the postulate or theorem that you can use to prove that they are similar. If not, write *not similar*.

1.

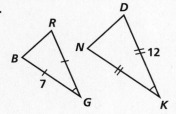

2.

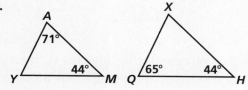

3. The lengths of three sides of a triangle are 5 in., 8 in., and 10 in. Describe the triangle as acute, right, or obtuse.

Find the value of *x*. Round your answers to the nearest tenth.

4.

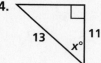

5.

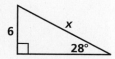

6. Express sin *A*, cos *A*, and tan *A* as ratios.

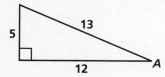

Find the coordinates of the vertices of the image of $\triangle XYZ$ for each transformation.

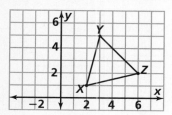

7. $T_{<2,5>}(XYZ)$

8. $R_{y=0}(XYZ)$

9. $r_{(180°,\,0)}(XYZ)$

10. What is $m\angle A$ to the nearest whole degree?

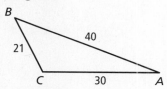

11. What is the image of $B(7, 2)$ for $T_{<3,\,-2>}(B)$?

12. Is a rotation an isometry? Explain.

13. A triangle has side lengths 17, 8, and 15. Is the triangle a right triangle? Explain.

14. Find the value of *x*. Leave your answer in simplest radical form.

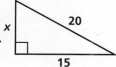

Quarter 3 Test (continued)   Form K

Chapters 7–9

Find the values of the variable(s) for each pair of similar figures.

15.

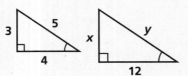

16.

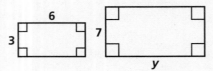

17. **Algebra** Find the measure of the acute angle that a line with slope 1 makes with a horizontal line.

18. In △ABC , a = 30 ft, b = 50 ft, and m∠D = 20. Find m∠F to the nearest tenth.

19. Describe the figure that results from rotating the figure at the right 180° about A.

20. △XYZ has vertices X(0, −6), Y(7, −4), and Z(6, 2). Find the image of △XYZ for a dilation with center (0, 0) and a scale factor of $\frac{1}{2}$.

21. Two buildings are 180 ft apart. The height of the taller building is 120 ft. The angle of depression from the top of the taller building to the top of the shorter building is 10°. Find the height of the shorter building to the nearest foot.

Find the value of each variable. If your answer is not an integer, leave it in simplest radical form.

22.

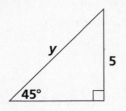

23.

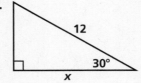

24. A photographic negative is 1 in. by 1.5 in. A print from this negative has a length of 8 in. as its shorter side. What is the length of its longer side?

25. What is the value of x?

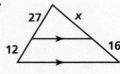

A 20.25   C 34

B 32   D 36

Quarter 4 Test

Chapters 10–13

Form K

1. Find the volume of the sphere to the nearest tenth.

6 in.

2. Find the area of the triangle. Round your answer to the nearest tenth.

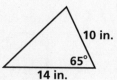

10 in.
65°
14 in.

Find the value of x.

3.

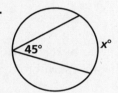

45°   x°

4.

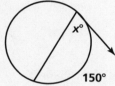

x°

150°

5. Find the area of the kite.

2 3 6
   3

6. Find the area of the shaded region to the nearest hundredth.

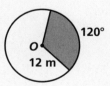

O
12 m
120°

7. Find the value of x.

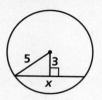

5   3
  x

8. Describe the locus of points in a plane 8 units from $(-4, 6)$.

9. What is the volume of the cylinder in terms of π?

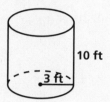

10 ft

3 ft

10. Find the area of the trapezoid.

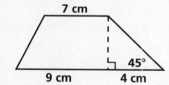

7 cm

9 cm   4 cm   45°

11. Use the figure below.

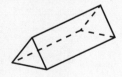

   a. How many faces does the figure have?

   b. How many edges does the figure have?

12. **Coordinate Geometry** Graph the circle $x^2 + y^2 = 25$. State the center and the radius of the circle.

Quarter 4 Test (continued)   Form K

Chapters 10–13

Find $m\widehat{AB}$.

13.

14.

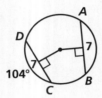

15. Find the volume of the pyramid.

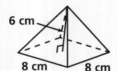

16. The surface areas of two similar containers are 74 in^2 and 52 in^2. The volume of the smaller container is 67 in^3. What is the volume of the larger container? Round your answer to the nearest whole number.

Find each measure in $\odot P$.

17. $m\angle MPL$

18. $m\widehat{LM}$

19. $m\widehat{LQN}$

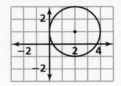

20. Find the area of a regular decagon with side length 5 in. and apothem 7.7 in.

21. Find the value of x.

22. What is the equation of the circle?

F $x^2 + y^2 = 4$
G $(x - 2)^2 + (y - 1)^2 = 4$
H $(x - 1)^2 + (y + 2)^2 = 4$
J $(x + 2)^2 - (y + 1)^2 = 2$

23. Find the area of a regular hexagon with radius 10 in. Round your answer to the nearest tenth.

24. Find the length of $\widehat{PQ}$. Leave your answer in terms of π.

25. Find the area of a label on a soup can that has a height of 10 cm and a diameter of 6 cm. Round your answer to the nearest tenth.

Mid-Course Test

Chapters 1–6

Form K

1. Reorder the reasons of the following proof to match the correct statements.

Given: $\overline{XY} \cong \overline{XZ}$, and $\overline{XB}$ is the angle bisector of $\angle X$.

Prove: $\angle Y \cong \angle Z$

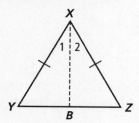

Statements	Reasons
1. $\overline{XY} \cong \overline{XZ}$	**a.** Given
2. $\angle 1 \cong \angle 2$	**b.** Corresp. Parts of $\cong \triangle$s are $\cong$.
3. $\overline{XB} \cong \overline{XB}$	**c.** Definition of $\angle$ bisector
4. $\triangle XYB \cong \triangle XZB$	**d.** Reflexive Property of $\cong$
5. $\angle Y \cong \angle Z$	**e.** SAS

2. If the four trapezoidal pieces shown below fit together to form a rectangular frame, what must be the measures of $\angle 1$ and $\angle 2$?

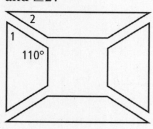

3. Find the value of x.

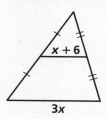

4. $\triangle ABC$ is similar to $\triangle PQR$. Find the value of x.

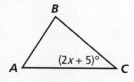

5. Graph quadrilateral $ABCD$ with vertices $A(-5, 2)$, $B(-5, -3)$, $C(2, -3)$, and $D(2, 2)$ to determine its most precise name.

6. Find the value of x if $DT = 100$.

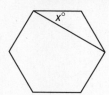

7. Find the value of x, given that the figure is a regular hexagon.

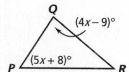

Mid-Course Test (continued)   *Form K*

Chapters 1–6

8. Graph a line perpendicular to $y = -\frac{1}{3}x + 2$ that contains (1, 1).

9. Find the value of *x*.

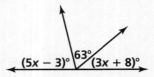

$(5x - 3)^\circ \quad 63^\circ \quad (3x + 8)^\circ$

10. What is the measure of ∠*HKL*? Classify the angle as *acute, right, obtuse,* or *straight*.

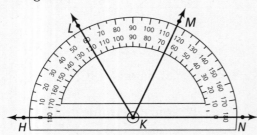

11. What is the measure of an exterior angle of a regular octagon?

12. Name two triangles that share a common angle. What is the common angle?

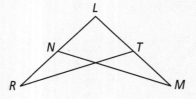

13. For rhombus *PQRS*, give the coordinates of *S* without using any new variables.

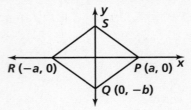

14. Refer to the diagram.
   a. Name a pair of same-side interior angles.
   b. Name a pair of alternate interior angles.

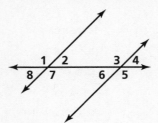

15. Find the value of *x*.

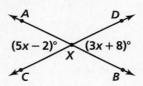

$(5x - 2)^\circ \quad (3x + 8)^\circ$

16. Find the values of *x* and *y*.

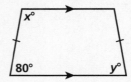

x°

$80^\circ \qquad y^\circ$

17. What is the name of the point of concurrency of the angle bisectors of a triangle?

18. What is the name of the point of concurrency of the medians of a triangle?

Mid-Course Test (continued)

Form K

Chapters 1–6

19. What conditions in the figure below will *not* prove $m \parallel n$?

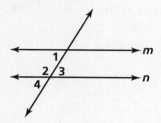

   A $\angle 1 \cong \angle 3$
   B $m\angle 1 + m\angle 2 = 180°$
   C $\angle 1 \cong \angle 4$
   D $m\angle 2 + m\angle 3 = 180°$

20. Line m is parallel to line ℓ. Line m is also parallel to line n. How are lines ℓ and n related? Justify your answer.

21. If $\triangle DLQ \cong \triangle EMR$, then which of the following is NOT necessarily true?

   A $\angle LDQ \cong \angle MRE$
   B $\angle DLQ \cong \angle EMR$
   C $\angle RME \cong \angle QLD$
   D $\angle MRE \cong \angle LQD$

22. Explain why a square is always a rhombus, but a rhombus is not always a square.

23. Write an inequality relating side lengths MN and QS.

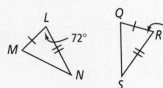

For Exercises 28–33, give *ABCD* the most precise name possible. Choose from *quadrilateral, parallelogram, rectangle, rhombus, kite, square,* and *trapezoid.*

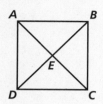

24. $ABCD$ parallelogram, $AB = BC$

25. $AC = BD, m\angle DEA = 90$

26. $\overline{AB} \parallel \overline{DC}$, $\angle A$ and $\angle B$ are supplementary

27. $AE = EC = BE = ED$

28. $\overline{AD} \parallel \overline{BC}, AD = BC$

29. $ABCD$ parallelogram, $AB = BC, AD = DC$

30. $\overline{QX}$ bisects $\angle PQR$. What is PX?

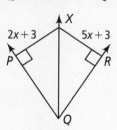

31. Find the measures of $\angle 1$ and $\angle 2$ in rectangle $ABCD$.

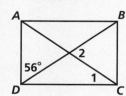

Mid-Course Test (continued)

Form K

Chapters 1–6

32. Find the value of *x*, given $\overline{AE} \perp \overline{EC}$ and $\overline{AE} \parallel \overline{BD}$.

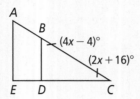

33. Find the midpoint of $\overline{AB}$ with $A(7, -2)$ and $B(-5, 6)$.

34. In parallelogram *BCKM*, find $m\angle 1$, $m\angle 2$, and $m\angle 3$.

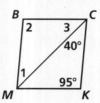

35. What is the distance between $(-1, 6)$ and $(5, -2)$?

36. A circle has radius 16 in. Find its circumference and area to the nearest tenth.

37. Find $m\angle 1$ and $m\angle 2$.

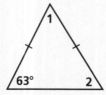

For each pair of triangles, state the postulate or theorem you can use to prove the triangles congruent. If the triangles cannot be proven congruent, write *not possible*.

38.

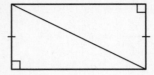

39.

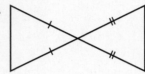

40.

41.

42.

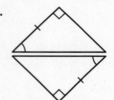

43.

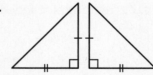

44.

45.

Final Test

Form K

Chapters 1–13

1. Find the measure of an exterior angle of a regular octagon.

2. Find the midpoint of $\overline{AB}$ with $A(0, 12)$ and $B(10, 4)$.

3. Explain why $\ell \parallel m$.

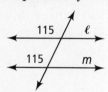

115   ℓ

115   m

4. What postulate or theorem can you use to prove the pair of triangles congruent?

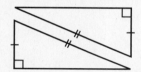

5. What is the image of $B(-3, 4)$ for $T_{<2, -5>}(B)$?

6. Find the area of the parallelogram.

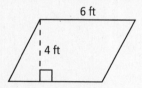

6 ft

4 ft

7. Find the area of a rhombus with diagonal lengths of 12 cm and 8 cm.

8. Find the perimeter of the square $KIRA$ with vertices $K(-6, 2), I(2, -4),$ $R(-4, -12),$ and $A(-12, -6)$.

9. Find the area of the square in Exercise #8.

10. Which of the following transformations are not isometries?
    I. rotation   II. dilation   III. translation
    F   I only
    G   II only
    H   I and III only
    J   II and III only

11. Find the length of $\widehat{AB}$. Round your answer to the nearest tenth.

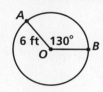

A

6 ft   130°

O B

12. Find the value of x.

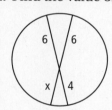

6   6

x   4

13. Find the area of a regular octagon with side length 5 cm and apothem 6 cm.

14. Find the volume of a square pyramid with height 12 cm and slant height 15 cm.

15. Sketch and describe the locus of all points in a plane 3 units from the point $(1, 0)$.

Final Test (continued)   *Form K*

Chapters 1–13

16. The base of a triangle is 8 m, and the height is 10 m. Find the area.

17. Find the value of x. Round your answer to the nearest tenth.

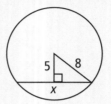

18. Which is the equation of a circle with center $(-5, -1)$ with radius 10?

A $(x - 5)^2 + (y - 1)^2 = 10$
B $(x - 5)^2 + (y - 1)^2 = 100$
C $(x + 5)^2 + (y + 1)^2 = 100$
D $(x + 5)^2 + (y + 1)^2 = 10$

19. Find the value of x. Round your answer to the nearest tenth.

20. Find the value of x.

21. Two figures have a similarity ratio of 4 : 5. If the area of the smaller figure is 112 cm², what is the area of the larger figure?

22. Two buildings are 200 ft apart. The height of the taller building is 135 ft. The angle of depression from the top of the taller building to the top of the shorter building is 7°. Find the height of the shorter building to the nearest foot.

23. In ABC, $m\angle A = 53$, $b = 6.2$ cm and $c = 7$ cm. Find $m\angle B$ to the nearest tenth.

24. Find the value of x.

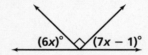

25. What is the image of $(-6, 1)$ rotated 90° about the origin?

Final Test (continued)

Form K

Chapters 1–13

26. Give the missing reasons to complete the following proof.

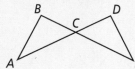

Given: $\overline{AC} \cong \overline{EC}$

$\overline{BC} \cong \overline{DC}$

Prove: $\angle A \cong \angle E$

Statements	Reasons
1. $\overline{AC} \cong \overline{EC}$	1. Given
2. $\overline{BC} \cong \overline{DC}$	2. Given
3. $\angle BCA \cong \angle DCE$	a. ?
4. $\triangle ABC \cong \triangle EDC$	4. SAS Postulate
5. $\angle A \cong \angle E$	b. ?

Complete each statement with the word *always*, *sometimes*, or *never*.

27. Two intersecting lines are _?_ coplanar.

28. If two lines are cut by a transversal, then corresponding angles are _?_ congruent.

29. A rhombus is _?_ a square.

30. What theorem or postulate would you use to prove that the pair of triangles are congruent?

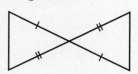

31. Find the value of x, given $\overline{DE}$ is a midsegment.

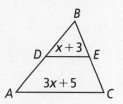

32. $ABCD \sim PQRS$. Find x.

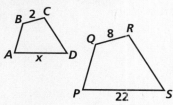

33. Find the value of x.

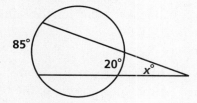

34. Find the area of the triangle. Round your answer to the nearest tenth.

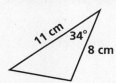

35. Find the measure of $\overset{\frown}{XY}$.

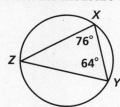

36. Find the volume of the cylinder in terms of π.

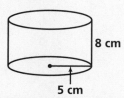

37. Find the area of the shaded region to the nearest tenth.

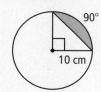

Final Test (continued)   Form K

Chapters 1–13

38. Find the value of *x*. Round your answer to the nearest tenth.

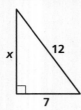

39. What type of transformation has the same effect as $R_{x=5} \circ T_{<0,\,-2>}$?

40. a. Find the surface area of the figure below. Round your answer to the nearest tenth.

b. Find the volume of the figure below. Round your answer to the nearest tenth.

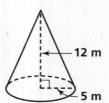

41. *ABCD ~ EFGH*. Complete the proportion and the congruence statement.

a. $\dfrac{AB}{EF} = \dfrac{?}{FG}$

b. $\angle D \cong$ __?__

42. Find the value of *x*. Round your answer to the nearest tenth.

43. Find the lengths of $\overline{AC}$ and $\overline{CD}$. Round your answers to the nearest tenth.

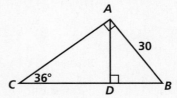

44. Find $m\angle ABC$.

45. What is the equation of the line parallel to $y = 3x - 7$ that contains (6, 8)?

End-of-Course Assessment

Selected Response

Read each question. Then circle the letter(s) of the correct answer(s). There may be more than one correct response.

1. What value of x makes $\triangle FGH$ similar to $\triangle MNP$?

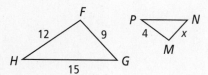

A 3

B 3.75

C 5.3

D 27

2. Write an equation of a circle with center $(-1, 2)$ passing through the point $(2, 4)$.

A $(x + 1)^2 + (y - 2)^2 = 13$

B $(x - 1)^2 + (y + 2)^2 = 13$

C $(x + 1)^2 + (y - 2)^2 = 169$

D $(x - 1)^2 + (y + 2)^2 = 169$

3. Which equation(s) can be used to find the value of x?

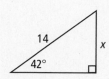

A $\cos 48° = \dfrac{x}{14}$

B $\sin 42° = \dfrac{x}{14}$

C $\cos 42° = \dfrac{14}{x}$

D $\sin 48° = \dfrac{x}{14}$

4. Find the volume of a cone with diameter 16 cm and height 12 cm.

A 100.5 cm^3

B 804.2 cm^3

C 2412.7 cm^3

D 3217.0 cm^3

5. A railway club provides free train rides on their large circular tracks. There are two tracks. The distance from Track 1 to the center is 30 m. The distance between Track 1 and Track 2 is 5 m. How much farther is the train ride on Track 2 than Track 1?

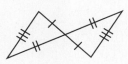

A 15.7 m

B 31.4 m

C 78.5 m

D 157.1 m

6. Which theorem(s) can you use to prove that the two triangles are congruent?

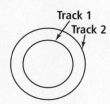

A ASA

B AAS

C SSS

D SAS

7. Choose all the ways you can correctly name plane *P*.

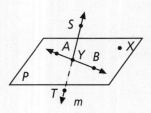

- **A** plane *AYB*
- **B** plane *AYX*
- **C** plane *YBP*
- **D** plane *YBX*

8. Choose all angle pairs that are congruent.

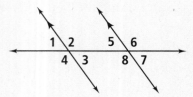

- **A** ∠1 and ∠5
- **B** ∠1 and ∠6
- **C** ∠2 and ∠8
- **D** ∠4 and ∠6

9. A dilation maps points *B*, *C*, and *D* onto *B′*, *C′*, and *D′* respectively. Choose all of the true statements.

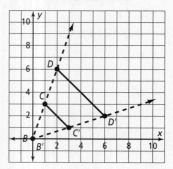

- **A** $\overline{CD} \parallel \overline{C'D'}$
- **B** The scale factor is $\dfrac{1}{2}$.
- **C** $\dfrac{BC}{B'C'} = \dfrac{BD}{B'D'}$
- **D** $\triangle BCD \cong \triangle B'C'D'$

10. Which equation(s) represent a line that contains the point $(-8, 3)$ and is perpendicular to $y = 4x - 7$?

- **A** $x + 4y = 4$
- **B** $y = 4x - 20$
- **C** $y = -\dfrac{1}{4}x + 1$
- **D** $y = -\dfrac{1}{4}x + 35$

11. Which statement(s) are true?

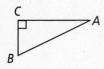

- **A** $\cos A = \sin B$
- **B** $\sin A = \cos A$
- **C** $\sin A = \cos B$
- **D** $\tan A = \tan B$

12. Which edges of the prism are parallel to $\overline{AD}$?

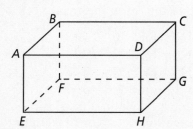

- **A** $\overline{BC}$
- **B** $\overline{EF}$
- **C** $\overline{FG}$
- **D** $\overline{DH}$

13. The map below shows a section of a city. Which statement(s) are true?

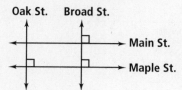

Oak St.   Broad St.

Main St.

Maple St.

A Oak Street is perpendicular to Main Street.

B Broad Street is parallel to Oak Street.

C Main Street is parallel to Maple Street.

D Oak Street is perpendicular to Broad Street.

14. Which shape is formed by a vertical plane intersecting the cone below? [G.GMD.4, Lesson 11-1]

A circle

B trapezoid

C triangle

D parallelogram

15. A bar of silver is shaped like a trapezoidal prism. The dimensions of the base are shown below. If the height of the bar is 12 cm, what is its volume to the nearest tenth?

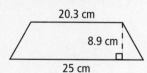

20.3 cm

8.9 cm

25 cm

A 325.3 cm^3

B 2419 cm^3

C 2670 cm^3

D 3261.6 cm^3

16. Find the area of the sector.

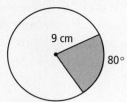

9 cm

80°

A $4\pi \text{ cm}^2$

B $9\pi \text{ cm}^2$

C $12\pi \text{ cm}^2$

D $18\pi \text{ cm}^2$

17. What are all of the correct ways to describe why the triangles below are congruent?

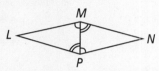

M

L   N

P

A ASA Congruence Theorem

B A reflection of $\triangle MNP$ across $\overline{MP}$ is a rigid motion that maps $\triangle MNP$ onto $\triangle PLM$.

C A translation, followed by a reflection, and then another translation is a series of rigid motions that will map $\triangle MNP$ onto $\triangle PLM$.

D A rotation of $\triangle MLP$ about point M, followed by a translation is a series of rigid motions that maps $\triangle MLP$ onto $\triangle PNM$.

18. What are all the possible coordinates for point M such that $SM = \frac{1}{2}MT$?

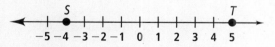

S   T

−5 −4 −3 −2 −1 0 1 2 3 4 5

A -13

B -2

C -1

D 13

19. A lifeguard sits on the shore in a chair that is 6 ft above the ground. She sees a swimmer at an angle of depression of 10°. About how far away from shore is the swimmer?

A 6.1 ft
B 34.0 ft
C 34.6 ft
D 95.1 ft

20. Which of the following statements is sufficient to show that a similarity transformation exists that maps $\triangle PQR$ to $\triangle P'Q'R'$?

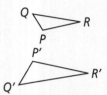

A $\angle P \cong \angle P'$ and $\angle Q \cong \angle Q'$
B $\overline{PR} \cong \overline{P'R'}$
C $\dfrac{PQ}{QR} = \dfrac{P'Q'}{Q'R'}$
D $QP = Q'P'$ and $QR = Q'R'$

21. Triangle ABC is reflected across line m. Which statement(s) are true?

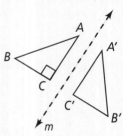

A $\overline{A'C'}$ is perpendicular to $\overline{C'B'}$.
B $AB = A'B'$
C $m\angle A = m\angle A'$
D $CC' = BB'$

22. $LMNK$ is a parallelogram. What are the values of x and y?

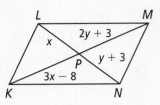

A $x = 4, y = 4$
B $x = 5, y = 2$
C $x = 9, y = 3$
D $x = 8, y = 11$

23. If an angle of one triangle is congruent to an angle of a second triangle, and the sides that include the two angles are proportional, then what is true about the two triangles?

A The triangles are similar.
B The triangles are congruent.
C The triangles are neither similar nor congruent.
D There is not enough information to make a determination.

24. Find the value of x to the nearest tenth.

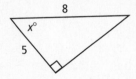

A 32.0   C 51.3
B 38.7   D 58

25. What is the length of $\overline{PQ}$?

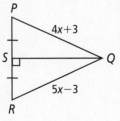

A 24   C 30
B 27   D 32

Constructed Response

In this section, show all your work in the space beneath each test item.

26. Write an equation of a line parallel to $y = \frac{1}{2}x + 3$ that passes through (2, 5).

27. If $\sin F = \frac{3}{5}$, what is $\cos G$?

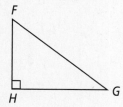

28. An environmental group is making signs for an upcoming community recycling day. They want the signs to be equilateral triangles with heights of 35 in. How long in inches will each side of the signs be? Round your answer to the nearest tenth of an inch.

29. Is $D_{(n, X)}(\triangle XYZ) = \triangle X'Y'Z'$ an enlargement or a reduction? What is the scale factor n of the dilation?

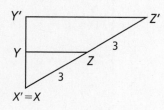

30. What are the vertices of $T_{<3, -1>}(\triangle FGH)$? Graph the image of $\triangle FGH$.

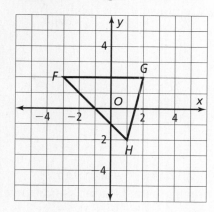

31. Construct $\overleftrightarrow{AB}$ that is perpendicular to line m.

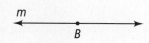

32. Constructs $\angle S$ congruent to $\angle R$.

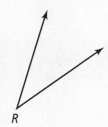

33. Determine whether the parallelograms are similar. If so, write a similarity statement and give the scale factor. If they are not similar, explain why.

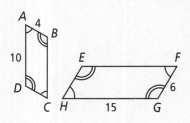

34. Which can has a greater volume? How much greater? Round your answer to the nearest cubic inch.

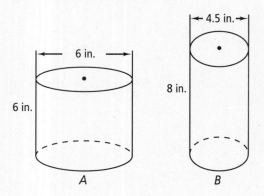

35. The measure of ∠5 is 110. Write each angle in the correct column.

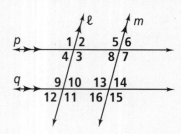

Angles that are congruent to ∠5	Angles that are congruent to ∠8

36. Does the transformation appear to be a rigid motion? Explain.

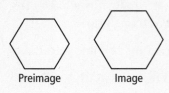

Preimage   Image

37. The diagonals of a quadrilateral are congruent and perpendicular. Identify the quadrilateral.

38. A student says that if two sides and one angle of one triangle are congruent to any two sides and one angle of another triangle, then the two triangles are congruent. What mistake did the student make? Draw two triangles that show the student is incorrect.

39. Draw and label the reflection of square *LMNP* across line *t*. Then describe how you know that *LMNP* and its image are congruent in terms of rigid motions.

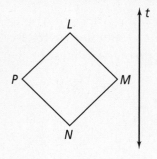

40. The coordinates of the vertices of $\triangle ABC$ are $A(0, 0)$, $B(6, 2)$ and $C(2, -4)$. What are the coordinates of the vertices after a dilation of $\frac{1}{2}$, followed by a reflection across the y-axis?

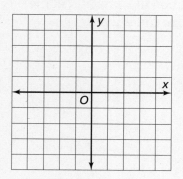

41. Draw the lines of symmetry and give the angle(s) of rotation for the figure below.

42. Describe the shape of the vertical and horizontal cross-sections of the cylinder below.

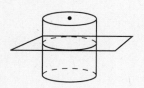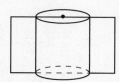

43. Determine if there is a similarity transformation that maps one figure onto another. If so, describe the transformation and write a similarity statement. If not, explain why.

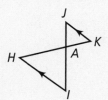

44. Rectangle $ABCD$ has vertices $A(3, 5)$, $B(5, 5)$, $C(5, 1)$, and $D(3, 1)$. What are the coordinates of the vertices of $r_{(90°, O)}(ABCD)$?

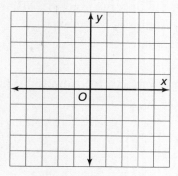

45. Find the perimeter of $\triangle TAP$ with vertices $T(1, 4)$, $A(4, 4)$, and $P(3, 0)$ to the nearest tenth.

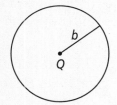

46. Show that the circles are similar by finding a scale factor and describing a similarity transformation that maps circle P to circle Q.

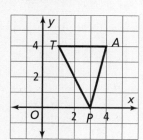

47. How can you use a congruence transformation to show that the figures are congruent?

48. Annie will use two right triangles to make a square for a logo. The triangles have the same side lengths and angle measures. What must also be true about the triangles in order to guarantee that the opposite sides of the square are parallel? Explain.

49. Find a congruence transformation that maps $\triangle CDF$ to $\triangle HJK$.

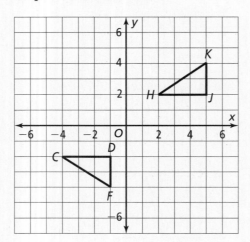

50. You can find the density of an object by using $d = \dfrac{m}{V}$, where m is the mass of the object in grams and V is the volume in milliliters. What is the density of a can of tomato sauce with diameter 10 cm, height 11.5 cm, and a mass of 822 grams? Use the conversion factor $1 \text{ cm}^3 = 1 \text{ mL}$.

51. Describe the transformations that map Figure 1 onto Figure 3.

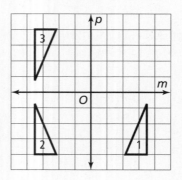

52. Construct an equilateral triangle. Label any congruent sides or angles.

53. The three sides of $\triangle RST$ are congruent to the three sides of $\triangle XYZ$. Describe a rigid motion that proves that the triangles are congruent.

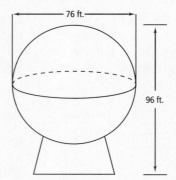

54. A diagram of a water tower is shown below. How can you use a geometric model to find the volume of the water tank at the top of the tower? Find the approximate volume. Use 3.14 for π.

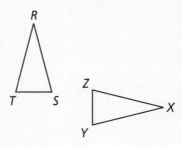

55. Write a congruence statement relating triangles in the figure below.

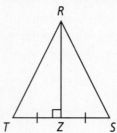

Extended Response

In this section, show all your work in the space beneath each test item.

56. Write a two-column proof to prove the Vertical Angles Theorem.

   Given: ∠1 and ∠3 are vertical angles.

   Prove: ∠1 ≅ ∠3

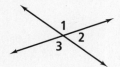

57. Write a proof to show that the diagonals of a rectangle are congruent.

   Given: Rectangle *ABCD*

   Prove: $\overline{AC} \cong \overline{BD}$

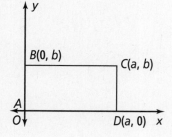

58. Given: $\overleftrightarrow{DL} \perp \overline{GP}$, $\overleftrightarrow{DL}$ bisects $\overline{GP}$

Prove: $GD = PD$

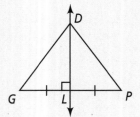

59. Prove that the diagonals of a parallelogram bisect each other.

Given: $\square ABCD$

Prove: $\overline{AC}$ and $\overline{BD}$ bisect each other at point E.

60. The state of Colorado is shaped like a rectangle with an approximate width of 280 mi and length of 380 mi. What is the population density of Colorado in people per square mile if the population is 5,116,800?

61. The figure shows a pyramid inscribed in a cube. The volume of the pyramid is 72 cm^3. Use the diagram and explain the relationship between the volume of the cube and the volume of the pyramid.

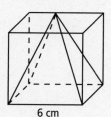

6 cm

62. Quadrilateral *ABDC* is inscribed in a circle. Prove that $m\angle A + m\angle D = 180$.

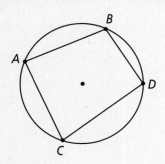

63. Write a two-column proof.

Given: $\triangle XYZ$ with $\overleftrightarrow{PQ} \parallel \overleftrightarrow{XZ}$

Prove: $\dfrac{XP}{PY} = \dfrac{ZQ}{QY}$

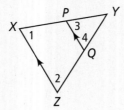

64. Prove the Triangle Angle-Sum Theorem.

Given: $\triangle GHK$

Prove: $m\angle G + m\angle H + m\angle K = 180$

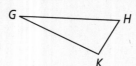

65. *GMPA* and *GRJF* are parallelograms. GRA is an equilateral triangle. Prove that $m\angle F = m\angle P$.

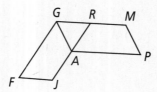

End-of-Course Assessment Report

Common Core State Standards	Test Item(s)	Type	Geometry Student Edition Lesson(s)
Experiment with transformations in the plane			
G.CO.A.1 Know precise definitions of angle, circle, perpendicular line, parallel line, and line segment, based on the undefined notions of point, line, distance along a line, and distance around a circular arc.	7 12	SR SR	1-2 3-1
G.CO.A.2 Represent transformations in the plane using, e.g., transparencies and geometry software; describe transformations as functions that take points in the plane as inputs and give other points as outputs. Compare transformations that preserve distance and angle to those that do not (e.g., translation versus horizontal stretch).	30 44	CR CR	9-1 9-3
G.CO.A.3 Given a rectangle, parallelogram, trapezoid, or regular polygon, describe the rotations and reflections that carry it onto itself.	41	CR	9-3
G.CO.A.4 Develop definitions of rotations, reflections, and translations in terms of angles, circles, perpendicular lines, parallel lines, and line segments.	21	SR	9-2
G.CO.A.5 Given a geometric figure and a rotation, reflection, or translation, draw the transformed figure using, e.g., graph paper, tracing paper, or geometry software. Specify a sequence of transformations that will carry a given figure onto another.	51	CR	9-2
Understand congruence in terms of rigid motions			
G.CO.B.6 Use geometric descriptions of rigid motions to transform figures and to predict the effect of a given rigid motion on a given figure; given two figures, use the definition of congruence in terms of rigid motions to decide if they are congruent.	36 39 49	CR CR CR	9-6 9-1 9-5
G.CO.B.7 Use the definition of congruence in terms of rigid motions to show that two triangles are congruent if and only if corresponding pairs of sides and corresponding pairs of angles are congruent.	55	CR	4-4
G.CO.B.8 Explain how the criteria for triangle congruence (ASA, SAS, and SSS) follow from the definition of congruence in terms of rigid motions.	17 47 53	SR CR CR	9-5 9-5 9-5

*Selected Response (SR) = 1 point, Constructed Response (CR) = 2 points, Extended Respsonse (ER) = 4 points.

Common Core State Standards	Test Item(s)	Type	Geometry Student Edition Lesson(s)
Prove geometric theorems			
G.CO.C.9 Prove theorems about lines and angles. *Theorems include: vertical angles are congruent; when a transversal crosses parallel lines, alternate interior angles are congruent and corresponding angles are congruent; points on a perpendicular bisector of a line segment are exactly those equidistant from the segment's endpoints.*	8 35 56	SR CR ER	3-2 3-2 2-6
G.CO.C.10 Prove theorems about triangles. *Theorems include: measures of interior angles of a triangle sum to 180°; base angles of isosceles triangles are congruent; the segment joining midpoints of two sides of a triangle is parallel to the third side and half the length; the medians of a triangle meet at a point.*	64	ER	3-5
G.CO.C.11 Prove theorems about parallelograms. *Theorems include: opposite sides are congruent, opposite angles are congruent, the diagonals of a parallelogram bisect each other and conversely, rectangles are parallelograms with congruent diagonals.*	37 59 65	CR ER ER	6-4 6-2 6-2
Make geometric constructions			
G.CO.D.12 Make formal geometric constructions with a variety of tools and methods (compass and straightedge, string, reflective devices, paper folding, dynamic geometric software, etc.). *Copying a segment; copying an angle; bisecting a segment; bisecting an angle; constructing perpendicular lines, including the perpendicular bisector of a line segment; and constructing a line parallel to a given line through a point not on the line.*	31 32	CR CR	3-6 1-6
G.CO.D.13 Construct an equilateral triangle, a square, and a regular hexagon inscribed in a circle.	52	CR	4-5
Understand similarity in terms of similarity transformations			
G.SRT.A.1.a A dilation takes a line not passing through the center of the dilation to a parallel line, and leaves a line passing through the center unchanged.	9 40	SR CR	9-6 9-6
G.SRT.A.1.b The dilation of a line segment is longer or shorter in the ratio given by the scale factor. Derive the quadratic formula from this form.	29	CR	9-6
G.SRT.A.2 Given two figures, use the definition of similarity in terms of similarity transformations to decide if they are similar; explain using similarity transformations the meaning of similarity for triangles as the equality of all corresponding pairs of angles and the proportionality of all corresponding pairs of sides.	1 33	SR CR	7-2 7-2
G.SRT.A.3 Use the properties of similarity transformations to establish the AA criterion for two triangles to be similar.	20 43	SR CR	9-7 9-7

*Selected Response (SR) = 1 point, Constructed Response (CR) = 2 points, Extended Respsonse (ER) = 4 points.

Common Core State Standards	Test Item(s)	Type	Geometry Student Edition Lesson(s)
Prove theorems involving similarity			
G.SRT.B.4 Prove theorems about triangles. *Theorems include: a line parallel to one side of a triangle divides the other two proportionally and conversely; the Pythagorean Theorem proved using triangle similarity.*	63	ER	7-5
G.SRT.B.5 Use congruence and similarity criteria for triangles to solve problems and to prove relationships in geometric figures.	6	SR	4-2
	22	SR	6-2
	23	SR	7-3
	25	SR	5-2
	38	CR	4-2
	58	ER	7-5
Define trigonometric ratios and solve problems involving right triangles			
G.SRT.C.6 Understand that by similarity, side ratios in right triangles are properties of the angles in the triangle, leading to definitions of trigonometric ratios for acute angles.	3	SR	8-3
	24	SR	8-3
G.SRT.C.7 Explain and use the relationship between the sine and cosine of complementary angles.	11	SR	8-3
	27	CR	8-3
G.SRT.C.8 Use trigonometric ratios and the Pythagorean Theorem to solve right triangles in applied problems.	19	SR	8-4
	28	CR	8-2
Understand and apply theorems about circles			
G.C.A.1 Prove that all circles are similar.	46	CR	10-6
G.C.A.2 Identify and describe relationships among inscribed angles, radii, and chords. *Include the relationship between central, inscribed, and circumscribed angles; inscribed angles on a diameter are right angles; the radius of a circle is perpendicular to the tangent where the radius intersects the circle.*	5	SR	10-6
G.C.A.3 Construct the inscribed and circumscribed circles of a triangle, and prove properties of angles for a quadrilateral inscribed in a circle.	62	ER	12-3
Find arc lengths and areas of sectors of circles			
G.C.B.5 Derive using similarity the fact that the length of the arc intercepted by an angle is proportional to the radius, and define the radian measure of the angle as the constant of proportionality; derive the formula for the area of a sector.	16	SR	12-2
Translate between the geometric description and the equation for a conic section			
G.GPE.A.1 Derive the equation of a circle of given center and radius using the Pythagorean Theorem; complete the square to find the center and radius of a circle given by an equation.	2	SR	12-5

*Selected Response (SR) = 1 point, Constructed Response (CR) = 2 points, Extended Respsonse (ER) = 4 points.

Common Core State Standards	Test Item(s)	Type	Geometry Student Edition Lesson(s)
Use coordinates to prove simple geometric theorems algebraically			
G.GPE.B.4 Use coordinates to prove simple geometric theorems algebraically.	57	ER	6-9
G.GPE.B.5 Prove the slope criteria for parallel and perpendicular lines and use them to solve geometric problems (e.g., find the equation of a line parallel or perpendicular to a given line that passes through a given point).	10 26	SR CR	3-8 3-8
G.GPE.B.6 Find the point on a directed line segment between two given points that partitions the segment in a given ratio.	18	SR	1-3
G.GPE.B.7 Use coordinates to compute perimeters of polygons and areas of triangles and rectangles, e.g., using the distance formula.	45	CR	1-7
Explain volume formulas and use them to solve problems			
G.GMD.A.1 Give an informal argument for the formulas for the circumference of a circle, area of a circle, volume of a cylinder, pyramid, and cone. *Use dissection arguments, Cavalieri's principle, and informal limit arguments*	61	ER	11-5
G.GMD.A.3 Use volume formulas for cylinders, pyramids, cones, and spheres to solve problems.	4 34	SR CR	11-5 11-4
Visualize relationships between two-dimensional and three-dimensional objects			
G.GMD.B.4 Identify the shapes of two-dimensional cross-sections of three-dimensional objects, and identify three-dimensional objects generated by rotations of two-dimensional objects.	14 42	SR CR	11-1 11-1
Apply geometric concepts in modeling situations			
G.MG.A.1 Use geometric shapes, their measures, and their properties to describe objects (e.g., modeling a tree trunk or a human torso as a cylinder).	15 54	SR CR	11-4 11-6
G.MG.A.2 Apply concepts of density based on area and volume in modeling situations (e.g., persons per square mile, BTUs per cubic foot).	50 60	CR ER	11-4 10-1
G.MG.A.3 Apply geometric methods to solve design problems (e.g., designing an object or structure to satisfy physical constraints or minimize cost; working with typographic grid systems based on ratios).	13 48	SR CR	3-4 3-4

*Selected Response (SR) = 1 point, Constructed Response (CR) = 2 points, Extended Respsonse (ER) = 4 points.

About Performance-Based Assessments

Starting in the 2014–2015 school year, students will likely be taking a new assessment that will assess their mastery of their state standards and determine their readiness for college or career work. This new assessment is expected to include Performance-Based Assessments or Performance Tasks.

With the Performance-Based Assessments, students will be expected to show not only their mastery of mathematical concepts and skills that they have learned up through Geometry, but also their proficiency with the Standards for Mathematical Practice, including their skills at making sense of problems and developing a solution plan to solve them, at reasoning abstractly and quantitatively, and at developing mathematical models to represent problem situations. These real-world problems will be multi-part, complex tasks.

Students will be given two (or more) class periods to complete these tasks that will require students to analyze given information, and based on their analysis, students will be expected to make decisions about options presented, develop mathematical or visual models to represent problem situations, and present and defend solutions to the problem situation presented. Students should expect to be asked to defend their decisions and justify their models. Writing will be an important element of these tasks.

You will find four (4) practice Performance Tasks to help your students begin to prepare for these new assessments. For each Performance Task, you will find a scoring rubric in the Answers section that you can use to evaluate students' work.

Performance Task: Designing a Container

Complete this performance task in the space provided. Fully answer all parts of the performance task with detailed responses. You should provide sound mathematical reasoning to support your work.

Three teams of students are designing containers that will hold 1000 mL of liquid. The containers must be 10 cm high and be open at the top. The shapes that the teams plan to use for their containers are listed below.

Team 1: rectangular prism with a square base

Team 2: cylinder

Team 3: cone

Task Description

Which team needs the least amount of material to make its container? Which team needs the most material? (Recall that 1 mL = 1 cm^3. Round your answers to the nearest hundredth.)

a. What are the dimensions of Team 1's container? Considering the outside of the container only, what is the surface area?

b. What are the dimensions and surface area of Team 2's container?

Performance Task: Designing a Container (continued)

c. What are the dimensions and surface area of Team 3's container?

d. Which team needs the least amount of material to make its container? Which team needs the most?

e. Suppose Team 2's cylindrical container does NOT have to be 10 cm high. Can you change the container's dimensions to use less material but still hold 1000 mL of liquid? Show your work.

Performance Task: Urban Planning

Complete this performance task in the space provided. Fully answer all parts of the performance task with detailed responses. You should provide sound mathematical reasoning to support your work.

Students are designing a new town as part of a social studies project on urban planning. They want to place the town's high school at point *A* and the middle school at point *B*. They also plan to build roads that run directly from point *A* to the mall and from point *B* to the mall. The average cost to build a road in this area is $550,000 per mile.

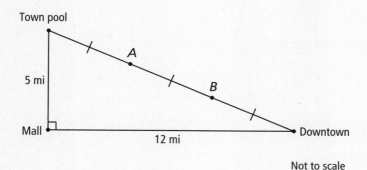

Task Description

What is the difference in the cost of the roads built to the mall from the two schools?

a. Find the measure of each acute angle of the right triangle shown.

b. Find the length of the hypotenuse. Also find the length of each of the three congruent segments forming the hypotenuse.

Performance Task: Urban Planning (continued)

c. Draw the road from point *A* to the mall and find its length.

d. Draw the road from point *B* to the mall and find its length.

e. How much farther from the mall is point *B* than point *A*? How much more will it cost to build the longer road?

Performance Task: Analyzing an Excavation Site

Complete this performance task in the space provided. Fully answer all parts of the performance task with detailed responses. You should provide sound mathematical reasoning to support your work.

Archeologists find evidence of three houses at a dig site. They believe the houses were arranged in a circle and want to excavate at the center of the settlement. The map shows the locations of the three houses, at points A, B, and C.

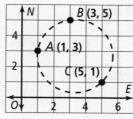

1 unit = 10 m

Task Description

Find the coordinates of the center of the settlement, and how far each house was from the center.

a. For any chord of a circle, the perpendicular bisector of the chord passes through the circle's center. Explain how you can use this fact to find the center of the circle.

Performance Task: Analyzing an Excavation Site (continued)

b. Find the midpoints of $\overline{AB}$ and $\overline{BC}$.

c. Find the slopes of $\overline{AB}$ and $\overline{BC}$.

d. Use the midpoints and slopes of $\overline{AB}$ and $\overline{BC}$ to write equations for the perpendicular bisectors of these segments.

e. What are the coordinates of the settlement's center? Explain.

f. How far was each house from the center of the settlement?

g. Give possible coordinates of another house in the settlement.

Performance Task: Applying Geometric Probability

Complete this performance task in the space provided. Fully answer all parts of the performance task with detailed responses. You should provide sound mathematical reasoning to support your work.

Students are competing in a class event, throwing darts at a square dartboard like the one shown below. The points for hitting each region are as shown. All triangles on the dartboard are equilateral triangles, and triangles with the same number of points are the same size.

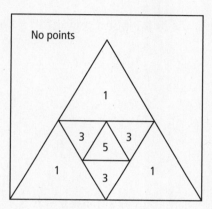

Task Description

You and your friend are playing a game of darts. You have 43 points and your friend has 48 points, but you have 2 darts left to throw and your friend has none. If each dart lands in a random location on the board, what is the probability that you can take the lead and win the game with your last 2 darts?

a. What is the probability that a dart hitting the board lands anywhere within the largest triangle?

Performance Task: Applying Geometric Probability (continued)

b. What is the probability that a dart hitting the board does NOT land in any triangle?

c. What is the probability that a dart lands in a 1-point region? In a 3-point region? In the 5-point region?

d. List each sequence of two dart throws that gives at least 6 points, and therefore wins the game. What is the probability of getting each winning sequence?

e. What is the probability that you get *any* of the sequences from part (d) and win the game?

SAT/ACT: Introduction

Each year, as a key step in their advancement toward college, more than two million high school students take the SAT Reasoning Test (SAT[*])[1] and the American College Test (ACT).[2] Many also take the more modest counterparts of these tests, the Preliminary SAT Reasoning Test (PSAT/NMSQT)[1] and the Preliminary American College Test, now known as PLAN.[2]

Experts disagree as to how well the SAT and the ACT predict college performance. However fair or unfair it may be, most colleges base their decisions on whether or not to accept a student, at least to some degree, on the student's SAT or ACT score. (PSAT/NMSQT scores are used to qualify students for National Merit Scholarships. Most students take the PSAT/NMSQT and PLAN, however, as practice for the SAT and ACT.) In general, the larger the college, the more importance it places on SAT or ACT test scores in assessing its applicants. Also, the more demanding a college's academic standards, the higher the test scores it expects of its applicants.

Whichever colleges you apply to, your high school transcript and activities, your college application form and supporting materials, and often letters of recommendation and personal interviews will have the greatest influence on whether you are accepted. Still, it's to your advantage to achieve the highest score that you can on the SAT or ACT. This section was designed in three parts to help you meet that goal on the math portions of the two tests.

The first part will tell you what you need to know about the two tests so that you won't be surprised when you sit down on test day and open your booklet. The second part will provide you with a host of test-taking tips. The third part is an SAT/ACT Practice Test you can take to apply what you've learned. If you feel you need more work with specific math content, you can turn to your textbook for a more comprehensive discussion of the relevant mathematics or for extra practice.

In the weeks leading up to whichever test you plan to take, you should spend a set amount of time each day preparing for it. Review key math topics, familiarize yourself with the test formats, and practice the test-taking skills described in this book. Of course, there's no telling how much your preparations will improve your score. Given the importance of the results, however, you have nothing to lose in preparing yourself fully for the test, and a great deal to gain.

[1] SAT is a registered trademark of, and the PSAT is a trademark owned by the College Board, which was not involved in the production of, and does not endorse, this product.

[2] ACT Assessment and the PLAN are registered trademarks owned by ACT, Inc., which was not involved in the production of, and does not endorse, this product.

SAT/ACT: Highlights

The SAT and PSAT/NMSQT

The SAT takes three hours. There are three sections in the math portion of the test.

Section	Length	Type of Question
I	25 minutes	Multiple-Choice
II	25 minutes	Multiple-Choice Grid-Ins
III	20 minutes	Multiple-Choice
Total	70 minutes	

The question types (multiple-choice and grid-ins) will be described later.

In each math section of the test, questions increase gradually in difficulty, with relatively easy questions in the first third of the section and relatively hard ones in the last third.

In addition to the sections listed above, there is a 25-minute "experimental" section, containing new SAT math, critical reading, or writing multiple choice questions that are being tried out. This section is not scored.

The PSAT/NMSQT is similar to the SAT, except that it only lasts for about two hours. In the math portion of the PSAT/NMSQT, the SAT's 20-minute, 16-question section is left out. There is no experimental section.

Both tests cover Knowledge of Number and Operations; Algebra, and Functions; Geometry and Measurement; and Statistics, Probability, and Data Analysis. You are not expected to know the fine details of math. Naturally, the more you know, the more likely you are to do well in the test. The SAT and PSAT/NMSQT, however, emphasize math reasoning and problem solving rather than comprehensive proficiency in mathematics.

The quadratic formula is one example of a fine detail. Neither the SAT nor the PSAT/NMSQT requires you to know it. To solve quadratic equations on the tests, you can use factoring or other elementary methods. Of course, if you *do* know the quadratic formula, you might find it useful, either to solve a problem or to check an answer. In general, however, you're better off using logic and clear reasoning to solve problems, rather than advanced mathematics.

You're allowed to bring a calculator to either test—in fact, you're encouraged to do so. None of the questions will *require* the use of a calculator. On the average, however, students who use calculators wisely do slightly better than students who do not use them at all, and considerably better than students who use them unwisely.

SAT/ACT: Highlights

Scoring

Multiple-choices are scored using the following guidelines: you receive one point for a correct answer and no points if you leave an answer blank. If you answer incorrectly, there's a penalty:

- one-fourth of a point is subtracted from your score if the question has five answer choices.

With grid-ins, you receive one point for a correct answer and no points for an incorrect or blank answer.

Here's how one SAT test was scored:

44 multiple-choice questions

28 correct	=	28 points
12 incorrect (5 answer choices)	=	$(-)$ 3 points $\quad (12 \times \frac{1}{4} = 3)$
4 blank	=	0 points

10 grid-in questions

6 correct	=	6 points
3 incorrect	=	0 points
1 blank	=	0 points
Raw Score	=	**31 points**

The policy of subtracting a fraction of a point for incorrect answers on multiple-choice questions is called a "guessing penalty."

The raw score is now rounded to the nearest point and converted to a "scaled" score between 200 and 800 (SAT), or 20 and 80 (PSAT/NMSQT). There are no passing or failing scores.

About a month after you take either test, you'll receive your results. These consist of your scaled score and a "percentile" score. The percentile score allows you to compare your results with those of all the other students who took the test. A score in the 64th percentile means that you did better than 64 percent of the people who took the test. The average SAT math score nationwide is 500 points.

SAT/ACT: Highlights

Question Types

There are two types of questions on the math section of the SAT.

Multiple-Choice Questions

Five answers are given for each multiple-choice question. Decide on the correct choice and fill in the corresponding oval on the answer sheet.

If 2 cans of tomatoes weigh 28 ounces, what is the weight, in ounces, of 7 cans of tomatoes?

(A) 2   (B) 8   (C) 56   (D) 98   (E) 196   Ⓐ Ⓑ Ⓒ ● Ⓔ

Grid-In Questions

Grid-in questions are called "student-produced responses" on the test. Each requires you to calculate the correct answer to a question and then write it on the answer grid. Gridding an answer incorrectly will result in a zero score even if your answer is correct. For that reason, you should review the method for gridding answers *before* you take the test, because there are several ways to grid incorrectly. The following pages will give you a chance to do that.

Sample Grids

Your responses are recorded on a special answer grid that provides ways of showing decimal points and fraction bars. You will be able to code decimal and fraction answers. For example, a student who gets an answer of 23.9 on a problem would code the answer as shown in this grid.

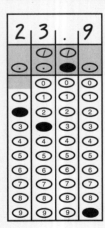

The grid is composed of four columns. If you look closely, you will notice that along with the digits 0 through 9, the division sign (/) and the decimal point (.) are available. *The first column cannot be filled with 0 or /.* Also, each character in the answer must occupy a single column in the grid. So the answer 23.9 requires all four available columns. Notice that there is no provision in the grid structure for coding negative values. *This is a clear message that there will be no questions in this part of the test that have negative answers.*

SAT/ACT: Highlights

The ACT and PLAN

The ACT takes three and one-half hours. The math section of the test lasts one hour and consists of 60 multiple-choice questions. Questions are arranged roughly in order of difficulty, from easiest to hardest. As with the SAT, you may use a calculator on the ACT.

Scoring

Unlike the SAT, the ACT is not scored by deducting a fraction of your incorrect answers from your correct ones. You get one point for a correct answer and no points for either an incorrect answer or an answer left blank. There is no penalty for guessing.

Here's how one ACT test was scored:

60 multiple-choice questions

38 correct	=	38 points
22 incorrect	=	0 points
Raw Score	=	**38 points**

The content of ACT test questions is invariable. There are always

- 24 questions on pre-algebra and elementary algebra;
- 18 questions on intermediate algebra and coordinate geometry;
- 14 questions on geometry;
- 4 questions on basic trigonometry.

The PLAN is a mini-ACT. The math section of the test lasts 40 minutes and consists of 40 multiple-choice questions, apportioned as follows:

- 14 questions on pre-algebra;
- 8 questions on elementary algebra;
- 7 questions on coordinate geometry;
- 11 questions on plane geometry.

As on the ACT, you can use a calculator when you take the PLAN.

Getting Your Results

You'll receive your ACT results in four to six weeks. Your math score (and your score in each of the other three areas of the test) will be a number from 1 to 36; 36 will be the highest possible score. (The PLAN is scored from 1 to 32.) As with the SAT, you'll also receive a percentile ranking so that you can compare your results with those of other students who took the test.

SAT/ACT: Test-Taking Tips

Taking the Test

The following are time-honored test-taking strategies.

Manage Your Time Efficiently.

The questions in each section of the test are arranged roughly in order of difficulty. As you begin, make a quick estimate of the average amount of time you have to answer each question. Use the estimate to guide you through the section. Allow yourself a little less than the average amount of time for the early, easier first questions so that you'll have extra time for the harder ones later on.

Starting with the first question, move as quickly as you can through the section. Consider each question in turn. Make a quick assessment as to whether you can solve it rapidly. If you think you can, do so. Work at a comfortable pace, but don't linger. Spending too much time on a problem in the fanciful belief that you've *almost got it* is a killer. Remember: all problems are worth the same number of points. You receive one point for each easy question that you answer correctly and one point for each hard one. How should you spend your time?

If you decide that you can probably solve a problem with a little more time, draw a circle around it. After you've made your first pass through all the questions, answering those that seem easy, return to the questions you've circled. This second look is often successful, so don't get discouraged if you find yourself circling lots of questions. Continue to pace yourself during the second pass. Work your way through the questions you think you have a chance on, but don't be reluctant to abandon them again and move on if they continue to tie you up. After the second pass, return to the questions that continue to stump you if time remains.

If you're sure that you won't be able to solve a problem, draw an **X** beside it and forget it. Throwing in the towel on questions you can't answer is simply good time management and nothing to apologize for. No one is expected to answer every question correctly and few people do.

Be careful.

Beware of the following:

- Under the pressure of test-taking, it's easy to make careless mistakes. Work through calculations methodically, rechecking them quickly at the end. Ask yourself if answers are reasonable. Is the price after a discount greater than the original price? Does one of the acute angles in a right triangle measure 150°? Use estimation whenever possible. On multiple-choice questions, an estimate may be enough to help you decide which of the given answers is correct without actually working it out.

- On multiple-choice questions, watch out for "obvious" choices. In the first part of a section, where the questions are relatively easy, an answer that seems obvious may be the right one. But in the last part, the obvious answer may have been put there to deceive you. After all, if an answer is obvious, what's the question doing in the hard part of the test?

SAT/ACT: Test-Taking Tips

- Check and double-check to make sure that you're writing your answers in the correct spots, and beside the correct numbers. To guard against potential disasters, many students write all their answers in their test booklets *only*, transferring them all at once to their answer sheets in the final minute or two.

- Beware of long computations. SAT and ACT problems can usually be solved with minimal calculations. If you find yourself in the midst of a multi-step nightmare, it's best to stop and look for a shortcut—or move on to the next question.

- If you're told that a figure is not drawn to scale, believe it. Don't assume that lengths and angles are drawn accurately.

- Measurements may be given in different units. If they are, convert and work the problem in one unit.

Be smart.

Use these ideas to simplify your work and improve your score.

- Write in your test booklet. There's no reward for a clean booklet and no penalty for one that's covered with pencil marks. If a question doesn't have a drawing and one would help, draw it. Write measurements and values on the drawing. When you calculate an answer, write out your calculations so that you can check them later. The next time, try doing them a different way. This is a good way to check your work and often reveals careless mistakes.

- On multiple-choice questions, draw a line through choices you know to be wrong. This will simplify the job of choosing the right answer.

- Look at the answer choices before working a problem. This will show you the form of the answer that is required (a fraction, for example), allowing you to work the problem in that form from the beginning rather than having to rewrite your answer later in a different form.

- Under "Reference Information," the SAT booklet provides a considerable amount of information on geometrical relationships. Use it.

- Know commonly used numbers. Recognize powers of 2, 3, and 5. Know the decimal equivalents for simple fractions with denominators of 2, 3, 4, 5, 6, 8, and 10. Know the common Pythagorean triples 3-4-5 and 5-12-13 and recognize their multiples.

SAT/ACT: Practice Test

Section I Multiple Choice

In the following problems you have five choices for an answer. Only one choice is correct. Mark your answer by filling in the correct bubble on the answer sheet that your teacher provides.

1. If $x - 4 = x^2 - 6$, then $x =$

   (A) 1 or 2

   (B) -1 or 2

   (C) 0 or 2

   (D) -1 or -2

   (E) -1 or 4

2. If a square is copied beside itself to produce a rectangle, $\dfrac{\text{perimeter of rectangle}}{\text{perimeter of square}} =$

   (A) 4

   (B) 3

   (C) 2

   (D) 1.5

   (E) 1

3. Mark bought 14 tapes, some priced at $6 each and the rest priced at $8 each. If he spent $94 altogether, how many tapes did he buy at each price?

   (A) 6 at $6 and 8 at $8

   (B) 7 at $6 and 7 at $8

   (C) 8 at $6 and 6 at $8

   (D) 9 at $6 and 5 at $8

   (E) 10 at $6 and 4 at $8

4. If $\dfrac{x - 2}{x + 2} = \dfrac{1}{2}$, then $x =$

   (A) 2

   (B) 3

   (C) 4

   (D) 5

   (E) 6

GO ON

SAT/ACT: Practice Test

Section I Multiple Choice (continued)

5. Jorge bought 16 CDs at a cost of $9 each. How many $12 CDs could he have bought for the amount he paid?

(A) 8

(B) 9

(C) 10

(D) 12

(E) 21

7. Jason worked 20 hours at $5 per hour and 30 hours at $6 per hour. What was his average hourly wage?

(A) $5.20

(B) $5.40

(C) $5.50

(D) $5.60

(E) $5.65

6. Five people split the following costs equally among themselves: $12.40, $10.95, $16.75, $6.10. How much did each person pay?

(A) $9.24

(B) $11.55

(C) $20.22

(D) $33.21

(E) $66.42

8. $2^2 + (2^3)^2 = \underline{\ ?\ }$

(A) $(2^2)17$

(B) 2^7

(C) 2^8

(D) 10^2

(E) $2^2(5)$

GO ON

SAT/ACT: Practice Test

Section I Multiple Choice (continued)

9. $x^2 - 4 = 3x$. Then $x = $ __?__

   (A) 2 or -2

   (B) 0

   (C) 4 or -1

   (D) 3 or 0

   (E) 2, -2, or 0

11. Ted bought 3 books at m dollars each. The sales tax on his purchase was 5% of the cost of the books. Which of the following expresses the total cost of his purchase?

   (A) $15m$

   (B) $0.15m$

   (C) $18m$

   (D) $3.15m$

   (E) $3m + 0.05$

10. In simplified form, $\dfrac{x^6 + x^4}{x^2}$ equals

   (A) $x^3 + x^2$

   (B) $x^4 + x^2$

   (C) x^5

   (D) x^8

   (E) x^{12}

12. If $-5x \geq 20$, which of the following is true?

   (A) $x \leq 15$

   (B) $x \leq 4$

   (C) $x \leq -4$

   (D) $x \geq 15$

   (E) $x \geq -4$

GO ON

SAT/ACT: Practice Test

Section I Multiple Choice (continued)

---

13. Which of the following pairs (x, y) is a solution of the system?

$$x + y = 4$$
$$-x + 2y = -1$$

- (A) $(1, 3)$
- (B) $(3, 1)$
- (C) $(2, 2)$
- (D) $(5, -1)$
- (E) $(-2, 6)$

15. A line segment is drawn from $A(14, 10)$ to $B(6, 4)$. Find the distance from A to the midpoint of the segment.

- (A) 3
- (B) 4
- (C) 5
- (D) 6
- (E) 8

---

14. If $\dfrac{1}{a + b} = 5$, then $b = \underline{\ ?\ }$

- (A) $\dfrac{1}{5} - a$
- (B) $-5a$
- (C) $1 - a$
- (D) $\dfrac{1 + 5a}{5}$
- (E) $\dfrac{1 - a}{5}$

16. Where does the line $6x - 2y = -10$ cross the y-axis?

- (A) -10
- (B) $-\dfrac{5}{3}$
- (C) 3
- (D) 5
- (E) 10

GO ON

SAT/ACT: Practice Test

Section I Multiple Choice (continued)

17. Which of the following points are on the line $y = 3x - 5$?

   I. $(2, -1)$
  II. $(4, 3)$
 III. $(0, -5)$

  (A) I only

  (B) II only

  (C) III only

  (D) I and III only

  (E) II and III only

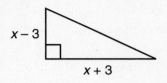

19. For what value of x is the area of the above triangle equal to 36?

  (A) $3\sqrt{2}$

  (B) 3

  (C) $3\sqrt{5}$

  (D) 9

  (E) 12

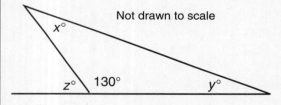

Not drawn to scale

18. Which statements could be true for this figure?

   I. $z = x + y$
  II. $z > y$
 III. $z = x$

  (A) I only

  (B) II only

  (C) I and II only

  (D) II and III only

  (E) I, II, and III

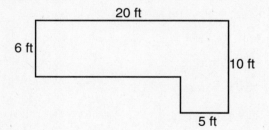

20. The perimeter of the above figure, in feet, is

  (A) 200

  (B) 140

  (C) 60

  (D) 52

  (E) 41

GO ON

SAT/ACT: Practice Test

Section I Multiple Choice (continued)

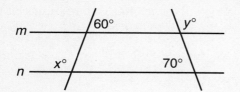

21. In the figure above, $m \parallel n$. What is the sum $x + y$?

(A) 130

(B) 180

(C) 200

(D) 230

(E) 270

22. The expression $\dfrac{\sin^2 x + \cos^2 x}{\sec x}$ simplifies to

(A) $\sin x$

(B) $\cos x$

(C) $\tan x$

(D) $\sec x$

(E) $\csc x$

23. The areas of the four sectors of the spinner are equal. The probability of spinning C *and* tossing a head with a penny is

(A) 8

(B) 1

(C) $\dfrac{3}{4}$

(D) $\dfrac{1}{2}$

(E) $\dfrac{1}{8}$

24. A spinner has 12 sections of equal area. The probability of spinning red is $\dfrac{1}{3}$ and the probability of spinning red or yellow is $\dfrac{3}{4}$. The number of yellow sections is

(A) 2

(B) 4

(C) 5

(D) 6

(E) 9

GO ON

SAT/ACT: Practice Test

Section I Multiple Choice (continued)

---

25. Which of the following is next in the sequence?

1, 5, 9, 13, 17, __?__

(A) 20

(B) 21

(C) 22

(D) 23

(E) 24

27. Which of these lines is perpendicular to the line $y = 2x + 6$?

(A) $2y = -4x + 3$

(B) $2y = 4x + 3$

(C) $2y = x + 3$

(D) $-2y = x + 3$

(E) $x + y = 6$

---

26. The coordinates of the midpoint of $\overline{LN}$ with endpoints $L(-1, -3)$ and $N(3, -5)$ are

(A) $(1, -4)$

(B) $(-2, 1)$

(C) $(-1, -4)$

(D) $(1, 4)$

(E) $(0, -4)$

28. Which of the following statements is *not* true for the equation $4x + 3y = 15$?

(A) The y-intercept is 5.

(B) The line has a positive slope.

(C) The x-intercept is 3.75.

(D) The line contains the point $(3, 1)$.

(E) none of the above

GO ON

SAT/ACT: Practice Test

Section I Multiple Choice (continued)

29. Which of the following is true?

(A) $5^0 = 0$

(B) $\dfrac{1}{5^0} = \dfrac{1}{5}$

(C) $\dfrac{x^6}{x^2} = x^3$

(D) $(2x)^4 = 8x^4$

(E) none of the above

31. Which of the following is an irrational number?

(A) $\sqrt{2}$

(B) 0.125

(C) $\dfrac{1}{3}$

(D) 101

(E) $\sqrt{81}$

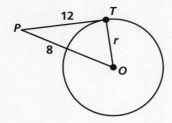

30. $\overline{PT}$ is tangent to $\odot O$ at T. Find the value of r.

(A) 4

(B) 5

(C) 6

(D) 8

(E) 10

32. For art class, you have constructed a model of your family's car. If your model is 4 inches high and your car is 5 feet high, what scale factor did you use?

(A) $\dfrac{4}{5}$

(B) $\dfrac{5}{4}$

(C) $\dfrac{1}{20}$

(D) $\dfrac{1}{15}$

(E) none of the above

STOP

SAT/ACT: Practice Test

Section II Student-Produced Responses

After you solve each problem on this section, enter your answer on the corresponding grid provided on your answer sheet.

1. What is the greatest value out of $\frac{3}{10}$, 0.03, and $\frac{2}{5}$?

2. If $\frac{1}{x} = \sqrt{0.04}$, then x equals __?__

3. The product of $(5-1)$, $(5-2)$, and $(5-3)$ equals twice the sum of x and 5. Then $x =$ __?__

4. Find the value of $n^4 - n^3$ when $n = -3$.

GO ON

SAT/ACT: Practice Test

Section II Student-Produced Responses (continued)

5. What is the positive solution to
$2x^2 - 5x - 3 = 0$?

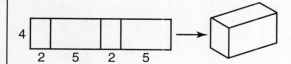

7. The figure on the left is folded to form a bottomless, topless box. If a top and bottom are put on the box, what is their combined area?

6. What is the sum of the measures of the interior angles of a 6-sided polygon?

8. The areas of two similar triangles are 98 in.^{2} and 162 in.^{2}. What is the ratio of their perimeters when comparing smaller to larger?

GO ON

SAT/ACT: Practice Test

Section II Student-Produced Responses (continued)

9. Two-thirds of 24 is equal to 25 percent of what number?

10. What is the constant term

of $\dfrac{3x^4 + 9x^3 - 2x^2 + 18}{x + 3}$?

STOP

Week 1

1. D

2. a. Check students' drawings

   b. $MJ = 6$ units

3. a. $x = 5$ **b.** $m\angle ABC = 25$, $m\angle CBD = 155$

c. Answers may vary. Sample answer:

$3(5) + 10 = 25$

$22(5) + 40 = 155$

$25 + 155 = 180$

Week 2

1. B

2.

3. a. $AB = 5$, $AC = 5$, $AD = 10$, $BC = 6$,

   $BD = \sqrt{97}$, $CD = 5$

b.

Length of Segment = 5	Length of Segment ≠ 5
$\overline{AB}$	$\overline{BC}$
$\overline{AC}$	$\overline{AD}$
$\overline{CD}$	$\overline{BD}$

Week 3

1. D

2. A

3. No valid conclusion; the hypothesis was not satisfied. For example, you could have gotten a ride or taken a taxi, etc.

4.

Statements	Reasons
1) $JK = KL$	1) Given
2) $JK = 3x + 9$	2) Given
3) $KL = 3x + 9$	3) Transitive Property of Equality
4) $JL = JK + KL$	4) Segment Addition Postulate
5) $JL = 3x + 9 + 3x + 9$	5) Substitution
6) $JL = 6x + 18$	6) Combining Like Terms
7) $JL = 45$	7) Given
8) $6x + 18 = 45$	8) Transitive Property of Equality
9) $6x = 27$	9) Subtraction Property of Equality
10) $x = 45$	10) Division Property of Equality

Week 4

1. C

2. $x = 24$

3.

Statements	Reasons
1) $m\angle 1$ and $m\angle 7$ are supplementary.	1) Given
2) $m\angle 1 = m\angle 4$	2) Vertical Angle Theorem
3) $m\angle 4$ and $m\angle 7$ are supplementary.	3) Substitution Property
4) $m\angle 7 = m\angle 6$	4) Vertical Angles Theorem
5) $m\angle 4$ and $m\angle 6$ are supplementary.	5) Substitution Property
6) $r \parallel s$	6) Converse of the Same-Side Interior Angles Postulate

Week 5

1. A

2. $m\angle B = 52$

   $m\angle C = 104$

3.

Statements	Reasons
1) ABC is a triangle with exterior angles 1, 2, and 3.	1) Given
2) $\angle 1$ and $\angle A$ are supplementary.	2) Angles that form a linear pair are supplementary.
3) $m\angle 1 + m\angle A = 180$	3) Definition of supplementary angles
4) $\angle 2$ and $\angle B$ are supplementary.	4) Angles that form a linear pair are supplementary.
5) $m\angle 2 + m\angle B = 180$	5) Definition of supplementary angles
6) $\angle 3$ and $\angle C$ are supplementary.	6) Angles that form a linear pair are supplementary.
7) $m\angle 3 + m\angle C = 180$	7) Definition of supplementary angles
8) $m\angle 1 + m\angle A + m\angle 2 + m\angle B + m\angle 3 + m\angle C = 540$	8) Addition Property of Equality
9) $m\angle A + m\angle B + m\angle C = 180$	9) Triangle Angle-Sum Theorem
10) $m\angle 1 + m\angle 2 + m\angle 3 + 180 = 540$	10) Substitution Property
11) $m\angle 1 + m\angle 2 + m\angle 3 = 360$	11) Subtraction Property of Equality

Week 6

1. A

2.

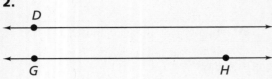

3. a. $3; -3; \dfrac{1}{3}; -\dfrac{1}{3}; -\dfrac{1}{3}$

b.

Perpendicular to $y = 3(x - 1)$	Not Perpendicular to $y = 3(x - 1)$
$5x + 15y = 1$	$y = 3x + 8$
$y = -\dfrac{1}{3}x - 5$	$y = -3x + 10$
	$3x - 9y = 14$

Week 7

1. A

2. $JK = \sqrt{16 + 9} = \sqrt{25} = 5$ and
$MN = \sqrt{16 + 9} = \sqrt{25} = 5$
$KL = \sqrt{16 + 9} = \sqrt{25} = 5$ and
$NO = \sqrt{16 + 9} = \sqrt{25} = 5$
$JL = \sqrt{0 + 36} = \sqrt{36} = 6$ and
$MO = \sqrt{0 + 36} = \sqrt{36} = 6$
So $\triangle JKL \cong \triangle MNO$ by SSS Postulate.

3. a. Graphs may vary. Sample:

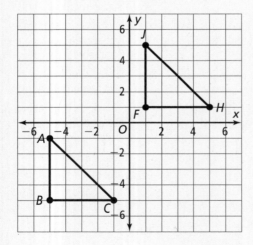

b. $m\angle F = 90$ because $\overline{FJ}$ is vertical and $\overline{FH}$ is horizontal. $AB = JF = 4$, and $BC = FH = 4$. Therefore, $\triangle ABC \cong \triangle FJH$ by SAS Postulate. (Note: Students could have also proved the triangles are congruent by SSS Postulate if they used the Pythagorean theorem to prove that $AC = JH = 4\sqrt{2}$.)

Week 8

1. B

2. $x = 5$

3.

Statements	Reasons
1) $\triangle LRN$ is equilateral; $\overline{MR} \cong \overline{PR}$	1) Given
2) $\overline{LR} \cong \overline{NR}$	2) Definition of equilateral triangle
3) $\angle LRM \cong \angle NRP$	3) Vertical Angles Theorem
4) $\triangle MLR \cong \triangle PNR$	4) SAS Postulate

Week 9

1. C

2. $x = 6.25$

3. a. Slope of $\overline{AB} = -1$; Slope of $\overline{DF} = -1$

b. $AB = 2\sqrt{2}$; $DF = 4\sqrt{2}$

Week 10

1. B

2. $x = 7$

3. a. $AD = \sqrt{(4 - 0)^2 + (-1 - 0)^2}$
$= \sqrt{4^2 + 1^2} = \sqrt{16 + 1} = \sqrt{17}$
$BD = \sqrt{(8 - 4)^2 + (0 - (-1))^2}$
$= \sqrt{4^2 + 1^2} = \sqrt{16 + 1} = \sqrt{17}$

b. $AD = DB$ from part (a). Draw $\overline{AB}$ and label its intersection with $\overline{CD}$ as point E. $\overline{AB} \perp \overline{CD}$, because $\overline{AB}$ is horizontal and $\overline{CD}$ is vertical. $AE = EB$, because both line segments measure 4 units. So, $\overline{CD}$ is the perpendicular bisector of $\overline{AB}$.

Week 11

1. D

2. $x = 4$

3. a.

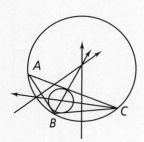

b. To draw the inscribed circle: Construct two angle bisectors. Their intersection is the center of the circle. Construct a perpendicular segment to any side from the center. The distance to the side is the radius. Construct a circle with this center and radius. To draw the circumscribed circle: Construct two perpendicular bisectors. Their intersection is the center of the circle. Draw a circle from that center passing through the vertices.

Week 12

1. B

2. $x = 3$, $y = 8$

3. $\angle LPO \cong \angle MPN$ and $\angle LPM \cong \angle OPN$ because vertical angles are congruent. Using Side-Angle-Side postulate, $\triangle LPO \cong \triangle NPM$ and $\triangle LPM \cong \triangle NPO$. Since corresponding parts of congruent triangles are congruent, $\angle OLP \cong \angle MNP$ and $\angle PML \cong \angle PON$.

Alternate interior angles are congruent, so $\overline{LO} \parallel \overline{MN}$ and $\overline{LM} \parallel \overline{ON}$. By the definition of a parallelogram, $LMNO$ is a parallelogram.

Week 13

1. D

2. $m\angle Z = m\angle Y = 74$; $m\angle W = m\angle X = 106$

3. From the given: $\overline{AC}$ bisects $\angle DAB$.
$\overline{AB} \parallel \overline{CD}$ by the definition of a parallelogram.
$\angle 1 \cong \angle 4$ and $\angle 2 \cong \angle 3$ because if parallel lines, alternate interior angles are congruent.
$\angle 1 \cong \angle 2$ by the Transitive Property of Congruence.
Therefore, $\overline{AC}$ bisects $\angle DCE$ by the definition of angle bisector.

Week 14

1. D

2. a.

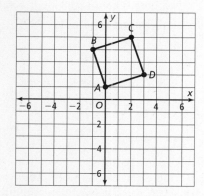

b. Yes, the slope of $\overline{AB}$ = slope of $\overline{CD} = -3$ and slope of $\overline{BC}$ = slope of $\overline{AD} = \dfrac{1}{3}$. So opposite sides are parallel. The product of the slopes is -1, so the sides are perpendicular by the definition of a rectangle.

3.

Can be Reached	Cannot be Reached
$\overline{XY} \cong \overline{ST}$	$\angle P \cong \angle O$
$\overline{JK}$ bisects $\overline{MN}$.	$m\angle K + m\angle L = 180$
$\overline{RS} \parallel \overline{TU}$ $\overline{WX} \perp \overline{YZ}$	
$\triangle ABC$ is a right triangle.	

Week 15

1. A

2. a. The triangles are similar because of the Angle-Angle Postulate. Vertical angles are congruent.

b. $x = 12$

3. Use slope formula to find slopes of the diagonals. The product of the slopes is -1, so quadrilateral $ABCD$ is a rhombus.

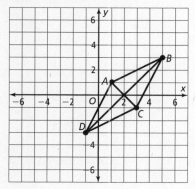

Week 16

1. A, C

2. a. The utility pole is about 10.8 ft tall.

b. Diagrams may vary, See sample.

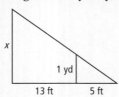

3. $\overleftrightarrow{SU} \parallel \overleftrightarrow{VW}$ is given. $\angle 1 \cong \angle 2$, $\angle 3 \cong \angle 4$ because if lines are parallel, then corresponding angles are congruent. By the Angle-Angle Postulate, $\triangle STU \sim \triangle VTW$. By the definition of similar triangles, $\dfrac{VT}{ST} = \dfrac{WT}{UT}$ because corresponding sides are proportional. $VT = VS + ST$ and $WT = WU + UT$ by the Segment Addition Postulate. By substitution, $\dfrac{VS + ST}{ST} = \dfrac{WU + UT}{UT}$. Simplify to find $\dfrac{VS}{ST} = \dfrac{WU}{UT}$.

Week 17

1. C

2. $w = 3$, $x = 41$

3. a.

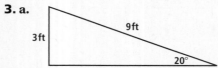

b. 3 ft

Week 18

1. C

2. 54.6

3. a.

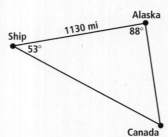

b. 1874 mi; First find the third angle measure: $180 - (53 + 88) = 39$. Next use the Law of Sines and solve: $\dfrac{\sin 88}{x} = \dfrac{\sin 39}{1130}$.

Week 19

1. D

2. a. $A'(-2, 0)$, $B'(1, 0)$, $C'(1, -3)$, $D'(-2, -3)$

b.

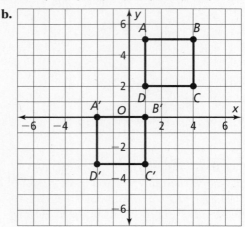

3. a.–b.

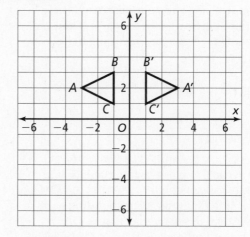

c. A reflection across the y-axis

Week 20

1. A

2. Answers may vary. Sample: Translate the top rectangle down 6 units, then translate 2 units right; reflect across x-axis, then reflect across the y-axis; rotate the bottom rectangle 180° about the origin; reflect the bottom rectangle across the x-axis, then translate 2 units to the left.

3. Translate $\triangle ABC$ so that points A and X coincide. Because $\overline{AB} \cong \overline{XY}$, you can rotate $\triangle XYZ$ about point A so that $\overline{AB}$ and $\overline{XY}$ coincide. Reflect $\triangle ABC$ across $\overline{AB}$. Because reflections preserve angle measure and distance, and because $\angle Y \cong \angle B$, you know that the reflection maps $\angle Y$ to $\angle B$ and $\overline{ZY}$ to $\overline{CB}$. Since points Z and C coincide, $\triangle ABC$ coincides with $\triangle XYZ$

Week 21

1. A

2.

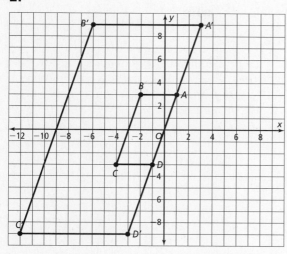

3. The triangles are similar because there is a similarity transformation between them (Angle-Angle similarity) and they can be mapped one onto another by rotation and dilation. Therefore, with triangle similarity and a ratio between corresponding sides, we can find the distance across the drop zone which is 161.5 mi.

Week 22

1. B

2. a. $\dfrac{7}{11}$ **b.** 7 : 11

3. a. Method 1: Use the formula $A = \dfrac{1}{2}ap$.

Method 2: Find the area of one equilateral triangle and multiply it by 6.

b. Area $= 162\sqrt{3}\,\text{m}^2$.

Week 23

1. C

2. 10π cm

3. a.

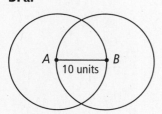

b. $\left(\dfrac{200\pi}{3} - 50\sqrt{3}\right)$ units^2

Week 24

1. D

2.

a.   **b.**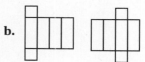

3. a. 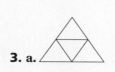 **b.**   **c.**

Week 25

1. B

2. 2,807,574 m^3

3. No, the volume of frozen yogurt is equal to the volume of the cone, both are about 180 cm^3.

Week 26

1. D

2. 128 cm^3

3. C, A, E, D, B

Week 27

1. B

2. Draw two chords. Then construct the perpendicular bisector to each chord. By Theorem 12–10, the perpendicular bisectors are diameters of the circle that contains the arc. Therefore they intersect at the center of the circle. Check students' drawings.

3.

Greater than 90	Less than 90	Equal to 90
$\angle c$, $\angle f$	$\angle a$, $\angle b$	$\angle d$

Week 28

1. A, E

2. $x^2 + (y + 8)^2 = 121$

3. a. $x^2 + y^2 = 11,532,816$
b. 59.3 km
c. about 296 days.

Week 29

1. D

2. a.

Number of Children in Family	1	2	3	4	More than 4
Frequency	38	42	30	27	13
Probability	$\frac{38}{150}$	$\frac{42}{150}$	$\frac{30}{150}$	$\frac{27}{150}$	$\frac{13}{150}$

b. about 191 families

c. about 457 families

3. He used a permutation instead of a combination. There are actually 792 ways.

Week 30

1. B

2. a. $\frac{1}{2}$ **b.** $\frac{1}{3}$

3. a. 54.5%

b. If the probability of the field being muddy decreases, the probability of the team winning will decrease, because it has a better chance of winning on a muddy field.

Screening Test

1. C **2.** H **3.** B **4.** H **5.** C **6.** J **7.** A **8.** F **9.** C
10. G **11.** C **12.** F **13.** B **14.** H **15.** C **16.** J
17. D **18.** H **19.** B **20.** J **21.** C **22.** H **23.** C
24. J **25.** B **26.** H **27.** D **28.** G **29.** D **30.** F
31. C **32.** F **33.** C **34.** J **35.** C **36.** G **37.** D
38. F **39.** B **40.** J **41.** C **42.** J

Common Core Readiness Assessment 1

1. C **2.** H **3.** B **4.** F **5.** D **6.** J **7.** B **8.** H **9.** A
10. G **11.** D **12.** F **13.** C **14.** G **15.** B **16.** J
17. B **18.** H **19.** D **20.** G **21.** A **22.** H **23.** C
24. H **25.** B **26.** H **27.** B **28.** F **29.** B **30.** F

Common Core Readiness Assessment 2

1. D **2.** G **3.** B **4.** F **5.** C **6.** J **7.** A **8.** H **9.** C
10. G **11.** A **12.** H **13.** C **14.** H **15.** B **16.** G
17. C **18.** H **19.** A **20.** H **21.** B **22.** F **23.** C
24. G **25.** C **26.** F **27.** C **28.** H **29.** B **30.** J

Common Core Readiness Assessment 3

1. A **2.** G **3.** A **4.** J **5.** C **6.** G **7.** A **8.** G **9.** C
10. F **11.** A **12.** F **13.** D **14.** H **15.** B **16.** G
17. A **18.** H **19.** C **20.** H **21.** B **22.** F **23.** D
24. G **25.** C **26.** H **27.** B **28.** H **29.** B **30.** G

Common Core Readiness Assessment 4

1. C **2.** G **3.** D **4.** F **5.** C **6.** H **7.** C **8.** G **9.** B
10. H **11.** A **12.** J **13.** B **14.** J **15.** D **16.** J **17.** B
18. H **19.** C **20.** J **21.** A **22.** F **23.** B **24.** H
25. B **26.** F **27.** B **28.** J **29.** A **30.** H

Common Core Readiness Assessment 5

1. C **2.** G **3.** C **4.** H **5.** D **6.** G **7.** B **8.** H **9.** C
10. G **11.** D **12.** J **13.** B **14.** F **15.** C **16.** H
17. A **18.** J **19.** B **20.** H **21.** B **22.** F **23.** D
24. G **25.** C **26.** G **27.** A **28.** F **29.** D **30.** G

Quarter 1 Test, Form G

1. $x = 3$

2. 25

3.

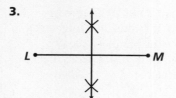

4.

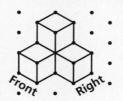

5. If two angles are complements of the same angle, then they are congruent. (Congruent Complements Theorem)

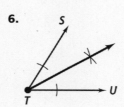

6.

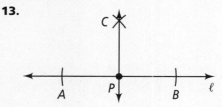

7. Line b is parallel to line c by the Transitive Property of Parallel Lines. **8.** 29

9. d, c, b, a **10.** $\overleftrightarrow{AC}$ **11.** 12π m
12. (10,6)

13.

14. (1, 2.5) **15.** $y = 3x + 1$ **16.** $\angle 2 \cong \angle 4$ by the Converse of the Corresponding Angles Postulate or $\angle 2 + \angle 3 = 180$ by the Converse of the Same-Side Interior Angles Theorem **17.** $2\sqrt{17}$

18. The intersection is a point, or there is no intersection. **19.** Two lines must not intersect *and* be in the same plane to be parallel. **20.** 40 **21.** 50 **22.** 90 **23.** 54° **24.** e, d, a, c, b **25.** Fern St. is perpendicular to Broad St.

Quarter 2 Test, Form G

1. $\overline{RS}$ **2.** 20 **3.** Reflexive Property of $\cong$; ASA **4.** 50 **5.** SSS Postulate **6.** SAS Postulate **7.** $(c - a, b)$ **8.** e, d, a, c, b

9.

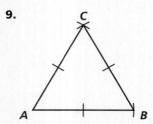

10. 20 **11.** AAS, $\triangle ABC \cong \triangle ABD$ **12.** 3
13. Answers may vary. Sample: You can use the distance formula to find the lengths of the diagonals $\overline{AC}$ and $\overline{DB}$. If the lengths are equal, then the diagonals are congruent, so the parallelogram is a rectangle.

14.

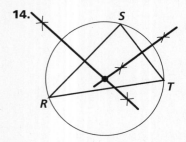

15. Answers may vary. Sample: The diagonals must be perpendicular bisectors of each other, or all sides must be congruent.

16.

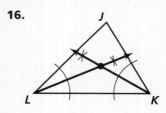

17. $P = 18$ units; $A = 12$ square units
18. Hypotenuse-Leg Theorem **19.** 9 **20.** Suppose that a triangle had more than one right angle. If this were true, then two of the angle measures alone would add up to 180, and the third angle would have a measure that would contradict the Triangle Angle-Sum Theorem. **21.** rhombus

22. 65 **23.** c, e, b, a, d or e, c, b, a, d **24.** No; AB is not half the length of the third side. **25.** a kite

Quarter 3 Test, Form G

1. $\triangle ABC \sim \triangle JKL$ by SSS $\sim$ Theorem
2. $\triangle TUV \sim \triangle WXY$ by AA $\sim$ Postulate **3.** obtuse
4. 56.3 **5.** 10.7 **6.** $\sin A = \frac{8}{17}$; $\cos A = \frac{15}{17}$; $\tan A = \frac{8}{15}$ **7.** $A'(7, 2), B'(11, 2), C'(10, -1), D'(6, -1)$ **8.** $A'(-5, 4), B'(-9, 4), C'(-8, 1), D'(-4, 1)$ **9.** $A'(-3, -4), B'(-7, -4), C'(-6, -1), D'(-2, -1)$ **10.** D **11.** $P'(3, 3)$
12. A **13.** Yes; $4^2 + 6^2 = \left(2\sqrt{13}\right)^2$, so it is right triangle by the Converse of the Pythagorean Theorem. **14.** $4\sqrt{3}$ **15.** 38
16. 6 **17.** 18.4 **18.** 76.3 **19.** 76.0 **20.** $A'(-2, 6), B'(0, 14), C'(8, 4)$ **21.** 48 ft **22.** $x = 3, y = 3\sqrt{2}$
23. $x = 2, y = 4$ **24.** 12 in. **25.** 8

Quarter 4 Test, Form G

1. 268.1 cm³ **2.** 66.3 cm² **3.** 25 **4.** 32 **5.** Answers may vary. Sample: Draw d_1, a diagonal of the kite that divides it into two congruent triangles. Let d_1 represent the base of each triangle. The area of one triangle is $\frac{1}{2}d_1h_1$. The area of the other triangle is $\frac{1}{2}d_1h_2$. Because the triangles are congruent, $h_1 = h_2$. The other diagonal, d_2, is the sum of h_1 and h_2. Therefore, the area of a kite is $\frac{1}{2}d_1d_2$. **6.** 14.14 cm² **7.** 12.5
8. a circle with center $(-2, -3)$ and radius 5 units
9. 28π m³ **10.** 81 m² **11.** 6
12. center: $(5, 6)$; radius: 4

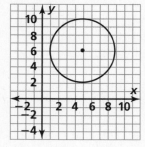

13. 73.7 **14.** 92 **15.** 400 ft³ **16.** 164 in.³ **17.** 30 **18.** 60 **19.** 270 **20.** 310.4 in.² **21.** 8 **22.** $(x - 2)^2 + (y - 2)^2 = 4$ **23.** 188.1 in.² **24.** 2π in. **25.** 284.7 cm²

Mid-Course Test, Form G

1. d, a, e, b, g, c, f **2.** m∠1 = 60, m∠2 = 150, m∠3 = 120 **3.** 19 **4.** 7 **5.** parallelogram **6.** 12
7. 36, 36 **8.** $y = -\frac{3}{2}x + 2$ **9.** 26 **10.** 125°; obtuse **11.** 60 **12.** $\triangle CAB \cong \triangle BDC$ by SAS.
13. $(a - b, c)$ **14a.** ∠3 and ∠5 or ∠4 and ∠6
14b. ∠1 and ∠5, ∠2 and ∠6, ∠3 and ∠7, or ∠4 and ∠8 **15.** 67° **16.** 115; 65 **17.** The circumcenter of a triangle is the point of concurrency of the perpendicular bisectors of the triangle. **18.** The orthocenter of a triangle is the point of concurrency of the lines that contain the altitudes of the triangle. **19.** ∠1 ≅ ∠3 or ∠2 ≅ ∠4 or $m∠1 + m∠4 = 180°$ or $m∠2 + m∠3 = 180°$ **20.** Line ℓ is parallel to line p; since lines ℓ and n are both perpendicular to line m, they are parallel to each other. Since lines ℓ and p are both parallel to line n, line ℓ and p are parallel to each other by Transitive Property of Parallel Lines.
21. $\overline{AC} \cong \overline{CF}$; $\overline{CB} \cong \overline{FD}$; $\overline{BA} \cong \overline{DC}$; ∠ACB ≅ ∠CFD; ∠CBA ≅ ∠FDC; ∠BAC ≅ ∠DCF
22. Answers may vary. Sample: A rectangle always has opposite sides parallel, making it a parallelogram. A parallelogram doesn't always have four right angles, so it is not always a rectangle.
23. $AD > CD$ **24.** rectangle **25.** rhombus
26. square **27.** parallelogram **28.** rectangle
29. rhombus **30.** 6 **31.** 48; 90; 42; 57; 33
32. $x = 25$; $y = 31$ **33.** (2.5, 1) **34.** 118; 34
35. 7.2 **36.** area = 452.4 in.²; circumference = 75.4 in. **37.** 74 **38.** HL **39.** not possible **40.** SSS
41. AAS **42.** not possible **43.** SAS **44.** ASA or AAS **45.** SSS or SAS

Final Test, Form G

1. 36 **2.** (2.5, 1) **3.** $\overleftrightarrow{AB} \parallel \overleftrightarrow{CD}$; Converse of the Same-Side Interior Angles Theorem
4. Hypotenuse-Leg Theorem; $\triangle ABC \cong \triangle EDC$
5. (6, −5) **6.** 128 cm² **7.** 96 in.² **8.** $12\sqrt{5}$ units
9. 40 square units **10.** D **11.** 14.0 in. **12.** 8.9
13. 47.0 cm² **14.** 1280 m³

15. two parallel, horizontal lines, one 3 units above and one 3 units below $y = -2$

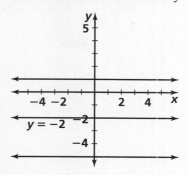

16. $144\sqrt{3}$ in.² **17.** 15.0 **18.** F **19.** 6.5 **20.** 7.5
21. 54 cm² **22.** 63 m **23.** 77.2 **24.** 11
25. (−2, −2) **26.** a, c, e, b, d or c, a, e, b, d
27. never **28.** sometimes **29.** sometimes
30. SAS; $\triangle ACD \cong \triangle CAB$ **31.** Yes; the length of $\overline{AB}$ is half the length of $\overline{DE}$. **32.** 18 **33.** 34
34. 92.3 in.² **35.** 100 **36.** 243π ft³ **37.** 199.0 cm²
38. 6

39.

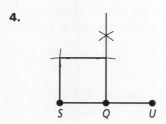

40a. 1809.6 cm² **40b.** 7238.2 cm³
41a. PQ **41b.** ∠F **42.** 13.0 **43.** $MW \approx 43.5$, $MX \approx 34.3$ **44.** 58° **45.** $y = -\frac{1}{3}x + 10$

Quarter 1 Test, Form K

1. 5 **2.** 9
3.

4.

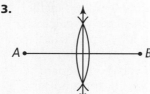

5. If two angles are supplements of the same angle, then they are congruent. (Congruent Supplements Theorem)

6.

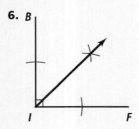

7. Line *a* is parallel to line *b* by the following theorem: In a plane, if two lines are perpendicular to the same line, then they are parallel to each other. **8.** 90° **9.** c, a, d, b **10.** $\overline{BF}$ **11.** 10π m **12.** (6,12)

13.

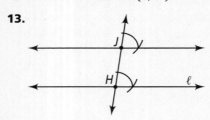

14. (−2, 4) **15.** −3 **16.** G **17.** 5 **18.** a line or no intersection **19.** noncoplanar lines that do not intersect **20.** 90 **21.** 60 **22.** 85 **23.** 55° **24.** 1. c, 3. a, 6. b, 7. d **25.** Pearl St. is not perpendicular to Wesley St.

Quarter 2 Test, Form K

1. $\overline{XZ}$ **2.** 4 **3.** b, a, d, c **4.** 56° **5.** SAS Postulate **6.** SSS Postulate **7.** $(c + a, b)$ **8.** c, b, a **9.** *Y* and *Z*; *X* **10.** 24 **11.** ASA Postulate **12.** 4 **13.** Answers may vary. Sample: show that the slope of diagonal $\overline{AC}$ is the negative reciprocal of the slope of diagonal $\overline{BD}$. **14.** perpendicular bisector; sides; circumcenter **15.** D **16.** angles; incenter **17.** *P* = 16 units and *A* = 12 square units **18.** HL Theorem **19.** 10 **20.** Suppose a triangle has more than one obtuse angle. Since the sum of two obtuse angle measures is greater than 180°, the sum of the measures of the angles in the triangle would be greater than 180°. This contradicts the Triangle Angle-Sum Theorem. **21.** rectangle **22.** 55° **23.** SAS **24.** Yes; $AB = \frac{1}{2}MN$ **25.** parallelogram

Quarter 3 Test, Form K

1. $\triangle BRG \sim \triangle NDK$ by SAS $\sim$ Theorem **2.** $\triangle AYM \sim \triangle XQH$ by AA $\sim$ Postulate **3.** obtuse **4.** 32.2 **5.** 12.8 **6.** $\sin A = \frac{5}{13}$; $\cos A = \frac{12}{13}$; $\tan A = \frac{5}{12}$; **7.** $X'(4, 6)$, $Y'(5, 10)$, $Z'(8, 7)$ **8.** $X'(2, -1)$, $Y'(3, -5)$, $Z'(6, -2)$ **9.** $X'(-2, -1)$, $Y'(-3, -5)$, $Z'(-6, -2)$ **10.** 40.3 mi/h; 29.7° north of west **11.** (10, 0) **12.** Yes; the preimage and image are congruent. **13.** Yes; $8^2 + 15^2 = 17^2$, so it is right triangle by the Converse of the Pythagorean Theorem. **14.** $5\sqrt{7}$ **15.** $x = 9$, $y = 15$ **16.** $y = 14$ **17.** 45° **18.** 134.8 **19.** The rotated figure is the same as the original figure. **20.** $X'(0, -3)$, $Y'(3.5, -2)$, $Z'(3, 1)$ **21.** 88 ft **22.** $5\sqrt{2}$ **23.** $6\sqrt{3}$ **24.** 12 in. **25.** J

Quarter 4 Test, Form K

1. 904.8 in.³ **2.** 63.4 in.² **3.** 90 **4.** 75 **5.** 24 square units **6.** 150.80 cm³ **7.** 8 **8.** a circle with center $(-4, 6)$ and radius 8 units **9.** 90π ft³ **10.** 40 cm² **11a.** 5 **11b.** 9 **12.** center: (0, 0); radius: 5

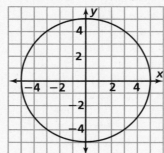

13. 90° **14.** 104° **15.** 128 cm² **16.** 114 in.³ **17.** 133° **18.** 133° **19.** 180° **20.** 192.5 in.² **21.** 11 **22.** B **23.** 259.8 in.² **24.** $\frac{7}{3}\pi$ ft **25.** 188.5 cm²

Mid-Course Test, Form K

1. a, c, d, e, b **2.** m∠1 = 70, m∠2 = 20 **3.** 12
4. 16 **5.** rectangle **6.** 11 **7.** 30

8.
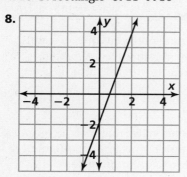

9. 14 **10.** 60°; acute **11.** 45
12. △LRT and △LMN; ∠RLM **13.** (0, b)
14a. ∠2 and ∠3 or ∠6 and ∠7 **14b.** ∠2 and ∠6
or ∠3 and ∠7 **15.** 5 **16.** x = 100, y = 80
17. incenter **18.** centroid **19.** J **20.** Line l is
parallel to line n by the Transitive Property of
Parallel Lines. **21.** A **22.** Answers may vary.
Sample: A square always has four congruent
sides, so it's always a rhombus. However, a
rhombus has 4 congruent sides but it doesn't
always have 4 right angles, so it's not always a
square. **23.** MN > QS **24.** rhombus
25. square **26.** parallelogram **27.** rectangle
28. parallelogram **29.** rhombus **30.** 3
31. m∠1 = 34°, m∠2 = 68° **32.** 13 **33.** (1, 2)
34. m∠1 = 40°, m∠2 = 95°, m∠3 = 45°
35. 10 **36.** C ≈ 100.5 in., A ≈ 804.2 in.²
37. m∠1 = 54°, m∠2 = 63° **38.** HL **39.** not
possible **40.** SSS **41.** AAS
42. ASA **43.** SAS **44.** AAS **45.** HL

16. 40 m² **17.** 12.5 **18.** H **19.** 6.4 **20.** 8
21. 175 cm² **22.** 110 ft **23.** 56.6 **24.** 7
25. (−1, −6) **26a.** vertical angles **26b.** CPCTC
27. always **28.** sometimes **29.** sometimes
30. SAS **31.** 1 **32.** 5.5 **33.** 32.5 **34.** 24.6 cm²
35. 80 **36.** 200π cm³ **37.** 28.5 cm² **38.** 9.7
39. glide reflection
40a. 282.7 m² **40b.** 314.2 m³ **41a.** BC
41b. ∠H **42.** 7.1 **43.** AC ≈ 41.3, CD ≈ 33.4
44. 50° **45.** y = 3x − 10

Final Test, Form K

1. 45 **2.** (5, 8) **3.** Converse of the Corresponding
Angles Postulate **4.** Hypotenuse-Leg Theorem
5. B(−1, −1) **6.** 24 ft² **7.** 48 cm² **8.** 40 units
9. 100 square units **10.** B **11.** 13.6 ft **12.** 4
13. 120 cm² **14.** 1296 cm³
15. circle with center (1, 0) and radius 3

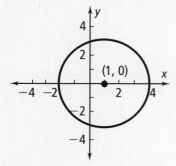

End-of-Course Assessment

1. A **2.** C **3.** A, B **4.** B **5.** B **6.** C, D **7.** B, D
8. A, C, D **9.** A, C, D **10.** A, C **11.** A, C **12.** A, C
13. A, B, C **14.** C **15.** B **16.** D **17.** A, D **18.** A, C
19. B **20.** A **21.** A, B, C **22.** B **23.** A **24.** C **25.** B

26. $y = \dfrac{1}{2}x + 4$

27. $\dfrac{3}{5}$

28. 40.41 in.

29. enlargement; $n = 2$

30. $F'(0, 1)$, $G'(5, 1)$, $H'(4, -3)$

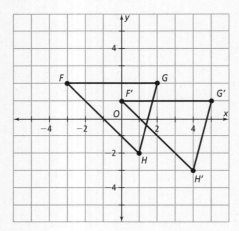

31.

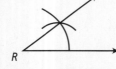
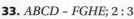

32.

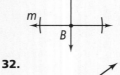

33. $ABCD \sim FGHE$; $2 : 3$

34. Can A; 42.4 in.³

35.

Angles that are congruent to $\angle 5$	Angles that are congruent to $\angle 8$
1; 3; 7; 9; 11; 13; 15	2; 4; 6; 10; 12; 14; 16

36. No; a rigid motion preserves distance and angle measure. The distances between the vertices in the image are not the same as in the preimage.

37. square

38. The SAS Postulate states that that the *included* angle between two sides must be congruent to the included angle of another triangle.

Sample drawing: Begin with an obtuse triangle, then move one of the legs so that it is an acute triangle.

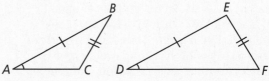

39.

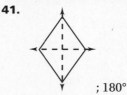

40. $A'(0, 0)$, $B'(-3, 1)$, $C'(-1, -2)$

41.

; 180°

42. vertical: rectangle; horizontal: circle

43. The similarity transformation is a rotation followed by a dilation about point A; $\triangle JKA \sim \triangle IHA$

44. $A'(-5, 3)$, $B'(-5, 5)$, $C'(-1, 5)$, and $D'(-1, 3)$.

45. 11.6 units

46. $\dfrac{b}{a}$; A translation followed by a dilation is a similarity transformation.

47. A reflection will map the congruent angles and the congruent sides onto each other.

48. The right triangles must have 45° angles.

49. $T_{<6, 0>} \circ R_{x\text{-axis}}$

50. 0.91 g/mL

51. $R_m \circ R_p$

52.

53. Because all sides are congruent, a rotation followed by a translation will map $\overline{RS}$ to $\overline{XY}$, $\overline{ST}$ to $\overline{YZ}$, and $\overline{TR}$ to $\overline{ZX}$.

54. The water tank has the approximate shape of a sphere; about 229,847 ft^3

55. $\triangle RZT \cong \triangle RZS$

56.

Statements	Reasons
1) $\angle 1$ and $\angle 3$ are vertical angles.	1) Given
2) $\angle 1$ and $\angle 2$ are supplementary. $\angle 2$ and $\angle 3$ are supplementary.	2) Angles that form a linear pair are supplementary.
3) $m\angle 1 + m\angle 2 = 180$ $m\angle 2 + m\angle 3 = 180$	3) Definition of supplementary angles
4) $m\angle 1 + m\angle 2 = m\angle 2 + m\angle 3$	4) Transitive Property of Equality
5) $m\angle 1 = m\angle 3$	5) Subtraction Property of Equality
6) $\angle 1 \cong \angle 3$	6) Definition of congruent angles

57. By the Distance Formula,
$AC = \sqrt{(0-a)^2 + (0-b)^2} = \sqrt{a^2 + b^2}$ and
$BD = \sqrt{(0-a)^2 + (b-0)^2} = \sqrt{a^2 + b^2}$.
So, $\overline{AC} \cong \overline{BD}$.

58. $\overline{GL} \cong \overline{PL}$ by definition of bisector. $\overleftrightarrow{DL} \perp \overline{GP}$, so $\angle DLG$ and $\angle DLP$ are right angles. Therefore, $\angle DLG \cong \angle DLP$ because all right angles are congruent. $\overline{DL} \cong \overline{DL}$ by the Reflexive Property of Congruence. So, $\triangle DLG \cong \triangle DLP$ by the SAS Postulate, and $GD = PD$ because corresponding parts of congruent triangles are congruent.

59.

Statements	Reasons
1) $ABCD$ is a parallelogram.	1) Given
2) $\overline{AB} \parallel \overline{DC}$	2) Definition of parallelogram
3) $\angle 1 \cong \angle 4$; $\angle 2 \cong \angle 3$	3) If lines are parallel, then alternate interior angles are congruent.
4) $\overline{AB} \cong \overline{DC}$	4) Opposite sides of a parallelogram are congruent.
5) $\triangle ABE \cong \triangle CDE$	5) ASA
6) $\overline{AE} \cong \overline{CE}$; $\overline{BE} \cong \overline{DE}$	6) Corresponding parts of congruent triangles are congruent.
7) $\overline{AC}$ and $\overline{BD}$ bisect each other at point E.	7) Definition of bisector

60. 48 people per square mile

61. The volume of the cube is 6^3 cm^3 or 216 cm^3. The cube and pyramid have the same base area and height, so the volumes differ by some constant factor, k.

$$V_{\text{pyramid}} = V_{\text{cube}} \cdot k$$
$$72 = 216k$$
$$\frac{1}{3} = k$$

So, the volume of a pyramid is equal to $\frac{1}{3}$ of the volume of a cube.

62. The Inscribed Angle Theorem states that

$m\angle A = \frac{1}{2}m\widehat{BCD}$ and $m\angle D = \frac{1}{2}m\widehat{BAC}$. There are 360° in a circle, so $m\widehat{BCD} + m\widehat{BAD} = 360$.

By the Division Property of Equality,

$\frac{1}{2}(m\widehat{BCD} + m\widehat{BAD}) = \frac{1}{2}(360)$ or

$\frac{1}{2}m\widehat{BCD} + \frac{1}{2}m\widehat{BAD} = 180$. By substitution, $m\angle A + m\angle D = 180$.

63.

Statements	Reasons
1) $\overleftrightarrow{PQ} \parallel \overleftrightarrow{XZ}$	1) Given
2) $\angle 1 \cong \angle 3,$ $\angle 2 \cong \angle 4$	2) If lines are perpendicular, then corresponding angles are congruent.
3) $\triangle YXZ \sim \triangle YPQ$	3) AA Similarity Postulate
4) $\dfrac{XY}{PY} = \dfrac{ZY}{QY}$	4) Corresponding sides of similar triangles are proportional.
5) $XY = XP + PY,$ $ZY = ZQ + QY$	5) Segment Addition Postulate
6) $\dfrac{XP + PY}{PY} =$ $\quad\quad \dfrac{ZQ + QY}{QY}$	6) Substitution Property
7) $\dfrac{XP}{PY} = \dfrac{ZQ}{QY}$	7) Property of Proportions

64.

Statements	Reasons
1) Draw $\overleftrightarrow{EF}$ through K, parallel to $\overline{GH}$.	1) Parallel Postulate
2) $\angle EKG$ and $\angle GKF$ are supplementary.	2) Angles that form a linear pair are supplementary.
3) $m\angle EKG + m\angle GKF = 180$	3) Definition of supplementary angles
4) $m\angle GKF = m\angle K + m\angle HKF$	4) Angle Addition Postulate
5) $m\angle EKG + m\angle K +$ $m\angle HKF = 180$	5) Substitution Property
6) $\angle EKG \cong \angle G$ and $\angle HKF \cong \angle H$	6) If lines are parallel, then alternate interior angles are congruent.
7) $m\angle EKG = m\angle G$ and $m\angle HKF = m\angle H$	7) Definition of congruent angles
8) $m\angle G + m\angle H +$ $m\angle K = 180$	8) Substitution Property

65.

Statements	Reasons
1) $GMPA$ and $GRJF$ are parallelograms.	1) Given
2) $\angle RGA \cong \angle P, \angle GRA \cong \angle F$	2) Opposite angles are congruent in parallelograms.
3) GRA is an equilateral triangle.	3) Given
4) $\angle GRA \cong \angle RGA$	4) All angles are congruent in equilateral triangles.
5) $\angle F \cong \angle P$	5) Transitive Property of Congruence
6) $m\angle F = m\angle P$	6) Definition of Congruence

Performance Task 1 Scoring Rubric

Designing a Container

The Scoring Rubric proposes a maximum number of points for each of the parts that make up the Performance Task. The maximum number of points is based on the complexity and difficulty level of the sub-task. For some parts, you may decide to award partial credit to students who may have shown some understanding of the concepts assessed, but may not have responded fully or correctly to the question posed.

Task Parts	Maximum Points
a. The prism has dimensions x cm, x cm, and 10 cm, with volume 1000 cm^3. So $10x^2 = 1000$, $x^2 = 100$, and $x = 10$. The dimensions are 10 cm, 10 cm, and 10 cm. This container is a cube with surface area $6(10^2) = 600$ cm^2.	2
b. The cylinder has radius r cm and height 10 cm, with volume 1000 cm^3. So $\pi r^2(10) = 1000$, $r^2 = 1000 \div (10\pi)$, and $r \approx 5.64$ cm. Surface area of the cylinder is about $2\pi(5.64)^2 + 2\pi(5.64)(10) \approx 554$ cm^2.	4
c. The cone has radius r cm and height 10 cm, with volume 1000 cm^3. So $\left(\dfrac{1}{3}\right)\pi r^2(10) = 1000$, $r^2 = 1000 \div \left(\dfrac{10\pi}{3}\right)$, and $r \approx 9.77$. To find surface area, first find slant height: $l^2 = 9.77^2 + 10^2$, so $l \approx 14.0$ cm. Surface area of the cone is about $\pi(9.77^2) + \pi(9.77)(14.0) \approx 729$ cm^2.	4
d. Team 2 needs the least amount of material to make its container (cylinder). Team 3 needs the most (cone).	4
e. Yes. One possible set of dimensions is $r \approx 5.4$ cm and $h \approx 10.9$ cm. Then volume is about $\pi(5.4)^2(10.9) \approx 999$ cm^3 and surface area is about $2\pi(5.4)^2 + 2\pi(5.4)(10.9) \approx 553$ cm^2.	4
Total points	18

Performance Task 2 Scoring Rubric

Urban Planning

The Scoring Rubric proposes a maximum number of points for each of the parts that make up the Performance Task. The maximum number of points is based on the complexity and difficulty level of the sub-task. For some parts, you may decide to award partial credit to students who may have shown some understanding of the concepts assessed, but may not have responded fully or correctly to the question posed.

Task Parts	Maximum Points
a. Downtown angle: $\tan^{-1}\left(\dfrac{5}{12}\right) = 22.6°$. Town Pool angle: $\tan^{-1}\left(\dfrac{12}{5}\right) = 67.4°$.	2
b. Hypotenuse h: $h^2 = 5^2 + 12^2 = 25 + 144 = 169$, so $h = 13$. Length of each of the three congruent segments $= \dfrac{13}{3}$ mi, or about 4.3 mi.	4
c. Let $a =$ length of the road from point A to the mall. Use the Law of Cosines: $a^2 = 5^2 + \left(\dfrac{13}{3}\right)^2 - 2(5)\left(\dfrac{13}{3}\right)\cos 67.4°$, so $a \approx 5.2$ mi.	4
d. Let $b =$ length of the road from point B to the mall. Use the Law of Cosines: $b^2 = 12^2 + \left(\dfrac{13}{3}\right)^2 - 2(12)\left(\dfrac{13}{3}\right)\cos 22.6°$, so $b \approx 8.2$ mi.	4
e. Since $8.2 - 5.2 = 3$, point B is about 3 miles further from the mall than point A is. At $550,000 per mile, the cost to build the longer road is $3(\$550,000) = \$1,650,000$ more.	4
Total Points	**18**

Performance Task 3 Scoring Rubric

Analyzing an Excavation Site

The Scoring Rubric proposes a maximum number of points for each of the parts that make up the Performance Task. The maximum number of points is based on the complexity and difficulty level of the sub-task. For some parts, you may decide to award partial credit to students who may have shown some understanding of the concepts assessed, but may not have responded fully or correctly to the question posed.

Task Parts	Maximum Points
a. You could choose any two of the chords $\overline{AB}$, $\overline{BC}$, or $\overline{AC}$. Find the midpoints of the chords, the slopes of the chords, and the slopes of the perpendiculars to the chords. Write equations of the two perpendicular bisectors and solve this system of equations.	3
b. Midpoint of $\overline{AB}$: $(2, 4)$. Midpoint of $\overline{BC}$: $(4, 3)$.	2
c. Slope of $\overline{AB}$: 1. Slope of $\overline{BC}$: -2.	2
d. The perpendicular bisector of $\overline{AB}$ passes through the point $(2, 4)$ and has slope -1, so its equation is $y - 4 = -1(x - 2)$, or $y = -x + 6$. The perpendicular bisector of $\overline{BC}$ passes through the point $(4, 3)$ and has slope $\frac{1}{2}$, so its equation is $y - 3 = \left(\frac{1}{2}\right)(x - 4)$, or $y = \frac{1}{2}x + 1$.	3
e. Solve the system of two linear equations, $y = -x + 6$ and $y = \frac{1}{2}x + 1$, to find the point of intersection of their graphs: $-x + 6 = \frac{1}{2}x + 1$, so $x = \frac{10}{3}$ and $y = -\frac{10}{3} + 6 = \frac{8}{3}$. The coordinates of the center of the circle are $\left(\frac{10}{3}, \frac{8}{3}\right)$.	3
f. Let r be the distance from the center to any point on the circle. Using $C(5, 1)$, $r^2 = \left(\frac{5}{3}\right)^2 + \left(\frac{5}{3}\right)^2$, and $r \approx 2.36$ m. Each house was about 2.36 meters from the center of the settlement.	3
g. Sample answer: $(2, 0.72)$. To get this answer, use the Distance Formula with the points $(2, y)$ and $\left(\frac{10}{3}, \frac{8}{3}\right)$ and distance $= 2.36$. Solving for y gives 0.72.	4
Total points	20

Performance Task 4 Scoring Rubric

Applying Geometric Probability

The Scoring Rubric proposes a maximum number of points for each of the parts that make up the Performance Task. The maximum number of points is based on the complexity and difficulty level of the sub-task. For some parts, you may decide to award partial credit to students who may have shown some understanding of the concepts assessed, but may not have responded fully or correctly to the question posed.

Task Parts	Maximum Points
a. Let the area of the dartboard equal 1 square unit. To find the area of the largest triangle, first find its height h: $h^2 + 0.5^2 = 1^2$, so $h \approx 0.866$. Area of the triangle is about $0.5(1)(0.866) = 0.433$. So the probability that a dart lands in the largest triangle is about 43%.	4
b. The probability that a dart does not land in any triangle is about $100\% - 43\% = 57\%$.	3
c. The probability that a dart lands in a 1-point region is about $(0.433)(0.75) = 0.32475$, or about 32%. The probability that a dart lands in a 3-point region is about $(0.433)(0.25)(0.75) = 0.0811875$, or about 8%. The probability that a dart lands in the 5-point region is about $(0.433)(0.25)(0.25) = 0.0270625$, or about 3%.	5
d. 1 and 5: Probability is $(0.32475)(0.0270625) = 0.0087885469$, or about 1%. 3 and 3: Probability is $(0.0811875)(0.0811875) = 0.0065914102$, or about 1%. 3 and 5: Probability is $(0.0811875)(0.0270625) = 0.0021971367$, or less than 1%. 5 and 1: Probability is $(0.0270625)(0.32475) = 0.0087885469$, or about 1%. 5 and 3: Probability is $(0.0270625)(0.0811875) = 0.0021971367$, or less than 1%.	5
e. Add the probabilities: $2(0.0087885469) + 0.0065914102 + 2(0.0021971367) = 0.0285627774$, or about 3%.	3
Total points	**20**

Multiple Choice

1. A **B** C D E
2. A B C **D** E
3. A B C **D** E
4. A B C D **E**
5. A B C **D** E
6. **A** B C D E
7. A B C **D** E
8. **A** B C D E
9. A B **C** D E
10. A **B** C D E
11. A B C **D** E

12. A B **C** D E
13. A **B** C D E
14. **A** B C D E
15. A B **C** D E
16. A B C **D** E
17. A B **C** D E
18. A B **C** D E
19. A B C **D** E
20. A B **C** D E
21. A B C **D** E
22. A **B** C D E

23. A B C D **E**
24. A B **C** D E
25. A **B** C D E
26. **A** B C D E
27. A **B** C D E
28. A **B** C D E
29. A B C D **E**
30. A **B** C D E
31. **A** B C D E
32. A B C **D** E

Student-Produced Responses

1. 2 / 5
2. 5
3. 7
4. 1 0 8
5. 3
6. 7 2 0
7. 2 0
8. .7 8
9. 6 4
10. 6

1.	Ⓐ	Ⓑ	Ⓒ	Ⓓ
2.	Ⓕ	Ⓖ	Ⓗ	Ⓙ
3.	Ⓐ	Ⓑ	Ⓒ	Ⓓ
4.	Ⓕ	Ⓖ	Ⓗ	Ⓙ
5.	Ⓐ	Ⓑ	Ⓒ	Ⓓ
6.	Ⓕ	Ⓖ	Ⓗ	Ⓙ
7.	Ⓐ	Ⓑ	Ⓒ	Ⓓ
8.	Ⓕ	Ⓖ	Ⓗ	Ⓙ
9.	Ⓐ	Ⓑ	Ⓒ	Ⓓ
10.	Ⓕ	Ⓖ	Ⓗ	Ⓙ
11.	Ⓐ	Ⓑ	Ⓒ	Ⓓ
12.	Ⓕ	Ⓖ	Ⓗ	Ⓙ
13.	Ⓐ	Ⓑ	Ⓒ	Ⓓ
14.	Ⓕ	Ⓖ	Ⓗ	Ⓙ
15.	Ⓐ	Ⓑ	Ⓒ	Ⓓ
16.	Ⓕ	Ⓖ	Ⓗ	Ⓙ
17.	Ⓐ	Ⓑ	Ⓒ	Ⓓ
18.	Ⓕ	Ⓖ	Ⓗ	Ⓙ
19.	Ⓐ	Ⓑ	Ⓒ	Ⓓ
20.	Ⓕ	Ⓖ	Ⓗ	Ⓙ
21.	Ⓐ	Ⓑ	Ⓒ	Ⓓ
22.	Ⓕ	Ⓖ	Ⓗ	Ⓙ
23.	Ⓐ	Ⓑ	Ⓒ	Ⓓ
24.	Ⓕ	Ⓖ	Ⓗ	Ⓙ
25.	Ⓐ	Ⓑ	Ⓒ	Ⓓ
26.	Ⓕ	Ⓖ	Ⓗ	Ⓙ

27.	Ⓐ	Ⓑ	Ⓒ	Ⓓ
28.	Ⓕ	Ⓖ	Ⓗ	Ⓙ
29.	Ⓐ	Ⓑ	Ⓒ	Ⓓ
30.	Ⓕ	Ⓖ	Ⓗ	Ⓙ
31.	Ⓐ	Ⓑ	Ⓒ	Ⓓ
32.	Ⓕ	Ⓖ	Ⓗ	Ⓙ
33.	Ⓐ	Ⓑ	Ⓒ	Ⓓ
34.	Ⓕ	Ⓖ	Ⓗ	Ⓙ
35.	Ⓐ	Ⓑ	Ⓒ	Ⓓ
36.	Ⓕ	Ⓖ	Ⓗ	Ⓙ
37.	Ⓐ	Ⓑ	Ⓒ	Ⓓ
38.	Ⓕ	Ⓖ	Ⓗ	Ⓙ
39.	Ⓐ	Ⓑ	Ⓒ	Ⓓ
40.	Ⓕ	Ⓖ	Ⓗ	Ⓙ
41.	Ⓐ	Ⓑ	Ⓒ	Ⓓ
42.	Ⓕ	Ⓖ	Ⓗ	Ⓙ
43.	Ⓐ	Ⓑ	Ⓒ	Ⓓ
44.	Ⓕ	Ⓖ	Ⓗ	Ⓙ
45.	Ⓐ	Ⓑ	Ⓒ	Ⓓ
46.	Ⓕ	Ⓖ	Ⓗ	Ⓙ
47.	Ⓐ	Ⓑ	Ⓒ	Ⓓ
48.	Ⓕ	Ⓖ	Ⓗ	Ⓙ
49.	Ⓐ	Ⓑ	Ⓒ	Ⓓ
50.	Ⓕ	Ⓖ	Ⓗ	Ⓙ
51.	Ⓐ	Ⓑ	Ⓒ	Ⓓ
52.	Ⓕ	Ⓖ	Ⓗ	Ⓙ

STUDENT ANSWER SHEET: TEST _____

1. Ⓐ Ⓑ Ⓒ Ⓓ
2. Ⓕ Ⓖ Ⓗ Ⓙ
3. Ⓐ Ⓑ Ⓒ Ⓓ
4. Ⓕ Ⓖ Ⓗ Ⓙ
5. Ⓐ Ⓑ Ⓒ Ⓓ
6. Ⓕ Ⓖ Ⓗ Ⓙ
7. Ⓐ Ⓑ Ⓒ Ⓓ
8. Ⓕ Ⓖ Ⓗ Ⓙ
9. Ⓐ Ⓑ Ⓒ Ⓓ
10. Ⓕ Ⓖ Ⓗ Ⓙ
11. Ⓐ Ⓑ Ⓒ Ⓓ
12. Ⓕ Ⓖ Ⓗ Ⓙ
13. Ⓐ Ⓑ Ⓒ Ⓓ
14. Ⓕ Ⓖ Ⓗ Ⓙ
15. Ⓐ Ⓑ Ⓒ Ⓓ
16. Ⓕ Ⓖ Ⓗ Ⓙ
17. Ⓐ Ⓑ Ⓒ Ⓓ
18. Ⓕ Ⓖ Ⓗ Ⓙ
19. Ⓐ Ⓑ Ⓒ Ⓓ
20. Ⓕ Ⓖ Ⓗ Ⓙ
21. Ⓐ Ⓑ Ⓒ Ⓓ
22. Ⓕ Ⓖ Ⓗ Ⓙ
23. Ⓐ Ⓑ Ⓒ Ⓓ
24. Ⓕ Ⓖ Ⓗ Ⓙ
25. Ⓐ Ⓑ Ⓒ Ⓓ
26. Ⓕ Ⓖ Ⓗ Ⓙ

27. Ⓐ Ⓑ Ⓒ Ⓓ
28. Ⓕ Ⓖ Ⓗ Ⓙ
29. Ⓐ Ⓑ Ⓒ Ⓓ
30. Ⓕ Ⓖ Ⓗ Ⓙ
31. Ⓐ Ⓑ Ⓒ Ⓓ
32. Ⓕ Ⓖ Ⓗ Ⓙ
33. Ⓐ Ⓑ Ⓒ Ⓓ
34. Ⓕ Ⓖ Ⓗ Ⓙ
35. Ⓐ Ⓑ Ⓒ Ⓓ
36. Ⓕ Ⓖ Ⓗ Ⓙ
37. Ⓐ Ⓑ Ⓒ Ⓓ
38. Ⓕ Ⓖ Ⓗ Ⓙ
39. Ⓐ Ⓑ Ⓒ Ⓓ
40. Ⓕ Ⓖ Ⓗ Ⓙ
41. Ⓐ Ⓑ Ⓒ Ⓓ
42. Ⓕ Ⓖ Ⓗ Ⓙ
43. Ⓐ Ⓑ Ⓒ Ⓓ
44. Ⓕ Ⓖ Ⓗ Ⓙ
45. Ⓐ Ⓑ Ⓒ Ⓓ
46. Ⓕ Ⓖ Ⓗ Ⓙ
47. Ⓐ Ⓑ Ⓒ Ⓓ
48. Ⓕ Ⓖ Ⓗ Ⓙ
49. Ⓐ Ⓑ Ⓒ Ⓓ
50. Ⓕ Ⓖ Ⓗ Ⓙ
51. Ⓐ Ⓑ Ⓒ Ⓓ
52. Ⓕ Ⓖ Ⓗ Ⓙ

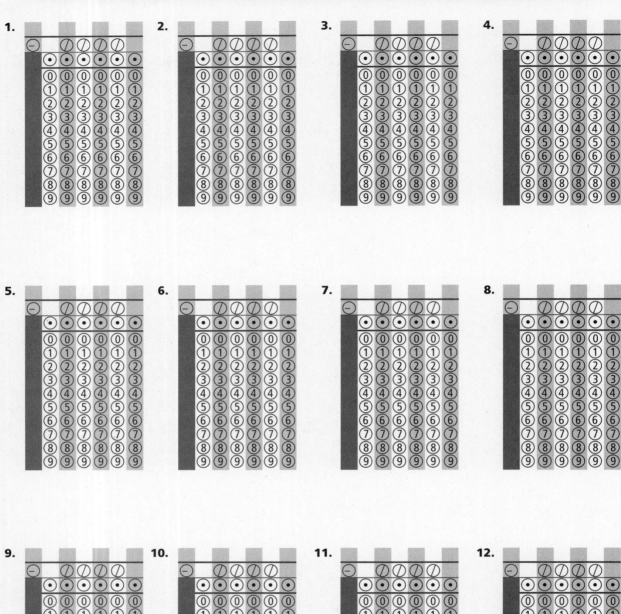

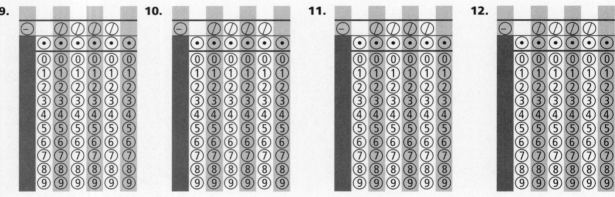

Multiple Choice

1. Ⓐ Ⓑ Ⓒ Ⓓ Ⓔ
2. Ⓐ Ⓑ Ⓒ Ⓓ Ⓔ
3. Ⓐ Ⓑ Ⓒ Ⓓ Ⓔ
4. Ⓐ Ⓑ Ⓒ Ⓓ Ⓔ
5. Ⓐ Ⓑ Ⓒ Ⓓ Ⓔ
6. Ⓐ Ⓑ Ⓒ Ⓓ Ⓔ
7. Ⓐ Ⓑ Ⓒ Ⓓ Ⓔ
8. Ⓐ Ⓑ Ⓒ Ⓓ Ⓔ
9. Ⓐ Ⓑ Ⓒ Ⓓ Ⓔ
10. Ⓐ Ⓑ Ⓒ Ⓓ Ⓔ
11. Ⓐ Ⓑ Ⓒ Ⓓ Ⓔ

12. Ⓐ Ⓑ Ⓒ Ⓓ Ⓔ
13. Ⓐ Ⓑ Ⓒ Ⓓ Ⓔ
14. Ⓐ Ⓑ Ⓒ Ⓓ Ⓔ
15. Ⓐ Ⓑ Ⓒ Ⓓ Ⓔ
16. Ⓐ Ⓑ Ⓒ Ⓓ Ⓔ
17. Ⓐ Ⓑ Ⓒ Ⓓ Ⓔ
18. Ⓐ Ⓑ Ⓒ Ⓓ Ⓔ
19. Ⓐ Ⓑ Ⓒ Ⓓ Ⓔ
20. Ⓐ Ⓑ Ⓒ Ⓓ Ⓔ
21. Ⓐ Ⓑ Ⓒ Ⓓ Ⓔ
22. Ⓐ Ⓑ Ⓒ Ⓓ Ⓔ

23. Ⓐ Ⓑ Ⓒ Ⓓ Ⓔ
24. Ⓐ Ⓑ Ⓒ Ⓓ Ⓔ
25. Ⓐ Ⓑ Ⓒ Ⓓ Ⓔ
26. Ⓐ Ⓑ Ⓒ Ⓓ Ⓔ
27. Ⓐ Ⓑ Ⓒ Ⓓ Ⓔ
28. Ⓐ Ⓑ Ⓒ Ⓓ Ⓔ
29. Ⓐ Ⓑ Ⓒ Ⓓ Ⓔ
30. Ⓐ Ⓑ Ⓒ Ⓓ Ⓔ
31. Ⓐ Ⓑ Ⓒ Ⓓ Ⓔ
32. Ⓐ Ⓑ Ⓒ Ⓓ Ⓔ

Student-Produced Responses